The Musical Structure of Plato's Dialogues

Also by J. B. Kennedy and published by Acumen

Space, Time and Einstein: An Introduction

The Musical Structure
of Plato's Dialogues

J. B. Kennedy

ACUMEN

© J. B. Kennedy 2011

This book is copyright under the Berne Convention.
No reproduction without permission.
All rights reserved.

First published in 2011 by Acumen

Acumen Publishing Limited
4 Saddler Street
Durham
DH1 3NP

www.acumenpublishing.co.uk

ISBN: 978-1-84465-266-2 (hardcover)
ISBN: 978-1-84465-267-9 (paperback)

British Library Cataloguing-in-Publication Data
A catalogue record for this book is available
from the British Library.

Printed and bound in the UK by Berforts Group Limited

For Louise Crascall

But, friend, when you grasp the number and nature of the intervals of sound, from high to low, and the boundaries of those intervals, and how many scales arise from them, which those who came before handed down to us, their followers, to call "harmonies," and when you grasp the various qualities inhering in the motions of the body, which they said must be measured with numbers and named "rhythm" and "metre," and when you apprehend that every One and Many should be so investigated, when you have grasped all of that, then you are wise ...   Plato (*Phlb.*, 17c11–e1)

Nothing is so characteristic of the Pythagorean philosophy as symbolism (*to symbolikon*), a kind of teaching which mixes speech and silence as in mystery rites ... what they signify is immediately lucid and clear for those who are accustomed to it, but dark and meaningless to the inexperienced ... with the Pythagorean symbols what seems to be affirmed is really being concealed, and what seems to be concealed is discerned by the mind.   Plutarch (in Stobaeus iii.i.199 [Wachsmuth & Hense])

Our discussion will be adequate if it has as much clearness as the subject-matter admits of, for precision is not to be sought for in equal degree in all arguments ... it is the mark of an educated mind to look for precision in each kind just so far as the nature of the subject admits; it is evidently equally foolish to accept probable reasoning from a mathematician and to demand demonstrative proofs from a rhetorician ...
          Aristotle (*Eth. Nic.* 1094b11ff. [after Ross])

Les anciens philosophes avoient une double doctrine; l'une externe, publique ou exotérique; l'autre interne, secrete ou ésotérique. La premiere s'enseignoit ouvertement à tout le monde, la seconde étoit reservée pour un petit nombre de disciples choisis ... Ce qui a fait prendre le change aux anciens & aux modernes sur le but de la double doctrine, & leur a fait imaginer qu'elle n'étoit qu'un artifice pour conserver la gloire des sciences & de ceux qui en faisoient profession, a été l'opinion générale que les fables des dieux & des héros avoient été inventées par les sages de la premiere antiquité, pour déguiser & cacher des vérités naturelles & morales ...   Diderot and D'Alembert (*Encyclopédie ou Dictionnaire raisonné des sciences, des arts et des métiers*)

Contents

Preface	xii
Abbreviations	xvii

1. The nature and history of philosophical allegory — 1
  1.1 Rehabilitating ancient ways of reading — 2
  1.2 Allegory, Socrates and Plato — 5
  1.3 Symbols, reserve and Pythagoreanism — 9
  1.4 Persecution and the politics of allegory in classical Athens — 12
  1.5 Plato and Pythagoreanism: two puzzles — 14
  1.6 The allegorical Plato in history — 18
  1.7 Methodological precedent: early Christianity — 23
  1.8 Methodological precedent: Renaissance Platonism — 25

2. Introducing the dialogues' musical structure — 29
  2.1 Structuring a dialogue — 31
  2.2 Ancient Greek music: three key ideas — 32
  2.3 Plato's symbolic scheme — 36
  2.4 Harmony and consonance, disharmony and dissonance — 37
  2.5 Sevenths and mixture — 38
  2.6 Guide to the strongest evidence — 40
  2.7 Methodology for line-counting — 45
  2.8 Canons of criticism — 46
  2.9 Responses to possible objections — 48

3. Independent lines of evidence — 52
- 3.1 Simple, objective measurements — 52
- 3.2 Parallel passages at the same relative location — 54
- 3.3 Ranges of positive and negative concepts — 56
- 3.4 Preview of the musical structure in the *Republic* — 57
- 3.5 A control: falsifiability and the pseudo-Platonica — 59

4. An emphatic pattern in the *Symposium*'s frame — 61
- 4.1 A theory of music — 62
- 4.2 Recurring clusters of features in the frame — 63
- 4.3 A new kind of commentary — 64

5. Making the *Symposium*'s musical structure explicit — 78
- 5.1 Phaedrus — 78
- 5.2 Pausanias — 84
- 5.3 Eryximachus — 96
- 5.4 Aristophanes — 104
- 5.5 Agathon — 116
- 5.6 Socrates and Diotima — 126
- 5.7 Alcibiades — 154

6. Parallel structure in the *Euthyphro* — 178
- 6.1 The same scale and the same symbolic scheme — 178
- 6.2 Guide to the strongest evidence — 179
- 6.3 The sevenths — 180
- 6.4 The connection to music — 181
- 6.5 Another kind of evidence: parallels between dialogues — 183
- 6.6 The *Euthyphro* is not aporetic — 184
- 6.7 Marking the notes — 185

7. Extracting doctrine from structure — 236
- 7.1 Aristotle on virtues and means — 236
- 7.2 Stichometry and the divided line — 238
- 7.3 Reading the dialogues in parallel — 240
- 7.4 The logic of the argument and its consequences — 241

8. Some implications — 244
- 8.1 Summary of the case — 244
- 8.2 Interpreting the dialogues — 245
- 8.3 Problems with anonymity and intentionality — 246

8.4	Interpreting Plato, Pythagoras and Socrates	247
8.5	History of music and mathematics	249
8.6	History of literature and literary theory	251
8.7	Ancient book production, papyrology, textual studies	251
8.8	The forward path	252

APPENDIX 1: More musicological background	253
APPENDIX 2: Neo-Pythagoreans, the twelve-note scale and the monochord	260
APPENDIX 3: Markers between the major notes	265
APPENDIX 4: The central notes	271
APPENDIX 5: Systematic theory of the marking passages	274
APPENDIX 6: Structure in Agathon and Socrates' speeches	287
APPENDIX 7: Euripides and line-counting	288
APPENDIX 8: Data from the *Republic*	291
APPENDIX 9: OCT line numbers for the musical notes	294

Notes	297
Bibliography	309
Index	315

Preface

The following arguments and evidence for the musical structure of Plato's dialogues were refined and strengthened in lectures for classicists at the University of Manchester, University College London, the University of Leeds and the Classical Association Conference at Durham University. They amplify many times over the grounds for the conclusions first reported in my "Plato's Forms, Pythagorean Mathematics, and Stichometry" (2010), and I am grateful to Acumen for bringing this book out promptly in response to the debate they occasioned.

At a time when the study of the humanities in universities is endangered, this debate has brought an extraordinary degree of attention to classics and ancient philosophy. The scholars and journalists who discussed this research in newspapers, broadcasts and online forums throughout the world have reminded many of the living importance of ancient Greek philosophy and literature.

These findings open up new lines of research, many more than can be pursued by any one scholar, and it may take time to assess their implications. As my title indicates, this book has a limited aim. It is a study of the *musical structure* in two dialogues, prefaced by some general and historical evidence.

However tantalizing, there are two reasons for proceeding in this way. First, Plato's musical symbols are repeated at regular intervals through the text of each dialogue and so can be studied rigorously and objectively. Claims can be verified first by making comparisons within a dialogue and then by showing that the same structure recurs in different dialogues. Second, the study of the symbols with doctrinal content depends on first establishing that the dialogues have a stichometric and musical structure. Thus the musical symbols are prior both methodologically and logically.

Nonetheless, a glimpse of doctrine is afforded by Chapter 7, "Extracting Doctrine from Structure", which focuses on a single, ethical doctrine but shows generally that stichometry will yield up revisionist insights into Plato's philosophy.

This research has already stimulated new work and led to a number of collaborative projects. Given the nature and the magnitude of these findings, however, scholars coming to these claims for the first time will naturally and properly react with scepticism. Although it was common for some fifteen hundred years to regard Plato as a symbolic writer and although Plato's familiarity with Pythagorean numerology is well attested in his writings, modern scholars have uniformly denied that Plato's dialogues are in any general way symbolical, allegorical or numerological.

Researchers in the history of science have, for a generation or so now, become accustomed to the idea that the study of primitive pseudo-sciences is essential to understanding the growth of modern science. The births of astronomy, chemistry and mathematics are to be found in astrology, alchemy and numerology. Historians of science have also become accustomed to stories of the neglect or marginalization of the histories of these pseudo-sciences in earlier work. The "discovery" of Newton's alchemical experiments and Pythagoreanism by Keynes and others is the most prominent case. Similar cases of neglect and rediscovery, more closely related to Platonism, are discussed below to establish certain methodological precedents.

This research grew out of a project on Greek mathematics, particularly on the connections between Plato's *Republic* and Euclid's *Elements*. The University of Manchester encouraged me to shift my teaching into related areas. In the philosophy department, therefore, I was teaching an advanced course on the *Republic* and found myself lecturing on the literature about its rather puzzling narrative structure by Lear, Annas and Rutherford. In the history of science centre, I was teaching another course on the history of mathematics, which dealt in part with Pythagorean mathematics and music theory. A series of unexpected insights led to the gradual realization that Pythagorean musical theory was key to the *Republic*'s narrative structure. Discussion of Plato's doctrines, that is, the consequences for interpreting Plato's philosophy, must be postponed. They will be the subject of future research.

For better or worse, making sense of these insights forced me to draw on research in many fields: classics, the history of philosophy, the history of literary criticism, musicology, papyrology and the history of mathematics. Like all "multidisciplinary" research, therefore, this book will commit sins of omission and commission. I was trained in an analytic philosophy department with a speciality in the history and philosophy of science. For help in other areas, I am grateful for conversations and correspondence with many friends and colleagues, but errors no doubt remain.

Scholars should not underestimate the epistemological complexity of the claims advanced here. They require not only the revision of certain accepted views about Plato and his philosophy, but employ novel argumentative strategies whose strength may not be at first apparent. I find that philosophers see the care with which each major assertion has been buttressed with independent lines of evidence, but tend to be unfamiliar with scholarly methods for interpreting allegorical literature. Some make evidentiary demands that would wipe out the study of allegory in great swathes of the literary tradition. Musicologists are experts in the traditional scales and modes of ancient Greek music, but often have little appreciation of Plato's innovations and reformist agenda in the mathematical sciences. To my surprise, classicists have a living disciplinary memory of spurious numerologists within their midst, and so may not recognize the degree to which numerology of various kinds was mainstream and even normal within elite science in ancient times.

Most importantly, the use of allegory and symbols to "reserve" doctrines, although surprisingly common (Ch. 1), will challenge the canons of criticism regularly employed by scholars in the history of philosophy. In modern times, interpreters of philosophical texts have placed great emphasis on rigour and objectivity, and sought to achieve these by means of literal, textual evidence and carefully analysed arguments.

The study of allegory confronts these methods with several problems. Allegorists seek a peculiar combination of communication and concealment. Great cunning and ingenuity are applied precisely to deny readers clear and distinct evidence for the secondary layers of meaning, and yet also to ensure that readers willing to do the detective work and follow the surface clues through a series of inferences will arrive at a definite doctrine. Allegorists are subtle. They use red herrings, disrupt patterns that threaten to become too clear, and invent a *sui generis* private language that must be unravelled by careful study of each individual work.

In some cases, allegorists have separately and explicitly unveiled their methods in later, informal ways. The letter to Can Grande attributed to Dante details the four layers of meanings built into the *Divine Comedy*. James Joyce laid out the subterranean correspondences between his *Ulysses* and Homer's *Odyssey* in a handwritten schema for his friend Stuart Gilbert. In most cases, however, literary scholars must infer the nature and content of allegories from clues within the compositions themselves. Generally, this means the literal meaning of the texts is only the starting-point, and not the final arbiter of interpretations. Figurative meanings are found only by making a series of comparisons and inferences and following a trail of clues. Such methods may be unfamiliar to historians of philosophy but, as the evidence in Chapter 1 makes clear, they were quite familiar in the late classical period when Plato was writing.

This research is, at least, a methodological victory for the new digital humanities movement. This growing field hopes to show, in various ways, that computers, new databases, online collections of literature and the internet can make decisive contributions to research in the humanities. The findings reported here could not, as Chapter 1 explains, have been made without computers. The musical patterns in Plato's dialogues were, it will be argued, more accessible when the dialogues were in their original format: papyri arrayed with neat and mathematically uniform columns of Greek letters. Modern critical editions of Plato, like the Oxford Classical Texts (OCT) used here, are the product of many centuries of editorial interventions. Although clearer in many ways, they obscure the regular patterns in Plato's dialogues, which explains in part why they were not discovered sooner. After the first, tentative insights, I obtained electronic versions of the texts and used new software to restore the OCT texts to their classical format. At once, the patterns became more visible. Much of the rigour, generality and objectivity that was finally achieved was made possible by these new digital technologies.

I have presented this research in a series of scholarly lectures and enjoyed discussions about it with what now may amount to hundreds of scholars. I have learned much, both from their queries and suggestions, and have revised much of this book to reflect their contributions and clarify my methods. I encourage any future critics to correspond with me.

Earlier stichometric studies of Plato's dialogues are reviewed in Chapter 2, but it is important to recognize several anticipations of the claims made about the *Republic* in Chapters 3 and 7, which already implied that Plato's works have a stichometric structure. After my "Plato's Forms, Pythagorean Mathematics, and Stichometry" appeared, several scholars contacted me about their earlier work. Vittorio Hösle of the University of Notre Dame published an important article, "Did the Greeks Deliberately Use the Golden Ratio in an Artwork?" (2008) suggesting that the *Phaedrus* and *Republic* had a mathematical design. Maya Alapin of Oxford University, in a thesis that follows up the work of John Bremer, explores the mathematical structure of the *Republic*.

The direction my research took would not have been possible without my teachers. At Princeton, while specializing in mathematics and computers, my sometime advisor Carlos Baker made me take a course in literature nearly every term. For four years, I was at least exposed to the rigours of the art of close reading in the preceptorials of the English and comparative literature departments, and became acquainted with the various structures used to unify their compositions by writers such as Dante, Spenser, Mann and Ashbery. Later, while working on a PhD in philosophy at Stanford University with Nancy Cartwright, Peter Galison and John Dupre, I also studied Greek philosophy with Julius Moravcsik, Wilbur Knorr and Jean Hampton. Although more of my time was spent with Aristotle's physical and cosmological treatises, Knorr was kind enough to debate his research on structure in Plato's *Laws* with me.

I would like to thank two Plato scholars here in Manchester who encouraged this work in its early stages. The late David Melling was the first to say, in a scrawl across a draft, "The patterns that you see exist". Harry Lesser greeted me after reading another draft with a mischievous smile and said, "It's just the kind of thing Plato would do".

This work has been supported in the first place by my friends and colleagues at the University of Manchester, whose critical enthusiasm and encouragement survived a long series of draft papers, several formal and informal lectures and many animated conversations. I would like to thank the Centre for the History of Science, Technology and Medicine, especially the director Michael Worboys and the former director John Pickstone, the administrator Gillian Mawson, Ian Burney, Jeff Hughes, Vladimir Jankovic, James Sumner, Carsten Timmermann, Elizabeth Toon and Simone Turchetti, for providing a welcoming home for this research; the philosophers who read my drafts, Harry Lesser, David Melling, John Shand,

Michael Rush and Thomas Uebel; and the philosophy and classics departments for their hospitality over the years. My friends and former colleagues in the philosophy department at Notre Dame encouraged me to teach courses on Aristotle, and I would especially like to thank Patricia Blanchette, David Burrell, Marian David, Chris Hamlin, Don Howard, Lynn Joy, Ernan McMullin, David O'Connor, Bill Ramsey, Ken Sayre, Leopold Stubenberg and Paul Weithman.

For conversations and correspondence, both great and small, about this book as well as other help, I would like to thank Peter Adamson, Tara Ahamed, Maya Alapin, Andrew Barker, John Bremer, Tad Brennan, Miles Burnyeat, David Creese, Armand D'Angour, John Dillon, Silvia Fazzo, Kirk Fitzpatrick, Peter Gainsford, Peter Goldie, Roberto Grasso, Christopher Green, Andrew Gregory, Michael Griffin, Penny Gouke, Jim Hankinson, Malcolm Heath, Angela Hobbs, Vittorio G. Hösle, David Howlett, Carl Huffman, Laura Jones, George Kenney, David Langslow, Brian Leiter, Alex Long, Regine May, M. M. McCabe, David Meadows, Gabriele Meloni, Kenneth Royce Moore, Maria-Ruth Morello, Andrew Morrison, Marcus Mota, Ian Mueller, Debra Nails, Liz Pender, Gerald A. Press, Lorna Robinson, Ken Sayre, Bob Sharples, Frisbee Sheffield, Mikaela Sitford, Suzanne Stern-Gillet, Peter Tallack, Harold Tarrant, Lauren Ware, James Wilberding and Colin Wilson.

The excellent John Rylands Library at the University of Manchester provided unstinting support, but thanks must also be given for essential online resources such as JSTOR, the Thesaurus Linguae Graecae, the Internet Archive, and the Perseus Digital Library. Several open-source software projects were key: the TeXShop Latex program from the University of Oregon, the Python programming language from the Python Software Foundation, and the Unicode Consortium.

For their conversations, support, and encouragement during these busy years I would also like to thank Melanie Horton, H. P. Tinker, Amanda Williamson, Andrew Read, Steve Gingell, Andrew Grose, Iyabo Fatimilehin, Justin Hayes, Joanne Goldfeld, Tammy Goldfeld, Sylvia Berryman, Mim Kennedy, Scott Kennedy, Sheryl Coe, Dan Kennedy, Jennifer Bush, Andrew Kaufman, Nathaniel Dahl, Michael Tippner, Chris Scarlata, Cornelius O'Boyle, Evelyn Donegan, Lilian Crascall-Kennedy, John Crascall-Kennedy, Carole Crascall, John Crascall and Louise Crascall.

Abbreviations

Translations throughout are my own unless otherwise indicated.

Aesch. Aeschylus
    Sept. *Septem contra Thebus*

Ar. Aristophanes
    Nu. *Nubes* (*The Clouds*)
    Pax (*Peace*)

Arist. Aristotle
    An. post. *Analytica poteriora* (*Posterior Analytics*)
    De an. *De anima* (*On the Soul*)
    Eth. Nic. *Ethica Nicomachea* (*Nicomachean Ethics*)
    Gen. corr. *De generatione et corruptione* (*On Generation and Corruption*)
    Int. *De interpretatione* (*On Interpretation*)
    Metaph. *Metaphysica* (*Metaphysics*)
    Poet. *Poetica* (*Poetics*)
    Pol. *Politica* (*Politics*)
    Rh. *Rhetorica* (*Rhetoric*)
    Top. *Topica* (*Topics*)
    fragments Aristotelis 1955; Aristotle 1952.

Aristox. Aristoxenus
    Harm. *Harmonica*

Clem. Al. Clemens Alexandrius
    Strom. *Stromateis*

Diels & Kranz H. Diels & W. Kranz, *Die Fragmente der Vorsokratiker* (1959)

DL Diogenes Laertius

Euripides
    Bacch. *Bacchae*

ABBREVIATIONS

Iambl. Iamblichus
       VP *Vita Pythagorae*

LSJ   H. G. Liddell *et al.*, *A Greek–English Lexicon*, 9th edn (1996)

Macrobius
       In Somn. *Commentarius ex Cicerone in Somnium Scipionis*

OCT   Oxford Classical Texts (line numbers in OCT editions are used throughout)

Ov.   Ovid
       Met. *Metamorphoses*

Pl.   Plato
       Cra. *Cratylus*
       Epin. *Epinomis*
       Euthd. *Euthydemus*
       Euthphr. *Euthyphro*
       Grg. *Gorgias*
       Leg. *Leges* (*Laws*)
       Phd. *Phaedo*
       Phdr. *Phaedrus*
       Phlb. *Philebus*
       Plt. *Politicus* (*Statesman*)
       Prm. *Parmenides*
       Resp. *Respublica* (*Republic*)
       Symp. *Symposium*
       Tht. *Theaetetus*
       Ti. *Timaeus*

Plut.   Plutarch
       De aud. po. *De audiendis poetis*
       De Is. et Os. *De Iside et Osiride*
       Vit. Marc. *Vitae Parallelae: Marcellus* (*Parallel Lives: Marcellus*)

pseudo-Plutarch
       De Mus *De Musica* (Laserre 1954)

Porph.   Porphyry
       Plot. *Vita Plotini*

Procl.   Proclus
       In R. *In Platonis Rempublica commentarii* (*Commentary on Plato's Republic*)
       In Ti. *In Platonis Timaeum commentarii* (*Commentary on Plato's Timaeus*)

Ptol.   Ptolemaeus mathematicus
       Harm. *Harmonica* (Ptolemy 1930)

Stob.   Stobaeus (Wachsmuth & Hense 1884–1912)

Vitruvius
       De arch. *De architectura*

Xen.   Xenophon
       Symp. *Symposium*

CHAPTER 1

The nature and history of philosophical allegory

There is a musical scale embedded in each of Plato's dialogues. Symbolic passages at regular intervals are used to mark successive notes.

The surface conversations in the dialogues can seem meandering. Some of the dialogues are even thought to be composites of material written at different times and in different styles. The musical scales give each dialogue an elegant formal unity.

The dialogues often end aporetically. They reach important conclusions at intermediate points and then end negatively with unresolved puzzles. The musical scales explain this. The dialogues each reach their climax at more consonant, intermediate notes and then peter out with the last dissonant notes of the scale.

Platonic forms are generally found by making comparisons and measurements. Applying the same methods to the dialogues themselves reveals the forms beneath their surface narratives.

The early Pythagoreans reportedly held that the entire cosmos was filled with an inaudible "harmony of the spheres", an unheard melody accessible only to philosophers. Plato has filled his dialogues with a similar music.

The early Pythagoreans reportedly held that each object had an inner, mathematical constitution. Vitruvius believed they even gave their writings a mathematical organization. Perhaps for the first time since antiquity, the dialogues are presented below in the style characteristic of classical, literary papyri and so of Plato's own autographs: as a parade of mathematically uniform columns. This restoration of the classical format makes the regular, musical patterns in the dialogues visible almost at once.

This preliminary chapter is an analytical literature review, and relies on quotations and summary reports of conclusions established by other scholars. There are two reasons for resorting to such an economical presentation. First, this chapter draws on scholarship in a range of fields and adequate justifications of the results surveyed here would require several volumes. Second, while this chapter establishes the plausibility and perhaps the intelligibility of the interpretations advanced in the chapters that follow, they must finally stand on the particular evidence given there. This chapter is stage-setting; later chapters turn to advancing novel claims buttressed by argument and evidence.

1.1 Rehabilitating ancient ways of reading

There has been a decisive shift in recent scholarship on classical conceptions of reading and interpretation. There is now a growing consensus that certain roles played by language have been neglected or misunderstood. This change significantly corrects our picture of various literary activities in the circles around Socrates and Plato. Today's philosophers, trained in the analysis and testing of arguments, may be unfamiliar with the strategies of ancient allegory. Even the attention paid over the past generation to the dramatic and dialogical strategies of Plato's writings has proceeded without extensive grounding in this recent research on ancient allegory.

Early in the Hellenistic era, a fire in a tomb charred and preserved a scroll of Orphic and philosophical commentary perhaps dating from the fifth or the fourth century BCE. Excavated by Italian archaeologists, this Derveni papyrus has been called the most ancient, surviving philosophical papyrus, and is now the subject of an extensive literature (Laks & Most 1997; Betegh 2004; Janko 2009). Perhaps the most prominent theme in the recovered text is a kind of allegorizing commentary, and this has contributed to a broad re-evaluation[1] of the significance of ancient allegory among classicists, literary theorists and historians of ancient philosophy:

> A number of pieces of evidence had suggested the existence at a relatively early date of allegorical interpretations of a "philosophical" nature, whether their perspective was physical or moral. Little information on Theagenes or the circle of Anaxagoras was available, but that little was confirmed by what we knew about the Sophists, in particular via Plato. No work of this kind, however, had survived. The Derveni papyrus permitted scholars to glimpse for the first time directly and concretely a literary genre to which access had previously only been indirect and abstract.
> (Laks & Most 1997: 4)

In short, recent scholarship has come to distinguish between two rival traditions of understanding and interpreting language in ancient times. The "rhetorical tradition" looked back to Aristotle's *Rhetoric*, passed through Longinus and Quintilian, and until recently was perceived as dominant. This tradition was oriented towards the needs of the public orator, whose speeches succeeded when they were clear and persuasive. In contrast, the "philosophical tradition" of reading and interpretation was oriented towards wisdom, and regarded texts as repositories of arguments and symbols, of exoteric and esoteric knowledge in need of careful interpretation. In the rhetorical tradition, language immediately worked its effects or was defective; in the philosophical tradition, difficult texts were potentially deep.

These two traditions were centrally divided over the nature of "allegory". Today, this term is usually applied to literary works in which one extended story is concealed beneath another by a sequence of metaphors or symbolic names, as in *Pilgrim's Progress*. In contrast, recent literature on ancient "allegory" treats it as a more diverse, evolving range of linguistic subterfuges, including "undermeanings" (*hyponoia*), riddling or oracular speech (*ainigmata*), "symbols", etymological interpretations, metaphors, similes and puns.[2] In classical studies, at least, "allegory" thus designates any language that intimates some meaning beneath, or in tension with, its ordinary or apparent sense. In the rhetorical tradition, perhaps inspired by some remarks in Aristotle's *Poetics* (1458a18–26), allegory in this broad sense was generally regarded as a blemish to be avoided. In the philosophical tradition of interpretation, on the other hand, allegory in its many guises was central.

Before these recent developments, the neglect of the philosophical tradition had been resisted a generation ago in a pioneering monograph by James Coulter, which helps convey the distance travelled by the later scholarship discussed below:

> [It is] a fact that modern histories of ancient literary criticism and theory, for whatever reasons, generally exhibit an anti-allegorical bias … such histories are written as if the rhetorical tradition and the less widespread tradition of genre criticism were the only modes of literary interpretation in the ancient world with a respectable claim … This assumption is, I believe, historically and intellectually unjustified [and is] only a particular expression of prevailing critical prejudices … (Coulter 1976: 22)

The recent revisionist movement is broad but has in the main confirmed and amplified Coulter's conclusions. It has many sources and was in part galvanized by the Derveni papyrus. Here, a few passages from three significant contributors will concisely portray the nature and breadth of the progress made since Coulter.

David Sedley's monograph *Plato's Cratylus* (2003) is a defence of Plato's interest in etymological allegory. The relatively neglected *Cratylus* is mainly a catalogue of ingenious and seemingly implausible etymological interpretations of isolated words. Since the nineteenth century, it has often been considered an elaborate joke and dismissed. From a modern viewpoint, it may be easy to do so. Socrates, for example, there suggests that a man is called an *anthrōpos* because the word is a compact form of *anathrōn ha opōpe*, that is, "one who reviews or reflects on what he has seen" (Pl. *Cra.* 399c1ff.; Sedley 2003: 37). Sedley concedes that there is much jesting and irony in the *Cratylus*, and that the proposed etymologies are condemned by modern linguists (2003: 40), but nonetheless argues that etymological allegory was a serious philosophical enterprise for Plato and his contemporaries:

> Plato in his mature work – including the *Cratylus* – remained thoroughly committed to the principles of etymology, that is, to the possibility of successfully analysing words as if they were time capsules – encoded packages of information left for us by our distant ancestors about the objects they designate. This finding, although it may come as no surprise at all to most classicists, is I am afraid calculated to cause apoplexy among many of Plato's philosophical admirers. (*Ibid.*: 23)

Sedley argues that this view of language was "endemic to Plato's culture" (*ibid.*: 28) and concludes that "Hunting, by the science of etymological encoding, for the resemblances that bind names to their objects is [for Plato] an entirely legitimate and enlightening procedure" (*ibid.*: 153). In sum, for Sedley, the *Cratylus* is not a mystifying and ponderous joke, but rather a serious exposition of etymological allegory intermixed with Plato's typical humour and irony. As such, it is an approach to language entirely representative of its times.

Andrew Ford's *The Origins of Criticism* (2002) clearly registers the shift away from the Aristotelian rhetorical tradition in histories of textual interpretation. It canvasses a wide variety of social contexts in which textual interpretation and criticism were practised and treats the Derveni papyrus as evidence for an important tradition of allegoresis:

> In the classical period, then, allegorical interpretation remained one among a number of modes of seeking hidden meanings beneath the ostensibly literal purport of a text. Within this methodological melting pot, the promise of a recherché knowledge of Homer continued to hold out an appeal, as allegorists and other up-to-date explicators of old poetry sought students among the educated young men of the democracy … [This method] united sophists, allegorists, and those Plato refers to as "the ones who are so clever about Homer today": when they "explained" that Homer "intended" the name "Athena" to signify "divine intelligence".
> (Ford 2002: 87–8)

Ford is especially attentive to Plato's role in the debates over allegory and drives a wedge between Plato's subtle views and the anti-allegorical rhetorical tradition.

Peter Struck's *Birth of the Symbol* (2004) is concerned to contextualize and trace the history of symbolic language through early and late antiquity. His introductory chapter surveys the change in scholarship over the past generation, and concludes in part:

> with the discovery of the Derveni Papyrus some decades ago, alongside the fragments of other famous allegorists from the classical period, we

> have indication enough that allegoresis forms a more or less continuous strand of literary thinking through the classical, Hellenistic, and early and late Roman periods. For these reasons, it is difficult to accept that this method of reading was "never very popular" [as J. Tate had said], that it was exotic or clearly outside the mainstream, or that it was concentrated in late periods of literary thought. (Struck 2004: 18)

Like Ford, Struck is particularly concerned to contrast the positions of Plato and Aristotle:

> Aristotle's notion of clear language, sensible as it seems, was actually a radical departure from the intellectual currents of the day. It stands out in stark relief against the extent evidence for the linguistic theories that preceded him ... (*Ibid.*: 51)

> [Aristotle's] focus on clarity is in my view as strikingly novel as his ideas on *mimesis* and *katharsis* and serves as another of the foundational building blocks of his decisive contribution to poetics. (*Ibid.*: 67)

Stated so starkly, the conclusions presented here only gesture towards the broad rehabilitation of the philosophical approach to interpretation and allegoresis. In their own ways, Sedley, Ford and Struck are concerned not only to survey the extent of the tradition at various times and in various genres but also to defend its coherence and earnestness. Whether Platonists, Stoics, philosophers, literary scholars, poets, novelists, pagans, Christians or Jews, some of the best philosophical and literary minds of antiquity were engaged with allegory.

The results of recent scholarship may be summarized in a formula: Plato has been read through Aristotelian spectacles. Earlier scholarship underestimated the radical departure and disruption posed by Aristotle's conceptions of language, and marginalized the rival philosophical tradition of interpretation. Newer work on the dramatic and historical context in the dialogues (as in Zuckert 2009) inherits from and shares with the older analytic interpretation an unexamined commitment to literalism.

1.2 Allegory, Socrates and Plato

The rehabilitation of ancient allegory puts pressure on some old, overlooked problems and creates some new ones for scholarly research. In particular, the tension between ancient and modern approaches to reading Plato is thrown into a new and disturbing light. This section concisely reviews literature on the relation between Plato and allegory in order to frame the history and seriousness of the problem.

The circle around Socrates

It is now well established that a number of figures associated or acquainted with Socrates were engaged in the philosophical investigation of "symbolism" and "allegory" in their various guises, and especially with the question of whether ethical, theological or physical doctrines could be found in Homer. In short, Homer was at times treated as a theologian, philosopher or prophet. Before the Derveni papyrus was published, Rudolf Pfeiffer considered Metrodorus of Lampsacus the first "true allegorist" (1968: 35, 237). He was counted a student of Anaxagoras and a member of the circle around Socrates. Diogenes Laertius reported that: "Anaxagoras seems to be first … to assert that the poetry of Homer [is] about virtue and justice. An acquaintance of his, Metrodorus of Lampsacus advanced this doctrine at great length, and was the first to occupy himself with the poetry's systematic physical doctrine" (*pragmateian*; DL II.1).

Plato has the rhapsode Ion associate Metrodorus with those who do not merely learn the poet's words but also interpret his thoughts (*hermēnea … tēs dianoias*) and know "what" he said (*Resp.* 530c3–d3), which clearly signals Plato's familiarity with his approach. The few surviving, late testimonia about Metrodorus give examples of simple-minded allegorical identifications (Achilles with the sun, Helen with the earth, etc.; DK 61B), but we do not know if these are representative or whether they formed only a small part of Metrodorus' methods. Another Socratic, Antisthenes the Cynic made a "distinction between 'seeming' and 'truth' in the Homeric poems" (Pfeiffer 1968: 36).[3] In Xenophon's *Symposium*, in a conversation that included Antisthenes, we have attributed to Socrates the remark that those who recited Homer failed to draw out their ethical teachings because they did not understand the poem's allegories (i.e. *hyponoia*; Xen. *Symp.* III.6.24).

Apart from the association between particular philosophers and allegoresis, there are some indications that this approach to interpretation was a well-known and widespread fashion during the lifetime of Socrates. Brief examples of allegorical etymologies may be found in Euripides (e.g. *Bacch.* 296–7) and Herodotus (e.g. I.122). Struck interprets a passage in Aristophanes (*Pax* 38ff.) as a probable reference to the allegoresis of Anaxagoras and Metrodorus, and concludes that their methods were "familiar enough to an Athenian audience to get a laugh in the popular medium of comedy" (Struck 2004: 41). In a passage from the *Cratylus* referred to above, Plato's Socrates says, "Indeed, even the ancients seem to think about Athena just as those who are currently skilled concerning Homer do. For the majority of these in interpreting the poet say that he has made out Athena to be mind and thought [*noun te kai dianoian*]" (Pl. *Cra.* 407a8–b2, trans. Struck 2004: 44). That is, as Struck says, Plato's Socrates here asserts that most interpreters of Homer at the time of Socrates engaged in allegoresis to some degree.

Although only one of many themes in their thinking, there is thus some evidence linking allegoresis to Anaxagoras, Metrodorus, Antisthenes, Socrates and others in the circles from which Plato emerged.

Surveying novels and poems from late antiquity, Robert Lamberton devotes a chapter to an argument that critical discussions of allegory lead to the writing of allegorical literature: "The popular literature of late antiquity does indeed appear to develop the possibility of genuine allegory under the influence of a pervasive tradition of allegorical interpretation" (1986: 160). Plato, it will be concluded, is an early instance of this syndrome: theoretical interest in allegory inspires allegorical writing.

Allegory, hyponoia *and enigmas in Plato*

Plato's familiarity with allegory broadly conceived is widely attested in the dialogues, and only a few central passages need be recalled here. First, even apart from the *Cratylus*, the dialogues deploy many allegorical devices and explicitly call attention to them. In the parable of the cave, Plato deploys a symbolic tale and interprets its elements one by one (*Resp.*, 514a1ff.). In the *Phaedrus*, Socrates criticizes those who find rational explanations behind the myths (*Phdr.* 229c6ff.). Gregory Vlastos's late studies of Socrates' irony did not relate it to questions of allegory and riddling language, but if irony is "saying one thing and meaning another" then it also undercuts the surface meanings of language (Vlastos 1991; cf. Struck 2004: 45–50). That is, those who accept that irony is characteristic of Plato's Socrates already accept that Plato adopted a style in which surface language and meaning could diverge, a style that in the classical period would have been considered a kind of "allegorical" language. Second, the dialogues often impute allegorical and riddling language to other thinkers and writers, as Struck's survey shows (2004: 41–50).

Plato's own views towards allegory have been debated. Ford's final assessment is carefully modulated to capture the divergent tendencies in the dialogues:

> Allegoresis is viewed by Plato as an uncertain method and dangerous where children are concerned, but he never denies outright the possibility of its being used in a more philosophical way. In the passage rejecting allegory from the *Republic* (378d), the reasons are primarily pedagogical and social rather than theological or methodological … Plato's disquiet is focused on popularisers of subtle interpretation, not on the method itself.   (Ford 2002: 86–7)

Peter Kingsley agrees with this:

> There is still a general belief that Plato was resolutely opposed to allegory as a method of explaining literary texts. However, the fact is that his attitude to it was as ambiguous and complex as his attitude to myth itself … Plato's attack on allegorising in the *Republic* is not an attack on the method but only on its use in certain circumstances.   (Kingsley 1995: 166–7)

In sum, although allegory and *hyponoia* were not well-defined categories, the dialogues repeatedly raise the issue of riddling language that undercuts or subverts its ordinary sense. The nature of allegory is a theme of the dialogues.

In the modern period, literature and philosophy have at times been sharply distinguished, and tropes such as allegory have been considered inappropriate for philosophical texts. It would be anachronistic, however, to apply this to Plato and his predecessors. With figures such as Empedocles and Parmenides writing in verse, it was impossible to distinguish poets from "philosophers" by literary form alone. Plato was writing at a time when prose was still a new and evolving technology. His dialogues, of course, resemble plays more than Thucydides' or Aristotle's treatises. Struck argues that the separation between philosophy and literature, and thus between two approaches to composition and interpretation, was profoundly affected by Aristotle's innovations:

> Aristotle explicitly declares a separation between poetic issues and philosophical ones. Looking for philosophical truths in poetry entails a genre transgression … Demarcating a clear genre distinction between Empedocles and Homer has the side effect of undercutting the consistent allegorical inclination to find specifically philosophical kinds of knowledge inside poetic texts. (Struck 2004: 67)

Such a separation is not consistently made in the dialogues. Plato's Socrates often considered himself a rival to Homer and the tragedians,[4] and Plato has the Athenian Stranger assert in the *Laws* that:

> we ourselves are poets of a tragedy that is the fairest and best our abilities allow. At least, our city's constitution was put together as an imitation (*mimesis*) of the fairest and best life, which we, at any rate, say is really the truest tragedy. Thus we are poets; we are poets of the same [subjects], your artistic rivals and adversaries. (Pl. *Leg.* 817b2ff.)

Thus, although philosophy is sometimes an alternative to poetry, at other times Plato's dialogues seem to be saying they are a better kind of tragedy or poetry. Proclus, for example, did later treat the dialogues as a literary genre comparable to tragedy and dithyrhambic poetry (*In R.* 14.15ff.). A struggle to surpass Homer coupled with a belief that the power of his verse lay partly in its allegories, as some in the circles around Socrates thought, might have stimulated Plato's own interest in allegory.

1.3 Symbols, reserve and Pythagoreanism

It is difficult today, in our culture of open publication, to appreciate the many political and sociological motivations in ancient cultures for "reserving" doctrines. Walter Burkert made the point that secrecy was then "normal":

> All mysteries have secrets; the ritual is interpreted as a *hieros logos* which may not be disclosed to the uninitate, and the initiate also learns secret passwords, *symbola*, *sunthēmata*. All kinds of societies that are bound together by cult have their esoteric aspect – even political clubs, trade guilds, and those of the physicians. (1972: 179)

Regardless of their content, Burkert emphasizes, secrets played an important sociological role by fostering a sense of inclusiveness and elite privilege that helped hold groups together: "Above all, there was the obligation of secrecy, deemed essential for all true mysteries; those who were 'in' wished to be kept distinct from those who were 'out'. The main concern was not propagating a faith, but withholding the central revelation. This made mysteries attractive" (1987: 45–6).

From the Hellenistic period through late antiquity, there is extensive evidence that Pythagoreans were considered a paradigmatic secret society that used "symbols", reserved their doctrines and swore oaths to secrecy (Iambl. *VP*; Thesleff 1961, 1965; Burkert 1972). This late reputation for secrecy is already attested in the fourth century BCE by Aristotle (in Iambl. *VP*, 6) and by his sometime student Aristoxenus (DL VIII.15–16). Burkert accepts that these show that secrecy and reserve were in fact a feature of early Pythagoreanism:

> Pythagorean silence and secrecy should also be see in the context of cult and ritual. To be sure, the secrecy of Pythagorean doctrine later was misused by forgers as license to "discover" more and more Pythagorean writings. But the testimony of Aristotle and Aristoxenus, which proves the existence of Pythagorean *aporrēta*, cannot be ignored.
> (1972: 179; cf. n.96)

Late tradition treats religious persecution as an important motivation for Pythagorean secrecy. Burkert (1972: 112ff.), Carl Huffman (1993: 2ff.) and Charles Kahn (2001: 7) find the evidence for persecution in the mid-fifth century BCE credible. A report survives from Aristoxenus, who was himself a native of Italian Tarentum, about a pogrom of some sort against the Pythagoreans in southern Italy (where Pythagoras himself had taken refuge):

> Finally they became so hostile to the men [the Pythagoreans] that when the Pythagoreans were meeting in the house of Milo [the Olympic victor] in Croton and taking council about affairs of the city they set fire to the

house and burned all the men except two, Archippus and Lysis. These men, since they were the youngest and strongest got out.
(Iambl. *VP* 249–50, trans. Huffman)

It is difficult to form a picture of these fifth-century Pythagoreans, but E. L. Minar's account has a degree of plausibility. Relying on passages from fourth-century figures such as Aristoxenus, Dicaearchus, and Timaeus (the historian), which are preserved in later works, as well as numismatic evidence, he argues that the Pythagoreans ruled an "empire" larger than Attica and centred in Croton for some fifty years (1942: chs III, IV). They were, like other clubs and societies, typically secretive but were attacked and persecuted after they became a reformist political movement. It was the combination of secrecy and exclusivity with power that eventually led to rebellion and the massacre of their leadership council (*ibid.*: 55). In the turbulent second-half of the fifth century, after the collapse of their empire, the remnants of the Pythagoreans were welcomed in cities such as Rhegium, briefly returned to Croton, and came to power for the first time in Tarentum (*ibid.*: ch. IV). "But as time went on and the political situation grew progressively worse," Minar concludes, "all except Archytas of Tarentum left Italy altogether" (*ibid.*: 79).

Some credit the Pythagoreans with inventing literary "symbolism". There is little evidence that Pythagoras and others among the earliest Pythagoreans wrote anything, but the Pythagoreans were later widely reputed, already in Aristotle (1955: 135 = Porph. *Plot.* 41), to use oral or written "symbols". In Greek, this word originally meant a part of some small object that two parties split and later used to prove their identity (LSJ). The Pythagoreans seemed to extend this meaning to include short phrases that played the role of secret passwords or answered ritualized riddles, and may have been used by initiates to identify one another. Struck traces the way this, perhaps idiosyncratic, usage was further stretched to encompass a wider range of enigma, allegory and literary symbolism: "The Pythagorean context (and others like it [in the mystery religions]) pulls the term from its strict classical role of authentication over into its role as a label for enigmatic language that carries a hidden significance" (2004: 102).

The relation between the Pythagoreans' use of "symbols" and the wider interest in finding allegories in Homer and Hesiod (described in §§1.1, 1.2) has been debated. Struck's brief review concludes, in agreement with Lamberton (1986) and Marcel Detienne (1962), that "allegorical interpretation of the poets may have been a part of early Pythagorean tradition" (2004: 103–4). Thus, even before the time of Plato, it is difficult to distinguish the broad interest in philosophical allegory from the Pythagoreans' use of "symbolism".

There are many references to reserving, withholding or disguising doctrines in Plato's dialogues. The guardian's Noble Lie in the *Republic* is the best known, but there are brief and incidental references that may or may not be significant in many dialogues. Socrates, for example, accuses Euthyphro of not wanting to teach him (*Euthphr.* 14b8ff.). Cleitophon suspects that Socrates is deliberately holding back his doctrines (*Resp.* 410c6).[5] Phaedrus pretends he does not have a written copy of Lysias' speech until Socrates finds it concealed under his *himation* (*Phdr.* 228d7).

Some longer passages explicitly raise the issue of reserving doctrines. In the *Phaedo*, Socrates quizzes the two young Pythagoreans from Thebes:

> "What, Cebes, have you not and Simmias not heard about that, though you are followers of Philolaus [the Pythagorean]?"
> "Nothing definite, Socrates."
> "Well I will tell you what I have heard about that ... the doctrine about that which is spoken in secret (*aporrētois legomenos*) is that humans are in a sort of prison [in this life]." (*Phd.* 61c6–9, 62b2–4)

This is a teasing passage. Plato has Socrates refer to the practice of reserving doctrines and associates them with a known Pythagorean, but then reveals the doctrine. In the *Cratylus* too, Socrates refers to reserved doctrines but immediately shares them with his interlocutor:

> Up to this point, it is agreed by many that what I just said is justice. But I, Hermogenes, being very persistent about this, have been taught the following in secret (*aporrētois*): ... someone told me it is correct to call [justice] Zeus ... After having heard this, I none the less gently asked them "Whatever could this mean, my good man, if that is so?" And then I seem to be prolonging the question more than is fitting and to go too far. They say I have been told enough. (*Cra.* 413e3–b1)[6]

That is, Socrates seems to be saying that he was taught some reserved doctrines but others were withheld from him.

Although the following passage may merely say that technical philosophy is inappropriate for a general audience, it shows Plato's characters deliberating about what is suitable for open display and what is better for small groups. In the *Parmenides*, when Zeno reportedly suggested that Parmenides should speak, he said:

> We ought to ask that of Parmenides himself. It is no trifling matter what he says. Or don't you see how much work you are requiring? If, certainly, there were more of us, it would not be fit to ask. It's improper to say such things before many, especially at his age. The Many do not know that, without this detailed and digressive exposition of all of it, it is impossible for the mind to arrive at the truth. (*Prm.* 136d3–e3)

In the *Theaetetus*, Socrates contrasts the ancients who concealed their meanings from the more recent sophists who openly reveal their philosophy: "[T]he ancients concealed (*epikruptomenōn*) things from the many with poetry ... while later figures [who teach that everything is in motion] are wiser in as much as they exhibit openly, so that even cobblers may hear and learn their sophistries" (*Tht.* 180c8–d5).

These passages at least establish that Plato's Socrates was taught in secret and knew some reserved doctrines. They also provide more evidence for Burkert's contention that reserving doctrines was pervasive in antiquity, since the characters in these passages do not protest or express surprise at the existence of secret teachings.

The dialogues do not treat this motif with any apparent seriousness. The passages that refer to withholding doctrines or to secret teachings seem incidental and play no large role in the subsequent conversations. Socrates seems willing to share his esoteric knowledge.

In sum, these and similar passages can be read in two different ways. Those who read the dialogues literally will find little of significance here. However, the advocates of the view that Plato had "unwritten" Pythagorean doctrines have seized on these passages and treated them as broad hints that Plato's Socrates and therefore Plato had something to hide (see below and Findlay 1974: 350–51; Krämer 1990: 55ff.).

1.4 Persecution and the politics of allegory in classical Athens

Literary historians have treated enigmatic, symbolic and allegorical language as a rhetorical device deployed in certain social contexts. Other research connects allegory to the political and religious controversies that were so prominent in late classical Athens, and argues that Plato and other philosophers had strong, political motivations for adopting allegory.

Thomas Cole's 1991 monograph *The Origins of Rhetoric in Ancient Greece* is an extended argument that in the fifth century BCE the rise of allegoresis and the new science of "rhetoric" have the same cause and were both part of a broad, political transformation in Athenian society. The rise of popular democracy placed new power in the hands of skilful orators but also dramatized their supposed ability to "make the weaker argument the stronger". Rhetoric thus emerged out of a consciousness that the same ideas could be presented in many different ways, that is, that the content of language could be distinguished from its presentation. This led to the interest in mastering general techniques of persuasion that were independent of content. Allegoresis too, Cole points out, rests on a parallel sense that the content of language might be disguised by its presentation. Although the above literary evidence for the popularity of allegoresis in the fifth century does little in itself to illuminate its social origins or motivations, Cole's argument plausibly explains how allegoresis fits into a milieu of developing rhetorical and philosophical studies.

Richard Janko, an authority on the Derveni papyrus, has particularly investigated the political motivations for philosophical allegory in classical Athens. His important article "Socrates the Freethinker" (2009) illuminates the political role of allegory during Plato's lifetime and is worth quoting at length here. Janko makes way for his revisionist history by first countering the still common tendency to underestimate, despite the execution of Socrates and other episodes, the dangers faced by philosophers in the late fifth century:

> Scholars have often tried to minimize the Athenians' persecution of scientists and intellectuals ... But even if some of the evidence is contradictory or unreliable, more than enough remains to prove that there was an increasingly fierce anti-intellectual climate and that it was centred on "atheism". (2009: 56–60)

The persecution of atheists, as Janko argues, was not limited to those who denied the existence of the gods. The Athenians did not distinguish "between those who believed in new gods, different from those in which the city believed, only one god or no god at all" (*ibid.*: 55). Monotheists were thus, since they opposed the traditional gods, atheists.

The new rationalizing *Naturphilosophie* of the *physkoi* and of philosophers such as Anaxagoras and Socrates was therefore perceived as a kind of atheism. Although Plato's dialogues are very concerned to portray Socrates as some sort of theist, the fact is that Aristophanes' *Clouds* clearly characterizes him as an atheist (e.g. *Nu.* 828–30) and a central theme of Plato's *Apology* is the denial of that charge. The author of the Derveni papyrus advocated a combination of monotheism, pantheism, and teleology but this too counted as "atheism" (Janko 2009: 53ff.). This broad understanding of atheism meant that the nascent sciences and new natural philosophies were rivals to traditional religion.[7] The threat to the new philosophies was not subtle:

> We see [in the *Clouds*] Socrates' Think-Tank, the first university the world has seen, burned down with the thinkers inside. Aristophanes probably got the idea from a historically attested attack in about 454 on a meeting-house of the leaders of the Pythagorean sect at Croton in Southern Italy: most were burned alive. (*Ibid.*: 57)

Janko argues that persecution and the threat of persecution propelled the turn towards allegory among key figures in the Greek Enlightenment. The allegorical reinterpretation of the myths opened up a path towards reconciling the new philosophies with traditional religion:

> This sensationalist text [of the Derveni papyrus] reveals exactly how, after the outlawing of research into astronomy in the 430s, spiritually inclined freethinkers tried to reconcile their new scientific understanding with the Greeks' traditional polytheistic religion, with its shocking myths and peculiar rites ... These thinkers deemed their new belief [in teleological monotheism] compatible with the latest scientific theories and discoveries. Indeed, followers of Anaxagoras like Diogenes and Diagoras tried to

> prove this by applying the new techniques of allegory and etymology to the interpretation of holy texts like the poetry of Homer and Orpheus and of rituals like the Mysteries, arguing that they cannot be taken literally but convey scientific truth. (*Ibid.*: 60)

This drove, according to Janko, the wide interest in allegory among philosophers: "The combination of allegory and etymology became common later in the fifth century" (*ibid.*: 52).

This attempted reconciliation, however, strengthened the sense that the traditional gods were under attack and catastrophically failed to avert further persecution. The fashion for reinterpreting the myths was deemed atheistical and:

> caused a fundamentalist backlash, when death sentences were passed first on Diagoras and then on Socrates ... *After his execution his disciples had powerful reasons for concealing his real or alleged relations to such religious beliefs, and particularly so if they held similar beliefs themselves*: they wanted to continue to teach in Athens without being convicted of impiety. (*Ibid.*: 60, emphasis added)

As late as 322 BCE, when Aristotle was charged with impiety and fled Athens, he reportedly insinuated a connection to the earlier persecutions with his quip that he would not let Athens "sin against philosophy a second time" (DL V.5; Plut., *Vit. Marc.* 41). For Janko, then, the persecution of "atheists" powerfully affected late-fifth- and fourth-century thought: "The fundamentalist reaction had profound effects on the development of both science and philosophy ... the new monotheism of Anaxagoras' successors became the hidden faith of many intellectuals; its influence on ... Euripides, Antisthenes, Plato, Aristotle [and others was ...] enormous" (2009: 61).

Already in antiquity, the neo-Pythagorean Numenius explained Plato's use of allegory and reserve as a result of fear of persecution (fr. 23.9ff., 24.61ff.). Any debate over Plato's motivation for using allegory must take into account Janko's powerful, revisionist interpretation of the political dangers faced by philosophy during Plato's lifetime. The new sciences and new philosophies were allied with allegory until Aristotle's critiques in the mid-fourth century.

1.5 Plato and Pythagoreanism: two puzzles

Our knowledge of Pythagoreanism before Plato is fragmentary. Perhaps because of the relations to Archytas portrayed in the Platonic epistles, Plato has been thought to have been directly influenced by Pythagoreanism, perhaps even an initiate. Several of the dialogues do contain Pythagorean themes: the *Philebus*, *Timaeus*, *Republic*, *Phaedo* and so on. There is also evidence that the early Academy was occupied with the study of Pythagoreanism. Several of its associates (Speusippus, Xenocrates, Aristotle, and Heraclides) wrote books, in part or entirely lost, whose titles record their interest in Pythagoras.[8]

Burkert's influential *Lore and Science in Ancient Pythagoreanism* (1972) has reoriented views of the early Pythagorean tradition and its relation to Plato, as Miles Burnyeat (2007) recently emphasized.[9] Variegated and sometimes conflicting reports about Pythagoras and his doctrines slowly grew through antiquity into a substantial literature.[10] Burkert argued at some length that these reports were the product of two traditions that should be carefully distinguished. One stemmed from Aristotle, and was generally deflationary. His Pythagoras had little to say about metaphysics and seemed a half-legendary, religious figure.[11] Burkert traced the other tradition back to Plato's heirs in the Academy: Speusippus, Xenocrates, Herclides and others. This tradition promoted a more metaphysical and mathematical Pythagoras as the very source of the Platonic tradition.

Although Burkert is cautious about Aristotle's views of the Presocratics, he argues that only Aristotle's more modest picture accords with Pythagoras' early dates (Burkert 1972: 28–97, esp. 57, 79). Huffman surveys what he calls "Burkert's revolutionary work" in a review, and endorses his conclusion:

> Thus, Aristotle's presentation of Pythagoreanism, although it also needs correction, is much more likely to allow us to appreciate the actual contribution of Pythagoras and fifth-century Pythagoreans than the Academic tradition. As one of the central controls for developing an accurate account of early Pythagoreanism, Aristotle's presentation undermines the assumption that what the later tradition frequently assigns to Pythagoras must contain a kernel of truth. The Pythagoreanism of late antiquity was not motivated by documentary evidence but by Pythagoras' status as the ultimate sage. (Huffman 1999: 69)

This creates a puzzle about the aggrandizing views of Pythagoras disseminated by the Academy. Burkert and Huffman see relatively little evidence for a Pythagorean influence on Plato's dialogues. For them, Socrates, Anaxagoras and, in the later dialogues, Parmenides loom larger. The *Philebus*' treatment of the limited and unlimited is taken to reflect the genuine Pythagoreanism of Philolaus, but these modest doctrines accord with and confirm Aristotle's views (Burkert 1972: 85–90). Plato's dialogues mention Pythagoras and "the Pythagoreans" only in the *Republic* (530d8, 600b1–2).[12] Most importantly, Burkert and Huffman take the *Timaeus* for a "Platonic and not a Pythagorean work" (Huffman 1999: 84). Why, then, this apparent exaggeration of Pythagoras' importance for Plato? Burkert can offer only conjectures:

> Speusippus, Xenocrates and Herclides equate the doctrine of their master Plato, and therewith their own philosophical positions, with the wisdom of Pythagoras ... (1972: 82)

> Plato's school sees in its own philosophical treatment of the problem of ultimate principles a continuation of Pythagoreanism, so that ancient material is reinterpreted accordingly. This Platonic interpretation of Pythagorean philosophy became dominant in the ancient tradition. Aristotle was the only one to contradict it and shows us therefore what had been there before Plato ... Platonizing interpretation took the place of historical reality. *One can only guess at the reasons why Plato and his pupils saw themselves as continuators of Pythagoreanism.* (*Ibid.*: 91–2, emphasis added)

In these passages, Burkert and Huffman are arguing for a distinction between early Pythagoreanism and Plato's own philosophy. They compare the views of Plato with those attributed to Pythagoras, Philolaus and Archytas and find the distance so great that the Academy's identification of the two is puzzling (Huffman 1993: 21ff.). The issue at stake is the novelty of Plato's philosophy.

There is a second, related puzzle about Plato's supposed "unwritten" doctrines and their relation to Pythagoreanism. The view that there were esoteric, orally transmitted "unwritten doctrines", which had been advocated by Konrad Gaiser, H. J. Krämer and others associated with the Tübingen school, was widely rejected by anglophone philosophers such as Harold Cherniss and Vlastos.[13] However, there is now a consensus among scholars such as Kenneth Sayre, Dillon and Kahn that Plato did have a Pythagorean ontology that was not spelled out in the dialogues. They nonetheless disagree that there was any sustained effort among Plato's successors to withhold these views or transmit them orally and clandestinely alongside the "exoteric" dialogues, as has been suggested by the adherents of the Tübingen school.

Sayre's *Plato's Late Ontology* (1983) marked a decisive shift among anglophone philosophers towards the acceptance of Plato's Pythagorean ontology. He argued that a careful reading of clues in the dialogues themselves provided sufficient evidence to confirm the secondary reports about Plato's views. As he later summarized:

> there were two radically opposed positions on the significance of Aristotle's reports. One (represented by K. Gaiser and H. J. Krämer of Tübingen, among others) held that Aristotle was reporting a set of doctrines passed on orally by Plato but never committed to writing – the so-called unwritten teachings. The other position was championed by Harold Cherniss in *The Riddle of the Early Academy*, to the effect that Aristotle simply did not understand Plato's views and was reporting them erroneously. Opposed as they were in other respects, both camps maintained that the views attributed to Plato by Aristotle could not be found in Plato's dialogues.
> (2006: 1)

Plato's Late Ontology offered a third alternative. It argued that all of the theses attributed to Plato by Aristotle could be found in the *Philebus*. The reason they are not immediately apparent is that they are expressed in terms other than those used by Aristotle in reporting them (*ibid.*).

Sayre does not sufficiently explain, however, why Plato could not make his supposed views "immediately apparent", and expound them in the direct language of the later summaries.

Kahn's introduction to Pythagoreanism clearly registers the move towards acknowledgement of Plato's unwritten doctrines:

> Since Plato himself did not see fit to publish a written account of these teachings, and since the later reports largely depend on Aristotle [who was unsympathetic], we cannot fully understand what Plato had in mind. It is nevertheless clear that certain features of [Plato's] oral doctrine of first principles exerted a decisive influence on the philosophy of Plato's immediate students ... the theory as reported by Aristotle and later writers is not entirely unfaithful to Plato's thought. (2001: 58, 62)

Like Sayre, Kahn finds evidence in certain passages of the later dialogues that confirm the secondary reports. Dillon's monograph *The Heirs of Plato* similary embraces the unwritten doctrines:

> [O]ne must resolve to look beyond the dialogues ... There is in fact considerable secondary evidence as to the views entertained by Plato on certain basic questions ... it seems clear that Plato, at least in his later years, had become more and more attracted by the philosophical possibilities of Pythagoreanism, that is to say, the postulation of a mathematical model for the universe. (2003: 16–17)

Dillon goes on to sketch these doctrines at length and relate them to passages in the dialogues.

The positions of Sayre, Kahn and Dillon are compatible with those of Burkert and Huffman. That is, Plato's unwritten doctrines may have affinities with Pythagoreanism, for example in their emphasis on mathematics, but may also be innovative enough to count as a distinct philosophy. The Academy's reasons for so definitely associating Plato's doctrines with Pythagoreanism, however, remain unclear.

The puzzle of the so-called unwritten doctrines has important implications here. There is now agreement that the Tübingen school was correct to infer that Plato had an unwritten, quasi-Pythagorean ontology, but was incorrect to suppose there was any sustained effort at clandestine, oral transmission. There is, furthermore, agreement that it is a subtle reading of select passages, hints and suggestions in the dialogues that provides the evidence to confirm the later reports of the unwritten doctrines. In sum, there is now a consensus that Plato had a philosophy that he did not spell out openly and simply in the dialogues.

Kahn's "ingressive interpretation" of the dialogues defends at length the need to read the dialogues subtly because their true import does not lie on the surface. In a section entitled "Plato's Motive for Holding Back", Kahns writes:

> Why so much deviousness on Plato's part? Why do dialogues like the *Charmides*, *Meno*, and the *Euthydemus* obscurely hint at doctrines ...? In the clase of Plato, his lifetime loyalty to the dialogue form suggests a temperamental aversion to direct statement, reinforced by much reflection on the obstacles to successful communication for philosophical insight ... [Plato's indirect and subtle,] ingressive mode of exposition has, I suggest, been chosen by Plato because of his acute sense of the psychological distance that separates his world view from that of his audience ...
>
> Plato's metaphysical vision ... is recognizably that of Plotinus and the Neoplatonists ... For Plato's new world view, his only ally would be the Orphic-Pythagorean doctrine of reincarnation.   (1996: 65–7)

Kahn does not see any extensive use of allegory or symbolism in Plato's dialogues, and does not investigate the relation between the kind of reserve he sees in the dialogues and the culture of reserving doctrines in classical religion and philosophy. He does, however, contend that Plato adopted a style of writing in all the dialogues designed to hold back or reserve his doctrines, that they nonetheless can be found within the dialogues, and that these doctrines had affinities with Pythagoreanism.

This monograph accepts the evidence that the Aristotelian and Academic traditions portrayed Pythagoras differently, but suggests that this important puzzle can be resolved by an allegorical or symbolic reading of Plato's dialogues. Subsequent work on the symbols with doctrinal content will show that Plato concealed a primarily Pythagorean philosophy within the dialogues. This makes it more likely that his followers in the early Academy had good grounds for associating Plato with Pythagoreanism.

Sayre, Kahn and Dillon have already established that Plato had a philosophy with affinities to Pythagoreanism that he did not spell out openly and simply in the dialogues. They have argued in different ways that subtle intepretation will reveal this philosophy. Kahn has sketched Plato's philosophical motivations for reserving this Pythagorean philosophy.

1.6 The allegorical Plato in history

Although treated by some today as a curiosity of intellectual history, allegorical readings of Plato were a prominent and sometimes dominant theme shaping his reception for some fifteen hundred years. It is clear that, by modern standards, much of this commentary is uncontrolled and unverifiable and far from rigorous. Its fundamental motivation and currency have therefore at times baffled modern scholars. Here, the contours of the tradition are briefly outlined. It is important to distinguish in ancient times, too, between the sometime tradition of esoteric, "unwritten" or "oral" doctrines, according to which some privileged doctrines were supposed to have been kept out of the dialogues, and the tradition that ideas were embedded in the dialogues themselves using allegory.

Plato's first interpreters

Early approaches to interpreting the dialogues have been traced by Heinrich Dörrie (1976), Dillon (1977, 2003), Eugène Tigerstedt (1977), David Runia (1986), Harold Tarrant (2000) and Tarrant and Dirk Baltzly (2006). Surprisingly, although there was sustained interest in Plato's philosophy in the two centuries following his death, there is little surviving evidence of intensive and careful efforts to interpret the dialogues. In this regard, Aristotle's treatises seem typical of the approach taken by Plato's early successors. The focus is on problems and argument while the dialogues are referred to in a way that is sometimes casual and haphazard (Runia 1986: 38–57). There is little evidence suggesting that the then-current methods of Homeric interpretation were applied to the dialogues, nor anything like a modern, evidence-based attempt to construct a coherent and consistent reading of the dialogues. The dialogues do not, after all, purport to represent Plato's philosophy. In the eight or so generations after Plato, when a series of authoritative figures spoke for an authoritative tradition, the dialogues were used rather selectively to buttress that authority. Only later did the dialogues themselves move to the forefront of the tradition. When they did, their study slowly became more intensive, more sophisticated and more allegorical.

Dörrie's *Von Platon zum Platonismus* provides a useful, if schematic, periodization of the various ancient approaches to Plato's dialogues. The first generations of "dogmatists" after Plato in the Old Academy were generally concerned with doctrines, arguments and problems associated with Plato, but seemed to place little emphasis on detailed readings of the text. Commentaries on the dialogues were apparently not written in the early Academy.[14] However, in a well-known dispute over creation in the *Timaeus*, Speusippus and Xenocrates were apparently reading parts of the *Timaeus* not literally, but as mere heuristic or expository devices (Runia 1986; Tarrant 2000: 45). The fragments of Xenocrates indicate that he treated some terms allegorically in a way that is reminiscent of those in the circle around Socrates.[15]

The dogmatists were followed by the "sceptics". These used the dialogues primarily to show that they were aporetic, issuing merely in professions of Socratic ignorance (Hankinson 1994: ch. 5). When Antiochus reinstated dogmatic approaches to Plato about the beginning of the first century BCE, his Plato was an eclectic combination of doctrines from the Old Academy, Aristotle and the Stoics: the dialogues had no privileged or central position. As Dörrie says:

> Although Antiochus had had good reason to employ all that was held to be traditionally Plato's in his system, he made no use of Plato's dialogues. On this point – the renunciation of extracting doctrines from the written works – Antiochus remained where his predecessors stood ... When loud

and even urgent questions about Plato's views were raised, the Academy remained silent. It had lost any competence to interpret Plato. Increasingly, Plato was read and interpreted outside the Academy.

(Dörrie 1976: 15–16)

As interest in Plato spread to Alexandria and other cities across the Mediterranean, there is thus a detectable turn from scrutiny of the doctrines ascribed to Plato by tradition towards the dialogues themselves. Many scholars have thus found a new beginning in approaches to Plato during and after the first century BCE. Dörrie loosely organizes these new developments into two phases: "naive" and "critical" (*philologische*). During the first, the dialogues were sometimes treated as straightforward assertions of Plato's doctrines. The *Timaeus*, in particular, was read literally. Even Philo of Alexandria, known for his allegorical interpretations of scripture, read Plato's dialogues literally (Runia 1986). He accepted, for example, the historicity of the Atlantis myth and compared it to Noah's flood. Writing in 1976, Dörrie said of this naive period:

the hermeneutical question was not posed … (1976: 35)

Today, the demand that an interpretation must set out from an evaluation of the entirety (*des gesamten Habitus*) of a text would appear obvious and even banal. However, even in modern philology, this demand was first recognized as valid in the last two or at most three generations. (*Ibid.*: 42)

Dörrie detects the beginning of more critical approaches to the dialogues in Eudorus, who based his interpretative claims on comparisons between a variety of passages from different dialogues (*ibid.*: 40–41).

In short, there is little evidence that Plato's dialogues were read critically by Plato's successors in Athens. As soon as Plato was studied in other centres that could not rely directly on the oral and written tradition of Athens, the problem of interpreting the dialogues loomed ever larger. This led to a slow movement towards the allegorical approaches that later came to dominate.

The allegorical turn

This shift towards more intensive readings of the dialogues is concurrent with, and in some figures coincides with, an apparent resurgence of interest in Pythagoreanism.[16] The so-called "neo-Pythagoreans", also from about the first century BCE, claimed that Pythagorean doctrines were symbolically embedded in Plato's dialogues. One key figure here is Numenius (second century CE) who was said in antiquity to be a Pythagorean. His surviving fragments testify to an esoteric reading of Plato that was in opposition to some traditions of the Academy. One of his works was entitled *On the Disagreement of the Academics with Plato*, and another *On the Secrets or Reserved Doctrines in Plato* (Numenius of Apamea 1973). Tarrant summarizes the fragmentary remains of these neo-Pythagoreans:

> All this suggests [their] belief that Pythagorean doctrines are *hidden* in Plato, who for one reason or another is reluctant to reveal them, and that *true Pythagoreanism can be teased out of Platonic texts by in-depth interpretation*. Like Thrasyllus, [other Neo-Pythagoreans like] Moderatus, Numenius, and Numenius' friend Cronius were all supposed to have written on the first principles of Plato and Pythagoras in such a way that they had somehow anticipated Plotinus ... So it would seem safe to say that something quite esoteric is regularly being detected beneath Plato's text, concealing details of the allegedly Pythagorean metaphysic that Pythagoreans, almost as a matter of faith, supposed to exist there.
> (Tarrant 2000: 84–5)

The routine attribution of hidden meanings to Plato can be found in Plutarch (c.45–125 CE), a priest of the Elysian mysteries and perhaps a Platonic successor. He held, for example, that:

> Plato, while often obscuring and concealing (*epēlugēzomenos kai paradaluptomenos*) his opposing principles, names the one Sameness and the other Difference. In the *Laws*, when he was older, using neither enigmas nor symbols but literal language, he said the cosmos was moved not by one soul but probably by more.   (Plut. *De Is. et Os.* 370f; cf. Tarrant 2000: 24)

This tendency to read beneath the surface of Plato's dialogues culminated in the Neoplatonists, where we have a full-blown allegorical Plato. Plotinus' *Enneads* are oriented towards philosophical problems rather than commentary, but the allegorical approach to Plato is already robust there. He says several times, for example, that Plato "hints" or has *hyponoia*.[17]

In *Ennead* III.5, there is an extended allegorical interpretation of passages from Plato's *Symposium*. The approach of Plotinus and his follower Porphyry to the dialogues was later criticized as "piecemeal"; Porphyry was thought to interpret the same passage in several different ways, which were not reconciled with each other (Wallis 1972: 134–7). Perhaps, the innovations of Iamblichus, a sometime student of Porphyry's, were a reaction to this uncontrolled allegoresis. He is held to have instigated the practice of positing a single *skopos* or "aim" for each dialogue, and systematically demanding that interpretations of individual passages cohere into a unified interpretation of the entire dialogue (Praechter 1973). In Proclus and later Neoplatonists it is largely taken for granted that Plato's dialogues should be read allegorically.[18] Macrobius, in the fifth century CE, says, for example:

> That is why Plato, when he was moved to speak about the Good, did not dare to tell what it was ... philosophers make use of fabulous narratives

(*fabulosa*); not without a purpose, however, nor merely to entertain, but because they realise that a frank and naked (*apertam nudamque*) exposition of herself is distasteful to Nature, who, just as she has withheld an understanding of herself from the uncouth sense of men by enveloping herself in variegated garments, has also desired to have her secrets handled by more prudent individuals through fabulous narratives ... Only eminent men of superior intelligence gain a revelation of her truths.   (*In Somn.* I.17–18)

Thus the allegorical approach to reading Plato had its defenders from about the time of the Neo-Pythagoreans through late antiquity and beyond.

The anti-allegorical turn

The allegorical approach to Plato at the core of Neoplatonism was influential through the Renaissance, where it was spread in part by Marsilio Ficino's translations of Plotinus, Iamblichus, Proclus, Porphyry and others. The existence and persistence of this ancient tradition of allegorical readings is important here as a precedent and plausibility argument. The turn from allegory and Neoplatonist interpretations of Plato can be treated only briefly here, although it deserves renewed scrutiny.

Two points about the decline of allegorism are important. First, the leading figures in the Reformation attacked and rejected allegoresis.[19] The religious and political authority of the Roman Catholic Church had come to be associated with claims that it had special access to the true meaning of scripture, and this depended in part on the allegorical methods of interpretation it had inherited from antiquity. Memories of these disputes live on in contemporary histories of scriptural hermeneutics:

> [T]he most valuable of Luther's hermeneutical principles [was] his insistence on the primacy of the literal or grammatico-historical sense. He resolutely set aside the verbal legerdemain involved in the multiple exegesis of the Schoolmen, and firmly took his stand on the plain and obvious meaning of the Word ... he emphatically urged the priority and superiority of the literal sense. For a thousand years the Church had buttressed its theological edifice by means of an authoritative exegesis which depended on allegory as its chief medium of interpretation. Luther struck a mortal blow at this vulnerable spot. From his own experience in the monastery he knew the futility of allegorisation – and stigmatised it as "mere jugglery," "a merry chase," "monkey tricks," and "looney talk".
> (Wood 1969: 164–5)

The Reformation's turn towards literalism had many causes and many consequences. It has been associated with the increased attention paid to observation and experiment in the scientific revolution that followed in its wake. It also led to the distinctively modern, literalist hermeneutics important to some forms of religious fundamentalism today.

Second, the anti-allegorical turn in Plato studies and the novel distinction of Platonism from "Neoplatonism" were the product of the Reformation's rejection of allegory. Tigerstedt's useful history traces the emergence of the modern approach to Plato among Protestant theologians such as Johann Jakob Brucker and Friedrich Schleiermacher. The allegorical commentators on Plato were, in Brucker's words, "mad, liars, impostors, vain and foolish forgers of a most detestable and false philosophy" (Tigerstedt 1974: 58). Tigerstedt concludes, for example:

> many theologians, most but not all of them Protestants, were highly suspicious of the evil influence of Platonism on Christian theology ... the separation of Platonism from Neo-Platonism seems to have been inspired by the wish to dissociate Plato from his later followers, who were regarded as anti-Christian, and thus maintain the venerable view of Plato as *anima naturaliter Christiana*. (*Ibid.*: 48–9)

The academic study of Plato has long since left this theological context behind, but these episodes do raise questions. The early modern rejection of allegorical readings of Plato took place before the recent research into ancient allegory and allegoresis. It took place before rigorous and critical methods for explicating allegory were applied to Dante, Spenser and other authors. During the Reformation, in an atmosphere of hostility to allegory, in a period that lacked the critical tools needed for the study of allegory, it may be doubted whether the crude but persistent allegoresis of the Neoplatonists was accorded a fair hearing. Twentieth-century scholarship was surprised when E. R. Dodds (1928), Philip Merlan (1968) and other students of Neoplatonism discovered they could trace certain of its doctrines back through the Academy to Plato himself, and the tendency today is to deny any sharp distinction between Platonism and Neoplatonism.

That is, it was once thought that the Neoplatonists misread and so misunderstood Plato. Now it is thought that they misread him but nonetheless correctly understood him.

1.7 Methodological precedent: early Christianity

Scholars in two other fields have, during the past generation, pioneered the study of allegorical and esoteric traditions in classic philosophical or religious literature. Earlier research had either interpreted these literally or denied their esoteric dimensions outright. The following rather brief sections survey this work and draw some methodological lessons.

The academic study of esotericism in early Christian theology was once neglected in ways not dissimilar to the older neglect of the Neoplatonists in

Anglo-American philosophy. Although traces of esoteric traditions are clear in the Gospels and early Patristic literature, they were, especially in the nineteenth century, ignored or minimized. Partly under the influence of Oxford's Guy G. Stroumsa, recent research has aimed at recovering and contextualizing these early traditions: "the existence of secret traditions in the earliest strata of Christianity is now recognized by most scholars" (Stroumsa 2005: ix).[20]

The Gospels are quite explicit about the existence of some kind of esoteric teaching. Mark, for one example, notoriously says about Jesus:

> When He was alone, the Twelve and others who were round him questioned him about the parables. He replied: "To you the mystery (*to musterion*) of the kingdom of God has been given; but to those who are outside (*ekeinois de tois exō*) everything comes by way of parables, so that (as Scripture says) they may look and look, but see nothing; they may hear and hear, but understand nothing". (Mark 4:10–12; Stroumsa 2005)[21]

This and similar passages have been interpreted in many ways, but some early Greek theologians did view such esoteric teachings as central to the Christian tradition. Clement of Alexandria's *Stromateis* defends reserving secret theological doctrines at some length. They are "hidden teachings about true knowledge" that it is dangerous to reveal (*Strom*. I, 12.56.2, trans. Stroumsa 2005: 36). Even as late as the fourth century, Basil the Great, for example, thought of these esoteric traditions as orally transmitted:

> Among the doctrines (*dogmata*) and proclamations (*kerugmata*) preserved in the Church, one receives the former from written teaching [while] the latter have been collected, secretly transmitted from the apostolic tradition. (Pruche 1968: XXVII.66, quoted in Stroumsa 2005: 35)

> [O]ur fathers kept [this teaching] in silence without worry or curiosity, knowing well that by keeping silent one preserves the sacred character of the mysteries ... This is the reason for the tradition of unwritten things: to prevent the high knowledge of the doctrines from becoming, for lack of serious protection, an object of contempt for the masses.
> (Pruche 1968: XXVII.66, quoted in Stroumsa 2005: 35)

According to Stroumsa, these esoteric traditions were, already before the end of the second century, "played down, blurred and denied" by some of the Church Fathers (2005: 6). In late antiquity, both the Greek mystery religions and Christian esotericism suffered a complex, "simultaneous disappearance" at a time when efforts were made by the now official religion to combat paganism and heretical Christian sects (*ibid*.: 156ff.).

During the same period in which Platonism and Neoplatonism were first distinguished, modern Christian theologians seemed to have agreed at least on marginalizing the evidence for early esotericism:

> Since the Reformation, the study of early Christian esoteric traditions has been highly problematic for both Catholic and Protestant scholars. For Catholics, for whom secrecy is associated with heresy ... the existence of such traditions is difficult to accept. For Protestants, the traditions of the Catholic Church, which is suspected of being tainted with esoteric doctrines, reflect a degeneration of the pristine *kerugma* of Jesus and his apostles ... Consequently, any suggestion that Jesus, Paul and their disciples had a share in esoteric doctrines encounters deep suspicion.
> (*Ibid*.: 1–2)

These brief passages are sufficient to suggest that there are both analogies with, and disanalogies to, the study of symbolism in Plato. The various reports of Christian esotericism seem to consider both oral and written transmission; here, no claims are made about any supposed oral transmission of Plato's philosophy. It does seem, however, that scholarly study of both Christianity and Platonism grew out of traditions in the Reformation and Enlightenment whose admirable commitments to rigour and openness obscured the nature of earlier traditions.

In the case of Plato, the bias towards literal readings was compounded by the subtlety of his symbolic system. The next section reviews a scholarly struggle with similarly well-concealed allegories.

1.8 Methodological precedent: Renaissance Platonism

Dante is the most well-known example of an author who gave his works mathematical form, but Alastair Fowler (1964) surveys a surprisingly wide range of authors who overtly or covertly practised numerical composition. This section concisely presents a case study of one such author, Edmund Spenser, who has been the subject of much recent scholarly scrutiny.

There are a variety of reasons for examining an episode within Renaissance Platonism. No claim is advanced here about any influence of ancient Platonism on the Renaissance, nor of Plato on Spenser. Rather, the scholarly methods used to interpret Spenser's poems, from counting lines to semantic parallels, constitute a methodological precedent for the techniques deployed in the body of this monograph.

Spenser, a representative Renaissance Platonist, resorted to various forms of numerical composition. The following briefly surveys three stages in the debates over Spenser's Pythagoreanism: discovery and resistance, a second wave of reinforcing research, and finally general acceptance and inclusion in authoritative reference works.

Spenser's reputation, rivalling that of Chaucer and Shakespeare, was suddenly altered in the early 1960s when the university presses at Columbia and Oxford together published the seminal *Short Time's Endless Monument* (1960) by Professor A. Kent Hieatt of Columbia University. This work announced the discovery of elaborate allegories in one of Spenser's poems. Years of intensive scholarly study of Spenser's oeuvre had failed to spot these concealed mathematical and astronomical structures. The vigour of Hieatt's work is apparent from the opening pages:

> What this book attempts to show is the presence of a dominant, most surprising, and hitherto unsuspected symbolic structure and meaning in a marriage ode generally known as one of the dozen or so great poems of our language ... In a journalistic sense the facts and interpretations presented here are novel – in fact, staggering: they appear to have gone unnoticed for 365 years ... they affect our estimate of a great poem which is known far and wide ... [There is] an unexpected, very complex, and highly integrated symbolism which underlines the literal meaning.
> (1960: 3–5)

Spenser's *Epithalamion* was written to celebrate his wedding, which was held on the vernal equinox in 1594, and describes the various activities and ceremonies that occurred during the course of that day. Hieatt first noticed that the body of the poem consisted of 24 stanzas which contain an irregular pattern of 365 longer and 68 shorter lines. These numbers, he concluded, match the known structure of the calendrical year. That is, the counts correspond respectively to the 24 hours of the day, the 365 days of the year, and to the total sum of weeks, months and seasons ($52 + 12 + 4 = 68$). The second chapter of Hieatt's book penetrated further into the architecture of the poem. He argued that the twelve stanzas formed two parallel sequences:

> A further peculiarity of *Epithalamion* is that stanzas at some distance from each other in the poem contain elements which seem to pair, or match each other, in various ways, but generally in the form of conceits. Some of these pairings are more obvious than others. Stanza 9 and stanza 21, for instance, plainly contain two such elements. In stanza 9 the bride is said to come forth as does Phoebe, the moon-goddess ... In stanza 21 the moon herself ... looks in the window. (*Ibid.*: 16)

Hieatt proceeds to show that all the stanzas in the poem together form a sequence of paired parallels. He first canvasses the most evident examples (9–12 and 21–24), using the literary, philosophical and astronomical context to interpret the various conceits. Having established the pattern and some of the strategies of Spenser's symbolism, he moves towards less obvious links and is able to conclude that all twenty-four stanzas form matched pairs. Thus there is an oscillation between theory and evidence. Theory is abstracted from a small number of obvious examples, used as guide for locating further matches, and then further elaborated from the larger set of evidence.

In sum, Hieatt's slim volume uses several distinct strategies to map Spenser's intricate symbolic architecture: line counts, correlation with know sequences and patterns (here calendrical and astronomical), and comparisons between parallel passages. Similar methods are employed below.

The detection of these mathematical allegories in Spenser's poems shifted their interpretations and revealed new dimensions in the poem's meaning. The surface narrative of the *Epithalamion* celebrates the fleeting events of a particular day in a particular place. By enveloping those twenty-four hours in an entire year of an eternal, astronomical cycle, Spenser has identified the particular with the universal.

The resistance to Hieatt's discovery is documented by the wide range of publications that rallied to his defence. Fowler's important *Spenser and the Numbers of Time* (1964) is representative of the ensuing controversy.[22]

One strategy Fowler uses is to supply historical context, connecting the allegory of the *Epithalamion* to its background in Renaissance Platonism. Drawing on the wide range of research that had appeared in the wake of Hieatt, Fowler finds examples throughout European literature of poems with elaborate numerical structures that had been revealed and explicated in contemporary commentaries. Fowler also broadens the argument by surveying the range of Pythagorean influences on architecture, biblical commentary and music theory. He explores the ancient tradition of numerical composition beginning with a passage in Vitruvius (cf. Ch. 2).

Writing about the time of the Neo-Pythagorean revival in the first century BCE, Vitruvius justified the brevity of his own chapters by remarking that stichometric composition was in fact practised:

> Furthermore, Pythagoras and those of his school who followed him resolved to write [their] maxims in scrolls according to a cubic principle [or ratio?] and, having established that a cube was 216 lines [or six cubed], thought there could not be more than three of them in one composition ... Greek comic playwrights also divided the length (*spatia*) of their narratives ... (V, *Prol.* 5)

The reasoning here is obscure and no evidence is given, but Vitruvius is clearly reporting a tradition according to which the Pythagoreans and playwrights counted the number of lines in their writings and modified them for certain ends. Fowler concludes that this context shifts the burden in the argument onto the sceptic:

> One predictable attitude to the foregoing analyses of numerical patterns ... will be that of comprehensive disbelief... [But the] more one studies the literature and ideas of the Renaissance, the more probable it seems that our reluctance to admit the existence of numerical composition stems from an ignorance of the thought-forms of that period. Indeed the burden of proof ought properly to rest with the sceptic. For while literary

> numerical composition was an obscure practice, the widespread application of number symbolism to other spheres of life and art was either more openly acknowledged or has since been uncovered through the labours of scholarship. (Fowler 1964: 238–9)

One motivation for scepticism is the presumption, today, that such numerical schemes are numerological, mystical or somehow aberrant. Fowler's and Hieatt's other defenders reconstruct the worldview of a period before the Scientific Revolution when the recovery of Greek mathematics was felt in commerce, perspectival painting, music theory and astronomy. Across a wide range of disciplines and cultural activities, the avant-garde of the time associated itself with mathematics. To rehabilitate these practices, Fowler presents this fashion for mathematics as a precursor to the Scientific Revolution:

> It is now well known that the enthusiastic revival of Pythagoreanism played a considerable role in the development of Renaissance scientific thought. The Pythagorean conception of the universe in mathematical terms helped to open the way to a truer and more scientific description of nature than was possible within the concrete enclosure of Aristotelian thought. It seems unreasonable to suppose, therefore, that the numerological Pythagorean element in Renaissance literature reflects an obscurantist cleaving to outmoded thought-forms. On the contrary, we should see it as the resultant of neo-realist impulses, and the expression of sensibilities in touch with the best thought of the age. (*Ibid.*: 246)

The philosophy behind these allegories was explored in a range of works that supplied the historical context needed to make these literary strategies intelligible. Richard Neuse, for example, plausibly articulated one element in Spenser's background:

> Mr. Hieatt's discovery of a complex symbolism in the *Epithalamion*'s stanzas and line numbers is of capital importance … this framework of an ideal time fits in exactly with a cardinal feature of the Pythagorean aesthetic, namely the hidden or implicit harmony which the artist was supposed to impose upon his work. Thus the numerical-symbolic structure of the *Epithalamion* serves, in Pythagorean fashion to express its secret affinity with the mathematical order of the universe. (1966: 51)

The existence of numerical and other symbolic patterns in Spenser's poetry was in time widely accepted.[23] By the 1990s, authoritative review articles endorsing the claims of Hieatt, Fowler and others appeared in the *Spenser Encyclopaedia*, edited by A. C. Hamilton (1991).[24] Textbooks such as *The Yale Edition of the Shorter Poems of Edmund Spenser* (Oram *et al.* 1989) brought his Pythagorean allegories into the university curriculum.

CHAPTER 2

Introducing the dialogues' musical structure

The appraisal of the musical structure in Plato's dialogues proceeds through two distinct stages. The first, the stage of verification, aims at confirming the bare fact that the dialogues have a stichometric and musical structure. The evidence for this stage is strong, clear and objective. It consists, for example, of the measurements of the lengths of set speeches clearly demarcated from the surrounding text, or of charts of the distribution of musical terminology in the *Republic*. The evidence for this verification stage is collected in Chapters 2, 3 and the introductory sections of Chapter 6, especially in the pair of sections entitled "Guide to the strongest evidence".

This evidence does not essentially depend on measurements with an especially high accuracy. There is sufficient qualitative or approximate evidence to make the case. The accuracy of various measurements is surprisingly impressive, but these constitute only one of several, independent lines of evidence.

The second, the stage of explication, aims at interpreting Plato's musical symbols in detail and assessing their implications for understanding the particular passages in which they occur. Chapters 4, 5 and 6, which are mainly close readings of the symbolism in the *Symposium* and *Euthyphro*, are occupied with this task.

It is normal for Dante scholars or Joyce scholars to agree that a composition is allegorical, and conceals a structure beneath its surface narrative, and yet to debate the interpretations of particular passages. This monograph aims to establish a similar consensus about Plato's works. The evidence for the underlying structure is strong. It will be more difficult to reach consensus about isolated passages, but the major, general claims advanced here do not require that every detailed explication in Chapters 4–6 be beyond dispute.

This chapter introduces Plato's symbolic scheme, concisely surveys some of the strongest evidence and briefly responds to a number of common questions and objections. It may be helpful, at this point, to refer to passages in the *Symposium* where the symbolic structure is most clear. To facilitate occasional forays into the text in Chapters 4 and 5, the annotations there have been kept as self-contained as possible (and so are sometimes repeated).

Later chapters proceed through the *Symposium* and the *Euthyphro*, traversing the embedded musical scale note by note and examining the range of symbols used to mark them in the text. The novel format in which the dialogues are presented here places the clusters of symbols at the centre of each left-hand page. These uniform columns throw the musical structure into relief. The annotations on the right-hand pages briefly characterize and interpret the symbols for each musical note in the scale.

The central claim of this chapter is that certain patterns of musical symbols are repeated at regular intervals through Plato's *Symposium* and mark out the notes of a known musical scale.[1]

More specifically, the evidence below will show that passages containing subtle constellations of symbols are located at each twelfth of the way through the text of the *Symposium*. That is, clusters of terms with symbolic meanings are located at one-twelfth, at two-twelfths and so forth.

As mentioned above, the Pythagoreans' "harmony of the spheres" was believed, at various times and for various reasons, to be extremely subtle and accessible only to those advanced in philosophy. Plato was thought by many of his contemporaries and followers to have been influenced by the Pythagoreans (Ch. 1), and the commentary below will claim that Plato, adhering to a "Pythagorean aesthetic", built a similar, musical structure into his dialogues.

Plato used the underlying scale as an outline for his dialogues. Arguments and episodes fill out one or more of the intervals between notes. Major concepts or turns in the arguments tend to be located at the notes. Shifts in the narrative, such as the beginnings and ends of speeches, tend to occur near musical notes. Thus there are two major kinds of evidence for the underlying scale: the clusters of symbols at the locations of the musical notes and the correlations with important features of the narrative.

The first section below explains how it was possible for an ancient author to structure a long literary composition. The next section introduces a few ideas from ancient Greek music, which are needed to understand the symbolism. The following sections survey several different kinds of evidence within the *Symposium*.

Many or most writers who use literary symbolism aim both to conceal and communicate: to use subtlety in a way that at first puzzles and then seduces readers into unearthing the deeper meanings of their works. Plato's idiosyncratic symbolism has been rendered doubly subtle over time. Not only was he writing in another language and culture, but the musical ideas he used are distant from our own.

2.1 Structuring a dialogue

To structure the *Symposium* by locating symbolic passages at regular intervals, Plato needed a way of counting or measuring the lengths of long speeches.

Classical Greeks counted the number of lines in their literary works in ways perhaps similar to the way we count the pages in a book or the words in an essay. The practice of counting lines, "stichometry", has been carefully studied by scholars of ancient book production and by papyrologists interested in piecing together works from their fragments, some surviving examples of which have notations giving their total line counts.

The still standard work on stichometry, Kurt Ohly's *Stichometrische Untersuchungen* (1928), collects evidence (too extensive to be reviewed here) that the practice was already common during Plato's lifetime. Ohly finds the earliest explicit reference to measuring texts in hexameter lines in Plato's *Laws*, and concludes from a variety of pieces of evidence that "in Platos alter wurde also der Hexameter bereits als Maßeinheit verwandt" [(in the time of Plato the hexameter was already used as the standard line (*Masseinheit*)] (1928: 93).[2] Some surviving fragments of early Greek papyri with historical, philosophical or literary prose compositions are written in such lines.

Manual stichometric studies of Plato's dialogues have been carried out in various ways by Martin Schanz (1881), Theodor Birt (1882: 440ff.), J. Rendel Harris (1893), Dodds (1959: 46), E. Berti (1966) and others, but were primarily aimed at inferring the lengths of the lines and columns on the papyrus sources of surviving manuscripts. Computer-based stichometric investigations of Plato's dialogues have apparently not been carried out before. This lacuna is surprising in an era when computerized, stylometric studies have been undertaken by a number of scholars (reviewed in Brandwood 1992).

In addition to this "total stichometry", in a number of later manuscripts there is evidence of "partial stichometry", that is, line numbers noted at intervals in the margins alongside the text, like our Stephanus page numbers.[3] These practices alone do not show that any fourth-century authors thought their prose compositions had a mathematical structure. They do show that measuring the total length of prose narratives, as well as, therefore, counting through texts and implicitly associating a number with each line, was common in antiquity.

There is also evidence that classical literary papyri were typically produced with uniform columns each of which had a uniform number of lines.[4] Thus, when it came time to pay a scribe or purchase finished papyrus rolls, the total number of lines was easy to count. Library catalogues recorded these line counts, and used them at times to check that copies of texts, which could extend over several rolls, were complete.[5] Diogenes Laertius' report that Aristotle's writings amounted to 445,270 lines may have derived from the catalogues of the library at Alexandria (V.27). He also gives totals for Speusippus (43,475; IV.5), Theophrastus (232,800; V.50), Xenocrates (224,239; IV.14) and others. The evidence presented below indicates that Plato used this everyday practice of stichometry to structure his dialogues.[6]

The uniform lines and columns of classical papyri would have made detecting Plato's regular symbolism easier. Later copies, perhaps from the time of the library at Alexandria, generally did not have uniform lines and columns, and this would have made Plato's subtle symbolism even more obscure.

Since Henri Estienne's 1578 edition of the dialogues made no attempt to ensure that his columns, our Stephanus pages, were uniform, their length varied significantly to accommodate his notes and Latin translation. There are many anomalies in the Stephanus numbers.[7] Thus, from some time around the Hellenistic period until the invention of the word processor, it was effectively impossible to discover Plato's stichometric structure.

The dialogue below is presented with uniform "columns", and thus restores an approximation of the classical format (see §2.7). Even without the commentary, careful readers might notice that passages with similar structures recur in the middle of the columns.

In this historical context, a philosopher with Pythagorean leanings would have had the wherewithal to monitor the relative locations of passages within texts.

The musical structures in Plato's dialogues required some sort of pre-planning.[8] It may be conjectured that Plato wrote out some kind of outline for his dialogues, perhaps on a separate papyrus scroll or on wax tablets, and then allotted a certain number of lines to each episode, speech or argument before proceeding with the final composition.

2.2 Ancient Greek music: three key ideas

Plato used a simple, mathematically regular musical "scale" in his dialogues. It may therefore be introduced without reviewing much of the theory and terminology of ancient Greek music.[9] Strictly, this scale should be called a "division of the canon", as Appendix 1 discusses. The relative neglect of certain aspects of Greek musical theory by modern Plato scholars has been a barrier to detecting Plato's musical symbolism.

The scale

Plato's Socrates distrusted mere appearances and knowledge based on the outer senses. In the *Republic*, Socrates criticizes the scales used in the music of his time for being based on sensation and custom (e.g. 530d6ff.). The regular scale used to structure the *Symposium* avoids the peculiarities and irregularities of those Greek scales and, in this respect, is similar to the musical scale constructed in the *Timaeus* (see Appendix 1).

The Pythagoreans famously discovered that pairs of notes blended in a pleasing, harmonious way when they were produced by pairs of strings whose lengths had

INTRODUCING THE DIALOGUES' MUSICAL STRUCTURE

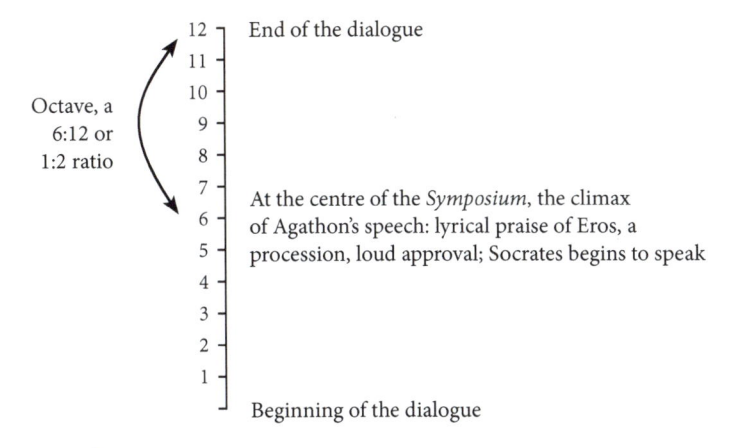

Figure 1 The twelve-note scale in each dialogue. The text is divided into twelfths and the beginning of each twelfth is marked by a symbolic passage. The twelfth note is at the end of each dialogue.

simple ratios such as 1:2, 2:3 and 3:4 (the octave, fifth and fourth). These harmonies will be produced when a long string is sounded together with another string of half, two-thirds or three-quarters of its length. Since twelve has many factors, it is convenient to choose to divide the length of the string into twelve units so that the harmonies will correspond to ratios between integers (6:12, 8:12 and 9:12).

This leads naturally to the idea of a scale of twelve notes produced by lengths of string corresponding to the integers from one to twelve (see Appendices 1, 2). In each of Plato's genuine dialogues, symbolic passages are located at each twelfth of the way through the dialogue. These points will be associated here with the integers 1–12. The midpoint of each dialogue is therefore note 6 in the musical scale, and the beginning will be note 0 (see Figs 1 and 2).

Thrasyllus, the editor of Plato's works and probably court philosopher to Tiberius, is paraphrased at length in Theon's *On the Mathematics Useful for Reading Plato* (Theon of Smyrna 1966). This work has puzzled historians because it reviews topics that seem to have little connection to the dialogues. In particular, it discusses at length the musical scale of twelve, regularly spaced notes, which is nowhere mentioned by Plato.[10] The author of the pseudo-Plutarchian *De Musica*, parts of which may also date from the first century, also explicitly associates a scale based on the number twelve with Plato (1138 = 120,26ff., 120,33ff. Laserre).

Quarternotes

There was a debate from the classical period onwards, mentioned in the *Republic*, Aristotle's *Metaphysics* and Aristoxenus, about the smallest, audibly distinguishable

THE MUSICAL STRUCTURE OF PLATO'S DIALOGUES

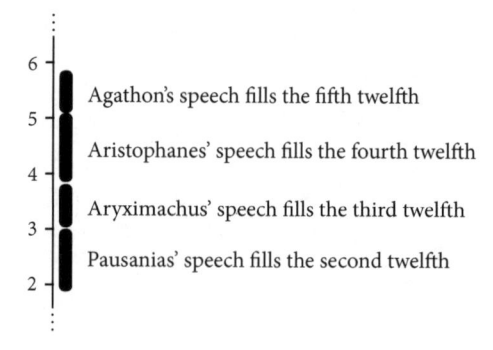

6 —
      ┃ Agathon's speech fills the fifth twelfth
5 —
      ┃ Aristophanes' speech fills the fourth twelfth
4 —
      ┃ Aryximachus' speech fills the third twelfth
3 —
      ┃ Pausanias' speech fills the second twelfth
2 —

Figure 2 The twelve-note scale organizes the narrative in each dialogue. The approximate fit between the beginning and end of the speeches and the locations of the musical notes is strong evidence that the early speeches of the *Symposium* fill successive twelfths. This is a good example of the imperfect patterns produced by literary interpretation. As the gaps between the speeches show, the speeches tend to begin or end near but not at the twelfths because those locations are marked by symbolic passages.

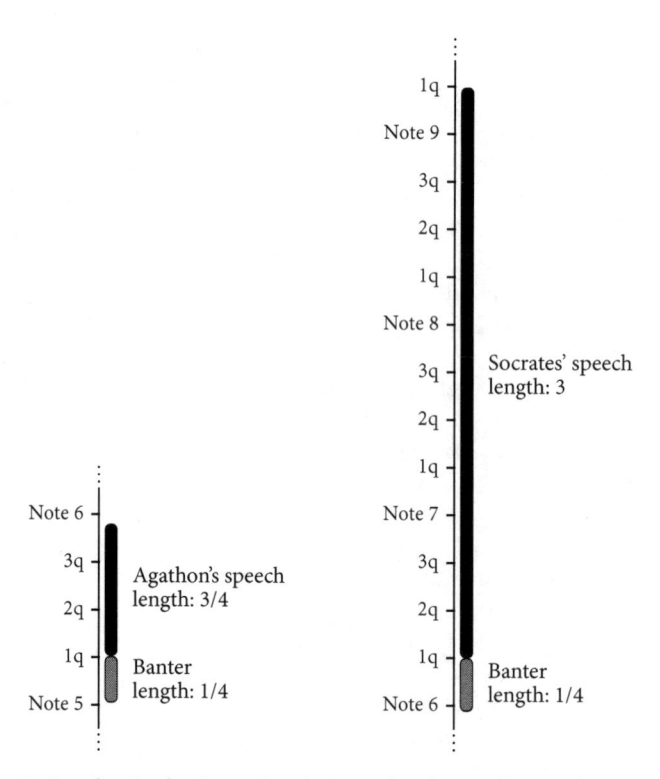

                                            1q
                                        Note 9 —
                                            3q
                                            2q
                                            1q
                                        Note 8 —
                                            3q   Socrates' speech
                                            2q   length: 3
                                            1q
                    Note 6 —   Note 7 —
                        3q   3q
                            Agathon's speech
                        2q length: 3/4   2q
                        1q   1q
                            Banter   Banter
                    Note 5 — length: 1/4   Note 6 — length: 1/4

Figure 3 Speeches in the *Symposium* begin and end near the quarternotes. Agathon's speech is three quarter-intervals long. Socrates' speech is three whole-intervals long, and so one-quarter of the entire dialogue. The banter before each speech is one quarter-interval.

intervals appropriate to musical scales (see Appendix 1). One view was that scales should include notes separated by a quarter of a "tone" (the unit interval between notes with an 8:9 ratio). The literature sometimes calls these intermediate notes "quarternotes" and makes the interval between them a "quartertone". These terms will be adopted here.

It was natural to use this terminology when *any* musical structure with regular divisions was further subdivided into quarter-intervals (even when each basic interval was not a single "tone"). Andrew Barker reviews evidence that, in the late fifth or early fourth centuries, "quarternote" and "quartertone" were used in this broad sense (see Appendix 1), and they will be so used here. So quarternotes mark the divisions between quarter-intervals.

Thus, in the *Symposium* symbolic passages are also located at quarter-intervals between each of the passages marking the notes from 0 to 12. For example, in addition to the symbolic passage at wholenote 6, at the midpoint of the dialogue, there are similar symbolic passages one quarter-interval past 6, two quarter-intervals past 6 and three-quarter intervals past 6 and so on (see Fig. 3).

Plato was not limited by the smallest intervals that the senses could distinguish. In the *Symposium*, there are very brief passages, usually only a single phrase or a sentence, that mark out even smaller, regular intervals between the major wholenotes and quarternotes, as will be discussed below.

Relative consonance

The theory of relative consonance plays a major role in Plato's symbolism (see Appendix 1). Each note in the scale has a property that depends on its relation to the twelfth note. If a note blends well with the twelfth note it is more "consonant"; if it blends less well it is more "dissonant". There were several algorithms for calculating the precise relative consonance of notes in ancient times (see Appendix 1), but the different approaches agreed that notes that formed small, whole number ratios with note 12 were consonant:

More consonant: 3, 4, 6, 8, 9

Similarly, notes that formed awkward ratios with note 12 were dissonant:

More dissonant: 5, 7, 10, 11

Other notes, such as note 2, were more or less neutral.

There is some uncertainty about how Plato calculated the relative consonance of the quarternotes, but some general trends are apparent. For example, quarternotes between consonant wholenotes tend to be more consonant, and those between dissonant notes tend to be more dissonant.

2.3 Plato's symbolic scheme

At each point in the text of the *Symposium* corresponding to a musical note, Plato included a passage with a special structure. To maintain a balance between concealment and communication, he varied the content of these passages. If they were all the same or obviously similar, the underlying musical structure would be too apparent.

The scheme for varying the passages accords well with Platonism. Generally speaking, a Platonic Form is recognized when a similarity between different particulars is recognized. A red hat and a red ball share a similarity, and this shared element is the "Form" of their colour. In the dialogues, the passages marking the notes have different contents but are also similar. Recognizing the similarity of the disparate passages, and thus the regular pattern that forms the musical scale, requires grasping their common Form. In short, the notes are marked by passages containing concepts that are many species of a single, overarching genus.

All the genuine dialogues and some of the so-called spuria use the same musical scale and the same scheme for varying the passages that mark the notes, but the genus differs from dialogue to dialogue. To take a hypothetical example, it is as if a dialogue mentioned roses at one-twelfth, lilies at two-twelfths, violets at three-twelfths and so on. Recognizing the musical scale depends on observing that the species of the genus "flower" are mentioned at regular intervals. The pattern of repetitions is itself a Form with the same structure as the known musical scale with twelve regularly spaced notes. Another dialogue might, hypothetically, mention different species of colour (red, yellow, orange, ...) at the twelfths.

In the *Symposium*, the notes are marked by various species of *harmonia*, that is by instances of the general notion of "fitting together". The Greek word may have had a wider range of meanings than the English "harmony". Its musical use was only one specialized sense.[11] The concept of harmony played a conspicuous role in the Pythagorean tradition, both early and late (Burkert 1972; Huffman 1993).

A theory of harmony appears in the *Symposium* itself, in Eryximachus' speech, and is key to understanding the various marking passages (the dialogues typically discuss the genus of the concepts used to mark their notes). For Eryximachus, *harmonia* has already become a philosophical term of art and means the blending of two opposites. Eryximachus emphasizes that two opposites cannot "harmonize" while they differ or disagree. Thus ideal "harmony" means a thorough kind of blending in which different ingredients are so "homogenized" that they somehow overcome their individual distinctiveness.

Three Greek words for blending ingredients play a role here. "Harmony" is used when the emphasis is on the ingredients fitting together. "*Krasis*" connotes a blending or fusion. "Synthesis" just means "putting together". In Greek generally, as well as in the *Symposium*, the overlapping meanings of these words were recognized, as in the definition reported by Aristotle: "a harmony is a *krasis* and synthesis of opposites".[12] Eryximachus' speech explicitly associates harmony and *krasis* (Pl. *Symp.* 188a4).

The following list surveys various species of harmony and *krasis* used to mark the musical notes in the *Symposium*:

- Verbal agreement in conversation (*homologia*)
- Acceptance of an invitation (a kind of verbal agreement)
- Unanimity or likeness of mind (*homonoia*)
- Logical agreement between reasons (also *homologia*)
- Physical *krasis* or blending
- Erotic partnership
- Beauty (a "harmony with the divine")
- Participation (of particulars in forms)
- Musical harmony (*harmonia*)

Appendix 5, on the systematic theory of the marking passages, analyses the connections between the concepts used to mark the notes and shows that the musical locations through the entire dialogue are marked by these concepts.

2.4 Harmony and consonance, disharmony and dissonance

Things fit together to different degrees. A smooth and thorough blend is more harmonic; a rough, tense or unstable blend may be termed "disharmonic". As the *Timaeus* says: "insofar as sounds are faster and slower, they appear higher and lower; sometimes their movements are disharmonic (*anarmostoi*) on account of the dissimilarity of the motion they make in us, and sometimes their movements are harmonic (*ksumphōnoi*) on account of similarity" (*Ti.* 80a3–6).

This spectrum, from more to less harmonic, was put to use in a remarkable way in Plato's musical scheme. It leads to some of the strongest evidence for Plato's musical structures.

The more consonant notes in the scale are marked with more harmonic combinations. For example, Hephaestus' offer to weld together the two lovers, to fuse and so "harmonize" the soulmates forever, marks a consonant note. Conceptual *krasis* marks musical consonance.

On the other hand, the more dissonant notes are marked by disharmonic combinations. The Socratic elenchus, for example, is an "agreement" (and so a kind of harmony) that the interlocutor has been self-contradictory (a kind of disagreement with oneself, or disharmony). Aristotle simply calls an elenchus a "combination of opposites" (*sunagōgē*; *Rh.* 1410a22–3). The conclusion of Socrates' elenchus of Agathon, for example, is located at a dissonant note. Here, cognitive dissonance marks musical dissonance.

As mentioned above, the structures of Plato's dialogues have often been found puzzling. The literature on the *Phaedrus* and the *Republic*, for example, has criticized their disjointed and sometimes meandering narratives. The *Republic* has even been thought, since the nineteenth century, to be a combination of separate tracts loosely stitched together.[13]

If it is possible to generalize, literary, philosophical and even musical compositions often build through a series of secondary climaxes or complications to a final climax. Although Plato's dialogues pioneered discussion of literary form (Halliwell 1998; Heath 1989), they themselves seem to fail to correspond to this or any other clear scheme. They often seem to reach major conclusions and then to move on to other, secondary subjects, or simply to peter out in puzzling myths.

The underlying consonance and dissonance of the musical notes accounts for the peculiar structure of Plato's dialogues. Major advances, the conclusions of arguments and dramatic highlights tend to occur at consonant notes. Refutations, discussions of Hades and portraits of tyrants mark dissonant notes.

In the *Symposium*, the good-humoured whimsy and benevolence of Aristophanes' speech stretches across a range of consonant notes. The two dramatic highlights near the end of Diotima's speech, the begetting with beauty and the vision of the great ocean of beauty atop her ladder, mark the two most consonant notes in the musical scale.

Agathon is a promiscuous poet whose speech is criticized by Socrates for failing to tell the truth. Alcibiades is a failed philosophy student who notoriously went on to betray his country. Their speeches occupy the two most dissonant ranges of notes in the musical scale.

In what follows, "consonance" and "dissonance" are always terms from musical theory, and measure the relative consonance of a musical note (combination with the twelfth wholenote is always presumed). "Harmony" and "disharmony" have the broad range of meanings listed above, and indicate a more or less successful "fitting together".

2.5 Sevenths and mixture

In the *Symposium*, the major notes in the twelve-note scale, the wholenotes and the quarternotes, are marked with various degrees of harmony or disharmony. There are other locations in the text, however, which are marked by different symbols. The passages located after each seventh of the way through the text, that is, at one-seventh, two-sevenths and up to sixth-sevenths, are very dissonant and are marked with the opposite of "harmony". To understand these passages, a few more ideas from the Greek theory of mixture will be needed.

Greek philosophers developed theories of how physical objects were combined, and tended to distinguish thorough blending from a mere "mechanical mixture" in which the ingredients retained their original characteristics. Thus blending a bucket of yellow paint with a bucket of blue paint to produce green paint was distinguished from mixing a bag of yellow marbles with a bag of blue marbles to produce a bigger bag of yellow and blue marbles. Combination without blending will here consistently be called "mixture" or "mere mixture".[14]

Aristotle analysed the process of blending in some detail, and his theory clarifies a point made in Eryximachus' discussion of harmonization. In particular, blending for Aristotle continued until the ingredients were all homogenized, that is, until their contrasting qualities altered and converged on some common, intermediate quality (as the yellow and blue paints each became green paint). Thus, in blending, the initially different becomes the same (see e.g. Arist. *Gen. corr.* 328a28ff.). This is the point Eryximachus is making when he criticizes Heraclitus for seemingly confusing harmony and mere mixture:

> It is quite absurd to say that a harmony differs or consists of things still differing. [Rather, harmony arises] out of high and low sounds which at first differ, and then later are made to agree by the art of music. A harmony, [in contrast,] would indeed not consist of high and low sounds still differing [which is mere mixture]. TWO-SEVENTHS A harmony is a *symphōnia* .... (187a6–b4)

This passage may seem commonsensical but, in the context of Greek natural philosophy, it makes the theoretical distinction between harmony and mixture explicit in the *Symposium*.

In the *Symposium*, the sevenths are marked by examples of mere mixture, temporary combinations or colocations in which the differing components commingle without blending and can emerge unchanged.

The traditional Greek lyre had seven strings,[15] and it is probable that the notes at the sevenths correspond to a scale used by such lyres. The semi-legendary musician Orpheus, for example, was associated with a seven-stringed lyre.[16] Within the scale of twelve notes used in the *Symposium*, notes at the sevenths would all be very dissonant (i.e. when played together with the twelfth wholenote) and this is the probable justification for marking them by mixtures.[17]

The passage from Eryximachus' speech quoted above, for example, is located two-sevenths of the way through the text (the point marked "TWO-SEVENTHS" in the quotation above). That is, an explicit reference to mechanical mixture and its distinction from harmony marks a seventh note.

Although the interpretation of a single passage cannot be confirmed without studying a range of similar examples, the passage at one-seventh of the way through the *Symposium* provides a concise example of the way Plato could use symbols to mark notes. Phaedrus says there:

> Orpheus the son of Oeagrus was ONE-SEVENTH sent out of Hades unfulfilled, receiving a mere phantasm of the woman he came to get – she herself was not given – because he seemed too cowardly – inasmuch as he was a lyre-player (*kitharōdes*), – and did not dare to die for the sake of his love ... but schemed to enter Hades while still alive. (179d2–6)[18]

Here, at one-seventh, we have a reference to the musician Orpheus, who had Pythagorean associations (Burkert 1972: 125ff.), and a reference to a musical instrument that often had seven strings. Comparison to the other passages at the sevenths shows (see below and Appendix 3) that the key idea here is that Orpheus was among the dead in Hades while still alive and later emerged unscathed. This is an example of a mere, temporary mixture between opposites, which, together with the negative tone of sneering derision, marks this dissonant note. Juxtaposing references to Orpheus and his lyre together with an example of mixture is a fairly heavy-handed way to draw the attention of any Pythagorean counting lines to this passage.

Since the contrast between mixture and harmony was well known, recognizing that the sevenths are marked by mixtures constitutes another kind of evidence that harmonies mark the wholenotes and quarternotes.

There are other locations between the wholenotes, quarternotes and sevenths that are marked by symbolic passages. For example, each interval between quarternotes is broken into eighths, and the end of each of these is typically marked by a brief phrase. In the following, the note located at the end of each such eighth will be called an "octad", for want of a better term. The brevity of the marking passages at the octads and at other locations between the major notes makes them difficult to interpret rigorously and so their discussion, except in a few cases where they are especially clear, is avoided.

2.6 Guide to the strongest evidence

An evaluation of the evidence for the musical structure in the *Symposium* should start with the strongest evidence listed here, and not proceed at the outset from the beginning of the dialogue. There are several reasons for this. First, the passages marking the first few notes have a clear but complicated structure that is not typical of the rest of the dialogue. Second, wholenote 2 is neither very consonant nor very dissonant and is marked in a less emphatic, neutral way. Thus it is best to begin with the highlights selected here.

The next section examines various objections to the following evidence and the conclusions drawn from it.

A simple notation for the musical notes will be used. The wholenotes in the scale are numbered with the integers 0–12. For brevity, the quarternotes between the wholenotes are numbered 1–3. For example, note 6.3 is the third quarternote after wholenote 6, and 3.0 is just wholenote 3. The interval between quarternotes is broken into eighths and these octads will be numbered 1–7. Thus, 3.2.4 will denote wholenote 3, quarternote 2, octad 4. The midpoints between the quarternotes, octad 4, are generally marked with harmonic or positive passages.

The cogency of the following evidence can be sampled by comparing a handful of key passages. This approach also uses a bare minimum of music theory: just the well-known fact that the Pythagoreans associated small whole number ratios like

2:3 and 3:4 with "harmonies". The first step is to examine passages at locations in the *Symposium* in Chapter 5 that correspond to fractions composed of small whole numbers: say two-thirds and three-quarters (i.e. notes 8.0 and 9.0). These passages are strongly positive and treat of topics such as beauty, love and the Forms. The second step is to compare these with locations that do not correspond to such fractions, such as ten-twelfths and eleven-twelfths (i.e. notes 10.0 and 11.0). These passages are strongly negative and treat of pain and rejection in a disharmonious relation. If these two correlations – positive passages at small whole number ratios and negative ones elsewhere – seem coincidental, the same notes in the text of the *Euthyphro* in Chapter 6 may be sampled.

The following sections survey some of the strong evidence. The first is restricted to objective features of the *Symposium*'s narrative; the second shows how harmonic theory is intertwined with content.

Narrative structure reflects musical structure

Plato uses the underlying musical structure as an outline for the dialogue. Major shifts in the narrative, such as changes between speakers, tend to occur at or near musical notes. Episodes fill out the intervals between notes and, within speeches, major developments or new topics occur at the notes.

This relation between the narrative structure and the musical structure is carefully modulated. There tends to be a closer relation near the intensely consonant or dissonant musical notes. Near more neutral notes, the relation is looser. It is as if some of the *Symposium*'s characters, such as Socrates, Aristophanes and Eryximachus, are more attuned to the underlying music and some less.

Here and below, a passage is *at* a note when it is within two or three lines of the calculated position of the note in the OCT edition of the dialogues; it is *near* a note when it within five or six OCT lines. In the *Symposium*, there are typically about forty OCT lines between quarternotes.

Dramatic climaxes at notes

As mentioned above, the rhetorical and philosophical peak of Socrates' speech, the vision of the Form of Beauty at the top of Diotima's ladder, lies *at* three-quarters of the way through the *Symposium*. This single fact is sufficient to establish a *prima facie* case for some underlying structure. It may, of course, be an accidental coincidence. The probability of this can be reduced by adducing more evidence. For example, the secondary peak of Socrates' speech, the begetting with beauty, lies *at* two-thirds of the way through the text. Together, these two passages, at notes 9.0 and 8.0, are strong, initial evidence for the underlying musical structure.

Lengths and locations of the speeches

Another kind of simple, objectively measurable evidence is the lengths of the speeches and their alignment with the musical scale. The *Symposium* provides a good introduction to these features because of the many changes in speakers. The locations of the notes themselves are marked with passages describing a harmony or disharmony, and the speeches tend to begin or end on either side of these marking passages (as shown in Figures 2 and 3).

Aristophanes' speech ends at note 5.0. Agathon's speech begins at the next quarternote 5.1. Thus the intervening banter between Socrates and Agathon fills a quarter-interval. Agathon's speech ends near note 6.0, and thus lasts for the three quarter-intervals from 5.1 to 6.0.

The banter between Agathon and Socrates that follows Agathon's speech also lasts a quarter-interval. Socrates agrees to make a speech at 6.1 and begins his cross-examination of Agathon there. Socrates finishes his speech at note 9.1. Socrates' speech thus lasts for the three whole intervals from 6.1 to 9.1, or a quarter of the entire dialogue.

It may, again, be a coincidence that Socrates' speech has such a length, but that its beginning and end are also aligned with notes in the scale requires two such coincidences.

The musical scale as outline

Aristophanes' speech clearly shows how the major sections and developments in the speeches are organized by the underlying musical scale. Each major step in his speech is lodged at a musical note:

- At 4.0, the three primitive wholes are introduced (male, female, androgyne).
- At 4.1, they are cut apart by Zeus to restore virtue.
- At 4.2, the halves are seeking re-unification through love.
- At 4.3, Hephaestus envisages the unity or "harmonization" of the lovers.

Episodes fill out musical intervals

Episodes or unified sections of the *Symposium* tend to occupy an integral number of quarter-intervals. One particularly clear example occurs in the second line of the dialogue where the narrator begins to recollect an earlier request to recount the events at Agathon's party. This passage of recollections lasts from the opening of the dialogue to the first quarternote, and thus fills one quarter-interval.

Octads

The musical structure is closest to the surface of the dialogue at the climax of Diotima's speech. As mentioned above, the quarter-intervals between the major notes are divided into eight short sections whose ends are each marked with a brief phrase. Diotima's ladder provides a clear example of these "octads". Each step up the ladder is located at an octad. The ascent begins at a quarternote and the steps are equally spaced in the text:

- Step 1 at quarternote: Love a single body (8.3).
- Step 2 at quarternote: General Form of Beauty in bodies (8.3).

- Step 3 at octad 1: Beauty in the soul.
- Step 4 at octad 2: Beauty in activities and customs.
- Step 5 at octad 3: Beauty in branches of knowledge.
- Step 6 at octad 4: Ocean of beauty: philosophy.
- Step 7 at octad 5: The vision of the final end or *telos* of erotics.

The description of the Form of Beauty that follows stretches from the fifth octad until the peak at 9.0.

Similarly, when Agathon ticks off features of Eros, his beauty and virtues, each of these is located at an octad:

- Octad 2: Beauty.
- Octad 3: Justice.
- Octad 4: *Sōphrosunē*.
- Octad 5: Courage.
- Octad 6: *Sophia*.

In both these examples, the equal spacing of the key phrases as well as their alignment with the musical structure militates against the possibility that these structures are accidental.

Sevenths

As mentioned above, Orpheus, who was known for his typically seven-stringed lyre, enters one-seventh of the way through the dialogue. Comparison with the passages at the other sevenths suggests they describe mere mixtures of opposites: live with dead, wise with foolish, and so on. Just such a mixture, wherein things are combined "while still differing", is discussed at the second seventh.

Musical symbols: the correlation with harmonic theory

Not just the lengths and positions but the contents of the speeches are carefully coordinated with the underlying musical scale. This correlation is surprisingly consistent.

Harmonies

The two climaxes of Diotima's speech, with their rarefied praise of beauty, are at two of the most consonant notes (8.0 and 9.0). Beauty is, she says, a kind of harmony with the divine, and this makes beauty an appropriate marker for these consonant notes.

Another form of harmony is a *krasis*: the thorough blending of once distinct elements. Hephaestus' offer to weld together the two lovers permanently is again the most vivid example of a *krasis* marking a consonant note (4.3).

Eryximachus' explicit definition of "harmony" in music, erotics and medicine marks a consonant note (3.2), and is part of a series of consonant notes marked by passages describing kinds of harmony:

- Harmony at 3.0: Heavenly Eros leads to virtue (participating in goodness).
- Harmony at 3.1: Medicine harmonizes bodily forces.
- Harmony at 3.2: Definition of musical harmony.
- Harmony at 3.3: Prophecy harmonizes gods and humans.

Disharmonies

In contrast, disharmonies mark the dissonant notes. For example, the passage at note 7.1 describes the opposing virtues and vices that Eros inherited from his parents, Resource and Poverty. The negative traits are lodged at the note and his discordant character marks this dissonant note. Here, the opposing elements are permanently harnessed together, but they remain an unhappy combination of positive and negative.

Socrates' elenchus of Agathon marks note 6.3. This is, again, an agreement (harmony) that assertions have been contradictory (disharmony), and this combination is a "fitting together" in a negative or jarring way – which is disharmonious.

The interval between the tenth and eleventh notes contains many of the most negative and vivid passages in Plato's dialogues. This is the location, for example, of the *Phaedo*'s tour of the underworld and the *Republic*'s account of the tyrant's vices (Ch. 3). In the *Symposium*, this quite dissonant range of notes is devoted to Alcibiades' frank retelling of his scandalous, failed attempt to seduce Socrates:

- Disharmony at 10.0: Socrates is compared to an ugly (and so "disharmonious"), piping satyr (killed by Apollo).
- Disharmony at 10.1: Alcibiades runs away from Socrates (breaking agreements, relationships), and again compares him to the satyr.
- Disharmony at 10.2: Alcibiades' first advances are rejected (disagreement); he feels distress and *aporia* (inner disharmony).
- Disharmony at 10.3: Alcibiades' awful offer to exchange sex and his patronage for Socrates' moral help.
- Disharmony at 11.0: Alcibiades is again rejected by Socrates and feels extreme distress and dishonour.

This dissonant range of notes is a sharp contrast to the consonant ranges surveyed above.

These highlights make a powerful, *prima facie* case for the existence of musical structure in the *Symposium*. In the following chapters, the annotations to all the notes in the musical scale show that the scheme introduced here is applied consistently throughout entire dialogues, and provides new evidence for the depth and richness of Plato's creation.

2.7 Methodology for line-counting

Locations of passages within each dialogue were measured here by stripping out everything but Greek letters from files containing the OCT editions of the dialogues, counting the letters, and inserting markers in the original files. That is, "invisible characters", punctuation, indications of changes in speaker and spaces were all deleted. Plato's autographs probably used little or no punctuation, but there is not universal agreement about this.[19] It is sufficient, given the fundamental limitations on accuracy caused by the many minor corruptions in the text, just to count Greek letters.

The computer programs were verified in several ways.[20] The algorithms employed were complicated and will be described separately.[21]

Although textual critics debate the point, some hold that Plato's texts survived repeated copying in relatively good shape,[22] and the investigations reported below accord with that view. However, the many small emendations, corruptions, possible interpolations and suspected losses of text listed in the OCT and other critical editions of Plato's dialogues suggest there will be a limit to the accuracy of any measure of distance within the dialogues. Fortunately, a certain benign averaging works to improve the accuracy of measurements of *relative* lengths and ratios within the dialogues.

The important musical relationships in the dialogues are all relative. This means that only relative measures and not absolute locations are important here. In this study, for example, it is essential to locate the approximate midpoint of the dialogues. Whether or not the total number of lines on either side of that midpoint differs appreciably from Plato's autographs is not important.

Several factors operate to improve the reliability of relative measurements. The effects of a fairly uniform distribution of smaller scribal errors, omissions and interpolations still uncorrected by textual critics would on average compensate for each other and would not therefore significantly disturb measurements of relative positions.

Chapter 7 will show, surprisingly, that the "error" in the measured position of the locations of passages can itself be measured. It is possible to measure "how corrupt" our texts are, and so to recalibrate and correct the measurements of relative location. Careful study shows that the measurements of relative location reported here are generally accurate to within a fraction of a per cent. This is a testament to the quality of the scribal tradition, to the extraordinary efforts of generations of modern textual critics and to the power of averaging.

As reviewed above, counting hexameter lines was routine even for prose by the late fifth or early fourth centuries BCE. There is strong evidence that Plato was counting such hexameter lines.[23] The software used here, however, counted only Greek letters.

To count hexameter lines, it would first be necessary to develop a general algorithm for separating Greek words into distinct syllables. This may seem easy, but there are difficult cases. Moreover, it is not clear to what degree *krasis* was used in

Plato's autographs. It may be that later editors combined syllables that were distinct in Plato. Finally, there is no obvious independent way to verify the segmentation into syllables, and thus to gauge the accuracy of hexameter line counts.

In one passage of Kennedy (2010) and in one section of this book, the sometime standard estimate[24] of thirty-five letters per Greek hexameter line is invoked in order to give estimates of the total number of lines in some dialogues. It is carefully stated there, however, that employing such a figure introduces a new source of error (perhaps as much as 1 or 2 per cent). Since directly counting letters verifiably gives measurements with smaller errors, it is better to avoid approaches that rely on this assumption.

2.8 Canons of criticism

In the first stage of analysis and interpretation, which aims to verify that the dialogues have a musical form, the form of the argument is inductive. Empirical, evidence-based theories are generally inductive and depend on the accumulation of many pieces of evidence that make the conclusion increasingly probable, whether in literary criticism or the empirical sciences.[25] Here, a variety of independent but mutually reinforcing kinds of evidence are given for every major claim.

Inductive arguments are difficult to mount and equally difficult to criticize. Their advocate must provide a broad range of evidence but the would-be critic must diagnose some wholesale problem with the evidence. Defending the theory that "the moon is full every twenty-eight days" depends on adducing many repeated coincidences between the count of days and the phase of the moon. A sceptic must find some repeated fault with the counts or with the observations, or reject the match between theory and evidence as a "mere coincidence". Persistently resorting to the last strategy amounts to "empty scepticism".

The principle of charity demands that a theory under scrutiny be construed in its strongest form.

Some of the evidence for the stichometric structure of the dialogues is objective and depends on simple measurements. The lengths of set speeches and their positions within the dialogues, as mentioned above, shows clear evidence for line-counting, which depends on straightforward counts of Greek letters. Such evidence is by itself sufficient to verify that the dialogues have a stichometric structure.

In the second stage of explication, some of the evidence depends on literary interpretation. For example, the claim that the more consonant notes are marked with more positive or harmonious concepts depends on interpreting some concepts as more positive. This is not as strong as a simple measurement, but is methodologically typical of textual interpretation in, say, the field of literary criticism.

In the natural sciences, inductive argument can be overthrown by a single counter-example ("black swans"). In literary interpretation, the possibility of red herrings and deliberately disrupted patterns is to be expected. To abandon interpretation in the face of such strategies would make much of the literary tradition, from Dante and Spenser to Mann and Joyce, inaccessible.

Platonism is widely thought to have at its core the notion that "Forms lie beneath appearances". The dialogues often inveigh against those who would restrict themselves to sensory evidence that can be touched by the hands or observed. Plato would seem, therefore, to have ample reason to make his structures subtle, to ensure that they remained unapparent. To this end, the evidence for them in his texts depends on measurement and comparisons: just the normal ways for seeking Platonic Forms.

We may want obvious and striking evidence for Plato's stichometric structures, literal evidence for figurative structures, but we must contend with the logical possibility that we have an author profoundly committed to denying us such evidence. Just as, in the sciences, we observe the phase of the moon but not the law of gravity, Plato wants us to move from the literal and apparent meanings of the text to their general but unobservable structure.

Counter-examples and the density of symbolism

A certain kind of argument often employed below relies on a correlation between the content of a passage and its mathematical location. Passages about harmony, for example, are found to occur at the locations of musical notes. An obvious response is to look for counter-examples: passages about harmony that lie at other locations which are not musically significant. This method of seeking counter-examples has proved an extremely fruitful means for investigating the nature of Plato's symbolism, as a brief example may show.

Note 6.3 in the *Symposium* is marked negatively by an elenchus of Agathon. Afterwards, about halfway between 6.3 and 7.0, there is another reference to an elenchus that even uses the verbal form of word "elenchus" (201e6). This puzzling passage is conspicuously in the wrong place. It is some twenty lines away from a major musical note but repeats the marker of a major note. Moreover, it is a negative marker and lies close to a midpoint between major notes, although these locations are often marked positively.

The recognition that Plato was marking the sevenths came while working elsewhere in the *Symposium*. This wayward occurrence of the verbal form of "elenchus" turns out to stand at just four-sevenths of the way through the dialogue (see annotations below). Interpreting it as a marker for the dissonant four-seventh note removed this "counter-example" from my list of problematic passages and helped confirm the pattern of the sevenths, which are generally marked with negative or dissonant passages.

This method of seeking and tabulating apparent counter-examples played a major role in detecting the patterns of the twelve-major notes, the quarternotes and other musical markers. Its use, however, depends on a surprising, concomitant insight: the symbolism in the dialogues is *dense*, as dense as that in Dante, Spenser,

Mann or Joyce. That is, as in other allegorical writers, many of the passages in Plato's surface narratives are related to the underlying symbolic scheme. They are doing some symbolic work.[26]

Unravelling all of Plato's symbolism will require much future work, but the immediate implications of this insight for criticism are delicate. Counter-examples are an important part of the process and call for explanation, but experience has shown that they are generally signals that more is to be understood.

Measurement and precision

As mentioned briefly above, the arguments here do not depend on reaching any especially high degree of precision. Literary criticism is not an exact science.

Plato's symbolism does not exactly correlate with the musical scale for several straightforward reasons:

- The alterations in the text imply that the measurements can claim only a statistical accuracy. Small variations are to be expected.
- The speeches do not precisely end or begin at notes because the locations of the notes are marked by symbolic passages that may stretch over several OCT lines. Thus the speeches naturally begin or end either before or after such passages, and only occasionally precisely at the exact location of a note.
- As shown below (§3.4, Ch. 5, etc.), the lengths of the marking passages vary with the consonance of the notes, thus the "symbol" marking a note may begin and end some lines on either side of the location of a note.
- In more consonant regions, the narrative seems more closely aligned with the scale than in more dissonant regions (cf. Alcibiades' speech). The degree of correlation varies.

Most importantly, Plato is not a machine. He does not slavishly follow the musical structure. The allegory aims to symbolically represent a musical scale, not exactly reproduce it. Thus the many lines of qualitative and approximate evidence collected in this and the following chapters are sufficient.

2.9 Responses to possible objections

The following briefly and somewhat informally responds to a few points that commonly come up in discussions, but these can only serve as starting-points for debate.

Aristotle was in the Academy together with Plato for some twenty years. If there were symbolic layers of meaning in the dialogues, there would be some evidence for it in

his treatises. But Aristotle's Politics, *for example, which discusses Plato's* Republic *at length, never treats it as a symbolic text.*
Aristotle repeatedly refers to the "so-called Pythagoreans" (e.g. *Metaph.* A.). His motivations for using this phrase have been debated, but it is at least clear that he is not saying "we Pythagoreans". His terminology is distancing.

The fragments collected by Ross (Aristotle 1955), show that Aristotle was a knowledgeable outsider to Pythagoreanism. He can contemptuously mock their scientific theories (e.g. at *Metaph.* 989b29ff.) and generally treats their lore as mere myth. There is no indication in Aristotle's writings that he was especially sympathetic to Pythagoreanism or an initiate.

Although Aristotle expresses admiration for Plato, there is little or no evidence in his treatises of any close relationship with Plato (who was some forty years older). Most of Aristotle's information about Plato comes from reading the dialogues or public lectures. Perhaps motivated by Aristotle's failure to succeed to the headship of the Academy, there were ancient rumours of hostility or some rupture in the relationship between Aristotle and Plato (Riginos 1976).

Burkert's (1972) history of Pythagoreanism is based on the fact that Aristotle and the early Academy had very different views about Pythagoras and his followers. Thus we know, on this very issue, that there was some rupture between Aristotle and the Platonists.

Aristotle did emphasize, like other members of the early Academy, that Plato followed the Pythagoreans, but there is no reason to think he would have been privy to any reserved knowledge.

The claims made here are a version of the "unwritten doctrines" school of interpretation, but that was refuted long ago by Cherniss and Vlastos.
The theses advanced here should be sharply distinguished from claims about the unwritten doctrines. In short, the claim made here is that there are structures hidden *within* the dialogues using various kinds of symbols.

However, the structures found here in the dialogues do tend to accord with and corroborate the ancient reports of Plato's Pythagorean metaphysics, which are accepted by Dillon, Kahn and Sayre (§1.5), and which form part of the motivation for Tübinger interpretations (§1.5).

The argument is circular. Evidence is taken from the dialogues, used to construct theories and then used to "confirm" these same theories.
Philosophers have clarified the way that evidence-based, empirical theories generally emerge from a virtuous circle: patterns are abstracted from data and generalized into theories; these are tested on broader sets of data; more refined patterns are abstracted; then more detailed or more exact theories are constructed; and so on. Theories generally rest on patterns abstracted from the evidence. The critical point is that new or broader sets of evidence are used in ever more general tests of the theory.

This is exactly what happened here. The patterns were first noticed in the *Republic*. In that longer dialogue, the passages marking the notes are longer and stand out in the somewhat meandering narrative. The question of whether the pattern was general was tested by examining all the genuine dialogues in turn. This is the reason that two dialogues are analysed here. The quite specific theory of the *Symposium*'s structure will be shown to fit the *Euthyphro* too.

The evidence consists of a series of coincidences.
All inductive theories are verified by matching theory to evidence, that is, "coincidences". This is no fault in itself. Inductive theories are accepted when it is judged that the coincidences they rest on are not mere accidents. Although any single case may be an accidental coincidence, inductive theories generally proceed by accumulating so many "coincidences" that the assertion that they are mere chance accidents becomes empty scepticism. The strategy here is therefore to provide an abundance of evidence, first by collecting particularly striking instances and then by showing that entire dialogues accord with and thereby confirm the musical patterns.

Patterns are being imposed on to, rather than discovered in, the text.
The claim here is that the patterns exist in the texts and are as objective as any observable pattern. Although it is sometimes fashionable to deride literary criticism as subjective, no sensible interpreter would deny that Dante, Spenser or Joyce use symbols or allegories in their compositions (however much the detail may be debated). The argument here is that Plato should be considered a similar writer, or, indeed, a progenitor of that tradition.

What safeguards against confirmation bias are there?
Confirmation bias, the tendency to cherry-pick evidence favourable to a theory, is a worry for any theory that rests on inductive evidence. Several safeguards are employed here. First, the case relies at the outset on objective measurements (the lengths of set speeches, etc.). Second, it is shown in the next chapter that the theory has proved falsifiable, in the sense that it fails to accommodate some data, and is stringently testable in this sense. Third, the same musical structure is shown *in extenso* to recur in different dialogues (Chapters 4–6). Fourth, each major claim is supported with a robust range of independent lines of evidence.

No ancient interpreter said that Plato was counting lines.
This may be true. Aristotle's failure to interpret the dialogues allegorically already tells us that an outsider to Pythagoreanism, even one familiar with Plato and his philosophy, could miss the dialogues' stichometric structures.

If this is true, it shows what we have ample evidence for: the stichometric structure and the musical symbolism are subtle. As soon as copies of the dialogues were made without regular columns, probably beginning in the Hellenistic period, detection of Plato's stichometry would have been doubly difficult.

However, there are reasons to be cautious here. The general stricture against the *argumentum ex silentio* applies (absence of evidence is not evidence of absence), but is even more important when studying a tradition that pays allegiance to a doctrine of reserve. As I shall discuss elsewhere, a number of Platonists in antiquity said both that there were hidden doctrines in the dialogues and that they would not divulge them. It is difficult to judge whether such claims are credible.

The neo-Pythagoreans, for example, did believe that there were Pythagorean doctrines in Plato and did associate him with a doctrine of reserve. Appendix 2 argues that there is evidence that they did see the musical structure in Plato but did not say so directly. They certainly emphasized just the key concepts needed to recognize Plato's musical structures. In the end, however, it is the evidence in the dialogues that matters most.

The class of concepts supposedly marking the locations of the musical notes, the genus of "harmony", is so wide and loose that anything might count as a marker.
The problem of finding rigorous criteria for distinguishing among less clear cases of what counts as "harmony" affects only the second stage of explication. As discussed in Appendix 5, the approach taken here has been to follow the explicit connections made in the dialogue. For example, beauty is said to be *harmostos* with the divine before note 8.0 in the *Symposium*, and this is why beauty counts in this dialogue as a species of harmony. Similarly, rehearsing or practising speeches is said to foster the participation of mortal in the immortal (after note 8.2), and so counts as a "harmonization". It is true, however, that problematic cases remain, as might be expected in all literary interpretation.

Plato could not have inserted so many symbols without awkwardly disturbing the surface narrative.
It does require great ingenuity to write at several levels at once, but this is common in allegorical literature. In this regard, Plato's writings are not exceptional.

A musical scale of twelve, equally spaced notes was not known to ancient Greek music.
It was not a common scale and may not have been used by musicians in performance. However, as the references in Appendix 1 show, this scale and its variants were well known to music theorists. Moreover, it is just the kind of scale the Socrates of Plato's *Republic* would embrace; its intervals are mathematically regular and are not determined by the limitations of our outer senses.

CHAPTER 3

Independent lines of evidence

Once the Stephanus numbers are replaced with accurate measures of relative location, the placement of key concepts and episodes at mathematically significant points in the dialogues is readily apparent. It is difficult to convey in short compass the regularity of these patterns, which extend through the length of a dialogue. Here, the strategy is to focus on a few easily measured features in a range of dialogues. Although each may appear trivial in itself, they provide a strong form of evidence for the stichometric structure of the dialogues.

3.1 Simple, objective measurements

Some dialogues, such as the *Phaedrus*, the *Menexenus* and the *Symposium*, contain set speeches clearly demarcated from the surrounding text. The lengths of some of these speeches provide evidence that the composition of each dialogue was stichometrically organized. In Chapter 7 it will be argued that such measurements are accurate to within a fraction of a per cent, but the arguments here generally do not depend on reaching this level of accuracy. As emphasized in Chapter 2, the qualitative and approximate evidence is sufficient by itself to make a strong case for the musical structures. These length measurements are one kind of evidence, and their importance lies in the fact that they are especially objective.

In the *Phaedrus*, Socrates' first speech is one-third as long as his second speech to within a fraction of a per cent (the first is 99.9 per cent of one-third of the second speech). The first speech is somewhat longer than one-twelfth of the dialogue and the second is somewhat longer than three-twelfths. The beginning of the second speech occurs shortly before the four-twelfths point and the end is aligned with the seven-twelfths point.[1]

In the *Menexenus*, for another example, Socrates' long speech is ten-twelfths of the length of the entire dialogue to within a fraction of a per cent (99.9 per cent of ten-twelfths).[2]

The structure of the early speeches in the *Symposium* was discussed in a qualitative way in the previous chapter. Their alignment with the underlying musical scale is clear but approximate.

Some speeches, for example, are separated by repartee which is located at the midpoint between two notes (and may be a way of blending two speeches). Thus the banter between the speeches of Eryximachus and Aristophanes is centered at the midpoint between 3.3 and 4.0, and stretches symmetrically for about ten OCT lines on either side of this midpoint. Thus the speeches themselves begin before and after the repartee.

Pausanias' speech, Eryximachus' speech and Aristophanes' speech are each thus about one-twelfth of the dialogue. Socrates' long speech, including his conversations with Agathon and Diotima, occupies three-twelfths or one quarter of the entire dialogue (it is 99.7 per cent of one-quarter of the dialogue). Alcibiades' speech lasts about two-twelfths of the dialogue.[3]

As discussed in Chapter 2, not just the lengths, but the relative locations of the speeches within the *Symposium* provide another form of evidence for the importance of the twelfths. The beginning of Pausanias' speech is aligned with the point two-twelfths of the way through the dialogue, the beginning of Eryximachus' speech (with hiccups) is aligned with the three-twelfths point, and the beginning of Aristophanes' speech is aligned with the four-twelfths point.[4] The climactic, rhetorical fireworks in praise of Eros that conclude Agathon's speech occur just before six-twelfths, the centre of the dialogue.[5]

The structure of arguments within individual dialogues is often organized around the scale of twelfths. Many examples could be given. In the *Phaedo*, Socrates concludes his argument for immortality from cyclic generation at the third twelfth; immediately thereafter he begins the argument from recollection, which concludes at four-twelfths.[6]

In the *Euthyphro*, the first definition of holiness is at three-twelfths and the second definition is at four-twelfths (Ch. 6).[7] In the *Apology*, Socrates begins his investigation of the oracle's claim that he is "wisest" at the two-twelfths point, and concludes it at three-twelfths.[8]

Measurements of the total number of hexameter lines in the dialogues also suggest that the number twelve has some architectural importance.[9] To calculate these absolute lengths from the letter counts it is necessary to introduce a further assumption about the approximate number of letters per hexameter line. The sometime standard figure of thirty-five letters per hexameter line is used here (see Ch. 2).

Although there is thus some additional uncertainty in the line length used in the present calculations, the round numbers that emerge here are another kind of evidence for a figure close to thirty-five for Plato's texts. Calculations of the total number of lines in the dialogues produce, here with only about 1 or 2 per cent accuracy, impressively round numbers involving multiples of the number twelve:

- The *Apology* is 1200 lines, or 100 per twelfth.
- The *Protagoras, Cratylus, Philebus* and the *Symposium* are each 2400 lines, or 200 per twelfth.
- The *Gorgias* is 3600 lines, or 300 per twelfth.
- The *Republic* is 12,000 lines, or 1000 per twelfth.
- The *Laws* is 14,400 lines, or 1200 lines per twelfth.

In sum, the lengths of speeches, the position of speeches within the dialogues, the location of significant turns in the arguments, and the absolute lengths of the dialogues all provide evidence for an underlying stichometric organization and, in particular, for the importance of a twelve-part structure.

3.2 Parallel passages at the same relative location

The evidence for a common twelve-part stichometric structure within individual dialogues suggests that they be read side by side, in order to compare their structures. Despite the different subjects of the dialogues, such comparisons reveal a surprising number of parallel passages: passages with similar content at the same relative locations in different dialogues. Here one, clear example is considered in a range of dialogues, both early and late. These passages suggest that Plato is employing the rhetorical figure of "variation", a technique common in symbolic and allegorical writing, in which the expression of a single idea is repeatedly altered to suit various contexts.

The *Republic*'s discussion of philosopher-kings and the form of the ideal just man occurs at the centre of the dialogue. Comparisons between the dialogues shows that passages describing the divine wisdom and justice of the ideal philosopher often recur near the centre. These terms also, of course, occur elsewhere in the dialogues, and that raises the chance that the following parallels are a coincidence. The immediate argument here against this possibility is simply the specificity, similarity and common locations of the passages (here "p" indicates a percentage):

- *Republic* (50.0–50.5p): Socrates seeks justice and the just man who "participates" in it, invokes Zeus, and first mentions the philosopher-kings who will lead (*hegemoneuō*) the city.[10]
- *Phaedrus* (49.5–50.3p): The followers of Zeus, the god of justice, seek a beloved with a "philosophical" nature, who is a leader (*hegemonikos*), and "participates" in the nature of god. The followers of Hera, on the other hand, seek a beloved with a "kingly" nature.[11]
- *Symposium* (49.4–50.0p): Agathon praises Eros for being "the best and most beautiful leader" (*hegemon*) and for being a "spectacle to the wise and admirable to the gods" (including Zeus), and Socrates, perhaps for Plato an ideal philosopher and embodiment of Eros, jocularly claims to be a prophet (generally, a kind of divine knowledge).[12]

Apart from the explicit repetition of forms of "hegemon", these three passages share a number of elements: Zeus and justice, the philosopher's relation to divinity and the notion of ruling or leading.

The *Cratylus* is useful for investigating parallels between the dialogues. Its series of etymologies is not organized in detail by any overarching argument or narrative; the locations of the various terms analysed there, which typically appear only once, is generally determined by the underlying network of parallels between the dialogues. Here, for example, our leitmotif occurs at the centre and nowhere else:

- *Cratylus* (47.7–51.3p): The etymologies of wisdom, knowledge, the good, justice, Zeus, and of *nous* which rules itself and orders all things.[13]

Some dialogues show this ideal philosopher in action at their centre, and repeat the cluster "philosophy, justice and god":

- *Apology* (49.1–50.7p): Socrates claims to be wiser because he knows nothing, except that injustice is wrong for man and god, he will not give up philosophy and he will obey the god.[14]
- *Euthydemus* (48.6–49.9p): One must philosophize, knowledge is more valuable than gold, and knowledge makes one immortal.[15]
- *Euthyphro* (48–50p): The gods dispute about justice, Socrates seeks to become wiser by being taught what the gods believe is correct (i.e. just) and will sing the praises of wisdom.[16]
- *Gorgias* (49.1–50.1p): Socrates asks about the nature of wisdom, behaves like an ideal philosopher by admitting his ignorance and seeking correction, and doubts whether justice is the stronger ruling over the weaker.[17]

Finally, the *Timaeus* interrupts a long passage on natural philosophy at the centre of the dialogue with a paragraph of Pythagorean theology. Since justice is sometimes for Plato a kind of harmony (e.g. *Resp.* 443c4ff.) this passage would itself constitute an example of just and divine rule:

- *Timaeus* (49.4–49.5p): Necessity willingly or unwillingly obeys God, who harmonizes everything in the universe according to precise proportions.[18]

Other examples could be given, but these passages are evidence that it is no coincidence that the *Republic*'s philosopher-kings are mentioned at the centre of the dialogue: the dialogues typically allude to the philosopher's divine wisdom and just rule at that point.

The *Cratylus* discusses "justice" at its centre but is evasive about its etymology (412e2ff.). Aristotle, however, offers an illuminating, allegorical etymology as if it were well known: "*dikaios* is so-named because it is [cutting] in half (*dicha*), as if someone would say *dichaios* [instead of *dikaios*], and call a judge a *dichastēs* [instead of *dikastēs*]" (Arist. *Eth. Nic.* 1132a30ff.). This may be one reason why references to justice are lodged consistently at the halfway point of the dialogues.

Although passages with puns alluding to their mathematical location within the text, such as the *Statesman*'s reference to "middle" at the midpoint (noted by Sayre 2006), are common in the dialogues, they are not pursued here since the brevity of puns makes them hard to interpret rigorously.[19]

3.3 Ranges of positive and negative concepts

Careful study of the parallels between the dialogues leads to another feature of their shared stichometric structure. The correlation of their contents with the consonance of the underlying notes, introduced in Chapter 2, is found in all the genuine dialogues. Side-by-side comparisons of passages at the same relative locations shows that concepts with negative valuations within the dialogues, such as disease, dishonesty, Hades, the body, difference and negation, tend to cluster in definite ranges and at a definite locations, such as around and between the dissonant notes ten and eleven. Similarly, positive concepts, such as the Forms, virtue, the gods, goodness, justice and the soul, tend to occur in distinct and equally definite ranges. These tendencies are never absolute but, as in the *Symposium*, the concepts in these ranges are clearly dominated either by more negative or by more positive concepts, as can perhaps best be made clear by the examples below.

It is common in literary scholarship to characterisze the tone, mood or style of extended passages. Of course, sceptics can always ferret out counter-examples and exceptions to such judgements, but to do so generally just shows a lack of familiarity with the methods of literary criticism. Such exceptions are easy to find. Nonetheless, the evidence for the general tenor of these passages is strong.

The following interpretations do make a particular assumption, namely that, for Plato, the good is good. More broadly, it is assumed that interpreters of Plato's texts can, unless there are reasons for proceeding otherwise, interpret good as better than bad, virtue as better than vice, truth as better than falsehood, justice as better than injustice, and so on. That is, although the specifics will vary from case to case, interpreters can as a rule classify the good, virtue, truth and justice as "positive" terms for Plato. If this is more than common sense, it is just the assumption that Plato is a moralist and generally uses such evaluative terms in their traditionally conventional senses.

The range of negative concepts from the tenth to the eleventh twelfth contain some of the more vivid passages in Plato's dialogues:

- *Apology* (10–11): Socrates is found guilty and then sentenced to death.[20]
- *Phaedo* (10–11): Wicked souls are condemned to Hades at ten-twelfths, our world is a mere muddy hollow, geography of the underworld, and, at eleven twelfths, abysmal Tartarus and the filthy River Styx.[21]

- *Phaedrus* (10–11): Rhetoric is like the groping of the blind at ten-twelfths, is merely persuasive, and needs not truth but probability; at eleven-twelfths, writing produces forgetfulness and the mere appearance of wisdom.[22]
- *Republic* (10–11): At ten-twelfths, the woes of the tyrant, murder, anarchy and lawlessness are described; the critique and banishment of merely imitative poets follows.[23]
- *Symposium* (10–11): The notorious Alcibiades begins his drunken speech just before ten-twelfths, Socrates is compared to a Satyr at ten-twelfths, Alcibiades' scandalous attempt to seduce Socrates, and, at eleven-twelfths, Alcibiades' pain, rejection and shame.[24]
- *Timaeus* (10–11): Old age and death, diseases and corruption of the body, and, at eleven-twelfths, madness and diseases of the soul.[25]

In contrast, positive concepts dominate around and between the points eight- and nine-twelfths of the way through the dialogues.

- *Apology* (8–9): The courageous conclusion to Socrates' first defence, and, at nine-twelfths, affirmation of his belief in God.[26]
- *Phaedo* (8–9): The theory of Forms is introduced at length and used to prove again that the soul is immortal.[27]
- *Phaedrus* (8–9): Socrates advocates a higher art of speaking (dialectics), which knows reality, employs the Method of Division to clearly define things, is well organized like a living body, and finds a single idea among particulars.[28]
- *Republic* (8–9): Ascension to reality by the true philosopher; at eight-twelfths the study of the One turns the soul to the vision of reality; mathematics and the sciences lead the soul upwards; dialectics; the nuptial number; the beginning of the transformation from aristocracy; and at nine-twelfths timocracy as an intermediate mixture of aristocracy and oligarchy.[29]
- *Symposium* (8–9): Intellectual reproduction stimulated by Beauty, the higher nature of love, and, at ninth-twelfths, the conclusion of Diotima's ladder, with an ascent to the form of the One.[30]
- *Timaeus* (8–9): The demiurge constructs all things, including the soul, according to the Good and harmonious proportion, the organ of divination and the ensouled body.[31]

Although all these ranges contain a combination of good and bad, the predominance of one or the other is clear.

3.4 Preview of the musical structure in the *Republic*

The passages marking the musical notes in the *Republic* are considerably longer than in the *Symposium* and must be analysed separately. Evidence from the

Republic, however, strengthens the case that Plato's symbolism is musical, as the following brief introduction will show. Moreover, since so many key terms are used repeatedly through the dialogue to mark the notes, their distribution provides remarkable, visual corroboration of the underlying scale.

In the *Republic*, the musical notes in the twelve-note scale are marked with clusters of words related to music, mathematics and measurement. These words include terms explicitly denoting musical concepts such as "music", "musician", "harmony", "pitch", "lyre" and "song". Some terms seem related to measuring intervals on a stringed instrument such as the monochord: "instrument", "string", "tension", "division" and so on. Other terms are metaphors: various kinds of "harmony" mark the more consonant notes, while war and *stasis* (i.e. civil war and factionalism) mark the more dissonant notes. Appendix 8 lists the words that mark two of the notes in the *Republic*, and so provides a concrete sample of the range of terms employed.

A first pass through the passages that mark the notes in the *Republic* issued in a list or lexicon of all the Greek words used to mark the musical notes. This made it possible, in a second pass, to count, rather mechanically, the number of words on the list in each Stephanus paragraph. The results of this simple census were summarized in graphs.

Figure 4 shows a small part of the entire graph, from the first to the second notes in the twelve-note scale.[32] This shows clearly that Plato uses larger clusters to mark the wholenotes. These are marked, on the left and right, with clusters of terms that are both taller (more musical terms per paragraph) and longer (stretching over more paragraphs). The three quarternotes between the wholenotes are marked by smaller clusters of musical terms.

Figure 5 shows that a similar pattern holds through the first four-twelfths of the text of the *Republic*. There is a very large cluster at the third, more consonant note

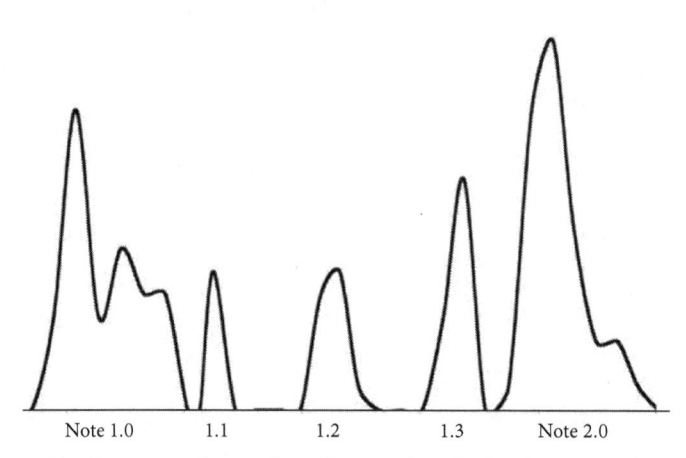

Figure 4 The frequency of musical, mathematical, and related terms in the *Republic*, from one-twelfth to two-twelfths of the way through the text. The two larger peaks are wholenotes; the three intermediate peaks are quarternotes.

(the discussion of Damon and the musical modes occurs there, a quarter of the way through the *Republic*). The clusters at the third and the fourth note, both very consonant, are so wide that their flanks merge with the smaller clusters that mark the surrounding quarternotes.[33]

The evidence in these graphs is not wholly objective. Some decisions had to be made about which terms to count as musical, and in cases where the terms were not explicitly musical this involved interpretation and judgements. This may account for the odd shapes of some of the peaks. However imperfect, the regularity of the pattern is nonetheless remarkable. Regardless of how the list may have been assembled, it is improbable than *any* sizable, fixed list of words would lead to a regular pattern, and even more unlikely that such a list would lead to a pattern matching the twelve-note musical scale described earlier.[34]

Since an explicitly musical terminology is used to mark its notes, the *Republic*'s stichometric structure is clearly associated with music, and is not merely a mathematical or acoustic pattern of some sort. This evidence, therefore, constitutes another kind of strong evidence for the underlying musical structure of the dialogues, which may excuse the novelty of these methods.

3.5 A control: falsifiability and the pseudo-Platonica

A widely discussed criterion for the cogency of evidence-based theories is "falsifiability". Some theories, such as Marxism or Freudianism are elastic enough to accommodate any data: they cannot be proved wrong (or so their critics claim). A good theory should be stringent enough to fail. It should be incompatible with some data.

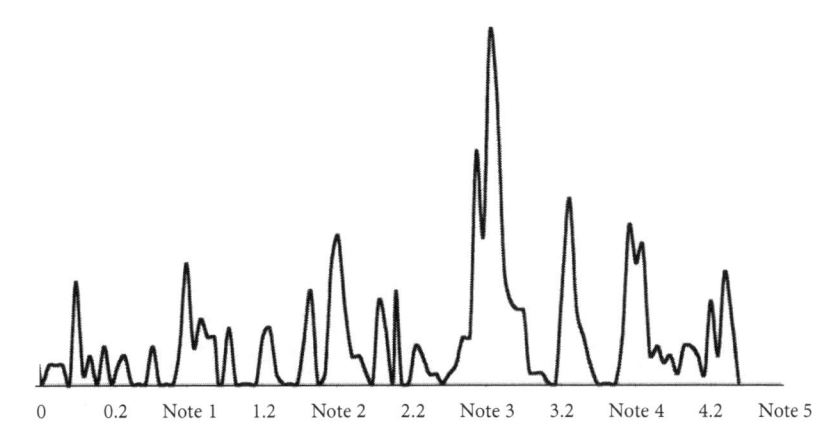

Figure 5 The frequency of musical, mathematical and related terms in the *Republic*, from the beginning of the dialogue to five-twelfths of the way through the text.

The present theory that there are musical patterns in Plato's dialogues is falsifiable in this sense. There are some ten dialogues, transmitted from antiquity, whose authenticity has been disputed. They are similar in content and style to the dialogues agreed to be genuine but are thought to be imitations or forgeries.[35]

No claim about the authenticity or spuriousness of any of these dialogues is made here. The presence of stichometric structure may only attest to an imitator's discerning acquaintance with the genuine dialogues.

The immediate importance of these dialogues for the present study is that they serve as a kind of check or control on the methods employed here. They show that, among texts written with a subject and style similar to Plato's, the methods can distinguish between those that have and do not have stichometric structure. That is, the tests for stichometric structure are stringent enough to be falsified by some data.

Four of the works that were investigated are generally agreed to be spurious: *On Justice*, the *Minos*, *On Virtue* and the *Eryxias*. These were found to have no detectable stichometric structure. On the other hand, the authenticity of the *First Alcibiades*, the *Cleitophon* and the *Epinomis* has been, however cautiously, defended by some modern scholars.[36] There is strong evidence in each of these last three dialogues for the presence of the twelve-part musical structure.

CHAPTER 4

An emphatic pattern in the *Symposium*'s frame

The two philosophers, the young narrator Apollodorus and Socrates, are often stopping and starting at the beginning of the *Symposium*. These motions seem incidental, but they are *equally spaced* through the frame: the same number of Greek lines occurs between each scene. In particular:

- Apollodorus is hailed on the road to Athens and stops walking.
- Apollodorus and his friend start walking towards Athens.
- Socrates departs for Agathon's party but stops in a neighbour's porch.
- Finally arriving, Socrates walks to, and sits down on, Agathon's couch.

Moreover, these passages occur at the locations in the text where, according to the theory outlined in Chapter 2, the musical notes should fall. This chapter argues that these passages contain a repeated cluster of symbols that can be understood only by comparing them to the theory of musical harmony expounded in Eryximachus' speech. Plato is marking the first four notes emphatically, and thereby firmly establishing the rhythm of the musical intervals within the dialogue, just as a musician begins a song by calling out "*one*, two, three, four".

This pattern is clear and definite, but not perfect. There are several references in the frame to being elsewhere (but not the act of travelling). There are brief references to motion by those who are less wise, the servants and Aristodemus, between the four marking passages (see below). However, for an allegorist aiming at subtlety, this pattern is daringly emphatic.

The frame of the *Symposium* is considered here in a separate chapter because its notes are marked with a series of symbols that does not continue unaltered into the rest of the dialogue. As suggested above, evaluation of the evidence for the musical structure should start with the short guide in Chapter 2.

My translations of the *Symposium* and the *Euthyphro* follow the recent trend in the history of science for plain and literal translations. To expose Plato's symbolism, an effort has been made to adhere closely to the Greek and use consistent translations for key terms even if this means my English is occasionally awkward or over-literal.[1]

The next section reviews Eryximachus' theory of music, and especially the roles of motion and musical harmony, and then uses his theory to elucidate the clusters of symbols at the opening quarternotes. The commentary that follows is a more expansive and detailed discussion of the passages at each note.

4.1 A theory of music

An important key to the dialogue's symbolism is found in Eryximachus' discursus on music theory (187a1ff.). In the passage that criticizes Heraclitus' theory of "mixture" as it is presented in the elliptical fragment about the bow and the lyre, Eryximachus offers in its place a theory that helps to elucidate the pattern in the frame.

Eryximachus' theory can be concisely presented as a series of theses:

- Music involves combinations of opposites, both of the fast and the slow (tempo) and of the high and the low (pitch) (187b1–3, b7–c1).
- The combination or steady balance between fast and slow is "rhythm" (b7), that is, the rhythmic temporal progression of the music as determined by the tempo of the beat or the pattern of short and long syllables in verse or song.
- The combination or blending of high and low pitches is "harmony" in its specialized musical sense, a "sounding together" (*symphōnia*) (a8–b2).
- Both rhythm and harmony are types of "agreement" (*homologia*). Agreement cannot consist, Eryximachus emphasizes, of differing or disagreeing elements while they disagree (2/7), but only of formerly differing elements that are somehow made to agree (a8–b7).
- Music establishes agreement in all these cases by implanting *eros* and *homonoia*, or love and sameness of nous (c2–4). Eros is the third mediating force that reconciles two opposite and disagreeing elements.
- Thus music is the knowledge or science of "erotics", a *technē* for harmonizing opposites and thereby creating rhythm and harmony (c4–8, 3.2).

Plato succinctly summarized this view of music in the *Laws*: "rhythm is the name for the order of the motion and harmony is the name for the order of the sound" (664e8–a2).[2]

The very word for the kind of agreement involved in music, *homologia*, suggests that the music of ordinary, prosaic speech may also be harmonized. The connection between music theory and speech is later made explicit when Alcibiades compares Socrates to a mythical musician:

> And aren't you, [Socrates,] an aulos player! You are much more marvellous than [the satyr Marsyas]. He enchanted humans with [musical] instruments by the power of his mouth ... You differ from [Marsyas] only in so far as you do this ... without instruments, by language naked and bare, [that is, by speaking unmetrical prose].　　　(215b8–d1, 10.0)

Alcibiades here says that Socrates' speech makes him a musician. This makes an important concept available for interpreting Plato's symbols: Eryximachus' theory of harmonization in music may apply to ordinary speech.

4.2 Recurring clusters of features in the frame

The following analyses similarities between four passages in the frame of the *Symposium*. These are similar enough to attract the attention of any reader attending to the possibility of Pythagorean symbols in the dialogue, and would introduce the musical structure to such readers. Careful study of all the passages located at similar intervals from each other would gradually reveal the whole musical scheme.

Four elements are repeated at the initial wholenote (0.0) and at the next three quarternotes (0.1, 0.2 and 0.3):

- *Activity/motion*: walking or "doing".
- *Opposition between wise and unwise*: some association between the wise and unwise, or between philosophers and non-philosophers.
- *Agreement/harmony*: an agreement or an assent to a call, request or invitation.
- *Inactivity*: some cessation of activity.

The three quarternotes stand out in a further way: cognates of the word *sophia* appear once at each note but not in between them.[3]

Eryximachus' theory explains this recurrent pattern. The clusters of features are a kind of symbol for a musical sound or note. The motion or activity that occurs at the locations of the quarternotes is the "motion" constitutive of musical rhythm. The resumption and cessation of the motion symbolizes the beginning and end of a musical sound. Eryximachus' "harmony of high and low" is here the "agreement of wise and unwise". The invitation and its acceptance are a harmonization produced in ordinary speech.

Eros or *philia* is arguably involved in each of these four agreements, and thus, as Eryximachus suggested, it is erotic forces that bring about each harmonization.[4]

In sum, there are two forms of interlocking evidence for musical structure in the opening frame. First, the emphatic recurrence of features in the four, equally separated passages suggest some sort of structure in the text. Second, the satisfying congruence with Eryximachus' theory of harmony suggests they are indeed symbols for musical notes.

4.3 A new kind of commentary

In order to recreate the experience of reading Plato on a classical, literary scroll, a five- or ten-metre strip of smooth papyrus with its row of neatly lettered, regular columns, the translated text of the *Symposium* is separated below into a succession of sections of equal length.

Each "column" on the left-hand page contains approximately one quarter-interval of text, with the calculated location of the wholenote or quarternote placed approximately in the centre of the page (except for the first and last pages).

This is a new kind of commentary. Its ambition is to make the structure beneath the surface of the text apparent. It exposes the regular patterns of symbols by making their relations to the overarching schema clear and distinct.

In the first verification stage of interpretation, in which the presence of the scale is established, a preliminary survey of these annotations might begin by surveying the more consonant and dissonant twelfths (3.0, 4.0, 5.0, etc.) and then reading through a entire interval such as that filled by Aristophanes' speech (4.0, 4.1, 4.2, and 4.3). The inferences and reasoning behind these annotations are collected and generally justified in Appendix 5.

Those who join in the further task of explicating every symbolic passage in the dialogue may proceed through the complete series of annotations. The interpretation of a fraction of the quarternotes is uncertain. These were ranked with stars, from three to one, to indicate whether their interpretation was clear and strong, middling, or uncertain, but as more and more received three stars the extraneous issues of the criteria for and boundaries between the categories seemed an unnecessary complication. Although the less certain interpretations will prove easy targets for those with little experience with allegorical literature, the important point is that extraordinary progress has been made.

We are like archaeologists unearthing the ruins of a forgotten city. The surface of the ground is covered with the familiar accumulations of many centuries. After laying down grids across the site, the first season of excavations will expose the bare outlines of the major streets and the foundation stones of a few grand houses. With a city plan in hand, the next season of digging turns towards understanding the confusing jumble of clues in every home and uncovering the treasures that will bring an ancient culture visibly back to life.

The following commentary uses several strategies:

- The locations of the musical notes and other mathematically significant locations in the text are marked. In classical literary papyri, the regularity of the columns and lines would have made these locations easy to track.
- The paragraph or so of text that marks each note is in bold type. The length of these marking passages varies. For example, the more consonant or dissonant notes may be marked more emphatically by longer passages.
- Plato's musical symbols are glossed in the text with their connections to the various species of harmony and disharmony. These species are analysed

systematically in an appendix, where arguments for the various identifications will be found, but the glosses should make immediately clear the musical significance of each passage.
- The correlation between the organization of the surface narrative and the underlying scale is similarly glossed. The beginnings and ends of speeches that coincide with musical notes, for example, are so labelled.
- The more extended annotations on the right-hand pages collect together the various elements of the marking passages, and assess, for example, whether they are as a whole harmonious or disharmonious. In order to make each annotation as self-contained as possible, some information may be repeated.

There are many brief passages or phrases that seem to have symbolic import but are so brief it is difficult to interpret them rigorously. Here and in the following chapters, underscoring is sometimes used to draw attention to a phrase even when there is no accompanying annotation.

Generally speaking, information that can be found in traditional commentaries is omitted.

After surveying the strongest evidence, collected in Chapter 2, a thorough page-by-page examination of the *Symposium*'s symbolism might proceed in the following way. The boxed glosses on the left-hand page will give a preliminary idea of the interpretation of each marking passage and its location on the scale. The discussion on the right summarizes the interpretation, and might be read before a close reading of each passage in boldface.

The glosses and commentary often depend on passages elsewhere in the *Symposium*. Appendix 5 constructs a typology of the dialogue's markers and discusses the connections between them, and is essential for clarifying the unity and rigour of Plato's symbolic system.

NOTE 0.0 = 172a1 I seem not to be unpractised in that about which you are enquiring (*ouk ameletētos*). HARMONY: RECITING SPEECHES And, indeed, I happened NARRATIVE SHIFT TO RECOLLECTED EPISODE; WILL END AT FIRST QUARTERNOTE recently to be going into MOTION the city from my house in Phalerum. Then an acquaintance OPPOSITES watching from behind called out from afar and, at once jokingly and invitingly, said "Hey, Phalerian! You, Apollodorus, won't you wait up?" And I stood and waited. 1/8 HARMONY: AGREEMENT; STOP And he said, "By the way, Apollodorus, a while ago I was searching for you, wanting to find out about that get-together at Agathon's, [172b] when Socrates and Alcibiades and the others of that time came together for the dinner-party – there were some speeches about erotics. Someone else was relating them to me, having heard from 2/8 Phoenix, son of Philip, and said you also knew them. But he had nothing definite to say. So you tell them to me! It would be most just for you to recite the speeches of your companion. But before that," he said, "tell me: were you yourself present at the get-together or not?" And I told him, "It seems that your relater related nothing 3/8 [172c] at all clear to you, if you think the get-together about which you ask happened so recently that I too was present." "But I did", he said. "Why so, Glaucon?" I said. "Don't you know that Agathon has not been resident here for many years,

Note 0.0 (172a1)

Plato is pioneering a new kind of symbolism. In the opening sentence of the *Symposium*, the narrator says he has practised reciting the story of Agathon's party: he is "not unpractised" (*ameletētos*). The symbolic import of this word is revealed by two facts. First, at the location of a later musical note, Diotima says just this kind of repeated practising preserves intellectual creations and thereby gives them and their authors a kind of immortality. "By this contrivance, a mortal thing participates in immortality" (note 8.1; 208b2–3). Second, such "participation" is an example of the blending or *krasis* that marks the notes in the *Symposium*. In this dialogue, participation is a species of the genus of harmony. This places a brief allusion to a kind of harmonization in the opening sentence, and this symbol serves to mark the initial wholenote in the musical scale.[5]

Since music is, for Plato, motion (through time) and harmony (of pitches), the initial notes are marked by references to motion and the agreement of opposites:

- *Activity/motion*: Apollodorus was recently going up to the city (a2).
- *Opposition between wise and unwise*: the narrator studies philosophy, the questioner, Glaucon, turns out to be ignorant (c3 ff., b8–9).
- *Agreement/harmony*: Apollodorus assents to a "call" from behind by stopping (a4 = 1/8).
- *Inactivity*: Apollodorus stops and waits (a5).

Much of the activity in the dialogue's frame serves as a pretext for introducing and repeating this symbolic structure.

Octads, the markers between the quarternotes: Brief phrases mark locations between the quarternotes. Here, the octads are marked by further references to harmony: 1/8 by agreement, and both 2/8 and 3/8 by "recitation" or practising of speeches.

THE MUSICAL STRUCTURE OF PLATO'S DIALOGUES

"and that from the time when I began mixing (*sundiatribō*) with Socrates, and made myself take care (*epimeles*) 4/8 each day to know what he might do or say, has not yet been three years? Before that, [173a] I was running around whichever way I might and thinking I was doing something though more miserable than anyone – not less than you are now, thinking that you must do all those things more than philosophize." And he: "Don't mock me. Just tell when the get-together ('being together', *sunousia*) 5/8 itself happened." And I told him that "We were still children when Agathon won with his first tragedy. It was the day after he and the chorus celebrated the victory feast." "Quite then a long time ago, it seems", he said. "But who related it to you? Was it Socrates himself?" "No, by God, it wasn't," I said, "rather he [who recited it to] to Phoenix. [173b] A certain Aristodemus, 6/8 from Cydathenaeum, short, always barefoot. He was there at the get-together, since he was Socrates' lover more than any of those at that time – it seems to me. Not indeed [from Socrates], but just afterwards I asked Socrates himself some things about what I heard from him, and he agreed with me that it was just as Phoenix had related it." "Why then," he said "won't you relate it to me? 7/8 Anyway, the road to the city is entirely suitable for speaking and listening while walking along." So at the same time as we were going along MOTION, we did the speeches about all that; [173c] thus, as I said at the beginning, I am not unpractised.

REFERENCE TO BEGINNING, RECOLLECTED EPISODE ENDS AT FIRST QUARTERNOTE
If, then, I must relate them to you (*humin*), it must be done.

HARMONY: AGREEMENT Anyway, when I myself either make some speeches NOTE 0.1 = 173c3 about philosophy WISE or hear them from others – HARMONY: RECITALS even apart from thinking of their benefits, I enjoy them PLEASURE preternaturally. When it's other things, especially [the speeches] of you men who are rich and money-makers, UNWISE – I'm myself distressed PAIN and pity you, my friends, since you think you do something DISHARMONY: DISAGREEMENT 1/8 although you are doing nothing. STOP

[173d] Probably you believe that I have an evil spirit (*kakodaimona*), and I think you think the truth. I, however, do not merely think so of you, but know it well.

Companion: You're always the same, Apollodorus. You're always criticizing yourself and the others, and you seem to me really to believe that everyone except for Socrates is wretched – 2/8 beginning with yourself. And wherefrom you ever came to be called by the nickname 'the crazy softie (*manikos/malakos*)', I don't know. In speeches anyway you are always like that: you irritate both yourself and others – but not Socrates!

Apollodorus: And it's clear indeed, my dear, that in thinking so, about myself and all of you, that I'm crazy and wacko. 3/8

Companion: It's not worth quarrelling about that now, Apollodorus. But don't do otherwise than what we've begged of you: just recite what those speeches were.

Apollodorus: Well, they were as follows [173e]

68

Note 0.1 (173c3)

The text itself calls attention to the interval between the first and second notes. Apollodorus' comment here, "as I said at the beginning, I am not unpractised" (173c1), points directly back to the first sentence of the dialogue. This repeated assertion bookends the recollected episode, which fills out the first quarter-interval. Apollodurus now returns, at the note, to direct discourse. In general, Plato uses the musical scale as an outline and makes passages dealing with an episode or topic stretch out over one or more quarter-intervals. The narrative structure reflects the musical structure.

Like the first note, the passage at this note describes a roadside scene. The four features of the motion-harmony pattern are found again in the paragraph around the location of the note:

- *Activity/motion*: the speakers are walking along the road to the city (b9).
- *Opposition between wise and unwise*: philosophy contrasted with worldly pursuits (c5ff.).
- *Agreement/harmony*: Apollodorus agrees to recite the speeches (c2).
- *Inactivity*: Apollodorus knows that his interlocutor is really "doing nothing" (d1).

Observe that positive terms cluster around the note, and negative ones afterwards: agreement, pleasure and wisdom are followed by disagreement, pain and ignorance.

Markers between the notes: The midpoints of the quarter-intervals are generally marked more emphatically. Here, at 4/8, there is a reference to Socrates, a synonym for *krasis*, and another allusion to "melody" (*epimeles*).

At 4/8, the word *sundiatribein* means "to spend time together", but *tribein* can mean "rub", "grind" or "knead" (as the *pharmakon* at *Phaedo* note 11.3 = 117a6–7), and so *sundiatribein* is etymologically "to knead or mix together", a symbol for *krasis* or harmony (its cognates will appear twice in the closing lines of the *Symposium* and twice in the opening lines of the *Euthyphro*).

At 5/8, *sunousia* is "social gathering", and generally means social or sexual intercourse, but literally means "being together" and is probably here another species of *krasis*. At 6/8, Aristodemus is one of Socrates' "lovers". Thus all three phrases allude to kinds of harmony.

THE MUSICAL STRUCTURE OF PLATO'S DIALOGUES

SPEECH BEGINS HALFWAY BETWEEN NOTES rather, I will try to recite to you from the beginning, [174a] as he recited it:
4/8 SOCRATES APPEARS

He said that Socrates met him after a bath and wearing his sandals, which he seldom did. And he asked him where he might be going so finely done-up. And he said, "To dinner at Agathon's. For yesterday I escaped the victory-feast, fearing the mob. I agreed 5/8 to be there today. That's why I've prettified myself, so that I might go beautiful to the beautiful one. But you," he said, "do you have any [174b] desire to go, uninvited, to dinner?"

And I said, he said [sic], "However you so bid." "Follow me, then," he said, "so that we may corrupt the proverb, turning it around so that it's 'good men 6/8 go automatically to the feasts of Goodman Agathon'. Homer, indeed, risks not only corrupting it but also outraging this proverb. Having made Agamemnon an especially good man in warfare [174c] and Menelaus a 'softie spearman', he made Menelaus 7/8 go uninvited to Agamemnon's feast when he was making offerings and entertaining: though the worse man, Menelaus went to the feast of the better man."

Hearing this, he said, Aristodemus said, "Probably, however, I will risk, not as you say, Socrates, but as Homer does: though I am inferior, I go to the feast of a wise (*sophou*) man uninvited. MOTION, OPPOSITES So see that, NOTE 0.2 = 174c8 if you take me there, you have a defence speech (*ti apologēsē*) to say, HARMONY: RECITE SPEECH as I will not agree to go uninvited [174d], unless I am invited by you."

HARMONY: AGREE, COUPLED "'Together as a couple walking along the road,'" he said, "we'll consider what we'll say. But, let's go." MOTION They went along, he said, discussing such things. Then Socrates, turning his mind towards himself as he walked along the road, 1/8 was being left behind. STOP As Aristodemus was waiting, he bid him go ahead. [174e] When Aristodemus got to Agathon's house, he found the door already opened, and there, he said, experienced something ridiculous. For right away one of the slave-boys from inside came to meet him and led him to where the others were reclining. 2/8 He found they were just about to dine. Right away, then, as Agathon saw him, he said, "Aristodemus! You've come at a good time (*eis kalon*), so that you may dine with us. If you've come for the sake of something else, postpone it to another time. Why, I was looking for you just yesterday so that I might invite you, but was not able to see you. But 3/8 why haven't you brought Socrates to us?"

And I, Aristodemus said, turning around saw that Socrates was not following. I said that I was coming with Socrates, having been invited by him to the dinner here.

Well, Agathon said, you did the right thing (*kalōs*). But where is he? [175a] He was just behind me. But I myself wonder where he can be.

Note 0.2 (174c8)

Like the two previous marking passages, this describes a roadside scene. That is, three passages in a row that fall at the calculated positions of musical notes all describe conversations and motion along a road. The passages filling the intervals between these notes do not refer to roadside conversations. The four features emphasizing the frame's quarternotes recur here:

- *Activity/motion*: Aristodemus jokes about "going", and they depart (c7, d4).
- *Opposition between wise and unwise*: Socrates and Aristodemus, who is a mediocrity, visiting a "wise man" (c7).
- *Agreement/harmony*: Aristodemus agrees to Socrates' invitation (*keklēmenos* or "call") to dinner (d1–3); Socrates agrees to give a "defence speech" (c8ff.).
- *Inactivity*: in a "fit of abstraction", Socrates stops on the road (d5–6).

Socrates' quip, "together as a couple walking …", emphasizes the harmony in motion: two friends are coupled together and travel along the road.[6]

There are some references to motion after the note. After Socrates has stopped, the less wise Aristodemus continues on alone (their coupling or harmony is thus broken). Agathon also refers, probably fallaciously, to going round to invite Aristodemus in the past, but this invitation was not made and so produced no agreement.

Narrative structure reflects musical structure: The narrator begins to recount the story of Agathon's party halfway between the quarternotes. This midpoint is also the place where Socrates first appears in the dialogue.

This midpoint in the dialogue is harmonically significant and therefore may be an appropriate place for Socrates to enter the dialogue. It is five "octaves" from the end of the dialogue, and is therefore faintly consonant with the twelfth note of the musical scale. That is, if twelve is divided by two five times (each division producing a note an octave apart), the resulting location is just the midpoint here between the quarternotes. Similarly, Socrates enters the andron at four octaves (see the appendix on the octaves).

Agathon said, he said, "Boy, 4/8 won't you go look and bring him here? And you, Aristodemus," he said, "recline by Eryximachus."

And then, he said, the boy washed [his feet] so that he might lie down. Another of the boys came back announcing that "That Socrates has withdrawn into the neighbour's porch here and is standing there. And when I called, he didn't desire 5/8 to come in."

"That's a strange (*atopon*) thing you say", he said. "Won't you call him? Will you not let him off?" [175b]

And Aristodemus, he said, said [*sic*] "Not at all. Rather let him be. This is a habit he has. Sometimes he stands aloof wherever he happens to stop. He'll come soon enough, I think. Don't try to budge him. Rather, let him be."

"Well, so it must be done, 6/8 if it seems so to you," he said Agathon said. "Boys! Serve the rest of us. In any case, you set out whatever you wish whenever no one supervises you – which I have never done – so now, holding that I was invited by you to dine as well as the others, take care of us so that we shall praise you."[7] [175c]

After that, he said, 7/8 they dined but Socrates did not come in. So Agathon many times bid that Socrates be sent for, but Aristodemus would not allow it.

Socrates came not much later, MOTION: SOCRATES ENTERS THE ANDRON as he'd passed time in his habitual way (*diatripsanta*), as they were right in the middle of dining. Then Agathon – who happened to be NOTE 0.3 = 175c7 reclining alone at the end – said, he said, "Here, Socrates, sit yourself down by me so that, touching [175d] your wisdom (*tou sophou*), WISE VS. UNWISE I shall enjoy what occurred to you in the porch. For it's clear that you found something and have it – otherwise you wouldn't have come away beforehand." So Socrates sat down HARMONY: AGREE; STOP and said that "It would be good, Agathon," he said [*sic*], "if 1/8 wisdom were such that it would flow from the more full to the more empty of us, if we just touched each other, as the water in cups flows through a wick from a more full into an emptier one. If wisdom were indeed that way, I would very much honour reclining next to you. [175e] I think I will be filled with much, 2/8 very fine wisdom from you. Mine were an inferior sort or disputable, being like a dream, but yours is brilliant and made much progress. Though you are young, it shone out from you so intensely and gleamed the other day before more than thirty thousand Greek witnesses." 3/8 "You're arrogant (*hubristēs*), Socrates", Agathon said. And this, about wisdom, we will shortly hereafter go to court, you and I, using Dionysius as a judge. But now, turn to your dinner first. [176a] After that, he said, Socrates lay down and dined as did the others.

Note 0.3 (175c7)

Once again, the narrative structure reflects the underlying musical structure. Socrates sets off for Agathon's at the previous note but stops. At this note, he finally completes the journey. Thus Socrates' period of inactivity fills out the interval between successive quarternotes.

This note, like the previous three, mentions motion along a road. Here, Socrates enters the andron and has his first exchange with Agathon.[8] The four features recur here when Agathon invites Socrates to sit and share the wisdom he has discovered:

- *Activity/motion*: Socrates starts again and arrives at Agathon's (c4).
- *Opposition between wise and unwise*: Agathon, who is no philosopher (as later criticism shows), wishes to hear Socrates' "wisdom" (c8).
- *Agreement/harmony*: Socrates accepts Agathon's invitation by joining him on the couch (d3).
- *Inactivity*: Socrates sits, and motion ceases again (d3).

Thus the first four notes in the dialogue have been emphatically marked by passages that describe motion and harmony, which are for Plato the two components of music.

There are references to motion at the midpoint between the notes (at 4/8). This passage may not represent a musical note because motion along the road is not mentioned explicity or because it involves only less wise characters: servants, Agathon and Aristodemus. There is also no agreement with the wiser Socrates (the servant is rebuffed). On the other hand, its location at a midpoint suggests it has some symbolic import.

THE MUSICAL STRUCTURE OF PLATO'S DIALOGUES

`SPEECH BEGINS HALFWAY BETWEEN NOTES` They performed the libations, `4/8` songs for the god, and the other customary things. Then they turned to the drinking. Then, he said, Pausanias, began a speech (*logos*) of the following sort.

"Well, gentlemen," he said, "in what way will we drink most easily? I say to you that I'm really having a lot of difficulty, because of yesterday's drinking, `5/8` and need a bit of a breather – and I think most of you do too for you were there yesterday. So consider in what way [176b] we might most easily drink."

Then Aristophanes said, "You say this well, Pausanias, by all means let's arrange for an easy way of drinking. For I was one of the ones who got drenched yesterday."

After hearing them, he said, `6/8` Eryximachus of Acumenus said, "You speak well. I need to hear from one more of you how he stands on easy drinking – from Agathon."

"Not at all," he said, "not even I have strength for it."[9]

[176c] "It would be a windfall (*hermaion*) for us, it seems," he said, "for me and Aristodemus and Phaedrus `7/8` and these here, if you, the strongest at drinking renounce it. We, indeed, are always incapable. Socrates I leave out of account. Either way will suffice as he will be satisfied whichever way we might do it. **Since, then, it seems to me that none of those present are eager to drink a lot of wine, perhaps it will be less a displeasure** `PLEASURE` **if I speak the truth about how intoxication is.** `NOTE 1.0 = 176c7` To me, indeed, I think this has become plainly clear from the art of medicine: [176d] that drunkenness is painful (*chalepon*) `PAIN` for humans. Neither would I wish, if I could help it, anyway, to drink to excess `MODERATION, MEAN` nor would I recommend it to another – `1/8` especially those still hung-over from the day before."

"But indeed," he said, Phaedrus of Myrrhinus said in response, "I, at any rate, am used to obeying you, especially when you say something about medicine. And now, if they consider it well, so too will the rest." Hearing this, [176e] all assented `HARMONY: AGREEMENT` they would not get themselves drunk in the present get-together (*sunousia*) `2/8`, but rather would drink at their pleasure. "Since then," said Eryximachus, "this has been resolved, each will drink as much as he wishes and none is under compulsion. The next thing I propose is to let the flute-girl who just came in depart, and play her *aolus* to herself or, if she wishes, to the `3/8` women in the inner rooms; we will entertain (*suneinai*) each other by means of speeches today. And, if you wish, I would propose to you by what sort of speeches."

All said that they so wished and bid him to make his proposal.

Note 1.0 (176c7)

This passage alludes to important Pythagorean themes. Self-control and finding a moderate path between the opposites of pleasure and pain was one goal of Pythagorean ethics.[10] Here, words for "pleasure" and "pain" occur near the note, and Eryximachus is recommending a moderate course.[11] Eryximachus will later assert that medicine, like music, produces agreement and harmony and especially moderates desire and pleasure (187c5ff., esp. e2ff.). In the *Phaedo*, notes are marked by what is explicitly called there a "*krasis*" of pleasure and pain.[12] Thus, this passage is an example of medicine producing an intermediate *krasis* or harmony between the opposites of pleasure and pain.

This is the first wholenote, one twelfth of the way through the text of the *Symposium*. From this point onwards, the notes are marked by species of "harmony between opposites" and usually do not mention motion explicitly. Of the four features that served to mark the previous notes, only "agreement", that is various species of harmony, continues.

This passage is marked by an important agreement – all the symposiasts consent to moderate their drinking – and so establishes a kind of harmony among the symposiasts. In the rest of the dialogue, threats to and restorations of this harmony will mark a number of notes.

Generally, in Plato's dialogues, the first wholenote and the next quarternote are where the topic and procedure (speeches or dialectical questioning, choosing an interlocutor, etc.) are established. Here, the speakers agree to drink moderately; at the next quarternote they agree on the topic. Although it remains implicit, the symposiasts are here agreeing on the way their wine will be served. Classical Greeks blended their wine in varying degrees with water in a large vase called the "*krater*" or "mixing bowl" in the centre of the room. Thus this passage is an allusion to a kind of physical *krasis*. When Eryximachus sends the flute-girl away, he says the symposiasts will entertain each other with speeches or, literally, "be together by means of *logoi*". This signals that language will replace ordinary, sensible music as the medium for harmonization.

SPEECH BEGINS HALFWAY BETWEEN NOTES So Eryximachus said that "Well, the beginning of my speech (*logou*) is from Euripides' play Melanippe. 4/8 'Not mine is the tale', but from Phaedrus here, which I am about to tell you. For Phaedrus is always saying to me, with some irritation, 'Isn't it terrible,' he says, 'Eryximachus, that hymns and encomia have been composed by the poets for some of the other gods, but to Eros, though being of such an age and so great a god, [177b] 5/8 not one of those many poets who have arisen has not yet composed not a single encomium?[13] If you wish, consider the excellent sophists, who composed encomia in prose of Heracles and others – as the superb Prodicos: this is not so very surprising, but I have already encountered a book by a wise man, 6/8 in which salt was marvellously praised for its benefit. And you will see many other such things [177c] so praised. They compose about such things with great seriousness, **but no person has as yet resolved up to this very day to hymn** 7/8 **Eros in a worthy way. And so such a great god has been neglected (*ēmelētai*)!'** SHAME It seems to me that Phaedrus has spoken this well. Thus I desire at once to make a contribution to him and to gratify him and, at the same time, it seems to me to be proper at present for those of us here to glorify the god. [177d] If you concur with that, then we might tolerably pass our time (*diatribē*) NOTE 1.1 = 177c8 with speeches. HARMONY: *KRASIS RESTORES VIRTUE* **It seems to me that each of us, [going] to the right, should declaim a speech, the most beautiful that's possible, praising Eros. We should begin with Phaedrus first, since he reclines on the first [couch]** and is at the same time the father of the speech (*logou*). **No one, Eryximachus, said Socrates, will vote in opposition to you.** HARMONY: ORDER, AGREEMENT 1/8 Indeed, nor would I refuse you, [177e] as I assert I know nothing other than erotics. Nor would Agathon nor Pausanias, nor indeed Aristophanes, for Dionysius and Aphrodite is all his pastime (*diatribē*). Nor would any other of those I see here. However, those of us reclining on the last [couches] 2/8 have no equal [chance]. But, if those at first were to speak suitably and nobly, we will be satisfied. So, with all good luck, let Phaedrus begin and let Eros be praised."

With this, all the others too concurred 1/9 [178a] and urged what Socrates had. Now, neither Aristodemus quite remembered 3/8 everything that each said, nor, in turn, do I remember all that he said. What he most remembered and those that seemed to me worth recalling – I will tell you the speech of each from those.

Note 1.1 (177c8)

This passage is, like the previous note, an important instance of harmony as agreement: the symposiasts all consent to make speeches in praise of Eros in a certain order, from left to right.

This passage is a model for many later passages that mark notes: something shameful outweighs its virtuous contrary, but this imbalance is put right by a harmony or *krasis*. Here the neglect of Eros is put right by an agreement to honour the god by passing the time with speeches.

This phrase "passing the time" is another instance of *diatribein* at a note. As mentioned earlier (see the comment following note 0.1), this word means, etymologically, "mix thoroughly", and thus plays the role in Plato's symbolic schemes of an allusion to mixing or forming a *krasis*.

Songs (hymns and paeans) are mentioned, which also puts an explicit reference to music and thus to musical harmony at the note.

Altogether, the constellation of symbols here has important implications for understanding later marking passages. Sharing speeches (*logoi*) is itself a way of forming a *krasis*, and this may be understood as a form of music. Again, Socrates' prose speeches will be explicitly called a kind of "music without instruments" by Alcibiades (note 10.0). Thus a harmony in or among the speeches – or their speakers – should be understood as analogous to a musical harmony.

Narrative structure reflects musical structure: Eryximachus begins his short speech (at least he calls it a *logos*) halfway between quarternotes.

CHAPTER 5

Making the *Symposium*'s musical structure explicit

This chapter annotates the locations of the musical notes in the *Symposium*'s speeches, in order to show that the symbolic scheme introduced in Chapter 2 is carried out in a consistent and comprehensive way through the rest of the dialogue. The introductions to each speech summarize the strategies for marking its notes.

Especially in the genre of allegorical or symbolic literature, explications of the details and meanings of symbols are often open to debate, even when there is a strong consensus that an author, such as Dante or Spenser, has adopted a symbolic or allegorical scheme.

Among the fifty or so wholenotes and quarternotes in the *Symposium*, some two or three are marked with passages whose relation to the genus of "harmony" is not clear (e.g. 6.2). The surprise is that most of the passages, especially at the more consonant or dissonant notes, can rather directly be read as species of harmony or disharmony. The commentary points out these residual problems, but generally does not attempt to assess the strength of each piece of evidence.

5.1 Phaedrus

As mentioned above, the notes between the first and third wholenotes are not emphatically marked, and verification of the bare existence of the musical structure of the *Symposium* should start with the third wholenote and the intensely consonant or dissonant notes that follow. The following is intended for readers making a thorough study of all the marked passages.

There is clear evidence in Phaedrus' speech for coordination between the narrative structure of the *Symposium* and the underlying musical structure. This evidence does not depend on the theory of relative consonance.

The midpoints between the quarternotes are typically marked in some significant way, often with more positive keywords or phrases. So far the midpoints have been, in particular, the place where characters announce that they are starting a *logos*, that is, an argument or a shorter or longer speech. The narrator began to recount the whole story of Agathon's symposium at a midpoint (0.1.4; see §2.6 for notation). Pausanias is said to begin a short *logos* at a midpoint (0.3.4). Eryximachus says he is beginning another short *logos* at the next such midpoint (1.0.4). These structural shifts in the narrative are pegged to musically significant locations.

This pattern continues in Phaedrus' speech. Both the beginning and the end of his speech fall at midpoints, halfway between quarternotes. His speech begins two OCT lines before one midpoint (1.1.4), and ends one line after another midpoint (1.3.4). Locating the beginning and end of the dialogue's first, major speech at midpoints underscores their importance. Moreover, this implies that Phaedrus speaks for two quarter-intervals. The length of the speech is a multiple of the basic musical interval. This is strong evidence for the stichometric organization of the dialogue. Many of the later speeches will also begin and end at musically significant locations, and similarly have lengths that are some integral number of quarter-intervals.

In content and style, Phaedrus' short speech is a young man's speech. It is full of talk of glamorous heroes and noble self-sacrifice, but is neither positively charged with Platonic philosophy nor negatively charged with the sort of relativism and sophistical doctrine that appears next in Pausanias' speech. In this sense, Phaedrus' speech is neutral. Comparison with later speeches suggests this is no accident. Unlike the more harmonious speeches at consonant notes (Aristophanes) or the more disharmonious speeches at dissonant notes (Alcibiades), Phaedrus' middling content is appropriate to the rather neutral consonance of the musical notes underlying his speech.

There are two quarternotes within Phaedrus' speech, and the symbolic passages that mark them are similar. At 1.1, he speaks of "a man in love", and claims that such love will lead to virtue. At 1.2, Phaedrus speaks of Achilles' love for Patroclus and claims that this love led to Achilles' heroic self-sacrifice. The notion that *eros* leads to virtue also marks a number of subsequent notes, since virtue and beauty are conceived of, in this dialogue, as kinds of "harmony" with the good. These passages are thus sufficiently harmonious to mark these mildly consonant quarternotes but, again, are not as emphatic or as philosophically definite as later passages.

Within the quarter-intervals of text that stretch between the wholenotes and quarternotes, a substantial number of musically or mathematically significant locations are marked with special symbols. Chapter 1 introduced the sevenths, and the first seventh lies here within Phaedrus' speech. The variety of symbolic passages between the major notes are surveyed in the appendices.

The connection between Phaedrus' assertions about virtue and the various species of harmony are only elucidated in later speeches. Only in Pausanias' speech, for example, does the pursuit of virtue become a philosophical project; only in Eryximachus' speech is the virtue *sōphrosunē* associated with harmony and *krasis* (see Appendix 5 for an overview of such connections).

SPEECH BEGINS HALFWAY BETWEEN NOTES First, then, as I said, he said, [sic] Phaedrus began to speak from here somewhere: "Eros is a great god and a marvel among humans and gods 4/8 in every which way, but not least for his genesis. [178b] The god is honoured for being among them the oldest," he said, "and the proof of this is: of the parents of Eros, neither are they nor are they said to be by no one, neither by a poet nor an ordinary person, and Hesiod says Chaos was born first,

'but then broad-breasted Gaia, 5/8 the abode of all, always safe, forthwith Eros'

Even Acusilaus concurs with Hesiod that after Chaos these two were born: Earth and Eros. Parmenides says of his birth:

'He devised Eros very first of all the gods'

[178c] "So it is agreed on all sides that Eros is among them the most old. 6/8 Since he is most old, he is the cause of great goods to us. I cannot say that there is a greater good, straightaway when a youth, than an excellent lover and, for a lover, than a boyfriend. What should guide people intent on living all their life nobly is this – not relatives 7/8 nor honours nor wealth [178d] – not anything other than *eros* can achieve it so well. What indeed do I say this is? The shame towards shameful things and ambition towards noble things. SHAME/VIRTUE Not without these does either an individual or a city produce great and noble works. Now I assert that any man in love, HARMONY: LOVE ESTABLISHES VIRTUE, NOTE 1.2 = 178d5 if he were revealed doing something shameful or suffering what he could not defend himself SHAME from on account of unmanliness, would not feel so much pain if he were seen by his father or by his companions or by anyone else as by his boyfriend. [178e] We shall see the beloved is the same as this, since he especially feels shame towards lovers 1/8 when he is seen involved in something shameful. Thus, if by some contrivance it came about that a city or army was composed of lovers and their boyfriends, there would be no better way to manage their affairs than by thus keeping away all shameful things and rivalries with each other [179a]; and if they fought together with each other, such fighters, although just a few, would, in a word, 2/8 vanquish all of humanity. A man in love would countenance being seen by his boyfriend deserting the ranks or throwing away his weapons less, I suppose, than by any others – and would often choose to die before that. Moreover – for he who might dare to abandon his boyfriend or not to rescue him 3/8 – no one is so bad that Eros himself would not inspire him towards virtue, so that he would be similar to those who are naturally best. [179b] And really, as Homer says, a god 'inspires with a fighting spirit' some of his heroes (*hērōōn*), and this, arisen from him, Eros provides to lovers (*erōsi*).

Note 1.2 (178d5)

The structure of this passage is similar to the previous note. There, the shameful neglect of Eros was remedied by the agreement to praise him in speeches; here, a man's shameful acts are eliminated by the erotic harmony between lovers. In both, there is an opposition between shame and virtue, and virtue is found through erotic harmony and agreement.

This passage does not say that love is a kind of harmony or *krasis*, but this theme will be made explicit in Eryximachus' theory of music (reviewed in Ch. 4). He will say that harmony may be an agreement or "like-mindedness" (*homonoia*) created by erotic bonds, and Aristophanes will comically treat true love as desire for a kind of fusion. Love as an erotic *krasis* or harmony will be a major marker of subsequent notes.

Eros as human love enters the dialogue at the note.[1] That is, Phaedrus turns here from Eros as a god or cosmic force to "a man in love".

Narrative structure reflects musical structure: Phaedrus' speech begins halfway between quarternotes, just as Eryximachus began speaking halfway between the last two notes.

"And, moreover, only lovers choose to die 4/8 for someone else – and not only men but women too. And of this, Alcestis, the daughter of Pelias, provides sufficient witness for this argument for all of Greece. She alone was willing to die for her own husband, although his father [179c] and mother were living. She so far surpassed 5/8 them in love (*philia*) on account of her *eros*, that she proved they were mere strangers to their son and were related to him in name only. And having effected this, her effecting this effect seemed so fine – not only to humans – but to the gods too that, although many have effected many, fine things, it is easy to count (*euarithmētois*) 6/8 those to whom the gods gave this right: to release the soul again from Hades. And they let hers go since they admired the effect [of her action]. [179d] So even the gods honour seriousness and virtue concerning *eros*. They sent Orpheus, the son of Oeagrus, ONE-SEVENTH away from Hades incomplete (*atelē*), showing him a phantom 7/8 of his wife, for whom he had come, but not giving her, since he seemed to be soft SHAME (in as much as he was a lyre-player) and did not dare to die for the sake of *eros* as Alcestis did HARMONY: VIRTUE FROM EROS but schemed to enter Hades while still living. Wherefore indeed, on account of this, they imposed a penalty upon him and made his death NOTE 1.3 = 179d8 [179e] happen by women. SHAME Not so did the gods honour Achilles, the son of Thetis, who they sent to the Isles of the Blest.

HARMONY: VIRTUE FROM EROS "He found out from his mother that he would die if he killed Hector but, if he did not do this, he would return home and end his life as an old man. He dared to choose to bring relief to his [dead] lover KRASIS Patroclus 1/8 [180a] and, having taken revenge, not only to die on his behalf but also to die in addition to the deceased. Whence the gods, exceedingly admiring him, especially honoured him since he had made so much of his lover. Aeschylus then talks nonsense when he says that Achilles was the [older] lover of Patroclus. Achilles was more handsome not only than Patroclus 2/8 but than all the heroes at once. And Achilles still had peach fuzz and was much younger than Patroclus, as Homer says. And indeed, in reality, [180b] the gods honour this virtue concerning *eros* most of all – they more marvel and admire and bless when a beloved loves (*agapa*) his [older] lover 3/8 than when the lover loves his boyfriend. Indeed, the lover is more divine than the boyfriend, for he is inspired. On account of this, they more honoured Achilles than Alcestis, and sent him to the Isles of the Blest.

Note 1.3 (179d8)

Here again, there is an opposition between shame and virtue, and virtue is found through the harmony of a love relationship. Orpheus acted shamefully, but Achilles – because of his erotic bond or "harmony" with Patroclus – acted virtuously.

There is a negative concept at the note, "death at the hands of women", which may have been considered shameful, and this may serve here to indicate that this note is dissonant.[2]

One-seventh (179d2)

In addition to the wholenotes and quarternotes on the twelve-note scale, there are marking passages placed at each seventh of the dialogue, that is, at one-seventh, two-sevenths and so on (see Ch. 2). The number seven had various symbolic meanings in ancient Pythagoreanism and was also the number of strings typically found on the classical lyre. Strikingly, the first mention of Orpheus' name occurs here one-seventh of the way through the dialogue. He was particularly associated with the seven-string lyre.

Study of all the passages at the sevenths shows that the essential marker here is the concept of "mixture" or "opposites that mix without blending". The use of mixtures, the conceptual opposite of harmony, to mark the sevenths is a qualitatively different and particularly compelling kind of evidence that harmonies mark the wholenotes and quarternotes.

Here, Orpheus is alive in the realm of the dead and emerges unchanged: his journey into Hades involved no *krasis* between the opposites of life and death. Phaedrus explains that Orpheus's shameful unwillingness to die in order to remain with his beloved in Hades was due to a weakness in their erotic bond: he was unwilling to die "for the sake of love" (cf. 179b4). Thus, an equation is made that will be important later: lack of Eros is lack of *krasis* or harmony, and this marks dissonance.

Narrative structure reflects musical structure: Phaedrus' speech will end midway between the notes, at the fourth octad, with a sentence referring to "virtue". The midpoints are often marked with emphatically positive elements.

5.2 Pausanias

Since the second wholenote is dissonant but only slightly so, the early notes in Pausanias' speech are marked by passages in which negative concepts such as shame only slightly predominate over more positive ones. Virtue will eke out a narrow victory at each note but it is built on weak, philosophically suspect foundations; only a weak, barely discernible harmony marks the notes. The neutrality of the marking passages in Pausanias' speech is another example of the correlation between content and relative consonance.

Pausanias' speech has often been thought to exhibit the influence of the sophists. His style and ethical relativism associate him with the sophistical movements in classical Athens (Bury 1932: xxvi–viii).[3] Moreover, the line following the end of Pausanias' speech, the jingling play on Pausanias' name and the reference to the *sophoi* who teach such puns, appears to connect him directly to the sophists (185c4–5). In the realm of the erotic, Pausanias makes the move that, for Plato, is characteristic of sophists: he declares he can teach virtue and thereby make the young good.

The following annotations, however, propose to modify this view. Reading the speech in a novel way, that is, by simultaneously tracking the relative consonance of the underlying notes, draws attention to a certain shift or evolution within Pausanias' speech. Near the more dissonant notes Pausanias is more sophistic. His ethical relativism makes mere convention or custom (*nomos*) the cornerstone of the pursuit of virtue. As Pausanias' speech approaches the very consonant third note, however, a more positive, Platonic philosophy emerges and the note itself is marked with effusive praise of "becoming good". The role of custom is minimized. That is, Pausanias seems to make progress towards a less sophistical, more Platonic, philosophy, and this progress is carefully aligned with the relative consonance of the underlying notes.

The same evolution occurs in Diotima's speech; in places Diotima is also explicitly associated with the sophists (see below). Near the dissonant seventh wholenote, she propounds dubious, mythological accounts of Eros' origins and of debauchery among the gods. As her speech approaches the more consonant eighth and ninth notes, her more rarefied, more Platonic philosophy of ascent to the form of Beauty emerges.

Focusing on the theme of harmony also makes it possible to see a kind of progression in the three speeches by Pausanias, Eryximachus and Aristophanes. They each represent stages in the ascent to ideal harmony, that is, to perfect unity:

- *Duality*: Pausanias proposes a duality between two kinds of love, virtuous and vicious. He makes no move towards bridging or overcoming this duality. Although he does discuss various forms of *krasis* or unification, his two loves remain separate and opposed to the very end of his speech.
- *Harmony*: Eryximachus makes Eros a harmonizer of disparate forces: distinct things come together and are somehow reconciled.

- *Unity*: Aristophanes' speech, at least metaphorically, recounts how an initial unity may be dismembered and then reunited. Hephaestus' final offer to the two lovers envisages a permanent fusion: "two will be made one". Hephaestus does not carry out his proposal, although Aristophanes is sure it will be accepted. True unity is not attained until the climax of Socrates' speech (note 9.0).[4]

The passages that mark the notes in Pausanias' speech contain assertions that "custom" suffices to make conduct "beautiful" or "noble". Debates over cultural relativism and the relative importance of "custom" (*nomos*) and nature (*physis*) were common in the Greek Enlightenment, and the sophists were generally portrayed as defending the priority of custom. Pausanias' relativism, his emphasis on *nomos* and his vague, undeveloped conception of moral virtue all point towards the influence of the sophists, and this is why his speech occurs in a somewhat dissonant range of notes.

"Therefore, indeed, I assert that, for <u>the getting of virtue and happiness, among the gods it is Eros who is the most venerable and most honourable and most powerful</u> 4/8 for humans both living and dead."

SPEECH ENDS HALFWAY BETWEEN NOTES Phaedrus delivered, he said, such a speech and after Phaedrus there were several others who he did not remember very thoroughly. Leaving those aside, he recited the speech of Pausanias. He said that:

PAUSANIAS BEGINS "Not beautiful (*ou kalos*), Phaedrus! 5/8 It seems to me the way the [subject of our] speech has been put forward is not beautiful: to so simply take it in turn to praise Eros. Indeed, if Eros were just one, it would be fine, but he is not one. And since he is not one it is more right [180d] to state beforehand how it is necessary to praise him. So I will attempt to set this up the right way: first describing the Eros which must be praised 6/8 and then praising the god in a worthy way. We all know that there is without Eros no Aphrodite. If she were one, then Eros would be one. But since there are indeed two, there must also be two Eros's. How could there not be two goddesses? On the one hand, there is the older and motherless daughter of Heaven, who moreover we therefore call Heavenly Aphrodite 7/8 and, on other hand, the younger daughter of Zeus and Dione, who we call Vulgar Aphrodite. [180e] Necessarily, then, the Eros which is partner (*sunergon*) to the one is to be called Vulgar Eros, and the other Heavenly Eros. SHAME VS. VIRTUE Now, it is necessary to praise all gods, and what each Eros is assigned must be described.

"For each action, the following holds. In and of itself an action NOTE 2.0 = 180e5 DISSONANT is neither beautiful nor ugly (*kalē oute aischra*). DISHARMONY: RELATIVISM [181a] The sort of thing we now do, drinking or singing or conversing, none of these is beautiful by itself but in action and as it is acted turns out to be so. When it is done beautifully and correctly it is beautiful WEAK HARMONY: VIRTUE FROM PRAXIS, BEAUTY ALONE but, when not done correctly, ugly. So indeed with loving (*to eran*) 1/8 and Eros himself: not all is beautiful or worth praising, but only that which turns us towards (*protrepōn*) loving beautifully.

"The Eros of Vulgar Aphrodite is truly vulgar [181b] and performs with (*exergazetai*) whatever he may meet. And it is he who the inferior sort of humans loves. That sort love, first, women not less than boys, 2/8 and then of these they love the bodies more than the souls, and then they love the most foolish they can; since they look only towards the deed, they do not care whether they love beautifully or not. Whence, indeed, it turns out that whatever they do, 3/8 it is the same for them whether it is good or the opposite. [181c] This is from the goddess, Vulgar Aphrodite, since she is much younger than the other and since her birth involved both male and female.

Note 2.0, dissonant (180e5)

This slightly dissonant wholenote coincides with the statement of Pausanias' relativism: no action is virtuous in itself, but only when done "beautifully" or "correctly" (*kalos, orthos*).

This structure of this marking passage note is similar to the preceding ones. Pausanias turns from talk of the gods to humans at the note. There is an opposition between virtuous and vicious actions. However, Pausanias only weakly characterizes the means for establishing virtue. Beauty and a vague "correctness" of actions suffice for virtue, a sort of harmony, but goodness goes unmentioned.

Pausanias' commitment to beauty, here without a deeper doctrine of truth or the good, is a kind of decadent aestheticism. Socrates will later criticize Agathon's praise of beauty as lacking truth, and remind him that beautiful things are among good things. Pausanias' suspect relativism and aestheticism, voiced by a sophist or one of their fellow-travellers, is appropriate to a dissonant note.

There are references to song and to the bond or "partnership" (*sunergon*; 180e2) between each Aphrodite and her Eros, but there is not much harmony at this dissonant note. Strong examples of harmony will not reappear until the very consonant region around and between wholenotes three and four.

Narrative structure reflects musical structure: Phaedrus' speech ends halfway between the quarternotes at the phrase "virtue and happiness". This is, again, a good example of Plato's technique: positive concepts are lodged at harmonically significant locations, while shifts in the narrative tend to occur just before or after them. Pausanias' speech begins at the fifth, less consonant octad with the words "not beautiful". This incipit and its lack of alignment with a major note are further ways of indicating his negative role.

Possible number pun: Each of Plato's dialogues seems to contain number puns, in which a number mentioned in a marking passage corresponds with the number of the note within the twelve-note scale. Given their brevity, however, it cannot be rigorously shown that they are in fact puns. Here, two kinds of Eros are introduced at the second note. The word "two" is used three times at 180d5–6. Similar examples will follow.

TURNS TO PRAISE OF HEAVENLY LOVE AT MIDPOINT "The Eros of Heavenly Aphrodite is free of hubris, first, since she has no share of the female but of the male alone 4/8 – and so he is the love of [teenage] boys – and, second, since she is older. Whence those inspired by this sort of love prefer the male, since they love (*agapōntes*) that which is more robust by nature and which has more intelligence. Anyone might recognize in this pederasty those who are genuinely moved by this sort of love. They do not love boys until after they already begin to have a mature intelligence, [181d] and this is near the time they grow a beard. 5/8 So prepared, I think those beginning at this point love as if they will be together for an entire life and lead their lives together and in common; and do not deceive the boy, having taking him when he was without reason (since young), and then depart with a laugh, running off to another. There should be a 6/8 law against loving [young] boys so that, [181e] through lack of clarity, much energy is not wasted. The end of a boy is unclear, that is, which will end good or bad in their soul or body. SHAME VS. VIRTUE Good men willingly impose such a law on themselves, but it is necessary to compel 7/8 those vulgar lovers [182a] to do some such, just as we compel them, as much as we can, not to love our free women. SHAME VS. VIRTUE These vulgar lovers are those who have made such a scandal, so that some [others] dare to say it is shameful to gratify lovers. And they say this, since they watch those vulgar lovers, and see the prematurity and injustice NOTE 2.1 = 182a4 DISSONANT of their actions – since, of course, any action done in an orderly (*kosmiōs*) and lawful way WEAK HARMONY: VIRTUE FROM BEAUTY, CUSTOM ALONE would not in justice bring censure. And moreover, the law concerning love in other cities is easy to understand, since it is simply defined. Here and in Lacedaimonia it is complex. In Elis [182b] and among the 1/8 Boeotians, and where they are not skilful (*sophoi*) at speaking, it is simply established in law that it is fine to gratify lovers, and not one – whether young or old – would say that it is shameful, so that, I think, they would not have the trouble of attempting to persuade their youths with words (as they would be incapable). It is established by law in Ionia and many other places 2/8 in as much as they live under barbarians. To the barbarians, [182c] this is, on account of their tyrannies, indeed shameful, as philosophy and gymnastics are as well. It is not, I think, expedient for the rulers for bold thoughts to arise among the ruled, nor strong affections nor associations, 3/8 which Eros and the others [i.e. philosophy and gymnastics] are most fond of implanting. In fact, the tyrants here also learned this. When the love (*erōs*) of Aristogeiton and the affection (*philia*) of Harmodius became steadfast, it destroyed their rule.

Note 2.1, dissonant (182a4)

Like the previous note, this is marked by an explicit opposition between virtue and vice, and by a suspect means for achieving virtue. Here, Pausanias suggests that behaving in a orderly or customary manner is sufficient to bring about virtue.[5] Plato typically portrays the sophists as identifying virtue with custom or law (*nomos*), and this weak sort of harmony is again appropriate to this relatively dissonant region in the musical scale. Negative concepts such as "scandal", "injustice" and "adultery" dominate this passage.

Narrative structure reflects musical structure: Pausanias makes explicit declarations of his relativism at this and the previous note, but not in between. At the previous note, a beautiful manner made a practice beautiful; here, whatever is customary or well ordered (*kosimos* has connotations of "decoration" or "ornament") avoids reproach.

"Thus, where it is established as shameful to gratify lovers, it is so by the wickedness of those who establish it: [182d] by the 4/8 greed of the rulers and the unmanliness of the ruled. Where it was simply established by law as fine, it was on account of laziness in the souls of the establishers. But here much more beautiful laws than these have been established, and as was said they are not easy to understand. 1/5 Considering that it is said more beautiful to love openly than in secret, 5/8 and especially to love the most noble and best, even though they may be more ugly than others, and that again the encouragement to the lover from all is astonishing [182e] – which would not be the case if he were doing something shameful – and finally that the successful seducer is deemed fine while the unsuccessful is shameful. Moreover, the law gives permission for the lover to be praised for performing marvellous deeds, 6/8 which if someone dared to do while pursuing or wishing to accomplish anything else than this, [183a] he would reap the greatest reproaches.[6] If indeed, wishing to get money from someone or to take up an office or some other power, he desired to do the sort of things lovers do towards their boyfriends 7/8 – making in his entreaties supplications and demands, swearing oaths, camping out in porches, and wishing to enslave himself in a slavery such as no slave ever would – he would be impeded from acting such actions NOTE 2.2 = 183a8 DISSONANT by both his friends and enemies: VIRTUE FROM NEGATIVES: COERCION, REPROACH [183b] those reproaching him for flattery and illiberality and the others admonishing him and being ashamed on his behalf.[7] SHAME VS. VIRTUE For the lover doing all these things it is an added grace, and it is permitted by the law to do them without reproach, as if something splendid is being accomplished. WEAK HARMONY: VIRTUE FROM CUSTOM ALONE

"The most terrible, 1/8 as the many at any rate say, is that only [a lover] swearing oaths is forgiven by the gods when violating oaths – they even deny lovers' oaths exist. Thus both the gods and humans [183c] have granted licence to the lover for all, as they say the law does here. Now someone might think that in this 2/8 city's laws it is splendid both to love and to return affection (*to philous*) to lovers. But since the fathers, having set minders over the beloveds, do not allow them to converse with their lovers, and since orders are given to the minders for that, both their peers and companions 3/8 will scold if they see something like that going on. [183d] Moreover, the elders in turn would not discourage or rail against the scolders as if what they are saying is incorrect. Seeing all that, someone might judge that, again, it is here established by law that such [behaviour] is the most shameful.

Note 2.2, dissonant (183a8)

Like the previous two notes, this is marked by an explicit opposition between virtue and vice, and by a suspect means for achieving virtue: custom or *nomos*. Other pairs of opposites, such as the friends and enemies of the lover (who are working in concert) or the slaves and free citizens, are not reconciled and so form no *krasis*. Negative concepts dominate this somewhat dissonant passage.

Pausanias does make the customs of Athens a blend or *krasis* of opposing foreign customs, but the most he can say is that Athenian practices are "not easy to understand" (182d5). This inability to grasp the harmonization of opposites is characteristic of Pausanias and appropriate to a slightly dissonant musical note (see Appendix 3).

Narrative structure reflects musical structure: Although the effect of various customs has been discussed since the preceding quarternote, only here, at the note, does Pausanias once again make a declaration that custom alone suffices for his conception of virtue. Three notes in a row have thus been marked in the same way.

"The following I think holds. As I said at the beginning, it is not simply either fine in and of itself 4/8 nor shameful, but fine if done in a fine way and shameful if shamefully. Now, 'shamefully' is to gratify someone wicked or with wickedness, and 'in a fine way' is to gratify a good person or nobly. That lover is wicked who is vulgar, who loves the body more than the soul; [183e] and neither is he steadfast in as much as he does not love something steadfast. 5/8 2/9 And again, when the bloom of the body, which he loves, fades, 'he flies off and away', dishonouring his many words and promises. The [Heavenly] lover, having a good character, remains a lover through life, [184a] since he is fused to something steadfast. Our law wishes to test these lovers well and nobly, 6/8 so that these are gratified and those avoided. On this account, it urges the lovers to pursue and the beloveds to flee, judging and testing which sort the lover could be and which sort the beloved. Thus, for this reason, in the first place, to be seduced quickly is considered shameful, SHAME FROM CUSTOM ALONE 7/8 so that time may develop, since time is thought to be a good test of most things, and in the second place since to be seduced by money or by political favours [184b] is shameful – whether one is treated badly and cowers with fear and does not resist or whether one is treated well with money or political favours and does not scorn them.

SHAME NOTE 2.3 = 184b3 DISSONANT "None of these seems either dependable or steadfast, even apart [from the fact] that no noble love (*philian*) has grown from them. One road, indeed, is left in our law if a boyfriend intends to nobly gratify his lover. WEAK HARMONY: VIRTUE FROM CUSTOM ALONE [184c] It is the law by us, just as it was for lovers not mere flattery nor disgraceful to enslave themselves deliberately in any kind of slavery to their boyfriends, 1/8 so indeed there is only one LEAVING DISSONANT, TURNING TO CONSONANT NOTES other voluntary slavery left that is not disgraceful. And this is a slavery for virtue. VIRTUE: *KRASIS* OF FREE AND SLAVE For it is believed by us that, if someone cares for another, judging that he will through him become better either in some skill (*sophian*) 2/8 or in any other kind of virtue whatsoever, then this voluntary slavery is neither shameful nor mere flattery. It is necessary to combine into one and the same thing this pair of laws: [184d] that one about pederasty and that about philosophy and the other virtue, NEARING CONSONANT NOTE, TURN TOWARDS PHILOSOPHY if the boyfriend gratifying the lover 3/8 is to turn out to be a noble act. When the lover and the boyfriend wish for the same thing, each upholds the law. The one, being gratified and serving the boyfriend in any way, justly serves him, and

Note 2.3, dissonant (184b3)

This note again has the same structure: an opposition between shameful and virtuous conduct, and a weak, sophistic conception of virtue established by custom. This dissonant note is similarly marked by a predominance of negative concepts: "contempt", "lack of steadfastness", "impossibility" and the fourth, firm declaration of the centrality of custom. Even the positive points in this passage are formulated negatively.

Immediately after this quarternote, there is a transition from dissonance to harmony, that is, from a negatively marked, dissonant range of notes towards the very harmonic third wholenote. There are several signs of change here:

- A clear *krasis* or blend of opposites: a lover freely becomes a slave.
- The assertion that love relationships aim at wisdom and the other virtues, and achieve them through a *krasis* of customs (4/8).
- A clear invocation of and turn towards "philosophy".[8]

Although it is traditional for a peroration to reach for more lofty heights, Pausanias is clearly, from this point, blending sophistic elements, his insistence on custom and his claim to teach virtue, with more Platonic concepts.

The octads are now marked with positive, Platonic concepts: *krasis* (1/8), wisdom and virtue (2/8), and goodness (3/8).

AT MIDPOINT: VIRTUE FROM *KRASIS* WITH PHILOSOPHY "the boyfriend in turn justly labours in any way for he who makes him wise and good. The one contributes a capacity for wisdom 4/8 and the rest of virtue and the other needs education and to acquire the rest of wisdom (*sophian*). [184e] When these laws come together towards the same (*suniontōn eis tauton tōn nomōn*) KRASIS, and only at that point, does it happen to be noble (*kalon*) for a boyfriend to gratify his lover – and otherwise never. In this case, it is not shameful even to be deceived. 5/8 In all other cases, both being and not being deceived brings shame. [185a] If indeed someone gratifies his lover, [supposing he's] a rich man, for the sake of money, and, being deceived, gets no money when the lover reveals he is poor, it is no less shameful. Such a person seems to exhibit his own self 6/8 since for the sake of money he would perform any service in any way, and this is not noble. According to the same argument, even if someone were gratifying his lover, [supposing the lover] a good man, and he, aiming at becoming better through his love (*philian*), [185b] was deceived by his lover, the lover thereby reveals he is bad and possesses no virtue – but the deception was nonetheless beautiful. 7/8 For it seems that [the beloved] too has made clear his own self: that for the sake of virtue and for becoming good he would eagerly do all for all HARMONY: VIRTUE, GOOD – and this, in turn, is the most beautiful of all. Thus it is all entirely noble to gratify a lover for the sake of virtue. HARMONY: VIRTUE, BEAUTY This is the *eros* of the Heavenly Aphrodite and is heavenly and worth much both to city and individual, NOTE 3.0 = 185b6 CONSONANT compelling the lover to take much care (*epimeleian*) himself of himself for virtue HARMONY: VIRTUE and compelling the beloved too. [185c] All the others are of the other goddess, Vulgar Aphrodite. DISHARMONY: SHAME

"So this, Phaedrus, however extemporaneous, he said, is my contribution to you about Eros." SPEECH ENDS NEAR NOTE

After Pausanias paused – the sophists (*sophoi*) teach me to speak 1/8 equally like this – Aristodemus said Aristophanes had to speak, but he happened to have come down with hiccups, whether because he was stuffed or something else, and was not able to speak. But he said [185d] – to Eryximachus who lay on the couch down from him – "Eryximachus, 2/8 it would be just for you either to stop my hiccups or to speak instead of me while I stop them myself." And Eryximachus said, "But I will do both. I will speak in your turn and, after you stop them, you will speak in mine. While I speak, if you would please hold your breath for a long time, the hiccups will stop. If not, gargle with water. 3/8 If, though, they are very severe, pick up something with which you could tickle your nose and sneeze."

Note 3.0, consonant (185b6)

The third wholenote is the first strongly harmonic note in the musical scale, and is clear evidence that such notes are marked with positive, more Platonic concepts. This note has a ratio of 3:12 or 1:4 with the twelfth note, which is composed of small whole numbers (belonging to the Pythagorean tetractys). This note is also two "octaves" from the twelfth note, since twelve divided by two twice gives three.

At the midpoint, halfway from the last quarternote, Pausanias finally reaches the conception that virtue results from a *krasis* or harmony (between pederasty and philosophy), which he states rather explicitly. He began his speech by drawing a distinction between the two kinds of love, but ends with a coalescence of two into one. Although still sophistical, since his *krasis* is of two "customs", Pausanias finally arrives at a more Platonic philosophy: that some conception of, and pursuit of, the good is central to virtue. The passage at the note explicates this coalescence or harmony:

- Positive concepts dominate. There is a clear cluster of positive concepts before the note (underlined).
- Explicit references to relativism and custom (*nomos*), which appeared in the previous four, disharmonious marking passages, now disappear. Virtue is now emphatically linked to the good and becoming good.
- Pausanias seems to reverse his earlier relativism: now it is not beauty that makes action virtuous but, instead, it is aiming at virtue that makes action beautiful.
- A variety of superlatives and intensifiers (e.g. "do all for all", "most beautiful of all", "entirely noble") are used to amplify and accentuate this harmonious musical note.
- There are no negations (e.g. no "not", "nothing" or "other") between the last octad (7/8) and the wholenote.
- The good, heavenly Eros is mentioned at the note.

Although overwhelmingly positive, this note is still a blend of virtue and vice.

Immediately after the note, there is a brief mention of the vicious, popular Eros in a sentence with two negations (*heteroi, heteras*; 185c2–3). His dualistic conception of love, personified by the two pairs of gods, remains to the end.

Narrative structure reflects musical structure: Pausanias' speech ends just after the note. There is generally a closer correspondence between the beginning and ends of the speeches and the major notes in the musical scale near the more consonant notes. This is a first example.

5.3 Eryximachus

The range of notes from the end of Pausanias' speech (3.0) to the end of Aristophanes' speech (4.3) is the most consonant in the first half of the dialogue. The speakers progress here from duality, through harmony, to a vision of ideal unity, and provide strong, clear evidence of the underlying musical structure.

The genus of the concepts used to mark the musical notes is typically discussed within each of Plato's dialogues. Here, in the *Symposium*, Eryximachus' theory of music expounds the nature of harmony, and makes explicit many of the connections needed to recognize its species, as discussed earlier. This introduction concentrates on the narrative structure of the speech.

The rhythm of musical intervals in the speech is clearly established by themes repeated in the marking passages at each of the three quarternotes in Eryximachus' speech. Each passage says that it is good to gratify the good but bad to gratify the bad. Moreover, each invokes a craftsman who has mastered the art of bringing about erotic harmony:

- 3.1: "Now I agree with what Pausanias was just saying,[9] that it is good to gratify good men, shameful to gratify the dissolute"; "the master-physician".
- 3.2: "Round comes the same conclusion: well-ordered men, ... should be gratified and their love preserved ... But the Popular Love"; "a good craftsman".
- 3.3: "For impiety is ... the result of refusing to gratify the orderly Love ... and of yielding to the Other"; "a craftsman of friendship".

As is often the case, the two back references at 3.1 and 3.2 call attention to musical intervals, that is, to the repetition of ideas at quarter-intervals. Both the gratification theme (i.e. sex) and the craftsmen serve to mark the notes: they are a form of "fitting together" and its cause.

At the outset of his speech, Eryximachus says that Pausanias began well but did not properly finish his speech and that he, Eryximachus, will remedy this. Other commentators, however, do not generally clarify how this speech forms a conclusion to the previous one.

The three quarternotes in Eryximachus' speech each introduce and extol different *technai*, which, proceeding beyond Pausanias, produce different and successively greater degrees of harmony:

- 3.1, *art of medicine*: This art produces an "alteration" or balance between two, distinct loves by replacing one with the other (at 3.1.1).
- 3.2, *art of music*: This erotic art produces "harmony", which is "agreement" and absence of difference. At the note, the two loves are said to be absent from this art itself, but they appear later when it is applied to human affairs (1/8–3/8).
- 3.3, *art of prophecy*: This produces a "communion"[10] between gods and humans, by supervising the two loves.

During this progression, the two loves remain distinct but the good, Heavenly Eros, becomes a causal agent producing harmonization. In an important phrase, it produces a "temperate harmony and *krasis*" between contraries (3.2.4). At the end of his speech, Eryximachus can speak of "Eros as a whole" (*ho pan Eros*; 188d4), as if it were singular and united, but then reverts to a division between the two loves.

Eryximachus, therefore, advances beyond Pausanias in two ways. Instead of a static duality of virtuous and vicious loves, Eryximachus makes heavenly Eros a dynamic cause of harmony. In addition, he theorizes various degrees of harmonization, but finally fails to reach true unity.[11]

"And if you do this once or twice, they will stop even if they are quite severe."

"Before you can even start speaking," said Aristophanes, "I will do so."

SPEECH BEGINS HALFWAY BETWEEN NOTES Eryximachus said, 4/8 "It seems to be necessary to me, since Pausanias did not adequately finish off his speech [186a] after starting so well, that I must try to place an end (*telos*) upon his speech. That Eros is double seems to me to have been well stated. That Eros is not only in the souls of humans and not only related to the beautiful 5/8 but is also related to many other things and in others – in the bodies of all animals, in plants in the earth, and in a word in all that is – that I seem to [186b] have learned from the art of medicine, my own art. The god Eros is great and marvellous and extends (*teinei*) over all, both human 6/8 and divine things. I begin my speech with the art of medicine in order too that we may honour this art. Indeed, the nature of bodies has this double Eros. The health of the body and its illnesses are admittedly different and dissimilar and, moreover, the dissimilar desires and 7/8 loves the dissimilar. The *eros* in the healthy is other than that in the ill. It is indeed, as Pausanias just said, fine to gratify the [186c] good lovers in the human [realm] but shameful to gratify the licentious. SHAME VS. VIRTUE Thus in our bodies it is fine to gratify the good and healthy within each body – and necessary. HARMONY: VIRTUE NOTE 3.1 = 186c1 CONSONANT This is what is named 'medical art'.

HARMONY FROM ART OF MEDICINE "It is also shameful to gratify the bad and diseased – and to be avoided, DISHARMONY: SHAME if one means to be technically apt. Indeed, to speak summarily, the art of medicine is knowledge of the erotics of the body in relation to filling and emptying, [186d] 1/8 and he who distinguishes between the good and bad love SHAME VS. VIRTUE in them is the master-physician (*ho itatrikōtatos*). And he who makes the alteration, so that one love is acquired instead of the other, and so that in those where there is no love but should be it develops, and so knows both how to implant love and, if already there, to expunge it – he would be a good craftsman. Indeed, it is necessary to be able to make the most hostile things existing in the body 2/8 friends (*phila*), and to love each other. HARMONY: LOVE BETWEEN OPPOSITES

"The most hostile things are the most opposite things: cold to hot, bitter to sweet, and all such things. Since our ancestor Asclepius knew how to implant love [186e] and unanimity (*homonoian*) among these, as those poets say and as I am persuaded, 3/8 he established our art. So all the art of medicine, as I assert, is governed through this god Eros, and so similarly are gymnastics and farming. [187a]

Note 3.1, consonant (186c1)

This is another clearly marked note. The opposition between virtue and shame is repeated several times. An agent is introduced, the art of medicine as a kind of erotic *technē*, which effects a balance between opposite extremes in the body: gratifying the good and disappointing the bad. Eryximachus will later make medicine an art of erotic harmonization. Here, it acts to encourage the good and fend off the bad but harmony is not explicitly mentioned. Thus this note is not as emphatically marked as the two succeeding ones.

The passages at this and the next note are generally important for understanding the scheme for marking the musical scale in the *Symposium*. At this note, the harmony between the opposed elements is explicitly constituted by an erotic bond, by "friendship and love" (186d6). *Eros* as an active mediating agent between opposites, as an art that produces harmony, will be a common marking concept through the dialogue.

Narrative structure reflects musical structure: Eryximachus begins his speech halfway between two quarternotes.

Just before the note, Eryximachus says he agrees with what Pausanias "was just saying" (186b8–9). He then repeats what was said in the last marking passage at note 3.0, which again calls attention to the interval between the notes. This theme, that it is good to gratify the good, will reappear at all three quarternotes in Eryximachus' speech – but not in between – and invests his speech with a definite rhythm.

MUSICAL ANALOGY INTRODUCED AT HALF-POINT "And it is clear to all who gives it even a little thought that the art of music too corresponds to these, as probably Heraclitus 4/8 too wished to say, although in respect of his words he did not speak well. For he said the one 'comes together while differing from itself, as in the harmony of a bow or a lyre'. It is very irrational to say that a harmony differs in itself or that it consists of things still differing. But probably he wished to say [187b] this: that it consists of high sounds and low sounds 5/8 which were differing before and then later were brought into agreement by the art of music. There doubtless would be no harmony of high and low sounds while they yet were differing. For harmony is a consonance, and consonance is TWO-SEVENTHS: HARMONY VS. STATE OF DIFFERING an agreement, and agreement is impossible between things 6/8 differing while they are differing.

"And in turn it is impossible to harmonize something differing and not agreeing – as too rhythm [187c] arises from fast and slow [speeds] which were differing before but later started agreeing. Agreement is put into all these, there by the art of medicine 7/8 and here by the art of music, by implanting love and unanimity (*homonoian*) between things. HARMONY: DEFINED AS LOVE AND AGREEMENT Music is, moreover, knowledge of erotics as it concerns harmony and rhythm. In the system (*sustasei*) itself of harmony and rhythm, HARMONY AND RHYTHM it is not difficult to discern erotics, nor is the double Eros yet there. But when it may be necessary to apply NOTE 3.2 = 187c8 CONSONANT [187d] rhythm and harmony to human beings, HARMONY either by creating, which they call 'composing melodies', or by correctly using the created tunes and measures, which is called 'education', here indeed there is difficulty and a good craftsman is needed. Again comes the same argument (*logos*): HARMONY: GOOD TO GRATIFY THE GOOD that the well ordered among humans 1/8 and those not yet well ordered but meaning to become more so should be gratified, and their *eros* should be safeguarded, for this is the beautiful *eros*, the heavenly *eros*, [187e] the *eros* of the Heavenly Muse. VIRTUE But the other is of Polymnia, the vulgar *eros*, which must be offered with care to those one may offer it to so that its pleasures may be enjoyed without implanting licentiousness. 2/8 SHAME Similarly, in my art, it is a great task to handle the desires associated with the art of gourmet cooking, so that one can enjoy its pleasures without illness. So in the art of music indeed and in the art of medicine and in all the others both human and 3/8 divine, as far as permitted, each *eros* must be safeguarded. [188a] For both inhere. Since too the system of the seasons of the year is full of both of them,

Two-sevenths (187b4)

The theory of the passages marking the sevenths comes first. Earlier, at one-seventh, Orpheus with his seven-stringed lyre was alive among the dead, and it was claimed that "mixtures" of opposites without blending would mark the following sevenths (as reviewed in Ch. 2). Here, two-sevenths of the way through the dialogue, Eryximachus says that differing things cannot be a harmony. Without using the word, he is distinguishing mixture from true harmonization. Thus the well-known distinction between mixture and harmony is articulated here, two-sevenths of the way through the dialogue, and serves to mark this location in the musical scale. Subsequent sevenths are also marked by mixtures.

Note 3.2, consonant (187c8)

This is one of the most emphatically marked notes. It lies midway between two of the most consonant wholenotes. The passage at the note is an explicit discussion of harmony in music, erotics and human affairs. The genus of the concepts that mark the notes is therefore used here to mark a note. This singularly important passage not only provides clear evidence of the underlying musical structure – that is, that instances of harmony are lodged at the notes – but also gives the essential theory of the marking scheme.

Plato's dialogues typically discuss the genus of the concepts used to mark their notes without, of course, announcing that the concepts will serve that purpose. This is the passage, in the *Symposium*, that provides the key to the marking scheme.

Note 3.2 is marked by a discussion of the genuine harmony that arises when things differing at first are later found in agreement. An ideal harmony thus somehow manages to blend or reconcile its elements in a way that overcomes their differences. Eryximachus makes the erotic bond a paradigm case of such harmonization. Erotics is the *technē* that produces harmony, even in cosmology, and true love is a harmonization.

MIDPOINT: HARMONY IS *KRASIS,* VIRTUES, LOVE "and after the things I just spoke of – hot, cold, dry and wet things – achieve an orderly love and take on a temperate (*sōphrosona*) 4/8 harmony and crasis (*harmonian kai krasin*), they come bringing prosperity and health to humans and to the other animals and plants, and do no wrong. But when the Eros with hubris gains the upper hand over the seasons of the year, he corrupts many things [188b] and does wrong. Plagues love (*philousi*) to arise 5/8 from such things as well as many other, dissimilar illnesses both to beasts and animals. And frosts, hail-showers and blight arise from overreaching and disorder towards each other of such erotic things, knowledge of which concerning the motions of the stars 6/8 and the seasons of the years is called 'astronomy'. Moreover, all the sacrifices too and those things supervised by the art of prophecy [188c] – these constitute the communion of gods and humans with each other HARMONY – concern no other thing than the safeguarding and doctoring of Eros. All impieties love (*philei*) to arise if someone does not gratify the orderly Eros 7/8 and does not honour and venerate him – rather than the other one – in all work (*ergō*), HARMONY: GOOD TO GRATIFY THE GOOD even that concerning parents, both living and dead, and the gods. VIRTUE VS. SHAME It is prescribed to prophecy to investigate and heal those in love, and it is again prophecy that is the craftsman of the love (*philias*) [188d] of gods and people HARMONY WITH GODS PRODUCED BY PROPHECY – in that it knows about erotics among humans NOTE 3.3 = 188d1 CONSONANT in so far as it extends to what is right and to piety. So manifold and great or rather so total is the power, taken together, that the All-Eros has. But the Eros who perfects whatever is good with temperateness and justice HARMONY: VIRTUES both for us and for the gods, he has the greatest power 1/8 and fashions all our happiness HARMONY: VIRTUE and makes us capable of keeping company and being friends with each other, as well as with the gods, our masters. HARMONY: FRIENDSHIP WITH GODS [188e]

"So probably I too, in praising Eros, omit many things – not, however, deliberately. But if I have left something out, it is your task, Aristophanes, 2/8 to fill it in. Or, if you have it in mind to praise the god in some other way, then praise him, since, moreover, your hiccups have stopped."

END OF SPEECH [189a]

Taking over, then, he said, Aristophanes said that "They very much stopped, but not before a sneeze was applied to them, which makes me wonder if the orderliness of the body desires 3/8 such noises and tickling, which is what a sneeze is. For they stopped straightaway after I applied a sneeze to them."

And then Eryximachus said, "Aristophanes, my good man,

Note 3.3, consonant (188d1)

This is another emphatically positive passage at a consonant note. The harmony between god and humans is produced by erotic bonds crafted by the art of prophecy.

As the passage in bold shows (especially after the note), while shameful impiety is mentioned, this note is marked by positive references to harmony, love, goodness, bliss, health, the Platonic virtues and friendship, which indicates that it is consonant.

Two points are important for interpreting later passages. The *Symposium* here briefly but explicitly associates "*krasis* and harmony" (188a4).[12] *Krasis* is the technical term for something thoroughly blended or fused, and the dialogue assumes throughout that harmony and *krasis* are closely related. Moreover, since the art of prophecy oversees what is "common" between gods and humans and establishes friendship between them, prophecy is – like music and medicine – another erotic art for producing harmonies. Thus references to prophets, as at note 6.0, will allude to agents that produce harmonies.

5.4 Aristophanes

Aristophanes' speech continues the pattern, from Pausanias' duality and Eryximachus' harmony to an envisaged unity, which runs through this range of consonant notes.

The fourth wholenote is the most consonant in the first half of the dialogue. The mischievous humour, appealing story and broad benevolence, which have made Aristophanes' speech the most popular part of the *Symposium*, now also attest to the careful coordination of style and content with the musical scale. Eryximachus' speech theorized harmony while Aristophanes' speech exhibits it, but both are designed to manifest the consonance of the underlying notes.

This speech is tightly organized by the musical scale (Ch. 2). Not only are major developments lodged at the successive quarternotes, but even the topics treated between them are allotted definite musical intervals. The major notes and the structure of the first quarter-interval are surveyed here. Each note takes a definite step from the initial, natural unity towards a higher, divine, erotic unity, and each is marked by the *agent*, natural or divine, that takes the step:

- 4.0, *Primordial wholes, nature*. After a brief introduction, Aristophanes says at the fourth wholenote that "human nature" must be learned. This consists, he says, of three genders. Each of these is a combination of two present-day humans, and the androgynes will later be described as the mutual participation, that is harmonization, of two opposites.
- 4.1, *Duality, Apollo*. At this first quarternote, Zeus cuts the creatures in two. Thus the text from the introduction of the globular creatures to their division fills one quarter-interval. This quarternote, like others that follow wholenotes, is marked less harmoniously than its neighbours: division is the opposite of harmonization (but see the annotations below). Apollo, the god of medicine and healing, makes each half a whole individual again.
- 4.2, *Love seeking unity, Eros*. The god of love makes his appearance in the passage that surrounds and marks the second quarternote. This very consonant quarternote is marked repeatedly and emphatically with several kinds of harmonization. Eros is figured as a "Uniter" implanted in human nature. Humans are each a "symbolon", a half that will be reunited with its counterpart. At the quarternote, reference is made to "androgynes", a symbol for *krasis*. Here pairs of creatures are bound together by love, but are still separate individuals.
- 4.3, *Envisaged unity, Hephaestus*. This is one of the most strongly marked quarternotes in the dialogue. At the note, Hephaestus offers to fuse the two lovers into one, in a relationship that will last even beyond death. This vision of unalloyed unity, the limit of harmonization, sits at the quarternote.

The gods Apollo, Eros and Hephaestus are introduced at successive quarternotes and serve to punctuate these points in the narrative with a regular rhythm.

Each interval that follows a major note is divided into three parts and each of these has a different topic. Two longer passages fill out the range from the note to the midpoint (4/8) and from the midpoint to the next note. The midpoint itself, in each interval, is briefly marked by some more emphatic species of harmony. For example, the interval after the fourth wholenote has the following structure:

- *Note to midpoint*: descriptions of the creatures.
- *Harmony at midpoint*: androgynes as a krasis like the moon.
- *Midpoint to note*: the creatures' hubris.

This repeated, fine-grained structure of the intervals shows again that episodes or themes occupy certain, definite intervals of text delimited by musically significant locations. The musical scale serves as an outline for the dialogue.

Aristophanes' speech ends one line before the fifth wholenote, and is approximately one-twelfth as long as the entire dialogue.

Eryximachus' speech does not end near a major note, and Aristophanes' speech does not begin near a major note. Plato is, however, still counting lines. The banter about hiccups that fills the gap between the two speeches starts about ten OCT lines before the midpoint and finishes about ten lines after it.[13]

"look what you're doing! You're making jokes even before you start to speak, and will force me [189b] to keep watch over your own speech, in case you say something absurd, though you could speak in 4/8 peace."

Aristophanes laughed and said, "Well spoken, Eryximachus, and let what was said be unsaid (*estō arrēta to eirēmena*). But don't keep watch over me, as I fear in what I mean to say not that I might say something funny – that would be a boon and right in the territory of my 5/8 muse – but that I say something ridiculous."

"Ballocks!", he said. "Aristophanes, you think you can get off scot-free! Just focus your mind and speak as if we'll hold you to account. [189c] But I'll probably, if it seems alright to me, let you off."

SPEECH BEGINS "And indeed, Eryximachus," said Aristophanes, "I intend to speak in a way different 6/8 than that in which you and Pausanias spoke. To me, humans seem in every way to fail to perceive the power of *eros* since, if they perceived it, they would have constructed the greatest temples and altars for him, and make great sacrifices VIRTUE – not as now there is nothing concerning him, though there should be the most of all. SHAME [189d] He is among the gods the most philanthropic, 7/8 being a benefactor of humans and a doctor for them who, once healed, would have the greatest happiness available to the human race. HARMONY: EROS' PHILANTHROPY, GREATEST HAPPINESS "So I will try to introduce his power, and you will be teachers for others. HARMONY: VIRTUE FROM TEACHING It is necessary that you first learn the nature of man NOTE 4.0 = 189d5 CONSONANT and its attributes. Our ancient nature was not that which it is now but of another sort. There were at first three kinds of humans, HARMONY: ANCIENT UNITIES not as now two, male and female, but there was also a third, [189e] additional combination (*koinon*) of these. Now only the name remains while it has disappeared. One kind was then the androgyne, 1/8 a combination in shape (*eidos*) and name of both male and female. HARMONY: KRASIS Now it is nothing except that the name remains as a form of reproach. Since the whole shape of each human was then round, having back and ribs in a circle, with four hands and legs 2/8 equal to the hands, and two faces similar in every way upon a [190a] cylindrical neck. There was one head for both faces, which faced oppositely, four ears, two private parts, and all the rest as one could guess from these. It moved upright as now, in either direction it wished. And whenever it would start to run quickly, 3/8 as those who tumble and bringing their legs upright tumble in a circle,

Note 4.0, consonant (189d5)

This very consonant note is marked by strong, positive praise of Eros and the great happiness he produces (underlined). There are two kinds of harmony here. First, the teaching relationship, when it is a bond of friendship or *eros*, is a kind of *krasis* or harmony between individuals. Similar erotic bonds will mark notes to come. Second, the man-woman represents a *krasis* of the two sexes.

This note has a now familiar pattern. There is a contrast between virtue and shame, and an erotic bond or *krasis* leads to virtue. Here, the shame of Eros' neglect will be remedied by a teaching relationship that spreads word of Eros' power.

At the note, Aristophanes describes the three sexes. The androgyne is "one thing" in name and form, and thus is a kind of primordial unity. At the following quarternotes, these unities will be cut in two (4.1), seek their other halves (4.2) and be offered a reunification (4.3).

Possible number pun: there are three kinds of human beings one-third of the way through the dialogue. On stringed musical instruments, the string was, the Greeks said, "cut" or "divided" to produce the various notes (see appendix). The string would have been divided into three parts to produce this fourth note on the scale of twelve. There is another possible number pun at the next note, which makes this one somewhat more probable.

Narrative structure reflects musical structure: This is an example of speeches that do not end and begin at quarternotes.

"there being eight limbs then, they pushed off from the ground and moved quickly [190b] in a circle. There were for these reasons three kinds, with such features: the male was at the beginning born of the sun, the female of the earth, and the kind sharing in both of the moon 4/8 since the moon shares in both. KRASIS AT MIDPOINT Both they and their motion were round because of their similarity to their parents. Their strength and robustness was terrific, and since they had self-aggrandizing ways of thinking they set upon the gods. What Homer says about [190c] Ephialtes 5/8 and Otus is said about them: they tried to make an ascent into heaven, as if intent on attacking the gods. So Zeus and the other gods deliberated about what they should do and were at a loss. There was no way they might kill them and, as with the giants, strike them with lightning 6/8 and obliterate them – for then the honours and the offerings from humans to them would be obliterated – and there was no way they might just let them behave so wantonly. After pondering with difficulty, Zeus said that 'I think', he said, 'I have a scheme whereby humans might exist and, by becoming weaker, stop their licentiousness. SHAME I will now, he said, cut each through into two, 7/8 [190d] and they will at once be weaker and at the same time be more useful to us since their number will become more copious – and they will walk upright on two legs. And if they still seem wanton and will not lead quiet lives, I will in turn, he said, again cut them in two, TALK OF QUARTERING AT QUARTERNOTE so that they will go about on one leg hopping.'

NOTE 4.1 = 190d6 CONSONANT "So saying, he cut the humans in two, UNITIES CUT IN TWO as those cutting apples and intending to preserve them, or as those cutting eggs with hairs. [190e] He would cut each one and bid Apollo to turn the face and the half-neck towards the cut so that, seeing their own cut, the human might be 1/8 more orderly (*kosmiōteros*) VIRTUE, and he bid him to heal the rest.

HARMONY: MEDICAL HEALING OF CUTS RESTORES VIRTUE "He turned the face and drawing together the skin every which way upon what is now called the belly (as if here were closing a purse with a drawstring), he finished it off by making one opening in the middle of the belly, which they now call the 2/8 navel (*omphalon*). And he smoothed out the many other wrinkles and fit together (*diērthrou*) the chest, [191a] having the sort of tool that cobblers use to smooth out the wrinkles in the leather on the last. He left a few, those around the belly and the navel, to be a reminder of their earlier condition. Since, then, 3/8 their nature had been cut in two, each desired and was coming together with its [other] half, throwing their hands around and intertwining with each other. Determined to grow together [again], they were dying from starvation and from [191b] general lassitude since they wished to do nothing apart from each other.

Note 4.1, consonant (190d6)

The unities described at the previous note are cut in two at this note, which makes this passage an apparent counter-example, since there is cutting rather than a *krasis* or harmony at the note. However, the structure is the same as before: a shameful impiety is put right by the art of medicine (according to Eryximachus, an erotic art that produces harmony), which heals its patients. This note is also positively marked by Zeus, the god of justice,[14] and Apollo, the god of medicine and music (who was also worshipped by the Pythagoreans). However, the presence of both cutting and healing make this a less consonant note (as 3.1 was the least consonant in the range between 3.0 and 4.0).

The quarter-interval following 4.1 is again broken into three parts:

- *Note to midpoint*: Apollo's healing and attempts to reunite with original other-halves.
- *Harmony at midpoint*: The search for and first "embrace" of a new half.
- *Midpoint to note*: Sex and reproduction with new partners (without mentioning love).

Possible number pun: A threat to slice into quarters occurs at the quarternote. In the *Republic*, musical "quarternotes" are discussed at the location of a quarternote, and this may be a similar reference. Such passages reinforce the interpretation of the notes between the wholenotes as "quarternotes". As mentioned at the previous note, "cutting" and "dividing" is often a pun for locating notes on a musical string, especially in the *Republic*. In general, however, such puns are too brief to interpret in any rigorous way.

"And whenever one of the halves would die, the one left behind 4/8 searched for and embraced another one left behind, and would meet either a half from a whole woman – which we now call a 'woman' – or from a man. And so they perished. Zeus pitied them and came up with another scheme: he repositioned their private parts towards the front – they had erstwhile had these too on the outside 5/8 and begat and gave birth [191c] not in each other but on the earth, like grasshoppers. So having repositioned these towards the front, he made them reproduce through these in each other (through the male into the female) with the following aim: so that, in their intertwining, 6/8 if a man met a woman, they would reproduce and the race would continue but, again, if a man met a man, he would have his fill of togetherness (*sunousias*) and they would take a rest and turn to their work and devote (*epimelointo*) themselves to the rest of their life. For so long, then, *eros* has been implanted [191d] in and among humans, the Uniter (*sunagōgeus*) 7/8 of our ancient natures, and tries to make one out of two and to heal human nature. HARMONY Each of us, then, is a broken half of a human whole (*symbolon*), inasmuch as we were cut like flatfish, from one into two. CUTTING: LIKE PREVIOUS NOTE Each of us is always in search of our other half. In so far as, among men, some are pieces cut from a whole (*koinou*) HARMONY that was formerly called an androgyne, NOTE 4.2 = 191d7 CONSONANT they prefer women. DIVIDED UNITIES SEEKING REUNIFICATION; SEX Many of our adulterers came from this type. [191e] Again, in so far as they are women, they prefer men and adulteresses come from this type. SHAME In so far as, among woman, the pieces are cut from a whole that was a woman, they do not pay much attention to men, 1/8 but rather are oriented towards women, and courtesans too come from this type. In so far as they are pieces cut from a whole male, they pursue males and, while they are boys, as they are slices of the male, love (*philousi*) men and enjoy lying down with [192a] and being intertwined 2/8 with men. And these are the best of the boys and youths, since they are by nature the most brave. And those who say, indeed, that they are shameless are lying. They do not do this out of shamelessness 1 – PHI but out of confidence and manliness and masculinity, since they cleave to what is similar to themselves. 3/8 Here is a great proof: once they are matured only these sort turn out to be [real] men in politics. After they have been reared up to manhood, [192b] they are pederasts and by nature pay no attention to marriage and reproducing, but are compelled to by the law (*nomos*).

Note 4.2, consonant (191d7)

This note is marked by the harmony of mutual love. Eros is now explicitly characterized as a healing "Uniter" making a *krasis* or harmony: "one out of two". At the note and after, there are various kinds of sexual or love relationships, that is, of erotic *krasis*: some are shameful and some are virtuous. Here Aristophanes seems to be speaking of mere physical couplings as part of a search for some true unity.

The unities described at 4.0 and divided at 4.1 are here seeking some higher reunification, but they will not find it until the next note.

The octads here and below seem to be marked with words referring to intimate love or sexual intercourse.

Aristophanes mentions a "*symbolon*" at the note (cf. §1.3). This was an ordinary Greek word for a sign or token, and more particularly was the corresponding half of something, like a bone or a coin, broken in two and kept apart, so that two parties could later recognize each other (LSJ). However, the word was also a term of art in ancient Pythagoreanism, and referred to their orally transmitted maxims and sayings or secret passwords (Burkert 1972: 166ff., 176; Struck 2004; cf. also 193a7).

The quarter-interval following 4.2 is broken into three parts:

- *Note to midpoint*: Various romantic inclinations and temporary relationships.
- *Harmony at midpoint*: First mention of a lifelong relationship.
- *Midpoint to note*: The joy of finding one's true other-half.

"Rather, they are content to lead out their lives with each other 4/8 and unmarried. This sort entirely becomes men who love boys and boys who love men, since they always cleave to what is related to them. When, then, one of these encounters his own half, whether a pederast or anyone else, [192c] then they are struck with astonishment by affection and 5/8 intimacy and *eros*, and, in a word, do not wish to part from each other even for a little time. And those are the ones who continue with each other through life, though they could not say what they wish to get from each other. To none would it seem that this is 6/8 sexual intercourse, that it is for the sake of this that one so delights being together with the other with such great ardour. Rather, it is clear that the soul of each wishes for something else, which it cannot express, [192d] but hints at and sends signs of what it desires. And if Hephaestus, with his tools, stood over them while they lay together 7/8 and would say, 'What is it that you wish, humans, to get from each other?' And if they were baffled (*aporountas*) APORIA he would again say, 'Is it then this that you desire, to become the same thing with each other as much as possible, HARMONY: TWO TO ONE, KRASIS OF LOVERS so that you will not leave each [192e] other by night or by day? If it is this that you desire, I will weld you together and join into the same thing so that, NOTE 4.3 = 192d8 CONSONANT from two, one will emerge HARMONY: TWO TO ONE, KRASIS OF LOVERS and that, while you live, you will be as one, both of you living in common. HARMONY And after you die, there too in Hades you will be one instead of two since you shared death. HARMONY But see if you desire this and it would satisfy you if you achieved this.' Hearing this, 1/8 we know that no one would deny it or would appear wishing anything else, but would utterly believe he had heard what of old he desired: to come together and be fused to one's beloved and to become one out of two. 2/5 The cause, indeed, of this is that our ancient nature was [as described], and we were wholes. The name for the desire and pursuit [193a] of the whole is *eros*. 2/8 And before this, so I assert, we were one, while now because of injustice we have been scattered by the gods, just as the Arcadians were by the Lacedaimonians. There is thus a fear, if our relations to the gods are not orderly, that we will again be cloven asunder, and go about like those who are molded on stelae in relief, 3/8 sawn in half down the nose, like broken dice. So on account of this every man should exhort in every respect piety toward the gods so that we may escape [the bad] [193b] and obtain [the good], as Eros is our leader and commander.

Note 4.3, consonant (192d8)

The climax of Aristophanes' speech is a clear, paradigmatic case of a note marked by an erotic harmony or *krasis*. Here the erotic craftsman is Hephaestus, who offers to fuse the two lovers. The notion of two fusing into one is expressed repeatedly and emphatically at the note. The emotional tone is also appropriate to this quite consonant note: Aristophanes warmly imagines the lasting fulfilment of true love.

This completes the cycle started at the beginning of the speech. At successive notes Aristophanes described unities, divided them, attempted to reunite them and finally described their reunification here. Hephaestus' offer, however, is merely contemplated; the true lovers are not actually fused together. A true, fully realized unity will have to wait until the ninth note, the climax of Socrates' speech, where the Form of Beauty itself is described.

Aristophanes here advances beyond the two previous speeches. Pausanias described a duality of two loves but foresaw no real commonality between them. Eryximachus described a harmony, in which two differing elements somehow overcame their differences. Aristophanes now envisages a true fusion and unification of two elements: the limiting ideal of harmonization.

In this case, it is not shame that is resolved by the erotic *krasis* but the epistemic equivalent: perplexity (*aporia*). This negative state will also feature in later notes. Night and Hades are also mentioned. Thus, although this passage is predominately positive, some negative elements remain: it is not wholly positive but a blend of positive and negative.

The theme of unification is repeated at and marks the two-fifths point.

After the marking passage, the tone of Aristophanes' speech turns markedly negative, as the dissonant fifth note is approached.

"Let no one do the opposite – 4/8 whoever does do the opposite will be hated by the gods. Having become friendly with and reconciled to the god, we will find and obtain our [true] boyfriend – which few now do. And do not reply, Eryximachus, by joking [193c] that in my speech I mean Pausanias and [his boyfriend] 5/8 Agathon. Probably these too happen to be among those and are both of the male nature. So I assert that about everything, and both among men and women, that in this way our race will achieve happiness: if we perfect love and each find the boyfriend who belongs to us, and so return to our ancient nature. 6/8 And if this is best, necessarily that which is nearest to this among those present now is best. And this is to find a boyfriend [193d] in spirit naturally akin to oneself. If we hymn the god who is the cause of this, it would be just if we hymn Eros, who provides us in the present with the greatest benefit, 7/8 leading us to what belongs to ourselves, and for the future with the greatest hopes: if we offer the gods piety, he will settle us in our ancient nature and, being healed, make us blessed and happy."

SPEECH ENDS AT NOTE "That," he said, "Eryximachus, is my speech about Eros – different from yours. As I requested of you, NOTE 5.0 = 193d7 DISSONANT do not make a joke of it, MOCKERY: DISHARMONY IN SPEECH so that we might hear what each of the rest will say – [193e] or rather what both will say: only Agathon and Socrates remain."

"But I will obey you", AGREEMENT: HARMONY he said Eryximachus said. "And for me the speech was delightfully delivered. And if I did not know that Socrates and Agathon were clever 1/8 about erotics, I would be very afraid that they might be at a loss (*aporēsōsi*) PLEASURE VS. FEAR, DISTRESS about speaking, since so much and such a variety has been said. As it is now, however, I'm confident."

Then Socrates said "You're a fine competitor, [194a] Eryximachus! If you were where I now am, or rather where I will probably be after Agathon has spoken well, you would be very afraid 2/8 and in every way as I am now."

"You want to cast a spell on me, Socrates," said Agathon, "so that I might be disturbed by thinking that the audience has high expectations that I will speak well."

"But I would be forgetful, Agathon," said Socrates, [194b] "if seeing your courage and self-confidence 3/8 when you were walking up to the platform with the actors, while you looked out over such an audience and got ready to exhibit your play (*logous*) – and were not in the least scared – that now I might think that you would be disturbed on account of the few humans here."

Note 5.0, dissonant (193d7)

This note is marked by harmony as agreement, with some negative elements: the notion of "mocking" is at the note, and "fear" and "*aporia*" occur after the note. The fifth wholenote is dissonant, but not as markedly so as later dissonant notes. This may be the reason that the negative elements are relatively mild here.

The verb "to mock" (*kōmōdein*) can mean satirize, ridicule or lampoon, and recalls the power in ancient Athens of comic theatre (cf. Socrates' remarks in the *Apology*, 18d1ff.). "Fear" is the opposite of desire, and these are the psychological correlates of pain and pleasure. *Aporia* marks epistemic failure, and is here analogous to moral shame.

Aristophanes asks not to be mocked and Eryximachus agrees. This is another example of the invitation and agreement theme that marked the notes in the frame.

Narrative structure reflects musical structure: Aristophanes declares his speech is finished just before the note and stops speaking, after some banter, just beyond the note.

5.5 Agathon

Agathon's speech occupies the dissonant range of quarternotes that follows the fifth wholenote. Agathon's character, his style, and the content of this speech are made disharmonious in various ways to match this range.[15]

Agathon is a prizewinning playwright but a decadent aesthete. He is the ageing beloved of Pausanias, who has sophistically argued that sex can be exchanged for moral edification. Aristophanes' *Thesmophoriazusae* caricatures Agathon as a camp and promiscuous, "passive" homosexual.[16] Socrates echoes Aristophanes' slanders by associating Agathon with "softness" at the outset of the *Symposium* (174c1). However fair or unfair, or crudely stereotypical, this portrayal may have been, many features of Agathon's speech attest to a kind of effeminacy that, even in classical Athens, was much maligned.[17]

Following Socrates' later quips about Gorgias (198c1ff.), Agathon's style has often been associated with the sophists, who generally play negative roles in Plato's dialogues. The content of Agathon's speech is also treated as sophistical. It is immediately criticized by Socrates for its lack of truthfulness (198d3ff.), and the elenchus of the younger Socrates by Diotima that opens Socrates' speech is an explicit refutation of Agathon (201e3ff.). Afterwards, Diotima makes many point-by-point rebuttals of Agathon's assertions.

For example, Socrates' speech replaces Agathon's definitions of the four virtues, which have a "Presocratic" tone, with more Platonic definitions:

(i) *Justice*: for Agathon, neither doing wrong nor being wronged (196b6ff.); for Socrates, harmoniously arranging the public and private spheres (209a5ff.);
(ii) *Sōphrosunē*: for Agathon, "mastery over desires" (196c5); for Socrates, also harmoniously arranging the public and private spheres (209a5ff.);
(iii) *Sophia*: for Agathon, skill in some technical or artistic craft (196d5ff.), so skilled poets are *sophos*; for Socrates, technical skill is inferior (*banausos*), while *sophia* is a wisdom about spiritual matters (203a4ff.), or an ideal sought by the philosopher (203e5, 204b2).
(iv) *Courage*: for Agathon, a matter of strength and mastery (196c8ff.); for Socrates, a willingness to run risks or make sacrifices in pursuit of some good (207b2ff.).

In short, both the style and content of this speech provide another example of the way disharmonious features of the surface narrative are matched to dissonant notes.

The length and structure of the speech gives more clear evidence of the musical scale. Agathon begins speaking at note 5.1 and stops just before the very harmonious sixth wholenote. Thus the beginning of the speech is aligned with a note, its length is three quarter-intervals, and its end is – less precisely – aligned with another note. Moreover, Agathon's discussion of beauty and the four cardinal virtues, as mentioned in Chapter 1, nicely illustrates the way brief phrases mark successive octads.

As in previous speeches, the marking passages in this speech exhibit a strong similarity that establishes its rhythm. Here, the three quarternotes are marked, among other things, by clusters of stylistic effects, a device appropriate to a wordsmith like Agathon:

- 5.1, *Cluster of rhetorical effects*: Although somewhat veiled in translation, the proem of Agathon's speech is packed with a dozen or so sophistic jingles, the kind of poetical prose popularized by Gorgias.
- 5.2, *Cluster of words for "softness"*: This trait was generally associated with the decadent, effeminate youths of the late fifth century (see below).
- 5.3, *Cluster of negative terms*: This very dissonant quarternote is marked by a string of words for privation, difference or negation.

These clusters associate Agathon and his Eros with more or less negative elements: the sophists, effeminancy and linguistic negation.

"What, Socrates?" said Agathon, "you surely don't think me so 4/8 full of the theatre that I don't know that a thoughtful few with sense are more frightening than the thoughtless many?"

"I would not be doing right, Agathon," he said, [194c] THREE-SEVENTHS "if I implied something crude about you. I well know that if you met some who you thought wise, 5/8 you would estimate them higher than the many. But we are not them – for we indeed were there too and we were among the many. If you met others who are wise, you would probably be ashamed if you thought you were doing something shameful. Or what do you think?"

[194d] "That's true", he said.

"And in front of the many, you would not be ashamed if you thought you were doing something shameful?" 6/8

Then Phaedrus, he said, replied by saying, "My dear Agathon, if you answer Socrates, it will make no difference to him whatever and whichever happens here, if only he can converse with someone – especially if he is handsome. I would gladly hear Socrates conversing, but I must take care (*epimelēthenai*) 7/8 of the praise of Eros and receive from each one of you a speech. So each of you giving your due to the god, let us converse."

"Yes, what you say is right, Phaedrus," said Agathon, [194e] "and nothing prevents my speaking. HARMONY: AGREEMENT Indeed, there will again be many times to converse with Socrates."

SPEECH BEGINS AT NOTE "I indeed intend NOTE 5.1 = 194e4 DISSONANT first to say what I must say and then say it. DISHARMONY: SOPHISTIC JINGLE Everything that has been said earlier seems to me not to praise the god DISHARMONY: CRITICISM but rather to felicitate humans for the goods that the god causes for them. How one should himself be [195a] so as to deserve these gifts, no one has said. 1/8 The correct approach to all praise about everything is to relate in words for what kind of things the person about whom the speech is, being himself of what kind, is actually responsible. DISHARMONY: SOPHISTIC JINGLE Therefore, indeed, it is just for us too to praise first how Eros is and then his gifts.

"I assert that, among all the gods, 2/8 Eros is happy and, if it is proper and inoffensive to say, the most happy of them, since he is the most beautiful and best. Being the most beautiful, he is as follows. First, then, he is the youngest of the gods, Phaedrus. He offers [195b] a great proof 4/9 for these words: always fleeing, he flees old age, clearly quickly (at any rate he catches us faster than he ought). By nature Eros hates 3/8 old age and will not approach it closely. He is always with the young and always young. The old saying is good, that the similar always draws near to the similar. Although I agree with Phaedrus about many other things, I do not agree about this: that Eros is older than Cronus and Iapetus. [195c]

Three-sevenths (194c1)

This passage, before the quarternote, is another example of mixture without blending or harmony. Just as Orpheus was alive among the dead at one-seventh, here wise Socrates is in the theatre with the "foolish" Many – but does not blend or harmonize with them. The whole passage, especially the suggestion that Agathon is crude, is sneering irony, which is appropriate for a dissonant seventh.

Note 5.1, dissonant (194e4)

Socrates' questions are a threat to the order of the speeches, but harmony is restored after Agathon agrees to speak as planned. At the note, there are negative criticisms of the others and jingles showing off Agathon's sophistical rhetoric. This is a negative passage marking a dissonant note.

Pausanias is directly associated with the sophists, and Agathon, Pausanias' beloved, has clearly absorbed the sophist's rhetorical ticks. As the thrice repeated "speak" in the translation suggests, the first paragraph is packed with over-clever, jingling sophisms. Rightly or wrongly, the dialogues typically portray the sophists as the enemies of philosophy, and Agathon's rhetorical posturing should be read in a strongly negative light.

Narrative structure reflects musical structure: Agathon begins to speak at the note and will speak for three quarter-intervals.

"I assert he is rather the youngest of the gods 4/8 and always young. The old matters about gods, which Hesiod and Parmenides relate, happened through [the goddess] Necessity and not through Eros, if they spoke the truth. For there would have been no castrations or bindings or other violent acts between the gods, if Eros were among them, but rather love (*philia*) and peace, as now, 5/8 through which Eros rules the gods. Now since he is young, he is tender to youth. There is need of a poet, such as Homer was, to exhibit the tenderness of the god. [195d] Homer said that Ate is a god and tender – at least her feet are tender. He says:

'Hers are tender feet: she does not approach 6/8 on the ground, but indeed walks upon the heads of men.'

DISHARMONY: CLUSTER OF WORDS FOR SOFT "It seems to be that he brings to light a fine proof of her tenderness, since she does not walk upon something hard, but upon something soft. [195e] Indeed, we too use the same as proof that Eros is tender. He does not walk upon the earth nor upon skulls, which are not so very soft, 7/8 but both walks and resides in the softest of existing things. He is seated in the characters and souls of gods and humans, and not in every soul that comes along, but when he encounters someone with a hard character he is off, and makes his home is a soft one. DISHARMONY: EROS AND SOFT SOULS So always touching, not only with his feet but all over, he necessarily is in the softest of the softest: NOTE 5.2 = 195e7 DISSONANT the most tender. He is the youngest [196a] and the most tender, and in addition has a pliant shape (*hugros to eidos*). Neither would he be able to fold himself up every which way nor, once he's entered into the entire soul, to depart unnoticed, if he were hard. A great proof of his proportioned 1/8 and pliant form (*symmetrou de kai hugras ideas*) is his gracefulness, which admittedly from all sides Eros especially has. There is always a war between Eros and the lack of gracefulness.

EVIDENCE FOR OCTADS: BEAUTY, FOUR VIRTUES 2/8 "The beauty of his complexion [196b] is a sign that the god leads his life among blossoms. For Eros will not sit in a body or soul or anything else whatsoever that is not blooming or has bloomed and withered; however, where there may be a good bloom and good perfume, there he both sits and remains.

"Concerning the beauty of the god, that will suffice although much yet remains. We must speak next concerning the virtues of Eros. The greatest is that Eros neither 3/8 commits injustice to any god or human nor is wronged by any god or human. Nor does he suffer violence – if he suffers anything. [196c] Violence does not touch Eros. Nor if he acts does he act with violence. All willingly serve Eros in everything. And what the willing agree to with the willing is just, say the laws that are 'the king of the city'.

Note 5.2, dissonant (195e7)

This note is marked by repeated references to "softness" (underlined), which is for Socrates a pejorative and thus appropriate to a dissonant note. Agathon represents the decadent, artsy, effeminate youths of late-fifth-century Athens. Socrates uses "softness" as a pejorative at 174c1 while thinking of Agathon, Phaedrus derides Orpheus as "soft" at 179d4, and Diotima makes Eros "hard" at 203c7.

At the note, there is a kind of *krasis* between Eros and "soft" souls. This is disharmonic. That is, making a home in a soft soul is a fitting together and so harmonic, but also negative because softness is here a negative trait.

Narrative structure reflects musical structure: After 5.2, there is clear evidence that Plato is counting lines between the quarternotes. He discusses, at equally spaced intervals, beauty, justice, courage, *sōphrosunē* and wisdom (the last four are the cardinal virtues). Both the length of these intervals and their alignment provide strong evidence that the octads are being marked by short phrases.

"In addition to justice, he has a copious share of temperateness (*sōphrosunē*). 4/8 It is agreed that it is temperate to master one's pleasures and desires, and no pleasure at all is master of Eros. If then they are weaker, they would be mastered by Eros and he would be their master; and if he masters pleasures and desires, Eros would be especially temperate. And as for courage 5/8 [196d], 'not even Ares can withstand' Eros. Ares does not possess Eros, but rather Eros (or Aphrodite, as per the story) possesses Ares: and the possessor is master of he who is possessed. Since he masters the most brave of the others, Eros would be the most brave of all. The justice and temperateness and courage of the god has been discussed; his wisdom (*sophia*) 6/8 remains. As far as possible, nothing must be omitted.

"And first, indeed, so that I in turn may honour my art, just as Eryximachus did his, [196e] the god is a poet so skilled (*sophos*) that he makes another [into one too]. At any rate, everyone becomes a poet, 'however uncultured (*amousos*) beforehand', who is touched by Eros. We properly use this as evidence 7/8 that Eros is a good poet, in sum, regarding all composition according to music: [197a] DISHARMONY: CLUSTER OF NEGATIVES for whatever we have not or know not we can neither give to someone different nor teach another. And, indeed, in respect of the procreation (*poiēsin*) of animals: of all [forms of creation], who will contradict that Eros not not [sic] skilled (*sophian*) in this, DISHARMONY: SOPHIA AS SKILL, SEX since all the animals come to be and grow through him? But, NOTE 5.3 = 197a2 DISSONANT do we not know that the craftsman in an art who has had this god as teacher will turn out a brilliant man of some account, and he who Eros does not touch will remain in the dark?

"Apollo invented the arts of archery, medicine and prophecy under the leadership of desire and *eros*, and so he too would be a 1/8 student of Eros; and so too the [197b] Muses [invented] the fine arts (*mousikees*), Hephaestus the art of metalworking, Athena the art of weaving and Zeus the art of governing both the gods and humans. Whence, it is clear that the occupations of the gods were established after the birth of Eros, who is clearly Beauty (for there is no ugliness with *eros*). Before him, as I said at the beginning, many, terrible things 2/8 happened to the gods on account of the rule of Necessity, as is said. After this god was born, all goods, for both gods and humans, arose out of the love for beautiful things. [197c]

"So it seems to me, Phaedrus, that Eros is himself first most beautiful and best, 3/8 and after that the cause to others of other such things. It occurs to me to say something in metre: that it is he who creates

> 'Peace among humans, on the open sea windless calm, allaying of winds and sleep when troubled.'

Note 5.3, dissonant (197a2)

A cluster of negative words marks this dissonant note, and illustrates the general connection between dissonance and negativity. There are some elements of harmony – the teaching relationship with Eros, reproduction and references to music – but disharmony dominates.

The more literal translation here brings out the number of words that contain "not", "different", "other" and so on (underlined). In contrast, the ten following lines contain not a single negative word.

There is probably a strongly disharmonic element in Agathon's use of *sophia* to mean "skill". Socrates and Agathon have been disagreeing over the nature of *sophia* since Socrates' entrance (175c8ff., 194c3ff.). Although the meaning of *sophia* changed and evolved during the fifth and fourth centuries, and could mean "skill" or "wisdom", a Platonist who makes wisdom one of the four cardinal virtues and who banishes poets from their republic would see Agathon's usage here as a travesty.

Agathon says Eros is skilful in creating life, that is, by inspiring reproduction. Sex is a kind of fitting together or harmonization, but is here treated as the merely physical fact of procreation.

This passage again associates Eros with music, and therefore with harmony and *krasis*. He is a poet skilled "in all composing that has to do with music", and a creator responsible for sexual reproduction (a kind of *krasis*). Thus, here too, a craftsman uses erotic bonds to create a *krasis* at the note. There are some positive, harmonic elements.

After the note, the concepts turn markedly more positive in the approach to the very consonant sixth note.

CLIMATIC PRAISE OF EROS, RHETORICAL FIREWORKS [197d] "Thus he empties us of estrangement and fills us with affection, he causes us to come together 4/8 with each other in meetings such as this, becoming our leader in festivals, choruses and sacrifices. He supplies gentleness and banishes crudeness. He loves to give good-will, and does not give bad-will; gracious, kind;[18] gazed upon by the wise, admired by the gods; coveted by those who have no share in him, a desirable possession to those whose share is large; the father of 5/8 tenderness, delicacy, voluptuousness, graces, desire. He cares for (*epimelēs*) goods and neglects the bad. He is, [197e] in pain, fear, desire and words, the steersman, defender, comrade and the best saviour, the cosmos of all gods and humans, most beautiful and best leader, who all men must follow, 6/8 hymning him beautifully, sharing in the song he sings, bewitching the thoughts of all gods and humans.

"There, he said, is the speech from me, Phaedrus. Let it be offered up to the god. It had its share of jokes and a measure of seriousness – as far as I was able." [198a] SPEECH ENDS BEFORE NOTE Once Agathon had spoken, Aristodemus said, all of those present applauded noisily, HARMONY: LOUD NOISE OF APPROVAL, AGREEMENT 7/8 as the youth had spoken so suitably both for himself and for the god. Then Socrates said, with a glance toward Eryximachus, "So do I seem to you," he said, "son of Acumenus, to have feared back then a fear not to be feared, or rather was I not speaking prophetically just now when I said that Agathon would speak marvellously and I would find myself at a loss (*aporēsoimi*)?" "The other point," NOTE 6.0 = 198a8 CONSONANT replied Eryximachus, [198b] "that he would speak well (*Agathon eu erei*), you seem to me to have spoken prophetically; SOCRATES IS PROPHET, HARMONIZES WITH DIVINE but as to your being at a loss (*aporēsein*), I do not think so." "And how, you fortunate man," said Socrates, "should I or anyone else whosoever not be at a loss when about to speak after the delivery of such a fine and variegated speech? Now, some of its other bits 1/8 were not uniformly marvellous, but who would not be amazed hearing the beauty of the words and phrases at the end? Since I was considering that I would not be able to speak [198c] as finely, not even close to it, I was on the verge of running away, if there were a way. Indeed the speech reminded me of 2/8 Gorgias, and so I felt like that bit in Homer: I feared that as he ended Agathon would send to me in his speech a head of Gorgias, terribly good at speaking, against my speech, and he would make me into a speechless stone. And I realized I'd then been ridiculous, when I agreed with you to praise Eros 3/8 in turn together with you [198d] and said that I was terribly good at erotics, when I knew nothing indeed about this matter of how one must praise anything. Out of stupidity, I thought it's necessary to tell the truths about each subject of praise,

Note 6.0, consonant (198a8)

The sixth note, at the centre of the dialogue, is the most consonant in the twelve-note scale.[19] This note is marked emphatically and loudly, in several complicated ways.

The strongest praise of Eros is at the centre of the dialogue. The rhetorical fireworks at the climax of Agathon's speech include references to singing and dancing, a cluster of positive terms ("best", "beautiful", etc.), and a long string of celebratory epithets. It concludes by enjoining all to "sing hymns beautifully, and participate in the song Eros sings to enchant the thought of every god and man". Approval is a kind of agreement, and the "tumultuous applause" that follows the speech is the loudest auditory sign of such harmony in the dialogue. This burst of rhetoric, noise and words for music appropriately marks this very harmonic note.

At the note itself, there are several kinds of harmony and *krasis*. Eryximachus, the theoretician of harmony, and wise Socrates are allowed to speak here. There is agreement: Socrates is a prophet. The art of prophecy, we learned, produces a common bond between gods and humans (188c6ff.), and thus Socrates as prophet embodies here at the centre of the dialogue a *krasis* between the human and the divine. The approach to the divine has often been thought the core of Platonism.

The apparently innocent banter between Socrates and Eryximachus contains certain negative elements and some complicated symbolic structures, which will be discussed in Appendix 5. As with the earlier interchanges between Eryximachus and Aristophanes, this banter may serve to blend together two speeches and so is appropriate to a harmonic note.

Narrative structure reflects musical structure: Agathon's speech ends shortly before the sixth note. He has spoken for about three quarter-intervals; Socrates will speak for three whole intervals.

5.6 Socrates and Diotima

Socrates' speech is the longest and most revealing in the dialogue. This introduction draws together evidence for patterns that stretch across many notes, so that the following annotations can concentrate on the structure of each marking passage.

This speech clearly rises to a climax. This progression is another example of the evolution seen in Pausanias, Eryximachus and Aristophanes, and generally confirms the pattern: the speeches pass from disharmonious material at relatively dissonant notes to harmonious material at relatively consonant notes, which are closer to the twelfth wholenote. Here, Diotima passes from discovering self-contradictions and dubious myths about debauchery among the gods to participation in immortality and the Form of Beauty.

Socrates, like Eryximachus earlier, is now a theoretician of "harmonization". He carefully expounds various types of combining, mixing or participating, and briefly introduces the theory of wholes and parts.

The narrative structure of Socrates' speech provides more clear evidence for stichometry (Ch. 2). The speech lasts for three whole-intervals, and thus for a quarter of the entire dialogue. The beginning of the speech is aligned with a quarternote (6.1) and the end with another quarternote (9.1). The two dramatic climaxes within the speech are one whole-interval apart, indicating again the importance of the division into twelfths, and are aligned with wholenotes (8.0 and 9.0).

The ascent up Diotima's ladder stretches over one quarter-interval, from 8.3 to 9.0, and provides particularly clear evidence that the octads between the quarternotes are marked; each step up the ladder is aligned with an octad.

The contents of the speech have been carefully correlated with the relative consonance or dissonance of the underlying notes. The range of more dissonant notes near the seventh wholenote at the beginning of Socrates' speech is more negative or disharmonious:

- 6.3, *Elenchus*: Socrates refutes Agathon.
- 7.0, *Elenchus*: Diotima refutes the younger Socrates by showing that Eros is no god (which may be blasphemy).
- 7.1, *Negative qualities*: Eros inherits poverty and lack of beauty from his mother.
- 7.2, *Love is acquisitive, aporia*: The younger Socrates supposes love aims to acquire beautiful things, and cannot answer Diotima's questions.
- 7.3, *Elenchus, amputation*: Diotima refutes Aristophanes' definition of love, and says we would cut off our hands if they were not good for us.

Except for the first quarternote, which is usually more dissonant, the range of notes spanning the very consonant notes 8.0 and 9.0,[20] is, in contrast, clearly marked with more positive, more harmonious material:

- 8.0, *Begetting in beauty*: Diotima says begetting with beauty is a harmony with the divine, a mortal sort of immortality.
- 8.1, *Contents of soul perishing (dissonant)*: Our knowledge and other characteristics are fleeting.
- 8.2, *Cardinal virtues*: Intellectual pregnancy with the virtues is a form of divinity.
- 8.3, *Perception of Forms*: The first step up Diotima's ladder is perceiving the Form of Beauty in bodies.
- 9.0, *Vision of the Form of Beauty*: The climactic description of the transcendental Form.

It has perhaps not been sufficiently emphasized that Socrates carries through on his promise to follow the structure of Agathon's speech. The correspondences between the two speeches are remarkably detailed: they begin with a cross-examination, outline their topics and follow the same topics in the same order: (i) the origins and nature of Eros; (ii) his goodness; and (iii) his works or function (*to ergon*).[21] In Agathon's speech, these breaks are not aligned with the notes, as if he was ignorant of the underlying structure, but in Socrates' speech they are: (i) at the midpoint between 6.3 and 7.0; (ii) at 7.2; and (iii) at the midpoint between 7.3 and 8.0.

"and making these the basis, to select from them the 4/8 most beautiful of them and to present the most good and proper bits. And I was very bold to think I would speak well since I knew the true way of praising anything. But, as it seems, this was not a fine way to praise anything. [198e] Instead, it was to attribute the greatest and most beautiful things to the subject, whether they might in fact be so or not. If they were false, 5/8 it was no matter. It was said earlier, as it seems, that each of us should appear to praise Eros, not how he was to be praised. On this account, I think, you stirred up every word and offered them to Eros, saying he was such and such and the cause of such things, so that he should appear [199a] the most beautiful and best 6/8 to, clearly, the ignorant – surely not to those who are knowledgeable – and this praise was, at any rate, beautifully and impressively done. But I did not know this way of praising and, in my ignorance, I too agreed with you to praise in my turn. 'The tongue promised, but not the mind.' So farewell to that. 7/8 I will not praise in this way – indeed I could not.

DISHARMONY: DISRUPTING AGREEMENT, SPEAKING ORDER [199b] "However, if you wish, I do desire to say nothing but the truth in my own way, not according to the way of your speeches, so that I don't earn a laugh. DISHARMONY: CRITICISM, RIDICULE Consider, then, Phaedrus, if you would need this sort of speech, to hear the truth said about Eros, NOTE 6.1 = 199b4 CONSONANT with whatever sort of words and arrangement of phrases that one might come upon."

HARMONY: SPEAKING THE TRUTH Then Phaedrus, he said, and the others urged him to speak, in just whichever way he thought he should speak. HARMONY: AGREEMENT; SOCRATES BEGINS AT NOTE "But more," Socrates said, "permit me to say a bit to Agathon, so that, having secured agreement with him, I may thus speak forthwith." [199c] "But of course I permit it," 1/8 said Phaedrus, "ask away."

HARMONY: AGREEMENT; QUESTIONING BEGINS After that, he said, Socrates started to speak from about here:

So indeed, my dear Agathon, you seemed to me to begin (*kathēgēsasthai*) your speech beautifully, saying that first one should exhibit what sort Eros is and later his works (*erga*). I very much admire this beginning. Come now, about Eros, since you beautifully and most appositely 2/8 related all the other ways he is, [199d] tell me this too. Is Eros such that he is "love of something" or "of nothing"? I do not ask if he is "of some mother" or "of some father" – 3/8 it would be ridiculous if the question were whether Eros was love of a mother or father. Rather, it is as if just this is asked of a father: whether the father is "father of someone" or not?

Note 6.1, consonant (199b4)

This note is marked by harmony as agreement: Socrates threatens to disturb the order and nature of the speeches by not making his speech but order is restored by his agreement with Phaedrus. As before, the shame of breaking his earlier agreement to make the speech is avoided, and virtue is restored by the harmony between the speakers.

This note is strikingly disharmonic before the note and strikingly harmonic afterwards. It is therefore only slightly harmonic or neutral.

The sentence at the note concerns "true speech" (*alēthēs logos*). It is later stated (215b8–d1) that prose speech can be a kind of music. The implication here is that the music of speech is harmonious when the speech is true, and that the rhetorical tricks of Agathon and Gorgias are not in themselves a kind of harmony.

Narrative structure reflects musical structure: Socrates begins his speech at note 6.1. After the note, he begins questioning Agathon, and this exchange will last for two quarter-intervals, until just after 6.3.

Surely you will say to me, if it pleases you to answer well, that a father is a father "of a son" or "of a daughter". Or not? "Very much so, indeed", said Agathon. And so the mother similarly? This too was agreed. [199e]

"And now," said Socrates, "tell me a few more things, 4/8 in order that you may better understand what I want. If I were to ask 'What then about a brother? Is he what he is since he is a brother of someone?'" He said he was. "Therefore, of a brother or of a sister?" He agreed. "Try then," he said, "to tell me about love. Is Eros love of no one or of someone?" [200a] 5/8 "He is indeed [love of someone]."

"Well, then," said Socrates, "keep watch over this yourself, remembering that it is love 'of something'. But tell me this much: whether that thing that Eros is love of he also desires – or not?" "Very much so", he said.

"And whether having that which he desires and loves, he then desires and loves it, or when he does not have it?" "When he does not have it, as is probable", he said.

6/8 "Consider if," said Socrates, "instead of probability, it is necessarily so [200b] that he who desires lacks what he desires, and does not desire if he does not lack it? Astonishingly, it seems to me, Agathon, that it is necessary. How does it seem to you?"

"Yes, it seems so to me too", he said.

"Well said. But would someone who is tall want to be tall, 7/8 or who is strong want to be strong?"

"Impossible, given what we've agreed."

"You speak the truth."

"If, indeed, being strong, he would wish to be strong," said Socrates, "and being fast to be fast, and being healthy to be healthy – maybe someone who thought [200c] these things and all such things, NOTE 6.2 = 200c1 that, being such and possessing these, he also desired the sort of things he possessed (I say this so that we may not be deceived) – these people indeed, Agathon, if you understand, necessarily have each of those things which they have in the present, whether they want them or not – and who would ever desire that? 1/8 But when someone says that 'I am healthy but also wish to be healthy' and 'I am rich but want to be rich' and 'I desire those things which I have', we would say to him [200d] that 'You, my fellow human, though possessing wealth, health and strength, wish also in time hereafter to possess these things that, now in the present, whether you wish it or no, 2/8 you have. So consider, when you say this – that you desire those things you presently have – if you mean anything other than this: that 'I wish what I have in the present also to keep in time hereafter'. Would he agree it was anything else?" Agathon concurred.

Socrates said, "Therefore, to love those things is 3/8 to love this: to have for himself in time hereafter, preserved and always present, those things which are not now to hand and not possessed."

"Entirely so", he said. [200e]

"And he and everyone else who desires desires what is not to hand and that which is not present,

Note 6.2 (200c1)

This passage is a puzzle. At this note in other dialogues, Socrates often discusses a hypothesis or premise that will be rejected at the dissonant notes to come (6.3, 7.0, …). Here, at the note, he reiterates the idea – to be rejected – that we desire what we already possess. It is not clear which species of harmony this is.[22]

Socrates does here restore the harmony of the argument. He wants assent to a logically necessary assertion (as he says at 6/8). The passage at and after the note browbeats Agathon into agreeing that the point in question is indeed necessary, and thus firmly establishes the key premise of the elenchus – as well as the harmony of the logos.

This passage interrupts the exchange with Agathon. Socrates invents a hypothetical speaker (*tis*) at the note and responds to him.

"and what he does not have and what he is not himself and what is lacking, it is such things 4/8 which desire and love are of?" "Entirely so," he said.

"Come then," said Socrates, "let us agree to what has been said. Is it anything else than that love is, first, love 'of something' and, next, that love is of those things which he lacks?" "Yes", he said. [201a]

"In addition to these, recall that you said in your speech that Eros was of certain things. 5/8 If you wish, I will remind you. I think you were saying something like 5/9 that among the gods their occupations were established through love of beautiful things. For love would not be of ugly things. Weren't you saying something like that?" "I did say so", said Agathon.

"And you spoke plausibly, my friend", said Socrates. "And if this holds in this way, 6/8 would Eros be anything else than love of beauty, but not of ugliness?" He agreed. [201b]

"Therefore, it is agreed that he loves this that he lacks and does not have?" "Yes", he said. "So Eros lacks and does not have beauty." "Necessarily", he said.

"What then? You say that which lacks beauty and in no way possesses beauty is beautiful?" 7/8 "No, indeed."

"Yet you agree that Eros is beautiful, even if these hold in this way?" And then Agathon said, "Probably, Socrates, I did not know what I was saying." DISHARMONY: ELENCHUS, EROS NOT BEAUTIFUL [201c] "But you spoke beautifully, Agathon", he said. "But tell me a little bit more. Don't good things also seem to you to be beautiful things?" "To me, yes."

"If, though, Eros lacks beautiful things, NOTE 6.3 = 201c5 DISSONANT and good things are beautiful things, then he would also lack good things." "I would not be able to contradict you, Socrates", he said. "So let it be as you say." DISHARMONY: ELENCHUS, NOT GOOD "It is the truth, my beloved (*philoumene*), [201d] that you cannot contradict; contradicting Socrates is nothing difficult." QUESTIONING ENDS, TURNS TO DIOTIMA AT NOTE

But I will let you be here. The speech about erotics, 1/8 which I once heard from the Manitean woman Diotima – who was wise about these things and many others, and who once by having the Athenians make sacrifices before the plague postponed the illness for ten years, and who also taught me erotics – this speech which she delivered I will try to relate to you from the agreements between 2/8 Agathon and me, as well as I can just speaking with myself [and not Agathon]. It is necessary, Agathon, just as you described, [201e] to describe him first – who Eros is and what sort – and then his works. It seems to me to be easy to relate the speech in this way, just as this foreign woman, while examining me, was then relating it. For I was saying to her 3/8 other things very much of the sort that now Agathon was saying to me: that Eros was a great god, and that he was love of beautiful things. She refuted (*ēlenche*) me FOUR-SEVENTHS using the sorts of arguments I used against him: that he is not beautiful according to my own argument, nor good.

132

Note 6.3, transition to dissonant seventh (201c5)

This quarternote is near a very dissonant note, the seventh wholenote on the twelve-note scale. It is marked by the conclusion of the elenchus of Agathon, which ends the questioning that occupied the previous two quarter-intervals.

The Socratic elenchus is a blend of agreement and refutation. When Agathon capitulates, he agrees (harmony) that his speech was self-contradictory (disharmony, negation). Their conclusion that "Eros is not beautiful" is negative, but there is also a cluster of positive terms (beauty, goodness and truth). Thus this note is predominately negative, appropriately so since it is near 7.0, but also transitional, and mixes positive and negative elements.

Narrative structure reflects musical structure: Socrates stops questioning Agathon after the note, and shifts to recounting his supposed discussions with Diotima. The placement of the elenchus at the note, and the duration of the questioning (two quarter-intervals) both reflect the underlying musical structure.

Four-sevenths (201e6)

This note is marked by another elenchus (the verbal form of "elenchus" occurs at the note, §2.8), which is appropriate to the dissonant sevenths. Here, Socrates recalls that Diotima refuted him, when he was young and using the same arguments as Agathon. It was just shown above, however, that these arguments are false. Thus Socrates is recalling a temporary mixture between a philosopher and falsehood. Just as Orpheus left Hades and remained alive, and Socrates left the theatre and remained wise, here Socrates has abandoned false arguments without any lasting stain. Like the other sevenths, this is an example of mechanical mixture without blending. It shows again that language or the *logos* is treated as a medium that may be harmonized (e.g. in verbal agreements) or merely mixed (e.g. when propositions are accepted and then rejected).

<mark>DIOTIMA BEGINS FIRST PART HALFWAY BETWEEN NOTES</mark> And I said, "Diotima, how do you mean that? Is Eros then ugly and bad?"

And she said, "Won't you hush!? (*euphēmēseis*) <mark>4/8</mark> Do you think that what is not beautiful necessarily has to be ugly?" [202a] "Of course."

"And what is not wise is ignorant? Or do you not perceive that there is something between wisdom and ignorance?" "What's that?"

"Don't you know," she said, "that to have a correct opinion without being able to give a reason is neither to know something – for how could an unreasonable thing (*alogon*) <mark>5/8</mark> be knowledge? – nor ignorance – for how would getting it right be ignorance? Surely there is something like correct opinion between thoughtfulness and ignorance." "You speak", said I, "the truth." [202b]

"So then what is beautiful does not necessarily have to be ugly, nor what is not good to be bad. Thus too, since you agree <mark>6/8</mark> that Eros is neither good nor bad, and do not any the more for that make it necessarily both ugly and beautiful, but rather something between these two", she said. "And yet," said I, "it is agreed by all that he is a great god."

"Do you mean by all of those who do not know," she said, "or even by those who know?" "By all of them." [202c]

Then she laughed <mark>7/8</mark> and said, "And how, Socrates, could those agree that he is a great god who say that he is not even a god?" <mark>DISHARMONY: EROS NO GOD</mark> "Who's that?", I said. "That includes you," she said, "and I am one too." And I said, "How can you," I said, [*sic*] "say that?"

And she said, "Easily. For tell me, don't you say that all the gods are happy and beautiful? Or do you dare <mark>NOTE 7.0 = 202c7</mark> <mark>DISSONANT</mark> to say that some of the gods are not beautiful and not happy?" <mark>DISHARMONY: GOD NOT BEAUTIFUL, HAPPY?</mark> "By god, not me!", I said. <mark>DISHARMONY: NEGATIVE AGREEMENT</mark> "And don't you call happy those who possess good and beautiful things?" [202d] "Very much so." <mark>HARMONY: AGREEMENT</mark> "But you have agreed that Eros on account of lacking good and beautiful things desires just those things which he lacks." "I agreed indeed." <mark>1/8</mark> "How could someone be a god who has no share in beautiful and good things?" "He couldn't, as it seems." "Do you see, then," she said, "that you believe Eros is no god?"

<mark>DISHARMONY: ELENCHUS</mark> "What then," I said, "would Eros be? A mortal?" "Not the least." [202e] "But what then?"

"Just as earlier," she said, "between mortal and immortal." "What's that then, Diotima?"

"A great daimon," <mark>2/8</mark> Socrates. For indeed, everything about daimons is between god and mortal." "What power does it have?"

"Interpreting and conveying to the gods things from humans and to humans things from the gods: on the one hand, entreaties and sacrifices and, on the other, orders and things exchanged for the sacrifices. Being in the middle of both, he would fill it altogether, <mark>3/8</mark> so that the All itself is bound together to itself (*amphoterōn symplēroi, ōste to pan auto autōsundedesthai*). Through him, the whole art of prophecy proceeds, and the art of priests and that of those concerned with sacrifices and rituals [203a] and spells and all prophetic utterances and sorcery.

Note 7.0, dissonant (202c7)

This dissonant note is marked by a strong negative statement at the note, the denial that the gods are beautiful and happy, and by Diotima's elenchus of the young Socrates.

As with the previous note, negative concepts dominate but there is harmony in their agreements, in the positive words for beauty, happiness and the gods, and finally in the capitulation to the elenchus. This passage also illustrates the relationship between teacher and student.

Diotima gives a theory of "harmonization" of the human and divine after the note. They do not "mix", but are bound together into one whole by the daimon, a mediating *krasis*.

Narrative structure reflects musical structure: Halfway between the quarternotes, Socrates shifts from direct to indirect discourse, and begins to recall his past conversations with Diotima. Her first word is at the midpoint.[23] This begins the first major part of the speech, which is devoted to Eros's nature and origins.

HARMONY WITH GODS HALFWAY BETWEEN NOTES "No god mixes (*ou meignutai*) with a human, but through him is all traffic and 4/8 conversation (*dialectos*) from the gods to humans, whether awake or asleep. And he who is wise about such things is a daimonic man; he who is wise about anything else, whether about some manual crafts or arts, is inferior. These daimons are indeed many and various, and Eros is one of them."

"Is he [the son] of some father and mother?", 5/8 I said. [203b]

"To relate that," she said, "is a long tale. Nevertheless I will tell you. When Aphrodite was born, the gods, including Poros, the son of Metis, held a feast. Once they had dined, Penia arrived and was begging, as happens when there's a feast. She was [loitering] around the doorway. Then Poros, drunk from the nectar 6/8 (there was not yet any wine), entered into Zeus' garden and, being overcome, slept. Penia, scheming 3/5 on account of her own poverty (*aporian*) to get a child from Poros, [203c] lay down next to him and became pregnant with Eros. Therefore, Eros became both Aphrodite's follower and attendant since he was conceived on her birthday (*gennētheis en tois ekeinēs genethliois*) 7/8 and, again, since he was by nature a lover of the beautiful and of Aphrodite (since she is beautiful). In as much as he is the son of Poros and Penia, Eros was established with the following lot. **HARMONY: *KRASIS* OF POSITIVE AND NEGATIVE** First, he is always in penury and, far from being tender and beautiful, as the many think, [203d] he is rather hard, dry, **NOTE 7.1 = 203d1 DISSONANT** barefoot and homeless. He is always camping on the ground without bedding, going to sleep in doorways or along roads under the open sky. Since he has mother's nature, he is always in need of company.

DISHARMONY: NEGATIVE QUALITIES AT NOTE "Because of his father, he is scheming to attain beautiful and good things. Since he is manly, he's rash and intense (*suntonos*) 1/8. He's a terrific hunter, always concocting some tricks. He is yearning after thought and well supplied with it. He philosophizes through all of his life. **POSITIVE QUALITIES** He is a terrific sorcerer, enchanter and [203e] sophist. He is by nature neither immortal nor mortal, but on his day he blooms and lives, and then will flourish; but when he dies, 2/8 he will be brought to life again on account of his father's nature. What he acquires is always flowing away, and so Eros is never in want nor rich and is, again, in the middle of wisdom and ignorance. The following holds. Among gods, none philosophizes nor desires to become wise [204a] (for they are wise), nor if any others are wise 3/8 do they philosophize. Nor, in turn, do the ignorant philosophize, nor desire to become wise. Just this is the difficulty with ignorance: those not already among the educated (*kalon kagathon*) nor wise seem to themselves to be adequate. Those who do not think they are in need do not desire that which they do not think they need."

Note 7.1, dissonant (203d1)

This marking passage has a particularly clear structure. It describes the birth of Eros from his parents, Resource and Poverty. There is a definite *krasis* at the note, the blending of the characteristics of the parents in their child. Moreover, since the note is dissonant, the negative qualities are described at the note and the positive ones afterwards. Here Eros himself is a *krasis*.

The assertion at the note that Eros is hard and barefoot, and not tender and beautiful "as the many think", is at once a pointed refutation of Agathon's earlier views (more dissonance), and is probably an allusion to Socrates himself.

Narrative structure reflects musical structure: The octads are again marked with significant concepts: 2/8 mentions the Pythagorean idea of rebirth and 3/8 refers to someone who is wise.

`PHILOSOPHERS HALFWAY BETWEEN NOTES` "Who then, Diotima," `4/8` I said, "philosophizes, if it is neither the wise nor the ignorant?" [204b]

"This would already be clear," she said, "to even a child: that it is those between both of these, among which Eros is too. Wisdom is among the most beautiful of things, and Eros is love of the beautiful. Thus, necessarily, Eros is a philosopher, `5/8` and since he is a philosopher he is between wisdom and ignorance. The cause of him and these is his birth. His father is indeed wise and resourceful, `PHI: PHILOSOPHER DEFINED AS MEAN` and his mother is not wise and resourceless. So then, the nature of a daimon, dear Socrates, is this. Given who you thought Eros was, [204c] this shouldn't have surprised you. For you thought, as it seems to me is proved from what you say, that Eros is the beloved, `6/8` not he who loves. On account of this, I think, Eros seemed all-beautiful to you. And it is indeed the loveable that is in reality beautiful and delicate and perfect and most blessed. But he who loves possesses another idea (*idean*) of the sort I described."

And I said, "Well, then, dear guest, you indeed speak beautifully. `7/8` Eros being such and so, what use (*chreian*) does he have for humans?" [204d]

"That," she said, "I will try to teach you next. `PART OF DIOTIMA'S SPEECH ENDS; NEXT BEGINS` Since Eros is such and so and born in this way, he is among the beautiful things, as you say. And if someone were to say to us 'Why is Eros "of beautiful things", Socrates and Diotima?' Or this is more clear:

`NOTE 7.2 = 204d5` `DISSONANT` 'When a lover loves something beautiful, what does he love?' And I said that 'To get it for himself (*genesthai autō*).'"

`DISHARMONY: LOVE IS ACQUISITIVE` "But," she said, "that answer craves a further question such as this: what will it be to him who gets beautiful things?"

"I don't yet," I said, "quite have an answer to that question."

`DISHARMONY: APORIA` [204e]

"But," she said, "it's as if someone, changing, `1/8` would make the inquiry using 'the good' instead of 'the beautiful': Come, Socrates, what does he love who loves good things?"

"This," I said, "I can more readily answer: that he will be happy." [205a]

"So, by acquiring good things," she said, `2/8` "the happy are happy, and it no longer needs also to be said 'What does he who wishes to be happy wish for?' Rather, your answer seems to contain the final end (*telos*)."

"You speak the truth", said I.

"Do you think that this wish and this love are common to all humans? And do all wish to have good things for themselves always? `3/8` Or how do you say?"

"Just so", I said. "It's common to all." [205b]

"Why then, Socrates," she said, "do we not say that everyone's in love, if all of them are in love all the time, but rather that some love and some do not?"

"I wonder too", I said.

Note 7.2, dissonant (204d5)

This passage is disharmonious because the younger Socrates treats Eros in a utilitarian manner. He asks "what *use* Eros is" and suggests that love is acquisitive. Socrates' *aporia* is also negative.

On the other hand, the passage is harmonic because it shows the cooperative exchange of questions and answers between teacher and student. At the note, Diotima momentarily joins the younger Socrates as respondent to a hypothetical questioner.

Phi: As will be discussed in Chapter 7, this location is often marked, in Plato's genuine dialogues, by references to the philosopher who finds the virtuous mean between pleasure and pain. Here, in the *Symposium*, we have a key definition of the philosopher: an intermediate sort who is a *krasis* between wise and unwise.

Narrative structure reflects musical structure: At 201e1–2, Socrates announced that Diotima's speech would have two parts devoted to the nature and the works of Eros. Here at the note, Diotima concludes the first and begins the second.

"But don't wonder", she said. "For, as we can now see, having separated off one species (*eidos*) of love, 4/8 we give the name attached to the whole to that and use other names for the rest." "Like what?", I said.

"Like the following. You know that creation is something various (*poēsis esti ti polu*). The cause of anything going from not existing to something existing is all creation, [205c] so that too production (*ergasiai*) in all the technical arts 5/8 is creation, and all the craftworkers in them are creators." "You speak the truth."

"Nevertheless," she said, "you know that they are not called 'poets' but have other names. From all of creation (*poiēseōs*), one species is marked off, that concerning music and metre, and addressed by the name of the whole ['poetry']. 6/8 Indeed, only this is called 'creation', and those possessing this form (*morion*) of creation are called 'poets'." "You speak the truth", I said.

"And so too with love. The main point is [205d] that all desire for good things and for becoming happy is for everyone 'love, the greatest and deceitful'. But those oriented in every other way toward love – 7/8 whether toward moneymaking, philo-gymnastics or philosophy – are neither said 'to love' nor called 'lovers'. But those proceeding earnestly in accordance with a single form (*hen ti eidos*) have the name of the whole [or its derivatives]: 'loving' and 'to love' and 'lovers'." "You probably speak the truth", I said.

"And an argument (*logos*) is made", she said, "that those who seek their NOTE 7.3 = 205d10 DISSONANT own halves [205e] are lovers. But my argument says that love is not of a half or of a whole DISHARMONY: CRITICISM OF DEFINITION OF LOVE if it does not, my friend, happen somehow to be good, since humans will want to cut off even their own feet and hands if to them their own things seem harmful. DISHARMONY: AMPUTATION, CUTTING APART Nor do I think humans will each welcome what is theirs 1/8 unless and if they say the good belongs to them and is their own while the bad is foreign to them. [206a] Thus there is nothing that humans will love other than the good. DISHARMONY: ELENCHUS Or do they seem [otherwise] to you?" "By God, not to me", I said.

"So then," she said, "is it simply to be said that humans love the good." 2/8 "Yes", I said.

"What? Must it not be added that they love the good to be theirs too?"

"It must be added."

"Then also," she said, "not only 'to be' but 'to be eternally [theirs]'?"

"This too must be added."

"So then, in short," she said, "love is of the good being theirs eternally."

"You speak most truly", I said. [206b] "Now that love is this eternally," 3/8 she said, "in which ways of pursuit and in which actions would zeal and exertion be called love? What happens to be love's work (*ergon*)? Do you have anything to say?"

"[If so,] I wouldn't be here admiring your wisdom, Diotima," I said, "and studying with you just to learn these things."

Note 7.3, dissonant (205d10)

This passage is predominately disharmonic because it is a refutation of Aristophanes' earlier doctrine that love seeks its other half (192e10ff.) This false argument is placed at the note. This negative passage is underscored by the reference to self-administered amputation that follows. This is a horrific thought, and cutting apart is the opposite of harmony understood as "fitting together". There are harmonic elements after the note: Aristophanes' view is replaced by the doctrine that loves seeks the good.

NEXT PART OF SPEECH, DEFINES ERGON OF EROS, AT MIDPOINT "Well, I will tell you", she said. "This [work of love] is 4/8 giving birth in beauty, both in relation to the body and in relation to the soul."

"A seer is needed whenever you speak like that: I don't understand." [206c]

"Well," she said, "I will tell you more clearly. All humans are, indeed, pregnant," she said, "both in relation to the body and in relation to the soul. After they reach a certain age, our nature desires to give birth. 5/8 It is not possible to give birth in the ugly, but it is in the beautiful. The sexual intercourse (*sunousia*) of man and woman is birth [of a sort]. This is a divine matter, and inheres as something immortal in the mortal animal: pregnancy and generation. These cannot occur in what is disharmonic (*anarmoston*). [206d] The 6/8 disharmonic is what is ugly for everything divine, and the beautiful is harmonic (*harmotton*). BEAUTY IS HARMONY WITH DIVINE The goddess of Beauty is Moira and Eileithyia at generation. On account of this, when those who are pregnant approach beauty, they become gracious and, gladdened, flow across and give birth and generate. HARMONY: APPROACHING BEAUTY, CLIMAX, PLEASURE When they approach ugliness, sullen and distressed, they shrink and turn away 7/8 and curl up and do not generate, holding in the pregnancy and carrying it painfully. Wherefore, then, DISHARMONY: APPROACHING THE SHAMEFUL, PAIN in someone pregnant and already swollen, [206e] an intense excitement arises about a beauty on account of the great travail to release what is carried. For, Socrates, DISAGREEMENT love is not of the beautiful, as you think."

NOTE 8.0 = 206e4 CONSONANT "But what then?"

HARMONY: REPRODUCING *IN* BEAUTY "It is of generation and birth in the beautiful."

"Ah, so", I said.

"Very much so", she said. HARMONY: AGREEMENT "Why then of generation? Because generation is the eternal and immortal in the mortal. HARMONY: KRASIS WITH IMMORTAL [207a] It follows from our agreements AGREEMENT that it is necessary to desire immortality together with the good, if love is for the good forever being theirs. 1/8 From this argument it is also necessary that love be of immortality."

She taught me, then, all these things when she would make speeches about erotics. TOPIC SHIFT: USE TO CAUSE Once she asked, "What do you think, Socrates, is the cause of this love and desire? Don't you perceive how all animals are in a terrible state 2/8 when they desire to reproduce, both those on land and in the air. They are all ill and erotically inclined, [207b] first about having sex with each other and then about rearing their offspring. Even the weakest is ready to battle against the strongest for them, even to die 3/8 for them or to be tortured (*parateinomena*) with hunger to rear them.

Note 8.0, consonant (206e4)

This important and very consonant note is two-thirds of the way through the entire dialogue. It is emphatically marked by several kinds of harmony, but most clearly by a sexual union with the beautiful that yields a further *krasis* of the mortal and immortal. This is the first of two dramatic high points in Socrates' speech; the second is at the ninth wholenote.

Before the note, there is a series of oppositions between harmony and disharmony, beauty and ugliness, pleasure and pain, and bringing forth and not bringing forth. These oppositions can be read as preceding the sexual copulation and successful begetting located at the note. The climactic *krasis* in and with beauty occurs at the note. After the note, harmony reigns in several ways. The begetting is a harmony of mortal and immortal. Diotima and the younger Socrates now agree with each other. The Good is mentioned. Harmony is thus here a quasi-divine, sexual reproduction that somehow blends mortal and immortal.

This note is also important for generally understanding the marking passages. Here, beauty is explicitly said to be "harmonious with the divine". That is, for the purposes of marking notes, beauty is one species of harmony. References to beauty are references to a kind of harmony.

Narrative structure reflects musical structure: At the note, Diotima interrupts a long passage of monologue for a quick exchange of question and answer: this dialectical cooperation and agreement is another species of harmony. After the note, Diotima shifts to a new, explicitly distinguished topic, the cause of love.

"They would do anything. One would think," she said, "that humans do these things rationally (*logismou*). But by what cause [207c] would animals be so erotically inclined? Do you have anything to say?"

And I once more said that I did not know. She said, 4/8 "Could you ever expect to become clever at erotics, if you do not understand this?"

"But, indeed, Diotima, as I just said, it was for this that I came to you, knowing that I needed teaching. So tell me the cause of this as well as of those other things about erotics." NEW PART OF SPEECH

"Well, then," she said, "if you are persuaded that love is by 5/8 nature that which we have often agreed it is, then don't be incredulous. The same argument here as there [for animals and humans]: [207d] mortal nature seeks, as far as it can, to be always and immortal. It can only in this way, by generation, because it always leaves behind something young and different instead of the old, since [during that time] in which one individual living creature is said 6/8 to be alive and to be the same … For example, it is said to be the same while it grows from a child to an elder. This, however, although it never retains the same things in itself, is nevertheless called the same. While it is always becoming new, some of it is perishing: [207e] its hair, flesh, bones, blood and its entire body. It's not since these are corporeal 7/8 but it's also so in relation to TURN TO SOUL, KNOWLEDGE the soul: the manners, habits, opinions, desires, pleasures, pains and fears – none of these ever remains the same as itself. Rather, some persist and others perish. DISHARMONY: PERISHING Much stranger (*atopōteron*) yet [208a] than these is that, with knowledge, it is not that some persists and the rest perishes, NOTE 8.1 = 208a1 DISSONANT so that we are never the same even with respect to knowledge, but, moreover, that each single piece of knowledge experiences the same [persistence and perishing]. DISHARMONY: NEVER THE SAME What is called 'practising' (*meletan*) exists because knowledge egresses. DISHARMONY: LOSING KNOWLEDGE Forgetting is the egress of knowledge, and PRACTISING SAVES KNOWLEDGE practising preserves knowledge 1/8 by again implanting a memory in the place of the departing knowledge, so that it seems the same. TURN FROM SOULS Indeed, in this way, everything mortal is preserved, not that it is entirely the same forever [208b] as with the divine, but rather by the departing and ageing thing leaving behind something different and new, yet as it was. By this contrivance, Socrates, the mortal participates in immortality, both the body and all the rest. 2/8 HARMONY OF MORTAL, IMMORTAL So don't be surprised if everything by nature honours its own offshoot. For the sake of immortality, this zeal that is love attends to all."

When I heard this argument, I was surprised [208c] and said: "Well," I said, [*sic*] "O most sophistical Diotima, does this in truth hold in this way?"

And she, as the perfect 3/8 sophists, said, "Know it well, Socrates.

Note 8.1, dissonant (208a1)

Before the note both our bodies and our knowledge are perishing, and this seems to mark a dissonant first quarternote.

After the note, practising or repeatedly memorizing our knowledge and younger replacements give us a kind of salvation and immortality. Here the *krasis* between mortal and immortal is explicitly called "participation" (*metechei*; 208b3).

The soul and knowledge are discussed only in the passage stretching from the octad just before the quarternote to the octad just after it.

It is not certain how to calculate the relative consonance of the quarternotes, although they seem to be more or less consonant according to which wholenotes they are near. This quarternote is between two very consonant notes, 8.0 and 9.0, but a negative sentence occurs at the note and the positive *krasis* afterwards. Although it is devoted to the soul, it seems to be as much negative and disharmonious as positive and harmonious (cf. 4.1).

This passage implies that the "practising" (*meletan*) mentioned in the first line of the dialogue is a reference to a kind of *krasis* or harmony between mortal and immortal.

"Since, at any rate, if you wish to glance toward the ambition among humans as well [as among animals], you would be surprised at the irrationality (about which I spoke) unless you understood and consider how terribly they are inclined to the love 4/8 of becoming one of the famous names and of 'laying up an immortal fame for time ever after'. For the sake of this they are all ready to hazard hazards [sic], even more than for their children, [208d] spend money, labour labours [sic] of whatever sort, and die for its sake. Do you think," she said, "Alcestis would have died for Admetus, or that Achilles would have added his death to Patroclus', 5/8 or that our King Codrus would have died to secure the kingdom for his children if they did not think that an immortal memory of their virtues would remain, a memory that we now have? Far from it", she said. "Everyone does everything for the sake of immortal virtue [208e] and that sort of reputation for good deeds – and the better person they are, the more they do it. 6/8 They love what is immortal. Those who are pregnant in a corporal way are oriented more toward women and they are eroticists in this way: they think that by producing children they will provide themselves with immortality, memory, and happiness for all future time. [209a] 7/8 Those who are pregnant in their souls TURN TO SOUL, VIRTUES – they are those,' she said, 'who are more pregnant in their souls than in their bodies – they conceive and bear what belongs to the soul: wisdom (*phronēsin*) and the rest of virtue.

HARMONY: VIRTUES "All the creators are the generators of these, and craft-workers in so far as they are said to be innovators. Much the greatest," she said, NOTE 8.2 = 209a6 CONSONANT "and the most beautiful wisdom (*phronēseōs*) is that concerning the well-ordering of cities and households, the name of which is 'temperateness' (*sōphrosunē*) and 'justice'. [209b] HARMONY: VIRTUES AT NOTE Moreover, when someone is pregnant in the soul HARMONY: DIVINE SOULS with these from childhood, when he matures (*ētheos*) and reaches the right age, he desires to reproduce and give birth straightaway; he runs around and seeks, I think, the 1/8 beauty in which he might give birth. TURN FROM SOULS TO BEGETTING, BODIES He will never give birth in ugliness. He welcomes beautiful bodies more than ugly ones since he is pregnant and, were he to meet a beautiful, noble and good-natured soul, would also very much welcome the combination (*sunamphoteron*). He would straightaway 2/8 abound with speeches about virtue and about how one [209c] must be a good man and what pursuits are suitable, and set about educating him. Touching (*haptomenos*) and socializing, I think, with the beauty, FIVE-SEVENTHS: BODIES MIXING, LOVERS TOUCHING he reproduces and gives birth to that which he was of old pregnant with. Keeping him in mind when he is present and away, he rears the newborn together and in common with him. Thus such [a couple] possess 3/8 a much greater common bond with each other than [ordinary] children and their love (*philian*) is firmer, since they have shared more beautiful and more immortal children.

Note 8.2, consonant (209a6)

This note is marked with strongly positive concepts: the four virtues and intellectual procreation.

As with the previous note, the passage from the octad before the note to the octad after it concerns the soul. Diotima turns from pregnancy of the body to pregnancy of the soul at 7/8 and then returns to beautiful bodies at 1/8. The soul is pregnant before the note, and gives birth afterwards. This shows that the passage concerns something harmonious (the soul may be more or less harmonious), and thus appropriately marks the musical note.

Five-sevenths (209c1)

Here again, the musical structure opens up new approaches to reading the content of the dialogues, to seeing the gap between Diotima and Plato.

The passage at five-sevenths is, for a Platonist, one of Diotima's morally dubious assertions. She here suggests that someone pregnant in soul will seek out a beautiful body, hopefully conjoined with a beautiful soul too, to "touch" and so to give birth. Locating this passage at a negative, dissonant seventh (5/7) and thus associating it with mere mixture, confirms that it should be interpreted negatively.

Socrates' aversion to such "touching" is vividly portrayed in the later scenes with the young Alcibiades (the so-called "Platonic love"). In contrast, Agathon joked, at the beginning of the *Symposium*, that by "touching" he could enjoy Socrates' wisdom, which Socrates immediately rejected (175c7ff.). Agathon's lover Pausanias, a sophist or fellow traveller, also suggested that sex could be exchanged for moral edification (e.g. 184d4–e4). Diotima's doctrines are sometimes Platonistic (the ascent to the Form of Beauty) and sometimes she is explicitly associated with the sophists (e.g. 208c1). She is a living character, and not just a mouthpiece for Socrates or Plato. That this passage is lodged at a dissonant note shows that its doctrines are not Platonic, that is, that Plato does not believe sex with beautiful bodies is a precondition for philosophical progress. Plato disagrees with Diotima here. Mere physical contact is an example of temporary mixture, and not of a lasting *krasis* or harmony between individuals.

"And everyone would prefer to produce such children for himself rather than the human sort, and envies, [209d] with a fixed gaze, Homer 4/8 and Hesiod and all the other good poets, who left behind them such offspring that furnish them with immortal fame and remembrance, being [as great] as they are. If you wish," she said, "[consider] such children as Lycurgus left behind in Lacedaemonia, the saviour of Lacedaemonia and 5/8 – in a word – of Greece. More honoured by us is Solon, on account of the laws he gave birth to, and other men, [209e] everywhere else, both in Greece and among the barbarians, who performed many, fine works, which gave birth to all sorts of virtue. Even many shrines to these have arisen for having such children [of the soul], but to none yet for having the human sort.

6/8 INITIATION ANNOUNCED AT OCTAD "Into these [elements of] erotics, Socrates, even you might be initiated. [210a] But I do not know if you are capable of the rites and final insights, for the sake of which these are (if one follows correctly). However," she said, "I will tell you and not lessen my zeal. Try to follow, if you are able. It is necessary," she said, "for he who is proceeding correctly 7/8 INITIATION BEGINS AT OCTAD with this enterprise to begin while still young to approach beautiful bodies and first, if the guide guides correctly, for him to love one body and there to give birth to beautiful speeches, HARMONY: LOVE ONE BODY; STEP ONE [210b] and then for him to understand that the beauty of any body whatsoever is NOTE 8.3 = 210b1 CONSONANT brother to that of any other body, and – if it is necessary to pursue the beauty of form (*eidei*) HARMONY: PARTICIPATE IN GENERAL FORM; STEP TWO – that it is very senseless not to believe that it is not one and the same as the beauty of all bodies; and having understood this, to become a lover of all beautiful bodies, HARMONY: GENERAL LOVE relaxing the intensity of his love for one body and judging it contemptible and paltry. After that, he must judge the 1/8 STEP THREE AT OCTAD beauty in souls more honourable than that in the body, so that if someone is suitable in respect of the soul, [210c] even if he has little of that bloom of youth, he will be satisfied with and love and care for him and seek to give birth to the sort of speeches which make youths better, so that he might 2/8 STEP FOUR AT OCTAD be compelled to observe the beauty in activities and customs (*nomois*) and to see that everything is in itself related to everything, and that the beauty in bodies is to be judged but a small thing; after activities, [the guide] must lead him to fields of knowledge, that he might in addition see their beauty and, gazing already 3/8 STEP FIVE AT OCTAD towards this manifold beauty and no longer towards that beauty in just one, as a lackey who, since he loves (*agapōn*) the beauty of one boy or of a certain human or of one activity, would be [210d] slavishly inferior and of little account;

Note 8.3, consonant (210b1)

This is a strongly positive note marked by erotic harmony. Someone in love with one body takes the first step up Diotima's ladder at the note; the top of the ladder is at the next wholenote, 9.0. The emphasis on bodies, however, is a disharmonic element.

Diotima announces the initiation into the *technē* of erotics at 6/8, and the journey begins at 7/8. Here again, we have the erotic craftsman, the "guide", encouraging erotic harmony. At the note, the lover first perceives a Platonic form (*katanoēsai ... to ep' eidon kalon*).

Narrative structure reflects musical structure: Plato is clearly placing significant or symbolic phrases at the octads. The first steps up Diotima's ladder occur at note 8.3 and each step after that is announced at the next octad. There is a progressive series of visions of various kinds of beauty, which are apparently stages in the initiation:

Rungs of Diotima's ladder at the octads:

- Step 1 at quarternote: love a single body (8.3).
- Step 2 at quarternote: general form of beauty in bodies (8.3).
- Step 3 at octad 1: beauty in the soul.
- Step 4 at octad 2: beauty in activities and customs.
- Step 5 at octad 3: beauty in branches of knowledge.
- Step 6 at octad 4: ocean of beauty: philosophy.
- Step 7 at octad 5: the vision of the final end or *telos* of erotics.

"but instead, turning toward the manifold ocean of beauty and surveying many, beautiful, even magnificent speeches (*logous*), he would 4/8 STEP SIX AT OCTAD give birth to thoughts in bounteous philosophy, and, while here, having grown and strengthened, would espy one single kind of knowledge, which is of the following sort of beauty. Try", [210e] she said, "to attend to me as much as you can. He who is led like a child thus far into erotics, seeing correctly and in order 5/8 STEP SEVEN AT OCTAD the beauties, and going forthwith toward the *telos* of erotics will suddenly behold something astonishing, naturally beautiful, that for which, Socrates, all the previous labours were for the sake of. First, then, it is always [211a] and neither becomes nor perishes, neither increases nor decreases and, then, is neither beautiful in this way and ugly in that way, and not once so and then not so, nor related in one way to beauty and in another to ugliness, and not here beautiful and there ugly, 6/8 nor in some respect beautiful and ugly in another. Moreover, beauty will not appear to him as some face nor as hands nor as anything else that participates in body, nor as some speech (*logos*) nor as some field of knowledge, 7/8 nor as being somehow in some other thing, as in an animal or in [211b] the earth or in the heavens or in anything else. Rather, by itself and with itself, as oneform (*monoeides*), HARMONY: THE SINGLE FORM OF BEAUTY it always is. All the other beauties participate (*metachonta*) in that in a certain way so as, HARMONY: PARTICIPATION while these others come to be and perish, that neither becomes greater nor NOTE 9.0 = 211b4 CONSONANT *KRASIS* OF CHANGING THINGS, UNCHANGING BEAUTY lesser. When someone, ascending from these here through correct pederasty, begins to see that beauty, he would then nearly touch the *telos*. This is, then, indeed the correct way to approach [211c] erotics or be led by another: HARMONY: EROTICS TO BEAUTY beginning from these [beauties] here, and for the sake of that beauty, 1/8 always to ascend, as if using upward steps: from one to two and from two to all beautiful bodies, and from beautiful bodies to beautiful activities, and from activities to beautiful studies, and from studies to finish with that study, 2/8 which is nothing other than the study of that beauty itself, so that he might know what beauty is itself. [211d] To live here, my dear Socrates," said the Mantinean guest, "if not somewhere else, while contemplating beauty in itself, is a life worthy of a human. If you ever were to see it, not gold nor robes nor those beautiful boys 3/8 and youths will seem to exist for you, which now, if you saw them, would astound you; and you and many others, upon seeing such boyfriends and being together with them, would be ready to neither eat nor drink (if it were somehow possible), but only gaze at and be together with them. [211e]

Note 9.0, consonant (211b4)

The literary and metaphysical peak of Socrates' speech occurs at the very consonant ninth note, three-fourths of the way through the entire dialogue. Diotima's ladder culminates here with a vision of the Form of Beauty itself. An important species of harmony is represented here: the participation of beautiful things in an abstract Form, that is, a *krasis* between changing things and the eternal, unchanging Form.

The series of negations before the note denies that transcendent Beauty has the kinds of properties that apply to ordinary things. These transcendent negations are a kind of "negative theology" of the Forms: the most positive description in our language is just the denial that its categories apply to the highest Forms.

Narrative structure reflects musical structure: In sum, the highlights of Diotima's speech occur at the eighth and ninth notes, two-thirds and three-quarters of the way through the entire dialogue. The steps of Diotima's ladder are located at successive octads, which is further clear evidence for the importance of the octads.

"Indeed, what would we think," she said, "if it were indeed possible to see 4/8 beauty itself uncorrupted, pure, unmixed and not filled up with human flesh, chromatics (*chrōmatōn*), and so much other mortal rubbish, and we could behold divine beauty itself? [212a] Indeed, do you think," she said, "it is an inferior life for a human looking thither and contemplating that in the necessary way 5/8 and being together with it? Or don't you realize," she said, "that only here with it, seeing beauty as it can be seen, will he give birth to – not images of virtue, since he will not be touching an image – but true virtue, since he will be touching the truth; and that, giving birth to and rearing true virtue, he commences becoming dear to the gods and, if any human can, will too be immortal?" DIOTIMA ENDS 6/8 [212b]

Indeed, Phaedrus and you others, so said Diotima and so am I convinced. And being convinced, I try to convince others that, for attaining this, **a better collaborator than Eros for our human nature will not easily be found.**

HARMONY: PRAISE OF EROS Therefore, I assert that every 7/8 **man must honour Eros, and I honour erotics** HARMONY: PRAISE OF EROTICS, HARMONIC *TECHNĒ* **and practise it especially, and so exhort others. And now and forever I praise the power and courage** [212c] **of Eros as far as I am able. Then, Phaedrus, believe this speech, if you wish, was delivered as an encomium** NOTE 9.1 = 212c2 **for Eros, but if not, whatever and however you please to name it, so name it.** HARMONY: PRAISE OF EROS; SOCRATES' SPEECH ENDS AT THE NOTE

After Socrates said that, they praised him, HARMONY: PRAISE, AGREEMENT but Aristophanes was attempting to say something, since Socrates while speaking about his speech had mentioned him, when suddenly there was a knocking on the courtyard door, which made a loud noise, as by revellers, 1/8 and the sound of a flute-girl was to be heard. Then Agathon said, "Slave-boys, won't you look? [212d] And if it's someone suitable, invite them in. But if not, tell them that we are not drinking and are already stopping."

And not much later they heard the voice in the courtyard of Alcibiades, who was very drunk and crying out loudly, 2/8 asking where Agathon was and demanding to be led to Agathon. So he was led in to them, supported by the flute-girl, as well as some other of his followers. He stood at the doors [212e] crowned with a bushy wreath of ivy and violets, 7/9 having very many ribbons on his head, 3/8 and said: "Gentlemen, greetings. Will you accept a very, extremely drunk man as a symposiast, or shall we leave as soon as we've crowned Agathon, which is what we came for?

Note 9.1 (212c2)

Socrates' speech ends harmoniously with an exhortation to praise Eros. This passage is positively marked in several ways: with words like honour and courage, with Socrates as a teacher, with the notions of paean and encomium, and with the applause at the end of the speech. Eros is here a Partner, bonded together with humanity.

Narrative structure reflects musical structure: Socrates finishes recounting Diotima's words and returns to his own voice at 6/8. Socrates finishes his speech at the quarternote.

5.7 Alcibiades

This speech includes the tenth and the eleventh wholenotes, the most dissonant in the twelve-note scale. The great theme of the *Symposium* is love as a force of harmonization, between humans or between humans and the divine. In contrast, Alcibiades' disharmonious theme is the wounding hurt of rejected love – until he turns to war.

His seductive brilliance notwithstanding, Alcibiades spurned philosophy and became the great villain of classical Athens's history. Here, he almost personifies disharmony. His actions are disruptive: he comes to the party uninvited, downs a bowl of wine, and threatens to derail the evening's congenial rhetorical contest. Throughout his speech, Alcibiades is pulled in opposite directions. Mingling condemnation and celebration, he half needles and mocks Socrates and half extols his love for him and his virtues. The speech is a bubbling turmoil of negative emotions and confused incident: anger, agony, resentment, distress, rejection, drunkenness, fanaticism, fraud, threat, criticism, sarcasm, cowardice, battle, seduction, squabbling, desire and jealousy. Just as the benevolent whimsy of Aristophanes' speech accorded well with the consonance of the fourth wholenote, here everything is *Sturm und Drang*.

Although we remember this speech for vividly and intimately lionizing Socrates, Alcibiades' praise is always double-edged. Socrates endured the cold while on campaign, but this made the other soldiers think he despised them. Socrates was brave at Potidaea, but this was a defeat; he was bold at Delium – while retreating. Alcibiades' comparison of Socrates to Marsyas, an ugly satyr, is clearly uncomplimentary, but contains further layers of threat: in most accounts, Marsyas was mutilated and killed by Apollo. When coupled with Alcibiades' wish that Socrates no longer existed (216c1), this joking banter seems to point towards Socrates' execution and explain the resentments of his fellow citizens. Even positive or jocular elements in Alcibiades' praise have a dark side, and this tense combination adds to the disharmony of the speech.

The musical scale, again, explains the odd structure of Plato's narrative. Instead of building to and ending with a final climax, the dialogues reach their Platonic peak three-quarters of the way through, and then degenerate. The *Phaedo* turns from the eternal forms to death and the underworld, the *Republic* has rule of the best decline into the savagery of tyranny, and here Diotima's ascent to the Form of Beauty ends in the intrusion of Alcibiades and the revellers.

Alcibiades makes several points important for the theory of the dialogue's allegory. Socrates' prose speech is a form of music without instruments, and needs to be "opened up" to see its inner, golden virtue. These remarks seemed innocent metaphor, but now read as a licence to look for the musical structure underneath the surface narrative.

Alcibiades says he will speak haphazardly (215a1–3), and neither the beginning and end of the speech nor the shifts from one topic to another within the speech are aligned with major notes. Nonetheless, the musical scale still supplies the scaffolding of the speech. For example, Alcibiades speaks for seven quarter-intervals, which, since the sevenths are associated with mixture and dissonance, may be significant (from 9.3.4 to 11.2.4). For another example, the several stages of the seduction story, as mentioned above, are pegged to quarternotes:

- *Disharmony at 10.2*: Alcibiades' first advances are rejected (disagreement), he feels distress and *aporia* (inner disharmony).
- *Disharmony at 10.3*: Alcibiades makes his awful offer to exchange sex and his patronage for Socrates' moral help.
- *Disharmony at 11.0*: Alcibiades is again rejected by Socrates and feels extreme distress and dishonour.

On the whole, however, the speech is less aligned with the musical scale than previous ones (see Appendix 6). This may be another way of making it "unfitting" and disharmonious.

"For I, indeed," he said, "was unable to come yesterday. But now I've come with bands on my head to bind up [with ribbons] from my head 4/8 the wisest and most beautiful head – if I may say so. Will you laugh at me then for being so drunk? [213a] Even if you laugh, I nevertheless know that I speak the truth. But tell me right now, may I enter on these terms or no? Will you drink with me or no?"

All then applauded and urged him to enter 5/8 and lie down, and Agathon invited him. He came led by his people. As he unwound the ribbons and was about to crown [Agathon], he did not see Socrates (having the ribbons before his eyes), but sat down next to Agathon in the middle [213b] between Socrates and him. Indeed, 6/8 Socrates had moved aside when he saw Alcibiades. Once he'd sat down, he greeted Agathon and crowned him.

Then Agathon said, "Take off Alcibiades' sandals, boys, so that he may lie down and make a third."

"Quite so," said Alcibiades, "but who here is our third symposiast?" And at once turning around 7/8 he saw Socrates, and seeing him he jumped up and said, "Hercules! What's this? That Socrates? You were lying here about to ambush me again, [213c] as usual suddenly turning up where I least expect you will be. And now why have you come? And why moreover are you lying down here? How not next to NOTE 9.2 = 213c3 Aristophanes or someone else who is laughed at and wants to be? DISHARMONY: RIDICULE, CRITICISM, LOVER'S QUARREL No, you've contrived how you might lie down next to the prettiest in here."

And Socrates said, "Agathon, see to it that you defend me! The love of this man has been no little trouble for me. Since that time when I fell in love with him, 1/8 it has no longer been possible [213d] for me either to look at or to converse with someone handsome, not even one, or he turns jealous and moody and abusive, makes a spectacle and with difficulty keeps his hands off me. Watch if he doesn't make one now! Reconcile us, or, if he attempts to use force, defend me. 2/8 I'm horrified by his mania, by his obsessive love for me (*philerastian*)."

"There will be," said Alcibiades, "no reconciliation between me and you. Rather, I will get revenge for this some other time. Now, however, Agathon," he said, "give over some of those ribbons, [213e] so that I may tie them up here on his marvellous head, 3/8 so that he doesn't complain that I tied up you, while he, though conquering all humans 4/5 in speeches – not only recently as you have but always – wasn't tied up." He at once, taking some ribbons, tied up some on Socrates and lay down.

Note 9.2 (213c3)

This quarternote is between the very consonant ninth and the very dissonant tenth wholenote. Socrates and Alcibiades declare their mutual love at the note. This passage is harmonious because it reveals the depth and duration of their erotic bond. It is disharmonious because of the lover's quarrel, that is, the ridicule and bickering. Their relationship combines good and bad, pain and pleasure, and admiration and distrust. Although it is uncertain how to calculate the relative consonance of the quarternotes, this seems somewhat more dissonant.

After he lay down, he said: "Well, gentlemen, you seem to me to be 4/8 sober. We can't entrust things to you, rather, we must drink! You've agreed to these terms! I choose as the symposiarch, until you've drunk enough, myself. So Agathon, if there's a big cup, have it brought here. Rather, there's no need," he said, "instead, boy, bring that wine-cooler" [214a] (he saw that it had room for more than eight cups). 5/8 Having this filled, he first drank it all and then urged some be poured in for Socrates and at the same time said: "In the case of Socrates, gentlemen, my trick will get me nothing. As many times as someone urges, so many times will he drink it all, but he will not the more be drunk – ever."

After the boy poured in [the wine], 6/8 Socrates drank. And Eryximachus said: "What's this that we are doing, Alcibiades? Do we drink so, just like dipsos, neither saying something over the cup [214b] nor singing something?"

And Alcibiades said, "Eryximachus! Best son of the best father, and most temperate (*sōphronestatou*) of all, greetings." 7/8

"And to you," said Eryximachus, "but what shall we do?" "Whatever you bid. One must obey you: HARMONY: AGREEMENT 'A medical man is worth many others.' Order whatever you wish." "Listen, then," said Eryximachus, "before you came in, we thought each should deliver a speech, the most beautiful he could, HARMONY: ORDER AND BEAUTY OF SPEECHES NOTE 9.3 = 214c1 CONSONANT about Eros, [214c] in turn and to the right, and praise him. HARMONY: PRAISE FOR EROS So, all the others of us have spoken. Since you've not spoken, and have finished your drink, it would be just if you spoke and, after speaking, ordered Socrates to do whatever you wish HARMONY: JUSTICE IF ORDER PRESERVED – and he likewise to the right and so on with the others."

"But, Eryximachus," said Alcibiades, "it's a beautiful thing you say, 1/8 HARMONY: AGREEMENT though for a drunk man to toss speeches next to those of the sober would not be equal terms. [214d] And besides, fortunate one, do you believe any of what Socrates just said? Or don't you know that everything is the opposite of what he said? Indeed, if I were to praise in his presence anyone other than him, whether god or human, 2/8 he would not keep his hands off me."

"Won't you hush!?", said Socrates. "By Poseidon!", said Alcibiades, "Don't say a word against it, as I would not praise anyone else while you are present." "Well, do so," said Eryximachus, "if you wish. Praise Socrates."

"What do you mean?!", said Alcibiades. "Does it seem I should, 3/8 Eryximachus, set upon the man and revenge myself in front of all of you?" [214e] "You!", said Socrates, "what do you have in mind? Will you praise me to make me a laughing stock? Or what will you do?" "I will speak the truth. Just see if you let me."

Note 9.3, consonant (214c1)

This note is marked by harmony as an agreement to conform to the order among the speakers, which is here associated with beauty and the virtue of justice. Alcibiades' arrival is a threat to this order, but his agreement, before and after the note, temporarily restores harmony.

"But indeed," he said, "the truth I will permit and bid you speak." 4/8

"I won't be beaten to it," said Alcibiades. "And you, however, do as follows. If I say anything untrue, [215a] interrupt in the middle, if you wish, and tell me that I lie. I never willingly state falsely that something is so. However, if while I'm remembering I say another thing another way, don't be surprised. It's not easy, in my condition, to reckon up your strangeness 5/8 fluently and in order."

"I will, gentlemen, in the following way endeavour to praise Socrates: through images. He will probably think it's for a laugh, but the image will be for the sake of truth, not for a joke. I assert [215b] that he is most similar to those *sileni* sitting in the shops 6/8 where they carve the herms, made by craftworkers with pipes or auloi, which – when they're opened up in two parts – are revealed to have statues of gods inside. And I moreover assert that he is an image of the satyr Marsyas. That in appearance (*eidos*) you are similar to them, Socrates, even you could not dispute. 7/8 For how you resemble other things too, listen up after this. You're arrogant (*hubristēs*). Or not? For if you don't agree, I will offer witnesses. DISCUSSION OF MUSIC STARTS And aren't you an aulos-player? DISHARMONY: PIPING [215c] At any rate, a more wonderful one than him. DISHARMONY: UGLY SATYR He bewitches humans with instruments by the power of his mouth. And even now, whoever plays his things on the aulos – what Olympus NOTE 10.0 = 215c2 DISSONANT played, I say is from his teacher Marsyas – HARMONY: TEACHING; DISHARMONY: PIPING, DEATH so his things merely produced, whether played by a good aulos-player or an inferior aulos-girl, HARMONY: *KRASIS* WITH DIVINE a possession that reveals who needs the gods and initiation rites, since the music is divine. But you differ from him only so far as, without instruments, you do this same thing using bare speech (*psilois logois*) 1/8. DISCUSSION OF MUSIC ENDS When we, anyway, hear another speaking (even other speeches of [215d] a very good speaker), it matters in a word not at all to anyone. But when anyone hears you or another delivering some of your speeches, even if the speaker is quite inferior, and whether a woman hears or a man or 2/8 a youth, we are amazed and possessed. I, at any rate, gentlemen, were I not at risk of seeming wholly drunk, would have told you on oath how I myself was affected by his speeches and still am now affected. [215e] When I hear him, my heart rate jumps and tears flow 3/8 under the effect of his speeches, much more than with the Corybantes, and I see very many others affected in the same way. When I heard Pericles and other good speakers, I thought they spoke well, but was not affected in such a way: neither was my soul disturbed nor was it irritated at being rendered so slavish.

Note 10.0, dissonant (215c2)

The very dissonant tenth note is clearly marked by a discussion of music, which starts an octad before the note and concludes an octad after the note.

This passage is harmonious in the sense that it is an explicit discussion of music, but is negative and therefore dissonant in several respects. First, Socrates is compared to an ugly satyr (perhaps with an implicit threat, since Marsyas was horribly killed). Second, aulos playing was thought vulgar in certain circles.[24] Third, although there is talk of divine inspiration here, the dialogues treat artistic inspiration with some suspicion (cf. the *Ion*), perhaps because it is unknowing and passive.

Prose speech, that is, words stripped of the metre and rhyme of poetry, is here identified with a kind of music played without instruments. This is again important for the theory of the symbolic scheme. References to harmony or agreement in language are therefore allusions to a kind of harmony analogous to musical harmony, and serve to mark musical notes.

"But, indeed, I was often so disposed by `4/8` this Marsyas here, so much so that it seemed [216a] the life I have was no more a life worth having. And this, Socrates, you will not tell me is not true. And I myself am still now well aware that, if I wished to lend him my ears, I could not withstand him and would be affected in the same way. He compels me to agree `5/8` that, although being in much need, I still neglect myself but practice [instead the political affairs] of the Athenians. Closing my ears with force, as from the Sirens, I run away, fleeing, so that I will not grow old sitting next to him. [216b] And I have been so affected in my relation with this human being alone that I feel what one might not think was in me: shame before anyone. `6/8` I feel shame before him alone. I am aware I am not capable of arguing against him that I need not do what he bids, but after I go away, I'm defeated by the honours of the many.

"So I desert him and flee and, [216c] when I see him, I am ashamed at what we've agreed. `DISHARMONY: SHAME AT BREAKING AGREEMENTS` `7/8` Often I would take pleasure in envisaging him no longer existing among humans, but if this were in turn to happen, I well know that I would feel a much greater distress. `DISHARMONY: PLEASURE AND PAIN` Thus I have no way of dealing with this man.

"So both I and many others have been affected in this way by the piping of this satyr here. `DISHARMONY: SATYR'S PIPING MUSIC` But you will hear from me how `NOTE 10.1 = 216c6` `DISSONANT` similar he is to those images I likened him to and how astonishing his power is. Know well that none of you knows him. [216d] But I will reveal him, since I've begun already. Observe that Socrates is erotically inclined toward handsome youths and is always around and bowled over by them and, moreover, that he is ignorant of everything `1/8` and knows nothing.

"As for his figure, isn't this the very form of a `SIX-SEVENTHS` silenus? Extremely. This was thrown around him, liked that carved silenus. Once opened up, how much do you think, symposiasts, the insides are full of temperateness? Know that it matters nothing to him whether someone is handsome `2/8` (rather, he despises [216e] this so much more than anyone could imagine) or if he's wealthy or if he has some other honour celebrated by the multitudes. He judges that all these possessions are worth nothing and that we are nothing – so I say to you. He spends his whole life being ironical in his way and making fun of people. `3/8` But when he's serious and he's opened up ... I don't know if someone has seen the statue inside. But I saw it straightaway once, and to me it seemed to be so [217a] golden and divine and splendid and wonderful that, in brief, whatever Socrates might urge had to be done.

Note 10.1, dissonant (216c6)

This dissonant note is marked by an explicit reference to music, and is preceded and followed by negative statements. There are two kinds of disharmony. Alcibiades says he is ashamed to have broken his agreements with Socrates. Moreover, he speaks of feeling a combination of pleasure and pain at the thought of Socrates' demise (more implied threat). These together, with the comparison to a satyr and his "piping", mark this dissonant note.

Six-sevenths (216d4)

This is another mixture without blending. Socrates is like Silenus but the satyr's negative qualities are external and do not contaminate his inner beauty. Socrates is outwardly "enraptured" by his erotic attraction to handsome youths, Alcibiades says, but inwardly calm or sober. Opening the statue to find the pure Socrates inside is, again, a kind of separation without taint (as Orpheus left Hades still alive, and Socrates left the theatre still wise).

STORY OF SEDUCTION BEGINS HALFWAY BETWEEN NOTES "Thinking that he was keen about my youthful bloom, 4/8 ... and I thought this was a windfall (*hermaion*) and wonderful good luck for me, since it was possible for me, by gratifying Socrates, to hear everything that he knew. I thought my youthful bloom was so wonderful. Although before it was not customary to be alone with him without an attendant, pondering this, 5/8 [217b] I then started sending away the attendant so we could be alone together – I must tell you the whole truth. So pay attention and, if I lie, Socrates, refute me. We were indeed together, gentlemen, one on one, and I thought he would straightaway converse with me as a lover converses with his boyfriend in private, and I was glad. 6/8 But nothing at all came of this. Rather, as his custom, after speaking with me and spending the day together, he'd be off and away. After this, I would invite him to exercise with me [217c] and I did exercise together with him, aiming to get something here. So he would exercise with me and he often wrestled me when no one was present. 7/8 And what can I say? I got nothing more. As I was accomplishing nothing at all in this way, it seemed to me that I must set upon the man with all my strength and not give up. DISHARMONY: REJECTION, ATTACK Since I had indeed started it, I had to know right away what the trouble was. I invited him to dine together, really [217d] like a NOTE 10.2 = 217c8 DISSONANT lover with designs on a boyfriend.

DISHARMONY: YOUNG BELOVED PURSUING OLDER LOVER "And he did not quickly heed this but nevertheless after some time acceded. DISHARMONY: GRUDGING AGREEMENT When he arrived the first time, he wished to leave as soon as we'd dined. And that time, as I was ashamed, DISHARMONY: REJECTION, SHAME I let him go. Another time, as I planned, after we dined, I conversed endlessly far into the night, and when he wanted to go 1/8 I pretended it was too late and made him stay. So, he was resting on the couch on which he had dined, next to mine, and nobody else except us was sleeping in the room. [217e] Up to here, then, my speech could properly be told to anyone. 2/8 You would not have heard me telling the sequel were it not, first, for the saying 'in wine – with or without slaves present – lies truth', and since it appears to me an injustice to allow Socrates' magnificent deed (*ergon*) to be forgotten once I've embarked on his praise. Moreover, I too have the condition of someone bitten by a snake. Indeed, they say someone in this condition does not wish [218a] to say how it was 3/8 except to those who have been bitten, as they alone understand and excuse it if he dared to do and say anything at all because of the pain.

Note 10.2, dissonant (217c8)

This note is marked by the harmony of erotic relationships, of "a lover scheming to ensnare his favourite", and the return of the theme of agreeing to an invitation (as at the frame's notes). On the other hand, it is negative and therefore dissonant because a youth is affronting Athenian custom by pursuing an older lover, because the invitation is accepted after some delay, and because the behaviour is shameful. The passage begins with rejection and ends with shame.

"I've been bitten by something more painful and in the most painful place where someone could be bitten – the heart or indeed the soul or whatever one must name it 4/8 – since I've been struck and bitten by speeches in philosophy, which get a grip more savagely than a snake when they take hold of a young, not ungifted soul, and make him do and say anything ... and seeing, moreover, those like Phaedrus, Agathon, Eryximachus, [218b] Pausanias, Aristophanes and Aristodemus ... and why do I need to say 5/8 Socrates himself, and all the rest? All of you have shared in common the mania and frenzy (*bakcheias*) 8/9 of philosophy – that's why all of you will listen. You will excuse what was then done and what is now said. You slaves (and if anyone else is profane and crude) set very big gates 6/8 upon your ears.

"So, then, gentlemen, when the lamp had been put out [218c] and the slaves were outside, it seemed to me that I must do nothing complicated toward Socrates, but freely say how things appeared to me. And, having given him a nudge, I said, 'Socrates, are you asleep?'"

"No, not at all," said he.

"Do you know what I've decided?"

"What could it be?" he said.

"You seem to me," I said, "to have been my only 7/8 worthy lover, and you appear to me shy about mentioning it to me. But I feel this way. I think it is very senseless not to gratify you in this and in anything else you need, either [218d] my property or my friends'. DISHARMONY: CLUMSY OFFER OF SEX For me, there is nothing more venerable NOTE 10.3 = 218d2 DISSONANT than that I become as good as possible, HARMONY: BECOMING GOOD, PARTNERSHIP and for this I think there is no more powerful partner for me than you. I indeed would feel much more shame before the thoughtful at not gratifying such a man, than I would feel before the unthoughtful many for gratifying him."

DISHARMONY: SOPHISTRY JUSTIFIES SEX

And he, after hearing this, replied quite ironically 1/8 and very much in his own, habitual way: "My dear Alcibiades, you're probably really no fool (*phaulos*), if it happens that what you say about me is true [218e] and there is in me a certain power through which you might become better. You must be seeing, I think, 2/8 an indescribable beauty in me and entirely different from your comely shape. If, beholding that, you attempt to start a partnership with me and exchange beauty for beauty, you intend to cheat me out of not a little. You're attempting to get true beauties instead of apparent ones [219a] and really mean to exchange 'gold for bronze'. But, fortunate fellow, 3/8 consider better lest you fail to notice that I am no such thing. Indeed, the mind's sight begins to see sharply when that of the eyes sets about fading from its peak. And you are far from that."

And I, hearing that, said "Well, that's the way it is with me, for I said nothing other than what I think.

Note 10.3, dissonant (218d2)

This passage combines strong harmonic and disharmonic elements, but the negative predominates. It describes an awful and clumsy moment when the most handsome young man in Athens offers to have sex in exchange for moral improvement. Alcibiades thereby puts into practice the sophistic philosophy advocated by Pausanias. More positively, the young Alcibiades at least has honourable aims, in wishing to "become good", and recognizes Socrates' worth as his teacher.

Narrative structure reflects musical structure: This and the next notes are the dramatic highlights – or lows – of the attempted seduction. Alcibiades' invitation to have sex occurs at this quarternote, but Socrates' rejection is not finally confirmed until the next, very dissonant note.

"You yourself must determine what you think is best for you 4/8 and me."

"Well," he said, "that's well spoken. In the time to come, [219b] we will determine to do what appears to the two of us (*nōn*) best about these and the other things."

After hearing and saying all that and, as it were, having shot my arrows, I thought I had wounded him. So, I stood up, not trusting this fellow to say anything more, and 5/8 wrapped my own cloak around him – for it was winter – and lay down under his short cloak (*tribōna*), while [219c] encircling this astonishing and truly spirited (*daimoniō*) fellow with my hands, and lay there the whole night. And not this either, Socrates, will you say is a lie.

Then, after I'd done that, 6/8 he was so superior to and so looked down on and so mocked my youthful bloom – and was so arrogant (*hubrisen*). DISHARMONY: CONTEMPT, HUBRIS And I had thought that my youthful bloom was really something, gentlemen of the jury. You are indeed judges of Socrates' contempt. DISHARMONY: REJECTION Know well, by the gods and goddesses, 7/8 that having slept soundly with Socrates [219d] nothing more odd (*perittoteron*) happened than if I'd slept with my father or older brother.

DISHARMONY: REJECTION After this, what frame of mind do you think I was in, believing that I'd been dishonoured, DISHARMONY: DISHONOUR but admiring this fellow's nature, temperateness, and courage, since I'd met a sort of man which, for his NOTE 11.0 = 219d6 DISSONANT wisdom (*phronēsin*) and strength, HARMONY: SOCRATES' VIRTUES I had not thought I would ever meet? Thus I felt I neither had grounds for becoming angry DISHARMONY: ANGER and withdrawing from my relationship (*sunousias*) with him, nor had I the means for [219e] winning him over. I well knew that he was much less vulnerable to money in every way than Ajax was to iron swords; and he'd fled from the only thing by which I thought he'd be seduced. 1/8 I was indeed in distress (*ēporoun*), and I went around DISHARMONY: REJECTION, APORIA enslaved to this human as no one has been to anybody else.

TOPIC SHIFT AFTER NOTE All these things had happened to me previously, and on top of that there was for us a shared campaign to Potidaea and we had meals with each other. He was, first, not only superior to me 2/8 when it came to hardships, but to all the others – when we were [220a] forcibly cut off somewhere without food, as happens on campaigns, the others were nothing compared to his endurance. And again, in the good times he alone enjoyed them completely. Although he didn't particularly want to drink, he beat everyone when he was forced to; and what was most astonishing of all 3/8 was that no one among men has ever seen Socrates drunk. Of this, it seems to me, there will straightaway be a test. Moreover, as for the resistance to winter – [220b] the winters there are terrible –

Note 11.0, dissonant (219d6)

The eleventh is the most dissonant wholenote in the scale of twelve notes. Accordingly, this is an extremely negative or disharmonic passage. It describes Socrates' rejection of Alcibiades' invitation and the consequent emotional turmoil: dishonour, contempt, *aporia*, subjugation and anger. Nonetheless, the note itself affirms Socrates' wisdom and virtues, and the relationship, that is, the erotic harmony or *sunousia*, is maintained.

Narrative structure reflects musical structure: After note 10.1, Alcibiades announces he will reveal the true Socrates and begins telling the story of his attempted seduction. Alcibiades is first rejected at 10.2, clumsily offers himself again at 10.3, and only here at 11.0 recounts his ultimate rejection. Major incidents in the narrative of the *Symposium* are lodged at musically significant locations.

Alcibiades changes the topic after the note. He has recounted the attempt to seduce Socrates for the last three quarter-intervals. Now Alcibiades turns to a description of war (disharmony) and Socrates' exploits (harmony).

he produced wondrous things, and once when there was a most terrible frost, and everyone either did 4/8 not go outside or, if someone did, they dressing up in clothes to an amazing degree, both wearing sandals and wrapping their feet in felt and sheepskin, but he went out among them wearing a cloak of the sort he usually wore before, he went barefoot through the snow and ice 5/8 more easily than the rest who were shod, and the soldiers looked angrily at him as though he despised them. [220c] And that is that. "But what a further feat the strong man dared and did" once there on campaign is worth hearing. Thinking, he was standing at dawn at a spot, investigating something, 6/8 and since he made no progress on it, would not give up and stood there searching. It was already the middle of the day, and the men were noticing him; amazed, one said to another that Socrates had stood there from dawn pondering something. Finally, then, since it was becoming evening, after some of the Ionians had dined [220d] – it was summer then – they brought out their bedding 7/8 and both slept in the cold and kept a watch on him in case he were to stand through the night. He stood until it became dawn and the sun rose. Thereupon he went away making his prayers to the sun.

And if you wish in the battles too. DISHARMONY: BATTLE It is just to render him his justice. HARMONY: JUSTICE When, indeed, that battle was – in which the generals gave me NOTE 11.1 = 220d6 DISSONANT the prize for courage – DISHARMONY: FRAUD, LIES [220e] none other among humans saved me than he.

HARMONY: SAVING A LIFE, EROTIC BOND Although I was wounded, DISHARMONY: BATTLE he did not want to abandon me and managed to save both me myself and my armor.

And I, Socrates, even then urged the generals to give you the prize for courage, and on this you will neither criticize me or 1/8 argue that I lie. The generals, however, were looking to my status (*axioma*) and wishing to give me the prize, and you became more eager than they that I take it rather than yourself. Moreover, gentlemen, [221a] it was worthwhile to see Socrates when the army retreated from Delium 2/8 and fled. I happened to be there with a horse, while he had [a foot-soldier's] weapons. The men were already scattered and he retreated together with Laches. I happened to be about and, as soon as I saw them, exhorted them both to take heart and said that I would not leave the two of them. There I observed Socrates 3/8 even more finely (*kallion*) than at Potidaea. I was less in fear since I was on a horse. First, how superior he was to Laches in self-possession! [221b] Then, it seemed to me, even there he passed along just as here [in Athens], "swaggering and looking from side to side" (this is your [line], Aristophanes),

Note 11.1, dissonant (220d6)

This is still a disharmonic range. A narrative about an extreme kind of disharmony, war and battle, is mixed with praise of Socrates. Like many of the quarternotes that follow a wholenote, this is disharmonic. At the note, Alcibiades is fraudulently awarded a prize for courage. Socrates does courageously save him, and so preserves their erotic relation. The disharmonic elements dominate the harmonic elements of the passage.

calmly scrutinizing 4/8 both friends and enemies, so that it was clear to all, even from quite afar, that if anyone touched this man, he would very robustly defend himself. On this account, both he and his companion got away safely. For the most part, those behaving so in war [221c] are not touched, while those in headlong flight are pursued. 5/8

There are many other things, then, that someone might have to praise Socrates for, and amazing things. However, in regard to his other pursuits, probably someone would say such things about another, but that he is similar to none among humans, not among those of ancient times nor of present times, this most of all is worthy of astonishment. For such as 6/8 Achilles was, one could compare Brasidas and others, and again such as Pericles was, one could compare [221d] Nestor and Antenor – and there are more – and yet others one could compare in this way. But such as this fellow, this strange man, has become, both himself and his speeches, even if one seeks, one would not come close to finding, 7/8 not among those of present times nor among those of ancient times, except and unless one would compare him to those I described: not to a human, but to satyrs and sileni, DISHARMONY: UGLY SATYR, PIPING both he and his speeches.

And so, indeed, I also left this out at the beginning: that even his speeches are extremely similar to [those statues of] sileni [221e] NOTE 11.2 = 221d8 DISSONANT that are opened up.

DISHARMONY: SOCRATES LIKE SATYR If one wishes to listen to Socrates' speeches, they would appear quite ridiculous DISHARMONY: CRITICISM at first: such names and phrases are put around the outside, like the hide of some arrogant (*hubristou*) satyr. DISHARMONY: HUBRIS He talks of pack-asses and some blacksmiths and cobblers and tanners, 1/8 and always appears by means of the same to talk of the same things, DISHARMONY: CRITICISM [222a] so that every inexperienced and senseless human would laugh at his speeches. When someone sees them opened up and enters into them, he will find at first that only these among all speeches have sense (*noun*) inside them and then that they are most divine, 2/8 and have very great statues of virtue in them, and extend over the greatest range – or rather to all, in so far as it belongs to the inquiries of someone intent on becoming good and great (*kalō kagathō*).

That is, gentlemen, what I praise Socrates for. And, moreover, mixed in together, I've told you what I criticize, his arrogance (*hubrisen*) toward me. [222b] He didn't do these things to me alone. 3/8 Rather, he deceives, as if he were a lover, Charmides, son of Glaucon, Euthydemus, son of Diocles, and very many others, and sets himself up more as the boyfriend instead of the lover.

Note 11.2, dissonant (221d8)

A negative discussion of Socrates' speeches is located at the note, and praise of their inner content follows after the first octad. The comparison to the Silenuses and satyrs recalls the discussion of their pipe playing and is therefore both musical and disharmonic.

After the note, Alcibiades issues a pointed invitation to look for the underlying meaning of Socrates' speeches, for something lying beneath the words and phrases of the surface narrative. Such references to allegorical interpretation are not uncommon in the dialogues.

THE MUSICAL STRUCTURE OF PLATO'S DIALOGUES

What I say to you, Agathon, is not to be deceived by this fellow but take care 4/8 being aware of our experiences. As in the proverb, don't like a fool be wise only after suffering. END OF SPEECH HALFWAY BETWEEN NOTES [222c]

After Alcibiades said that, there was laughter at his frankness, since he seemed still erotically inclined toward Socrates. Then Socrates said, "You look sober, Alcibiades. You would not ever, enclosing yourself 5/8 all around (*kuklō*) so cleverly, have undertaken to hide that for the sake of which you have said all this, and put it at the end, speaking as if in an aside, as if you have not spoken all for the sake of this: [222d] to set Agathon and I at odds, thinking I must love you and none other, and that Agathon must be loved by you 6/8 and not by anyone else. But you've not escaped notice: your drama of satyrs and sileni became obvious. So, my dear Agathon, don't let him gain anything by it. Arrange things so that nothing sets you and me at odds." [222e]

Then Agathon said, "Socrates, you probably speak the truth. 7/8 I see another sign: that he reclined in the middle between you and me, so he might separate us apart. DISHARMONY: THREAT TO EROS There will be nothing more for him! I will come and recline next to you." DISHARMONY: SPURNING A LOVER, CHANGING ORDER

"Quite so," said Socrates, "recline here, down from me."

"O Zeus," said Alcibiades, "how much do I suffer from this man! DISHARMONY: JEALOUS SQUABBLING You think it necessary to be superior NOTE 11.3 = 222e7 DISSONANT in everything. DISHARMONY: HUBRIS But, if nothing else, you marvellous man, HARMONY: EROS, PRAISE OF SOCRATES let Agathon settle down in the middle of us."

"But that's impossible", DISHARMONY: DISAGREE said Socrates. "For you have praised me, and I must praise in turn who's to my right. HARMONY: RESTORE SPEAKING ORDER If Agathon reclines down from you, won't he praise me again, instead of being praised, 1/8 rather, by me? So, let it be, you devil (*daimonie*), and [223a] don't begrudge this blessed fellow being praised by me. I do indeed very much desire to praise him."

"Alas," said Agathon, "Alcibiades, there's no way I could remain here. By all means I'll switch places, so I might be praised by Socrates."

2/8 "There we go again!" said Alcibiades, "The usual thing. With Socrates present, it's impossible for another to get a share of the handsome ones. And now how resourcefully he's found again a persuasive argument, so that this one will sit down next to himself."

[223b] Agathon was standing up to sit down next to Socrates when suddenly a multitude (*pampollous*) of revellers came 3/8 to the doors. Finding they'd been opened when someone was exiting, REVELLERS ENTER they walked straight on in to them and reclined.

Note 11.3, dissonant (222e7)

This passage is an artful jumble. There is talk of motion, jealousy and squabbling, but also good-humoured joking about the love triangle. Disharmony predominates. The banter includes threats to relationships and to the order of speaking. Harmonic elements, however, are still present. Socrates jocularly tries to restore harmony, various professions of love are made, and there is again praise of Socrates at the note.

There is much talk of disordered motion here, but none seems to occur until just before the revellers burst into the gathering (at 3/8).

Narrative structure reflects musical structure: Alcibiades' speech ends halfway between the quarternotes.

Everything was full of confusion and, no longer in order (*en kosmō*), everyone was compelled to drink a lot (*pampolun*) of wine. ORDER BREAKS UP AT THE HALFNOTE

Eryximachus, 4/8 Phaedrus, and some others, said Aristodemus, went away, [223c] and he took some sleep. He slept soundly for very much (*panu polu*) time, since the nights were long, and awoke towards day when the cocks were already singing. Once he was awake, he saw the others were sleeping or had gone. Only Agathon, Aristodemus 5/8 and Socrates were still awake and drinking from a large cup [which they passed] to the right. HARMONY: SOME ORDER OR HARMONY REMAINS Socrates was conversing with them. Aristodemus, he said, did not remember the rest of the conversation [223d] (he was not present from the beginning and kept nodding off), but the gist of it, he said, was that 6/8 Socrates was compelling the others to agree HARMONY: SPEECH, AGREEMENT that it is for the same man to know how to create comedy and tragedy, and to be by his art (*technē*) a tragic poet and a comic poet. HARMONY: FUSING OPPOSITES As they were being compelled to [accept] them, HARMONY: PERSUASION, AGREEMENT they were not following very much and nodding off. Aristophanes fell to sleep first and soon thereafter, as it was 7/8 becoming day, so did Agathon. Then Socrates, once he'd tucked them in, HARMONY: FRIENDSHIP stood up to go and Aristodemus followed as usual. Socrates went to the Lyceum, APOLLO (PYTHAGOREAN DEITY) washed himself off, and spent (*diatribein*) the rest of the day as at other times. And having so spent it (*diatripsanta*), HARMONY: REPEATS WORD FOR *KRASIS* towards evening, he rested at home. HARMONY: RETURN HOME, COMPLETE CIRCLE NOTE 12.0 = 223d12 CONSONANT

Note 12.0, consonant (223d12)

In music theory, as the twelfth note of the scale is approached, the notes become very dissonant. However, the region that is very close to and increasingly indistinguishable from the twelfth again becomes consonant. Accordingly, midway through the final quarter-interval (4/8) here, the revellers disrupt the series of speeches. They end the moderate drinking, trigger motion into and out of the andron, and create an "uproar", a tumultuous outburst of sound. Extreme disorder marks this dissonant midpoint. The interval that follows is dominated by friendship and a sense of peaceful completion.

At the very end, in the early hours of the morning, Socrates is still trying to preserve the "left to right" order or harmony of the speeches, at least with Agathon and Aristophanes, and still trying to reach agreements. Socrates is a force for harmony.

The sun rises and Socrates visits a shrine dedicated to Apollo. Both the sun and Apollo, the god of music, were sacred to the Pythagoreans. The last lines twice repeat the verb *diatribein*, which can also mean the kind of mixing that produces a *krasis*: a final, emphatic reference to harmony.

There is also here the motion and the cessation of motion that marks notes early in the dialogue: Socrates leaves the party and then stops at home. The dialogue therefore follows Socrates through an entire night. His return home completes the circle: the dialogue began with Apollodorus ("gift of Apollo") leaving his home. When the narrator says "Aristodemus followed as usual", there is a final shift of narrative level back to the topmost level of the opening frame.

The dialogue ends quietly, without reference to music or noise or conversation. This is surprising when compared to the applause and rhetorical fireworks that marked the consonant note at the midpoint of the dialogue. There may be two, related reasons for this. First, here, at the twelfth note, the "harmony" between two different notes may be said to have become an ideal unity. When a twelfth note is sounded in unison with another twelfth note, a single note is heard. In this case, the highest form of harmony is not "fitting together two different things" but unalloyed identity. But this would be quiet in the sense that no blending or "harmonization" is heard. Second, the concluding twelfth note may be quiet because, for the Pythagoreans, "silence is golden" (Burkert 1972: 178ff., 199).

CHAPTER 6
Parallel structure in the *Euthyphro*

6.1 The same scale and the same symbolic scheme

The *Euthyphro* is shorter and the passages marking the musical notes are more succinctly marked, but they suffice to show that this dialogue has the same twelve-note scale as the *Symposium*. Here too, the wholenotes and quarternotes are marked with different species of a single genus of concepts, and this regular pattern of concepts forms the underlying scale.

In the *Symposium*, the notes were marked by species of harmony. Here, they are marked by various species of *assertions of higher knowledge*. As Socrates says, Euthyphro "strongly asserted he clearly knows" the nature of piety (*saphōs eidenai diischurizou*, 5c8–9). This genus is not *prima facie* related to music, but a later section will argue for a surprising connection.

A survey of the notes shows that, in Euthyphro's assertions, this genus especially comprehends his supposed knowledge of the gods, the Good and wisdom. Socrates' higher knowledge tends to be limited to the human sphere. He will mark notes with assertions about, for example, human religious beliefs, but will ascend only as high as knowledge of the forms or of his mythical ancestor Daedalus. Euthyphro's epistemic assertions are other-worldly; Socrates' are this-worldly.

The genus of "assertions of higher knowledge" comprehends passages that include:

- assertions of knowledge about the gods or holiness (especially definitions of holiness);
- references to legal charges or prosecutions that depend on assertions of knowledge about the gods, holiness or the good (whether explicit or implicit);
- assertions of knowledge about piety, reverence and human religious practice;

- assertions of knowledge about technical arts (*technai*) or science (*epistemē*) or reason (*logismos*);
- assertions concerning wisdom (*sophia, nous, phronēsis*), the good (*agathos* and cognates) or divine inspiration (e.g. *mania*);
- references to teaching higher knowledge (a kind of asserting or professing).

The *Symposium* explicitly discussed the theory of its marking passages, especially in Eryximachus' theory of harmony. This dialogue too is careful to make the connections between its markers explicit, effectively supplying the clues needed to detect its musical pattern. For example, reiterations of legal charges frequently mark notes, and their connection to assertions of higher knowledge is a theme of the dialogue. At a note near the end of the dialogue, for example, Socrates says:

> If you had not clearly known (*ei gar mē ēdēstha saphōs*) the nature of piety and impiety, I am confident that you would never, on behalf of a serf, have charged your aged father with murder. NOTE 11.3 You would not have run such a risk of doing wrong in the sight of the gods, and you would have had too much respect for the opinions of men. I know well, [15e] therefore, that you think you clearly know (*hoti saphōs oiei eidenai*) the nature of piety and impiety.

This note is doubly marked. Socrates twice says that Euthyphro's legal charge is an implicit assertion of higher knowledge, namely, knowledge of impiety and the gods. Moreover, Socrates makes a typically this-worldly claim: he "knows" that Euthyphro thinks he knows about impiety. These two knowledge claims, Euthyphro's charge and Socrates' assertion about Euthyphro's religious beliefs, emphatically mark this note while they give, at the same time, part of the general theory of the marking passages.

6.2 Guide to the strongest evidence

As in the *Symposium,* the evidence consists of a large number of coincidences between significant passages and the notes of the underlying musical scale, as well as a correlation between their content and the relative consonance of the notes. Although the evidence is concisely summarized here, it makes a strong case for the musical structure of the *Euthyphro.*

Legal charges involving impiety and spiritual pollution are, as mentioned above, clear instances of assertions of higher knowledge. In the *Euthyphro*, these are carefully coordinated with musical notes. The charges against Socrates fall at notes (0.3, 2.3, etc.), and Euthyphro's surprising disclosure that he is charging his father with murder falls at another location of a musical note (1.2).

The very consonant third and fourth notes are marked with positive ideas. At the third, Euthyphro asserts his initial definition of holiness. At the fourth, Socrates expounds the theory of Forms, explaining he is asking for the "one idea" that makes many instances of holiness holy.

In the second half of the dialogue, the very consonant eighth and ninth notes are similarly marked with positive ideas. At the eighth, Socrates asserts descent from Daedalus, a human who approached the realm of the gods (see commentary). At the ninth, Socrates for the first time asserts his own definition of holiness: that it is a species of that cardinal Platonic virtue, justice.

Reversing this correlation between positive content and consonant notes, the more dissonant notes are, as will be expected now, marked with negative passages. The dissonant fifth and seventh notes are the conclusions of important elenchi of Euthyphro's positions. At the tenth, sacred relations between humans and gods are compared to mere technical arts such as house-building. The dialogue reaches its low point at the very dissonant eleventh note, where Euthyphro affirms that holiness is a kind of economic barter or trade with the gods.

The quarternotes also repeat the patterns seen in the *Symposium*. For example, those near discordant wholenotes are also markedly negative. Thus the quarternotes 5.1, 5.2 and 5.3, which are near the dissonant fifth wholenote are marked by strings of negations, privatives and words like "other", "difference" and "disputation".

As in the *Symposium*, there is evidence that finer divisions between the quarternotes are also marked. Significant, positive concepts, for example, are often lodged at the midpoint between quarternotes (i.e. at the fourth octad).

6.3 The sevenths

In the *Symposium*, the sevenths were marked by mechanical mixture, that is, by opposites that did not blend into a harmony. In the *Euthyphro*, they are marked by various kinds of failures to assert: by disjunctions, ignorance, disagreements or differences. These passages tend to be marked with negations or "otherness".

Since the passages are brief, three can be briefly analysed here. The passage at the first seventh contains a disjunction,[1] "it could be this or that", but no definite endorsement of either possibility is made: "The real question is whether the murdered man has been justly slain. If justly, then your duty is to let the matter alone; but if unjustly, ONE-SEVENTH proceed against him" (4b8–10).

The second seventh is marked by a reference to Socratic ignorance. Socrates says he knows nothing, and therefore perhaps asserts that he asserts nothing. This kind of negative confusion is appropriate to a dissonant seventh: "But, as you also know these things, and are a good knower, necessarily, then, as it seems, we must concede them too. What will we say, those of us who agree TWO-SEVENTHS we know nothing (*mēden eidenai*) about them?" (6a10–b3). The next seventh is marked by a list of opposite assertions or disagreements, unblended opposites, which collectively fail to assert any one thing, and is punctuated by a string of negatives:

> And therefore, Euthyphro, in thus chastising your father you may very likely be doing what is THREE-SEVENTHS loved by Zeus but hated by Cronos or Uranus, and what is dear to Hephaestus but hated by Hera, and there may be other gods who differ one from the other (*heteros heterōdiapheretai*) about this. (8b1–5)

In sum, the sevenths are clearly contrasted with the major notes in the scale. They are not merely marked by disharmonious or negative assertions, but by the absence of assertion or the co-location of unreconciled and so unblended opposite assertions.[2]

6.4 The connection to music

The major notes in the *Euthyphro*'s musical scale are marked with assertions of higher knowledge. The dissonant sevenths are marked with various failures to assert. Although the evidence for this pattern is clear, its rationale is not. To understand the connection of these epistemological or logical categories to music, a brief excursion into ancient logic is necessary.

The argument below has three steps. It begins with a brief exposition of certain ideas in Aristotle's logic, because his programme is relatively clear. It then uses these ideas to interpret a more complicated passage in Plato's *Sophist*. This leads, finally, to an explicit connection between logic and music. The aim here is not to give a complete analysis of these doctrines, but merely to establish that certain ideas were explicitly associated, and that this association is the basis for the musical symbolism in the *Euthyphro*.

The opening chapters of Aristotle's *De Interpretatione* lay the foundations for his logic. Among all sentences (*logoi*), some are "assertions" (*apophaniseis*: "declarations", "propositions", etc.), which will be either true or false, while other sentences are mere expostulations or poetry and make no definite truth claims. Assertions may be affirmations or negations. An affirmation is true, for example, when it rightly asserts that a predicate belongs to or inheres in a subject.

Strikingly, Aristotle conceptualizes the relation between predicate and subject as a kind of synthesis.[3] For example, he says: "Truth and falsity are about synthesis and division (*sunthesis kai diairesin*)" (16a12013); "[The various forms of the copula] are nothing in themselves, but indicate a certain synthesis, which is not to be conceived without the things it conjoins" (16b23–5). That is, when a predicate and its subject are really combined or "synthesized", the corresponding affirmative assertion is true; when they are separated or "divided", the assertion is false. The *Categories* uses slightly different terminology to express the same idea:

"Uncombined terms ... in and of themselves make no affirmation, only in combination with each other (*sumplokē*) do affirmation and negation arise" (1b25); "Terms without combination, such as 'man', 'white', 'runs' or 'wins', are neither true nor false" (2a4–10).

The synthesis or combination that is asserted involves a kind of unity: "A single assertion refers to one thing or something which is one by being bound together (*ho sundesmō heis*)" (17a15–16, cf. 19b5ff.).

Aside from the synthesis of predicate and subject, Aristotle's logic speaks of a second kind of synthesis, which will also appear in the *Sophist*: "In some cases, the predicates are synthesized (*suntithemena*) into one, entire predicate resulting from the separate predicates" (20b31–2).

In short, he says that predicates which are merely accidentally co-located in the same subject do not coalesce into a single, synthesized predicate, while essential predicates do. Thus Aristotle's theory of assertions involves various kinds of synthesis and combination, which produce some sort of fused unity.[4]

Plato's discussion of predication in the *Sophist* is sufficient to establish the points needed here, even though it is part of the dialogue's broader and more complicated argument. The Stranger recalls that the puzzle about how one thing can remain one and yet have many predicates has led to disputes. These arise when any sort of assertion is made: "We say '*a* man', while somehow attributing to him *many* named features," he says, "like shape, size, viciousness, and virtuousness" (251a8–10). A middle position is endorsed, according to which some predicates combine and some do not, and is described in language reminiscent of Aristotle's: "And indeed, those who sometimes combine or synthesize (*ksuntitheasi*) everything, and divide (*diairousin*) everything at other times, ... they would be saying nothing if there were no combining together (*ksummiksis*)" (252b1–6). As other passages also show, the Stranger here clearly supposes, as Aristotle did, that predication involves the synthesis and division of terms.

The Stranger proceeds to say that there will be a science of such syntheses and divisions, but introduces the syntheses that occur in logical assertions by way of analogies to grammar and music:

> Indeed, some things will [combine together] and some will not – just as letters of the alphabet would be combined. For some of these fit together or harmonize (*ksun-armottei*) [in syllables] with each other, and some do not so harmonize ...
>
> And is it not the same with high and low sounds? Isn't someone who has the technical art, which recognizes which commingle and which do not, musical, and isn't someone who does not know this unmusical?
>
> (252e9–253b4)

The Stranger finally declares that the general science of synthesis and division is dialectics. This makes the important, Platonic science of dialectics a science of harmony and disharmony (253b9–d3).

Several important points emerge from this brief detour into logic and predication theory.

The *Symposium* marked its notes with species of the genus of synthesis and harmony. The use of "harmony" as a symbol for a musical note is natural enough. It may at first have seemed odd that the *Euthyphro* marked its notes with species of "assertions". However, it is now clear that both Aristotle and Plato think of assertion as involving a kind of synthesis, namely that of predicate with subject or of predicate with predicate. In classical theories of combination and blending, however, this "synthesis" is just a synonym for "harmonization" and "*krasis*" (see Ch. 2). Thus there is a surprising similarity between the marking passages in both dialogues.

Moreover, the *Sophist* explicitly says that the kind of synthesis involved in assertion is analogous to the harmonization of sounds in music. Assertion so conceived could also, therefore, naturally serve as a symbol for musical notes.

In sum, the pieces of the puzzle fit together nicely here. The concept abstracted from a survey of the *Euthyphro*'s musical scale, "assertions of higher knowledge", at first seemed remote from the *Symposium*'s symbolic scheme, but now turns out to be just another kind of synthesis or harmony. Moreover, the *Sophist* explicitly makes the link between synthesis in assertions and harmonization in music. This mutually corroborating evidence reinforces the general claim that the same symbolic scheme is used throughout Plato's dialogues.

6.5 Another kind of evidence: parallels between dialogues

Plato's dialogues are distinguished from one another in many ways: by their subjects, their characters, their locations and their styles. Nonetheless, when read side by side there are a remarkable number of parallels between passages at the same relative locations, especially at the more harmonic or disharmonic notes. As was shown in earlier chapters, the network of parallels between the dialogues is a rich, untapped source of evidence for the dialogues' symbolic content. This section introduces a number of structural parallels between the narratives of the *Symposium* and the *Euthyphro*, and the commentary in the next section highlights many more.[5] The aim here is merely to establish the presence of these parallels, and thus to adduce another kind of evidence for the underlying stichometric structure.

It was mentioned, for example, in Chapter 3 that the topic and the procedure for the dialogues were often established at notes 1.0 and 1.1. At note 1.1 in the *Symposium*, Agathon's guests agreed to spend the evening making speeches.

Here, at note 1.1 in the *Euthyphro*, Socrates notes in passing his willingness, rooted in his "philanthropy", to talk to anyone who will listen. That is, he in effect explains why he would have a long, abstract discussion with someone he encounters on the street, just as he does in this dialogue. Although the *Euthyphro* is again more concise and merely gestures toward an explanation, both passages at notes 1.1, therefore, establish the form of what follows.

The nature of the conversation in both dialogues clearly follows the relative consonance or dissonance of the underlying notes. For example, from 4.0 to 4.3 tends to positive and amicable, and from 5.0 to 5.3 tends to negative and disputatious.

In the *Symposium*, Aristophanes' speech stretched from 4.0 to 4.3. His good-humoured benevolence matched the consonance of that range of notes. In the *Euthyphro*, this same range of notes is coloured by an unusual degree of agreement and cooperation between Socrates and Euthyphro. Socrates begins by congratulating Euthyphro for finally giving an essentialist definition, and then proceeds to draw him out further. They talk abstractly of quarrels, but agree about their character.

In the *Symposium*, the dissonant range of notes from 5.0 to 5.3 began with Socrates suggesting that Agathon's play was crude and was then mainly occupied with Agathon's speech, which was full of fancy rhetoric and suspect morality. In this dialogue, the harmony between Socrates and Euthyphro in the preceding consonant range has ended. Socrates drives Euthyphro into self-contradiction at the fifth, very dissonant wholenote. He accuses Euthyphro of not answering questions, refutes him again at 5.2, and replaces Euthyphro's doctrines with their opposites. This part of the dialogue is remarkably negative and conflicted. It is a dispute about disputing – even the gods are disputing – and this reflects the jarring dissonance of the underlying notes.

The broad structure of Diotima's speech is also mirrored in the conversation between Socrates and Euthyphro in the second half of this dialogue. Generally speaking, the first half of Diotima's speech is critical, negative and suspect. It contains elenchi, myths of dubious morality and demotes Eros to a daimon. The second half contains her more rarefied, more Platonic philosophy of love, and culminates in the ascent to the Form of Beauty. These two parts, one more negative and one more positive, correspond to the two underlying ranges of notes: the range from 6.3 to 7.3 is dissonant, and that from just after 7.3 to 9.3 is more consonant. The same twofold pattern in the same two ranges of notes is manifest in the *Euthyphro*. Up to 7.3 is critical and negative. Around the more consonant wholenotes 8.0 and 9.0, relative harmony between Socrates and Euthyphro reigns again. At note 9.0, Socrates reaches the high point of the dialogue, where he invokes the Platonic virtue of justice.

6.6 The *Euthyphro* is not aporetic

The *Euthyphro* is commonly classed among Plato's "aporetic dialogues of definition" because Socrates and Euthyphro fail in the end to agree on a definition of holiness. However, as the following commentary will argue in greater detail, the musical structure of the dialogue pinpoints the positive and definite conclusion of the dialogue.

Most scholars will agree that, in some sense, the philosophical climax of the *Symposium* is reached with the vision of the Form of Beauty at the top of Diotima's ladder, which it has been emphasized lies at the ninth, most harmonious note in the musical scale. As briefly mentioned in §6.2, at the ninth note here in the *Euthyphro*, Socrates propounds his own definition of holiness when he says "So holiness NOTE 9.0=12d3 is a species of justice? Shall we posit that ...". Burnet's commentary, for example, passes by this brief remark without paying it much attention (Burnet 1924: 55), but there are reasons to regard this passage as formulating the philosophical conclusion of the dialogue.

In the surface conversation of the dialogue, there are several indications that this passage has a privileged status. First, it is the only definition propounded by Socrates. Second, it is the only definition agreed to by Socrates and Euthyphro. Third, this definition is not overturned by any later argument. The following dispute turns, for example, on the question of *which* species of justice holiness is, not about whether or not holiness is a species of justice. Fourth, Socrates himself confirms that this definition was important when he later berates Euthyphro: "For just now, when we came to the point, you turned aside!" (*apetrapou*; 14c2).

Moreover, in this passage at 9.0, Socrates uses two words that, as Burnet emphasizes, are technical terms in Plato's theory of Forms (see commentary). Thus both the *Symposium* and the *Euthyphro* in parallel point to the Forms at the ninth note.

It is, of course, plausible that "holiness is a species of justice" is a genuine Platonic doctrine (Broadie 2003: 58; Bodéüs 2000: 138). As an ethical concept it must be related to the four cardinal virtues. In sum, the arguments in the surface conversation, the invocation of the theory of Forms, and, critically, the passage's location at a key, consonant musical note all point to its importance. Although other *aporia* remain, the *Euthyphro* does make positive progress towards a definition of holiness. Study of the other dialogues will provide more evidence for a general principle: the philosophical conclusions of the dialogues lie at the ninth note.

6.7 Marking the notes

Since the *Euthyphro* is a shorter dialogue, two quarternotes can be presented on each left-hand page. The commentary on the right-hand side is correspondingly brief.

THE MUSICAL STRUCTURE OF PLATO'S DIALOGUES

Euthyphro: [2a] NOTE 0.0 = 2a1 What's new Socrates? What's happened that made you leave your conversations (*diatribas*) in the Lyceum and now converse (*diatribeis*) here at the Royal Portico? It couldn't be that you happen to have a suit in the Royal Court as I do?

Socrates: The Athenians don't call it a "suit", Euthyphro, but an "indictment".

Euth.: [2b] What do you say? CHARGES An indictment? So someone, it seems, 4/8 has indicted you? I could not stoop to thinking that you've indicted someone else!

Soc.: No, not at all.

Euth.: So someone else indicted you?

Soc.: So indeed.

Euth.: Who then?

Soc.: I'm not entirely sure I recognize the man, Euthyphro. He seems to be some youth 6/8 and not well known. They call him, I believe, "Meletus". He's from the village of Pitheus. Do you recall a CHARGER Meletus of Pitheus with long hair NOTE 0.1 = 2b11 and a beard just starting (*eugeneion*)? With a hooked nose?

Euth.: No, I don't, Socrates, but what sort of indictment [2c] have you been indicted with?

According to Greek music theory, the notes after 3.0 are more harmonic or disharmonic than earlier notes which are far from the twelfth note. In Plato's dialogues, the notes after 3.0 are therefore marked more emphatically, and it is best to start assessing the evidence for the musical structure with those later notes, or with the guide in the previous sections.

Since there is also some uncertainty about how to calculate whether these early notes are consonant or dissonant, they are generally not so labelled.

Note 0.0 (2a1)

The opening sentence here twice repeats a symbolic word that was twice repeated in the closing sentence of the *Symposium*. The interpretation of *diatribein* as a symbol for harmony in that dialogue was discussed in Chapter 4 (cf. note 0.0.4). Here, Euthyphro mentions the Lyceum, Apollo's temple. Apollo was supposed sacred by the Pythagoreans. The *Symposium* also began and concluded with apparently incidental allusions to Apollo.[6]

The midpoint between the notes (4/8) here is marked by the first allusion to the charges against Socrates. At the next midpoint below, Socrates will make the connection between the charges and a presumption of "wisdom", that is, of some higher knowledge. Charges against Socrates as well as the charges made by Euthyphro will mark many succeeding notes. They are a species of assertions of higher knowledge.

Note 0.1 (2b11)

Here Socrates describes Meletus, who asserts the charges against him, and Euthyphro denies knowledge of him.[7]

At the midpoint (4/8), Socrates returns to the charges and connects them to "wisdom".

Soc.: What sort? Not an ignoble one, I think. Although he's just a youth, he's recognized a problem that's no trifle. This man knows, as he says, in which way the young are corrupted and who corrupts them. CHARGES FROM WISDOM He might even be wise! 4/8, And seeing that my ignorance has been corrupting his cohorts, he's run off to the city-court to accuse me as if running to his mother [for help]. [2d] And it seems to me that, among all the politicians, he's the only one to start off in the correct way. For, indeed, it's correct to take care (*epimelēthēnai*) first KNOWLEDGE OF GOOD of all that the young will become as good as possible (*aristoi*), just as a good farmer takes care (*epimelēthēnai*) of the young plants first of all and after that the others.

NOTE 0.2 = 2d2 Moreover, Meletus probably wants to purge (*ekkathairei*) those of us who are corrupting the young shoots, as he says. [3a] Then, later after taking care of the older people, it's clear he will have become the cause of great and superlative goods to our city. Anyway, that's probably how it will turn out, having 4/8 begun with such a beginning.

Euth.: I wish it were so, Socrates, but I shudder to think just the opposite may occur. It really seems to me that he is beginning at the very hearth by doing evil to the city if he is undertaking to wrong you. But tell me, what does he say you are doing to corrupt the youth?

Soc.: [3b] Well, my marvellous man, it's quite strange (*atopos*), as you shall hear. CHARGES ABOUT RELIGION For he says I am the creator of gods NOTE 0.3 = 3b2 and that, having created new gods, I do not believe in the ancient gods. He's indicted me on account of that, he says.

Note 0.2 (2d2)

This is marked by a clear assertion of knowledge of the "good", but here it concerns Meletus' apparent intention to make the young good and a farmer's knowledge of what is good for plants. Socrates' assertions of "higher" knowledge are typically restricted to the human sphere.[8]

Note 0.3 (3b2)

This quarternote is strongly marked with the first instance of the charges against Socrates; these are in effect the assertion of knowledge about Socrates and the gods.

Euth.: I understand, Socrates! It's because you say there's a daimon always about you. It's for these innovations about the gods that he's indicted this indictment. And with this slander he's gone off to the court, knowing that such 4/8 good (*eu*) slander appeals to the Many. It's the same with me. [3c] When I say something in the assembly about the gods, foretelling the future, they ridicule me as if I were raving. But nothing that I foretold wasn't true. ASSERTS RELIGIOUS KNOWLEDGE But all that sort envies us. There's no need to worry about them – just charge ahead (*all' homose ienai*). NOTE 1.0 = 3c6

Soc.: But, my dear Euthyphro, to be ridiculed is probably no trouble. Indeed, the Athenians, it seems to me, don't care much if someone thinks they are clever, as long as they don't think [3d] ASSERTS RELIGIOUS KNOWLEDGE their wisdom is for teaching. But if they think he makes others wise, they get angry, either on account of envy as you say or on account of something else.

Euth.: However that may be in my case, 4/8 I have no desire to find out.

Soc.: For probably you seem stingy about offering your wisdom and don't seem to want to teach it. But I fear, because of my love for humanity, I seem to them that I would speak in a torrent to everyone: not only without pay for myself, but I would SOCRATES' "TEACHING" NOTE 1.1 = 3d9 gladly pay out if someone else wished to listen to me. So if, as I just said, they do ridicule me as you say they did you, [3e] there would be nothing unpleasant in spending our time in the court playing and laughing. If though, they are more serious [about my indictment], how this will turn out is unclear except to you seers.

Euth.: But it will probably be no problem, 1/9 Socrates, if you contest the suit sensibly (*kata noun*) 4/8 as I believe I will do mine.

Soc.: And for you, Euthyphro, what sort of suit is it? Are you the accuser or defendant?

Euth.: Accuser.

Soc.: Who?

Euth.: [4a] Someone who to pursue makes it, again, seem like I rave.

Soc.: What? Do you accuse someone [young and] flighty?

Euth.: Far from being flighty, someone who happens to be very well advanced in years.

Parallel narratives reflect musical structure: There are many instances where the narratives of the *Symposium* and the *Euthyphro* seem to parallel each other, especially at the more consonant or dissonant notes.

For example, it was mentioned in Chapter 3 that the topic and the procedure for the dialogues were often established at notes 1.0 and 1.1. At note 1.1 in the *Symposium,* Agathon's guests agreed to spend the evening making speeches.

Here, at note 1.1 in the *Euthyphro,* Socrates notes in passing his willingness to talk to anyone who will listen. That is, he in effect explains why he would have a long discussion with someone he encountered on the street, just as he does in this dialogue. In both dialogues, the passages at notes 1.0 and 1.1, therefore, establish the form of what follows.

Note 1.0 (3c6)

This wholenote is emphatically marked. Before the note, Euthyphro strongly asserts that, as a seer, his knowledge is true: "I have said nothing but the truth".[9] After the note, Socrates refers to teaching and so asserting such wisdom.

Note 1.1 (3d9)

Characteristically, Socrates' assertions are limited and this-wordly. He here notes his habit of talking to everyone who will listen.[10]

Narrative structure reflects musical structure: The line after this quarternote, "So if, as I just said, they do ridicule me", refers back to the line one quarter-interval before, that is, just after the previous quarternote. In the *Symposium,* such back-references called attention to musical intervals of one or more quarternotes.

Soc.: Who have you accused?
Euth.: My own father.
Soc.: Your own father! My good man!
Euth.: Quite so.
Soc.: CHARGES What sort of charge is it, NOTE 1.2 = 4a9 and what kind of suit (*dikē*)?
Euth.: Of murder, Socrates.
Soc.: Hercules! Euthyphro! I guess most people are unsure of where right and justice lies, [4b] but I believe no ordinary person would bring such a charge unless they were already far advanced in wisdom.
Euth.: And, by God, I am indeed far advanced, Socrates.
Soc.: Is it someone from your household who was killed by your father? Surely so. You wouldn't prosecute him for murder on account of killing someone 4/8 outside the family.
Euth.: It's ridiculous, Socrates, that you believe it makes a difference whether the deceased was a member of the household or someone else. It's necessary to be vigilant only about this: whether the killer killed justly or not. And if justly, that's the end of it, but if not, ONE-SEVENTH prosecute – even if the killer eats with you at the same table. ASSERTS RELIGIOUS KNOWLEDGE [4c] Indeed, your sin is the same NOTE 1.3 = 4c2 if you knowingly live with such a killer and you do not purify both yourself and him by bringing a suit. The deceased was a neighbour of mine and, as we have a farm on the island of Naxos, worked there for us. Anyway, he got drunk and angry with one of household slaves and slew him.

Note 1.2, consonant (4a9)

This passage is generally important for the theory of the marking passages in this dialogue. Here, the charge of murder is first announced, and reiterations of charges will also mark later notes. But Socrates immediately makes the connection to epistemology: bringing a legal charge is an assertion of some higher "wisdom", about the good or the gods. Charges are a species of the genus of assertions of higher knowledge.

One-seventh (4b10)

The sevenths are marked by failures to assert. Here, the issue is whether a murder is just or unjust, and Euthyphro here does not assert either. (At one-seventh in the *Symposium*, Phaedrus asserted that Orpheus was justly slain by women.)

Note 1.3, consonant (4c2)

This is clearly marked by an assertion of higher knowledge about religion.

Then my father bound this neighbour's feet and 4/8 hands and threw him in a ditch. He sent a man here to Athens to ask the priest [4d] how he should proceed. During this time [when he was waiting], my father paid little attention to the bound man and neglected him – since he was a murderer and it mattered not at all if he were to die, which then is just what happened. He died from starvation and the cold and from being tied up, NOTE 2.0 = 4d4 before the messenger could arrive back from the priests. RELIGIOUS KNOWLEDGE

And that's why my father and the rest of the family are outraged: that I, on behalf of a murderer, prosecute my father for murder, although he's not a killer, as they say, and, if he really did kill, the victim was a murderer and we shouldn't worry about him 4/8 since it's [4e] unholy anyway for a son to prosecute his father for murder. Of course, they know little, Socrates, about what the divine holds to be holy and unholy.

Soc.: By God, Euthyphro, do you really think you know accurately enough about the gods, and about what's holy and unholy, to be doing what you say? Don't you fear that, NOTE 2.1 = 4e7 in judging your father, you may be in turn doing something unholy? CHARGES FROM RELIGIOUS KNOWLEDGE

Euth.: I would have no value, Socrates, and nothing would differentiate Euthyphro from the Many, if I did not know such all things accurately.

Note 2.0, dissonant (4d4)

This note is marked by mention of the religious exegete, whose pronouncement rests on claims to higher knowledge about the gods. The death of the bound and abandoned labourer marks a somewhat dissonant note.

Note 2.1 (4e7)

Socrates' question and Euthyphro's answer explicitly affirm that the charge of murder rests on higher knowledge about religion.

Soc.: But, my marvellous Euthyphro, it would be tremendous if I could become your student. Then, before Meletus' indictment is heard, I could challenge him, 4/8 saying that in earlier times I made much of knowing 1/5 about divine matters but now since he says I spoke ill-advisedly and erred in innovating about the gods, that I have become your student! I would say, "And if you, Meletus, agree that Euthyphro [5b] is wise about these things and thinks correctly, then think the same of me NOTE 2.2 = 5b2 and do not prosecute me. CLAIM OF RELIGIOUS KNOWLEDGE If not, then sue him, my teacher, before you sue me since he's corrupting the old, both me and your father, by teaching me and by criticizing and punishing him." And if he is not persuaded and neither abandons his suit nor indicts you instead of me, I will repeat all of that challenge 4/8 to him in court.
Euth.: By God, Socrates, if he attempts to [5c] indict me, I think 2/9 I'd ferret out his weak spot, and there would much sooner be an argument about him in court than about me.
Soc.: And I, my dear friend, recognizing all that, wish to become your student, since I know that this Meletus and others overlook you NOTE 2.3 = 5c5 CHARGES but observe me so sharply and easily that they indict me for impiety.

Note 2.2, consonant (5b2)

There are several assertions of knowledge here. Euthyphro is pictured as teaching his religious knowledge. Meletus may agree that Euthyphro is wise in these matters. Socrates makes a hypothetical assertion: "if my teacher were wise about religion, I would be too". Once again, the legal charges are connected to claims to higher knowledge.

This may be harmonious because it hypothetically considers the proposition that Socrates is wise about religion.

Note 2.3, consonant (5c5)

Socrates' assertions of knowledge are typically this-worldly. Here, he knows that no one observes Euthyphro. This is also a reference to Euthyphro's teaching activity, a kind of profession of knowledge.

Soc.: So now, before God, tell me what you have been so strongly asserting that you know, what sort of thing do you assert piety and impiety are, whether it's about murder [5d] or anything else? Is what is holy in and of itself 4/8 the same in every action (*tauton ... to hosion auto autō*)? And is the unholy again the opposite of everything holy? Is the unholy everywhere similar to itself and possessing one certain idea (*mian ... idean*) of unholiness insofar at it will be unholy?

Euth.: Entirely so, Socrates.

Soc.: Tell me then, what do you say holiness and unholiness are?

Euth.: I say, then, that holiness is that which I do now, prosecuting someone who does wrong NOTE 3.0 = 5d9 FIRST DEFINITION OF HOLY AT FIRST MORE-CONSONANT NOTE by murdering or stealing from a temple, or someone who sins by doing something else like that, whether a father [5e] or a mother or anyone else whosoever, and that not prosecuting such a person is unholy. Thus, Socrates, look, I will tell you a great proof that this law holds – a proof that I have already told others, that it is correct to prosecute for these crimes – never tolerate the 4/8 impious whoever they happen to be. Humans do believe that Zeus is the best and the most just of the gods, [6a] and yet they admit he tied up his own father because he unjustly swallowed his children and that Zeus' father in turn had castrated his own father for other reasons. But they criticize me NOTE 3.1 = 6a3 RELIGIOUS KNOWLEDGE, CHARGES for prosecuting my father for committing crimes. Thus they say the opposite of what they themselves say about the gods and about me.

Parallel structure: As Socrates approaches this consonant third note, he becomes, at 4/8, more philosophical and alludes to a Platonic form that is the same in every instance. In the *Symposium*, as Pausanias approached the third note, he similarly introduced, at 4/8, the more philosophical idea that the older lover would help the beloved pursue wisdom and virtue.

Note 3.0, consonant (5d9)

This very consonant note (three out of twelve is a 1:4 ratio) is emphatically marked by Euthyphro's first definition of holiness, an assertion of higher knowledge. This may be appropriate to a consonant note either because the act of defining is an important step in philosophy or because Euthyphro here says that piety is prosecuting those who are guilty, that is, those who "commit injustice". Later, consonant notes will also connect piety to justice, a central Platonic virtue.

Note 3.1 (6a3)

Euthyphro asserts higher knowledge in two ways here. He asserts that the stories about the gods are true (below, at 6a10–b1, Socrates emphasizes the claim to knowledge involved), and that he is prosecuting his father for injustice. (First quarternotes are often somewhat dissonant.)

Soc.: Indeed, Euthyphro, is it not just for the sake of this that I have been indicted: that after someone repeats such tales about the gods, I find them hard to accept? This is why, it seems, they say I sin. 4/8 So, if these tales seem true to you [6b], who know so well, then necessarily we must condone them. For what could those of us who say they TWO-SEVENTHS know nothing about all that say? Tell me, however, in the name of the god of friendship, do you truly believe these things happened in that way?

Euth.: Yes, and even more astounding things, Socrates, that the Many do not know. NOTE 3.2 = 6b7 RELIGIOUS KNOWLEDGE

Soc.: And do you believe there really was a war of gods against other gods, and hatreds and battles and many other such things, which are spoken of by the poets and with which our temples are decorated by the "good" painters? [6c] And, moreover, the tapestry woven for the Great Parade for Athena that's filled with such decorations [illustrating these tales], the one that's brought up to the acropolis – shall we really say all these tales are true, 4/8 Euthyphro?

Euth.: [Yes,] not only these, Socrates, but – as I was just saying – I will if you wish relate to you many other things about the gods which, if you heard, I know would amaze you.

Soc.: I wouldn't be surprised. But tell me these stories some other time when I'm free. Now, however, try to say clearly NOTE 3.3 = 6d1 what I just asked you. You have not adequately taught me what I was asking you earlier: what could holiness be? Instead, you've told me that just this which you are doing happens to be holy, namely prosecuting your father.

Euth.: And what I said was true, Socrates.

Soc.: Probably. But, Euthyphro, you say many other things are holy.

Euth.: And indeed they are.

Two-sevenths (6b2)

This is another example of a seventh marked by the failure to assert: Socrates knows nothing.

Note 3.2 (6b7)

This note is strongly marked by the strong claim to have esoteric knowledge, unknown to the Many, about the gods (repeated at 4/8).

Note 3.3 (6d1)

Socrates makes a negative assertion of his own: that Euthyphro has not taught him the definition of holiness. Euthyphro strongly reaffirms his earlier assertion.

Soc.: Remember, then, that that I didn't 4/8 request this, that you teach me one or two of all the holy things, but that idea in itself (*auto to eidos*) by which all the holy things are holy. You were saying that, somehow, it is by a single idea (*mia idea*) [6e] that unholy things are unholy and holy things holy. Don't you remember?

Euth.: I do.

Soc.: So teach me now what this very idea (*autēn ... tēn idean*), could be, so that by making comparisons to it and using it as a standard (*paradeigmati*) NOTE 4.0 = 6e5 ASSERTS FORMS I may say that such and such which you or someone else might do is holy, and if not so unholy.

Euth.: But if you wish, Socrates, I shall tell this to you too.

Soc.: But I do so wish.

Euth.: Well then, that which is dear to the gods is holy, and that which is [7a] not dear to the gods is unholy.

Soc.: Splendid, Euthyphro! Just as I besought you to answer, 4/8 so now you have answered. If, though, you have answered truly, this I do not yet know, but you, it's clear, will thoroughly teach me how what you say is true.

Euth.: Of course.

Soc.: Come then, we shall examine what we are saying. That which is dear to the gods and people dear to the gods are holy. That which is hated by the gods and people hated by the gods are unholy. Holiness and unholiness are not the same but diametric contraries. NOTE 4.1 = 7a10 ASSERTS DEFINITION Not so?

Euth.: So indeed.

Soc.: And it appears that was well said.

Euth.: [7b] It appears so, Socrates.

Soc.: Therefore too, Euthyphro, it was said that there are quarrels among the gods, and differences with each other, and that there are hatreds among the gods towards each other.

Euth.: So it was.

Soc.: Hatred and anger, my good fellow, are brought about by differences over what sort of thing? Let us examine it this way. If you and I were to differ 4/8 over which of two numbers was greater, would such a difference make us hateful and angry at each other? Or would we turn to counting and quickly be reconciled [7c] about such things?

Euth.: Entirely so.

Parallel structure: In the *Symposium*, Aristophanes' speech stretched from 4.0 to 4.3. His good-humoured benevolence matched the consonance of that range of notes. Similarly, here in the *Euthyphro*, this same range of notes is coloured by an unusual degree of agreement and cooperation between Socrates and Euthyphro.

Socrates begins by congratulating Euthyphro for his essentialist definition, and then proceeds to draw him out further. They talk of quarrels, but agree about their nature. Euthyphro does not see that the seeming harmony of their exchange will abruptly end with an elenchus at the next dissonant wholenote. The content of the conversations tracks the relative consonance of the underlying musical notes.

Note 4.0, consonant (6e5)

Socrates alluded to the Forms as he approached the consonant third note. Here, at this even more consonant note, Socrates expands upon the concept of a "single form", and uses one of the technical terms for a Platonic Form, "paradigm", at the note. Knowledge of the Forms is a kind of higher knowledge. He then challenges Euthyphro to "teach" him the Form of Holiness, which will enable him to assert whether an action is holy.

Euthyphro proposes a second definition, "that which is dear to the gods is holy and that which is not dear to the gods is unholy". Surprisingly, this appears between major notes – unlike the last definition which marked the third wholenote. There is a clear explanation for why this new definition does not suffice to mark a note. Euthyphro makes a logical error, which makes his definition faulty and perhaps no definition at all. In general, opposites must be defined by opposites, and contraries by contraries (see e.g. Arist. *Top.* VI.9, VII.3). If there is something intermediate or indifferent between the holy and unholy, they are mere contraries. Euthyphro, however, mistakenly defines these contraries, holy and unholy, by two opposites, "dear" and "not dear". Socrates silently corrects and rephrases Euthyphro's definition to leave room for intermediate cases (he later explicitly speaks of correcting Euthyphro's definitions at 9c7–d2). Socrates makes the holy "whatever is dear to the gods" and makes the unholy its contrary: "whatever is hated by the gods". This leaves room for something between holy and unholy that is indifferent to the gods. Corrected by this amendment, the definition marks the next note.

Note 4.1, consonant (7a10)

Socrates reiterates and corrects Euthyphro's second definition of holiness at a quarternote, which is now perhaps a proper assertion and marks the note.

Soc.: Therefore too, if we were to differ about which things were greater or lesser, we would turn to measurement and quickly cease NOTE 4.2 = 7c4 to differ?
Euth.: So it is.
Soc.: And turning to weighing, I believe, we would distinguish between the heavier and the lighter.
Euth.: How could it not be so?
Soc.: Well then, differing about what 1 – PHI and being unable to come to a decision about what would we become enemies to each other and angry? It's probably not easy for you to say, but I will. Consider if it is about [7d] 4/8 the just and the unjust, and the beautiful and the ugly, and the good and the bad. Is it not differing and being unable to come to an adequate decision about these that makes us enemies to each other, when we do, both you and I and all other people?
Euth.: Yes, it is just this sort of difference, Socrates, NOTE 4.3 = 7d7 and about these things.
Soc.: What about the gods, Euthyphro? If they differ, isn't it over just these things that they would differ?
Euth.: Quite necessarily. ASSERTS KNOWLEDGE OF HUMANS, GODS
Soc.: [7e] And among the gods, 2/5 then, my noble Euthyphro, they judge various things to be just according to your statement, and to be beautiful and ugly, and good and bad. They wouldn't be having quarrels with each other if they didn't differ about these things, right?
Euth.: That's correct. 4/8
Soc.: And so what they each judge beautiful and good and just, they each will find dear, and the opposites of these they will hate?
Euth.: Quite so.
Soc.: These things, as you say, some judge just [8a] and some unjust and, disputing about these, they quarrel with and war against each other. Is it not so?
Euth.: It's so.

Note 4.2, consonant (7c4)

Reason, measurement and weighing are routes to knowledge beyond disagreement. (The reference to "greater and lesser" at this consonant quarternote may allude to the Platonic "Great and Small".)

Note 4.3, consonant (7d7)

Euthyphro agrees with Socrates' suggestion about what makes differences irreconcilable among humans, and so asserts it. Then he answers Socrates' next question affirmatively, and so asserts higher knowledge about what makes differences irreconcilable among the gods.

Soc.: The same things, it seems, are hated NOTE 5.0 = 8a4 by the gods and loved by the gods, and [the adjectives] hated-by-the-gods and dear-to-the-gods would be the same.

Euth.: So it seems. ELENCHUS: ASSERTS CONTRADICTORIES ABOUT GODS

Soc.: And then the same things are both holy and unholy, Euthyphro, by this argument.

Euth.: Probably so.

Soc.: But this is not what I asked you to answer, my marvellous man. I did not ask you whether something is the same, both holy and unholy. Or, as it seems, whether something dear-to-the-gods is also hated-by-the-gods. [8b] Thus 4/8 Euthyphro, concerning what you do now, castigating your father, it would be no surprise if in acting so you were in this way doing something THREE-SEVENTHS dear to Zeus, but to Chronus and to Ouranus hateful, and dear to Hephaestus but hateful to Hera, and if any other of the gods differed with each other (*heteros heterō diapheretai*) about it, then to them too accordingly.

Euth.: But, Socrates, I think none of the gods NOTE 5.1 = 8b8 differ from another (*oudena ... heteron heterō diapheresthai*) about this, and hold that it is unnecessary to punish someone who kills another unjustly. ASSERTING NEGATIVE KNOWLEDGE OF THE GODS

Soc.: What? Among people, Euthyphro, have you ever before heard anyone [8c] 4/9 disputing that someone who killed unjustly or committed any other injustice whatsoever need not be given a punishment?

Euth.: They never cease disputing such things both in and out of the court. 4/8 There are lots of wrongdoers who do and say anything to escape punishment.

Soc.: But do they both agree, Euthyphro, that they have done wrong and, while so agreeing, nonetheless say there is no need to give them a punishment?

Euth.: No, not that.

Parallel structure: In the *Symposium*, the dissonant range of notes from 5.0 to 5.3 began with Socrates suggesting that Agathon's play was crude and was then mainly occupied with Agathon's speech, which was full of fancy rhetoric and suspect morality. In this dialogue, the harmony between Socrates and Euthyphro in the preceding consonant range has ended. Socrates drives Euthyphro into self-contradiction at the fifth, very dissonant wholenote. He accuses Euthyphro of not answering questions, refutes him again at 5.2, and replaces Euthyphro's doctrines with their opposites. This part of the dialogue is remarkably negative and conflicted. It is a dispute about disputing – even the gods are disputing – and this reflects the jarring dissonance of the underlying notes.

Note 5.0, dissonant (8a4)

This dissonant note is marked by Socrates' elenchus or refutation of Euthyphro's asserted definition of holiness. The inconsistency is exposed at the note, where Euthyphro affirms knowledge about the gods.

Socrates makes the contradiction explicit in the next line: "the same things are both holy and unholy". This refers back to the opposite claim made at note 4.1: "holiness and unholiness are not the same, but diametric contraries" (7a9–10). Thus the elenchus occupied three quarter-intervals.

Three-sevenths (8b2)

This seventh is marked by two failures to assert. Socrates' own statement is hypothetical ("it would be no surprise if in acting so"). Moreover, as discussed above, the disjunctions that follow would not have been considered assertions. Euthyphro had asserted that his action was loved by the gods, but now he concedes it could be loved or hated.

Note 5.1, dissonant (8b8)

This dissonant note is marked by a negative assertion about the gods, that they will not differ, and by clusters of negative words: "nothing", "other", "differing", "not". In the *Symposium*, a note in this same dissonant range was marked by a string of negatives (cf. note 5.3).

Soc.: Nor would they do and say everything. This I think they would not dare to say nor even propose for debate: that, if they do do wrong, NOTE 5.2 = 8d1 they need not be punished. Rather, I think, they deny doing wrong. Isn't that so?

Euth.: That's true.

SOCRATES ASSERTS NEGATIVE KNOWLEDGE OF HUMANS Soc.: Then they do not dispute that a wrongdoer must not be given a punishment, but they probably dispute who it is that has done wrong and what they have done and when.

Euth.: That's true.

Soc.: Do the gods too, therefore, experience just this if they quarrel 4/8 about just and unjust things, as per your statement: some say others among them do wrong while others deny it? Since doubtless no one, my marvellous man, [8e] among the gods or people would dare to assert that someone doing wrong need not be punished.

Euth.: Yes, what you say is true, Socrates, in the main.

Soc.: Rather, I think, those who dispute, whether they are gods or people NOTE 5.3 = 8e6 (if the gods do dispute), dispute each of the actions. Differing about the nature of the action, some say it was done justly and some unjustly. Is that not so? ASSERTING KNOWLEDGE OF THE GODS' DISPUTES

Euth.: Quite so.

Note 5.2, dissonant (8d1)

A negative assertion by Socrates about what humans will not say. Socrates' higher knowledge is generally negative and restricted to humans (see below on note 5.3). Another cluster of negative words and privatives also mark this dissonant note.

Note 5.3, dissonant (8e6)

Socrates makes an almost tautological assertion about discord, mentions the gods, but then carefully limits his assertion to humans. This note is again marked by a cluster of negatives – "dispute" (three times), "differing" and "unjustly" – as was note 5.3 in the *Symposium*.

Soc.: [9a] Come now, my dear Euthyphro, teach me too so that I may become wiser. What proof is there for you that all the gods 4/8 believe your neighbour died unjustly, who killed a man while he was labouring, was bound by the master of the deceased, and died on account of his bindings (just before the man who bound him could ask the priests what should be done about him), and indeed that on behalf of such a one it is correct for a son to charge and prosecute a father for murder? Come, NOTE 6.0 = 9b1 [9b] try to show me clearly what about this indicates, more than anything, that all the gods (*pantos mallon pantes theoi*) believe that this action is correct. And if you show this properly, I will never cease to sing the praises (*enkōmiazōn*) of your wisdom.

Euth.: But that's probably no small task (*ergon*), Socrates, since I could show you that quite definitively.

Soc.: I understand. 4/8 I seem to you to be a slow learner, or slower than the judges, since you will show them clearly that it is an injustice and that the gods all hate such things.

Euth.: Quite clearly, Socrates, if only they would listen to my speech.

Soc.: [9c] But they will listen, if you seem to speak well (*eu*). I thought of this while you were speaking and inquired of myself: "If NOTE 6.1 = 9c3 Euthyphro definitely would teach me that all the gods believe such a death is unjust, TEACHING KNOWLEDGE OF THE GODS what more have I learned from Euthyphro about what indeed is holy and unholy? Only that this event (*ergon*) would be, as it seems, hateful to the gods. But it just appeared that it is not by this that holiness is marked off from the unholy – for that which is hateful to the gods 4/8 appeared also to be dear to the gods." So, I will let you off on this point, Euthyphro. If you wish, let all the gods think this act unjust and all of them hate it.

Note 6.0, consonant (9b1)

Socrates abruptly halts the discussion to summarize the facts of the case at the midpoint of the dialogue, and so at its most consonant note. After 6.1, Socrates just as abruptly returns to the general question of the nature of piety.

Here there is a reference to the higher knowledge of the religious "exegetes", a reference to the correctness of the charges that implicitly assert higher knowledge, and to teaching knowledge claims about the gods. Socrates' concluding remark that he would never stop "singing the praises" of Euthyphro's wisdom is an allusion to music, which is rare in this dialogue. (See the appendix for a reading of the fine structure of this passage, and its similarity to the parallel passage in the *Symposium*.)

Note 6.1, consonant (9c3)

This note is marked by another reference to Euthyphro teaching his higher knowledge about the gods and holiness.

But shall we now make this correction in your statement: that were all the gods to hate something, it would be unholy, and were they all to love something, it would be holy. What some of the gods might love and some of the gods might hate, would be neither or both. So, do you now wish this NOTE 6.2 = 9d6 to define for us what is holy and unholy? ASSERTING A DEFINITION OF PIETY

Euth.: What would prevent it, Socrates?

Soc.: Nothing by me, Euthyphro, but you consider yourself if premising this will thus make it easy to teach me what you promised.

Euth.: [9e] I would say that this is holiness: what all the gods love; and its opposite, what all the gods hate, is unholiness.

Soc.: Then shall we in turn examine 4/8 if this, Euthyphro, is well said? Or shall we just admit it 5/9 and similarly just accept our own assertions and those of others, conceding they hold if only someone asserts they do? Or must we examine what the asserter asserts?

Euth.: It must be examined! But I think it is now well said.

Soc.: [10a] We will soon, my good fellow, be in a better position to know. Consider the following. Is holiness NOTE 6.3 = 10a3 loved by the gods since it is holy, or is it holy since it is loved by the gods? THE EUTHYPHRO DILEMMA

Euth.: I don't know what you're saying Socrates.

Soc.: Well, I will try to express it more clearly. We say something is "being carried" or (*kai*) "carries", and is "being led" or "leads", and is "being seen" or "sees", and all such: you understand that they are different FOUR-SEVENTHS from each other and by what they are different (*hetara allēlōn esti kai hē hetera*).

Euth.: Um, I think I understand.

Soc.: Therefore, there is "being loved" – and "loves" is different from it.

Euth.: Of course.

Soc.: [10b] Tell me then whether something is "being carried" because it is carried or because of something else.

Euth.: No, just by this.

Soc.: And something is "being led" because it is led, and something is "being seen" because it is seen?

Euth.: Of course.

Parallel narratives reflect musical structure: In the *Symposium*, notes 6.2 and 6.3 were marked by the sharp dialectical exchange between Socrates and Agathon over whether "we love what we lack" and Eros' beauty. Agathon accepted a logical distinction at 6.2 and then was driven to an elenchus at 6.3. Here, Euthyphro is similarly presented with a logical distinction at 6.2 and then the well-known Euthyphro dilemma at 6.3 (which, while not a strict elenchus, will undermine his definition of piety). The sharp attacks in both dialogues at 6.3 are appropriate to a quarternote near one of the more dissonant wholenotes.

Note 6.2 (9d6)

Euthyphro here endorses a proposed, revised definition of holiness, that unanimity among the gods implies holiness or unholiness, and so again marks a note with an assertion of higher knowledge.

Note 6.3, dissonant (10a3)

Socrates expounds the "Euthyphro dilemma" at the note, which is an attack on his definitions of piety.

Four-sevenths (10a9)

This is again marked by a failure to make an assertion. Just as at three-sevenths, this is marked by a list of disjuncts, none of which is asserted.

Soc.: Not because it is "being seen", then, is it therefore seen, NOTE 7.0 = 10b7 but, the opposite, because it is seen it is therefore "being seen". NEGATIVE LOGICAL ASSERTION Nor is it because something is "being led" that it is therefore led, but because it is led, because of this, it is "being led". Nor because something is "being carried" is it carried, but because it is carried it is "being carried". So is it plainly clear, Euthyphro, [10c] what I want to say? I want to say this: if something actively becomes or something passively suffers, it is not because it is passively "being something" that it is acted upon, 4/8 rather since it is acted upon it is passively "being something". It is not because something passively suffers [some action] that it suffers [that action], rather since it suffers [that action] it passively suffers. Don't you concede it's so?

Euth.: I do.

Soc.: So "being loved" too is either actively doing something 3/5 or passively suffering something [acting] on it?

Euth.: Of course.

Soc.: And it is so here as with the earlier ones. Not because it is "being loved" is it loved by what loves it, NOTE 7.1 = 10c13 but because it is loved it is "being loved".

Euth.: Necessarily. STEP ONE IN ELENCHUS

Soc.: [10d] What do we say then about holiness, Euthyphro? Is it anything else than "loved by all the gods" according to your statement?

Euth.: Yes, that's it.

Soc.: And is it loved just because of this, that it's holy, or because of something else?

Euth.: No, just because of that.

Soc.: Then, it is loved since it is holy, and not holy since it is loved?

Euth.: So it seems.

Soc.: But, on the other hand, since it is loved by the gods, 4/8 it is "being loved" and dear to the gods.

Euth.: Of course.

STEP TWO IN ELENCHUS

Soc.: But then that which is dear to the gods is not holy, Euthyphro, nor is holiness that which is dear to the gods PHI – as you asserted. Rather, these are different from each other.

Euth.: [10e] How's that, Socrates?

Soc.: Well you have agreed that holiness is loved just on account of this, that it is holy, and not that it is holy because it is loved. Not so?

Euth.: Yes.

Parallel narratives reflect musical structure: Generally speaking, the first half of Diotima's speech is critical, negative and suspect. It contains elenchi and myths of dubious morality, and demotes Eros to a daimon. The second half contains her more rarefied, more Platonic philosophy of love, and culminates in the ascent to the Form of Beauty. These two parts, one more negative and one more positive, correspond to the two underlying ranges of notes: the range from 6.3 to 7.3 is dissonant, and that from just after 7.3 to 9.3 is more consonant.

The same twofold pattern in the same two ranges of notes is manifested in the *Euthyphro*. Up to 7.3 is critical and negative. Around the more consonant wholenotes 8.0 and 9.0, relative harmony between Socrates and Euthyphro reigns.

Note 7.0, dissonant (10b7)

This dissonant note is marked by a series of negative assertions. There are several repetitions of "not" and also the word "opposite". After the note, Socrates emphasizes that he is making an assertion: "So it is plainly clear what I want to say". This passage secures the first, important premise for the following elenchus.

Note 7.1, dissonant (10c13)

Socrates reiterates the general point made at the previous note, but now takes the next step in the elenchus by applying it to the case at hand, namely, being loved by the gods. He then recollects Euthyphro's definition, an assertion of higher knowledge.

Phi (10d13)

Just as the divided line was first separated into two segments, one higher and one lower, here Socrates distinguishes "dear to the gods" from the "holy", which is "different from each other" (see Chapter 7).

Soc.: And that which is dear to the gods, since it is loved by the gods, NOTE 7.2 = 10e7 just by this fact that it is loved, is dear to the gods, and it is not loved because it is dear to the gods.
Euth.: That's true. CONCLUSION OF ELENCHUS
Soc.: But if "dear to the gods" and holiness were the same, my dear Euthyphro, if holiness is loved because it is holy and that which is dear to the gods is loved because it is dear to the gods, and again if "dear to the gods" 4/8 were dear to them because it is loved by the gods, then too holiness would be holy because it is so loved. Now, however, you see that they exist as opposites, as totally different from each other. The one is loveable because it is loved; the other is loved because it is loveable.

So probably, Euthyphro, when asked what holiness could be, you did not wish to reveal its essence (*ousian*) NOTE 7.3 = 11a8 to me, and told me some one of its qualities, that holiness's quality was this "to be loved by the gods". [11b] What it really is, you have not yet said. NEGATIVE, CRITICAL ASSERTION So, if you please (*philon*), do not hide it from me but once more, from the beginning, tell me what could holiness be, whether it is to be loved by the gods or whatever else it suffers – we will not differ over that – but earnestly tell me what holiness and unholiness are.

Note 7.2, dissonant (10e7)

This dissonant note is strongly marked by the key, concluding line of the elenchus. When Euthyphro assents to Socrates' assertion at the note, he has contradicted himself. This is not clear to Euthyphro until Socrates spells it out in the next paragraph.

Socrates is portrayed as casuistical and disputatious in this dissonant range of notes, but his logic is impeccable. For Euthyphro, "being holy" and "being dear to the gods" are identical. But he says something "being holy" causes the gods to love it, and not the reverse. But it is the reverse which is true for "being dear to the gods". So they cannot be identical. Euthyphro's definition fails again.

Note 7.3, dissonant (11a8)

This note is marked by a substantial negative, and highly critical, assertion by Socrates, that Euthyphro's definition deliberately hid the essence of holiness.

Euth.: But, Socrates, I'm not sure how I might tell you what I know. Whatever we propose is always somehow running around and doesn't want to stay where we fix it.

Soc.: Your statements, Euthyphro, resemble the [mythical, perambulating] statues of my ancestor [11c] SOCRATES ASSERTS RELATION TO GODS Daedalus. If it were me stating and asserting these things, NOTE 8.0 = 11c3 you would probably be mocking me, saying that my "works" (*erga*) in language were running off on account of my relation (*sungeneian*) to him, and that they did not want to remain where someone put them. But now the hypotheses are yours. Some other witticism is needed. They just do not wish to stay still for you, as it seems even to you yourself.

Euth.: To me the statements seem pretty much to stand in need of the same witticism, Socrates. 4/8 It's not me that incites them to run around and not remain in the same place. Rather, [11d] you seem to me the Daedalus. As far as I'm concerned, they would have remained just so.

Soc.: Probably, then, my friend, I have become technically more skilful than that man [Daedalus] SOCRATES ASSERTS HIGHER SKILL in that, while he only made his own statues not stand still, NOTE 8.1 = 11d6 I make, in addition to my own works, those of others move as well. And to be sure this in my technique is clever: that I am not deliberately so skilful (*sophos*). For I desired the statements to remain motionless and fixed – even more than [I would desire] acquiring, on top of the skill (*sophia*) of Daedalus, [11e] all the money of King Tantalus. But enough of this. Since you seem to me to put on such airs, 4/8 I will combine forces with you so that you might teach me about holiness. Just don't get tired now. See if you don't think that, necessarily, everything holy is a just thing.

Euth.: I do.

Parallel narratives reflect musical structure: Just before the eighth wholenote, Euthyphro admits defeat in the face of Socrates' critical dialectics. The dialogue enters a relatively positive and harmonious phase, corresponding to the climaxes at notes 8.0 and 9.0 in Diotima's speech.

Note 8.0, consonant (11c3)

The harmonious eighth note (2:3) is marked by Socrates' strongest positive assertion of higher knowledge in the dialogue, of his supposed relation to the Athenian hero Daedalus, a human who flew high near the sun and approached the gods. Just as the *Symposium* suggested an affinity between Socrates and Eros conceived of as a daimon intermediate between the gods and humans, at this note Socrates is associated with another such intermediary.

Socrates does not tell us enough to interpret his allusion rigorously, but Hoefmans' analysis of the earliest extant, substantial retelling of the myth (in Ov. *Met.*, 8.183–235) suggests one line of analysis. Daedalus, he says, there "asks Jupiter forgiveness for his audacity to trespass the realm of the gods; it is no *hybris* on his part, he argues, but necessity: in order to be free he has to 'stretch' the natural bounds of his human condition" (Hoefmans 1994). Daedalus would therefore represent the use of higher, "technical" knowledge to approach or temporarily reach divine realms, while yet remaining distinctly human. This interpretation of the myth fits here. Like Daedalus, Socrates is a human and his assertions of higher knowledge reach upwards but he does not claim to have knowledge of the gods – as Euthyphro does.

Socrates asserts here two kinds of "higher" knowledge: of his association with a mythic hero, and of his *technē*.

The following quarternotes are unusually all assertions of Socrates' knowledge, and all carefully restricted to the human realm.

Note 8.1, consonant (11d6)

This note is marked by Socrates' perhaps jesting but positive assertion that his art is more clever and wise than Daedalus' art, which reached the heavens. After the note, Socrates begins to expound, through questions, his own positive definition of holiness, which is connected to the cardinal virtue of justice.

Soc.: And is every just thing a holy thing? Or is everything holy a just thing, and not every just thing [12a] a holy thing, but rather some of them are holy while others are not?

Euth.: I don't follow what you are saying, NOTE 8.2 = 12a4 Socrates.

Soc.: [Well, try to follow.] You have the advantage of me in youth as much as in wisdom. But I say that you have put on airs because of the wealth of your wisdom. But, happy man, exert yourself. And it is not difficult to understand what I say. FIVE-SEVENTHS I say just the opposite of the versifier who versified these verses: "Even he who was the author of all these things will not revile Zeus who wrought it; 4/8 for where there is fear there is reverence." But I differ from this poet in this – shall I tell you how?

Euth.: Certainly.

Soc.: It does not to me seem to be that "where there is fear there is reverence". There are many who fear illnesses and poverty and many other such things but, although they are fearing, have reverence for none of these things that they fear. Does it not seem so to you too?

Euth.: Certainly.

Soc.: But where there is reverence, NOTE 8.3 = 12b9 there is fear too. Because wouldn't anyone with reverence and shame about doing something also at the same time fear [12c] and dread a reputation for wickedness [for doing it]?

Euth.: Anyone would indeed fear it.

Soc.: Then it is not correct to say "where there is fear there is reverence" but "where there is reverence there is fear". There is not reverence everywhere there is fear. For, I think, fear is more general than reverence. Reverence is 4/8 a species of fear just as odd numbers are a species of number. Thus it is not "where there is a number there is an odd number" but "where there is an odd number there is number". Do you follow now?

Euth.: I do.

Parallel narratives reflect musical structure: As this dialogue begins to ascend to the very consonant note at 9.0, there is a parallel with the *Symposium*. In both dialogues, the narrator has begun to expound a positive philosophy. In both dialogues, there is a reflective pause, a recognition of difficulties and the need for ability, and finally an exhortation to continue. Here, at note 8.2, Euthyphro says he does not "follow", and, after gauging his capability, his youth and wisdom, Socrates enjoins Euthyphro to exert himself. Similarly, after note 8.2 in the *Symposium*, Diotima says the younger Socrates might be able to complete the initiation and enjoins him to try to "follow", if he is able (209e5ff.).

Note 8.2, consonant (12a4)

Socrates raises the question of the relation between justice and holiness and then makes another positive assertion about wisdom.

Five-sevenths, dissonant (12a7)

This dissonant note falls at "opposite" and is marked by the two contradictory views of the relation between fear and reverence. Like the earlier lists of disjuncts, there are at this point two unreconciled assertions, and so no definite assertion.

Note 8.3, consonant (12b9)

Socrates makes a positive assertion about reverence, that is, about human religious feelings, and thus again limits his assertions of higher knowledge to the human sphere.

Soc.: It was this sort of thing, therefore, that I was also saying back there when I was questioning you. Is it that where there is a just thing, there is a holy thing? Or, instead, that where there is a holy thing, there is a just one, and that where there is a just thing there is not in every instance a holy thing. So holiness NOTE 9.0 = 12d3 is a species of justice? Shall we posit that or does it seem otherwise to you?

Euth.: Not otherwise, but so. It appears to me that you speak correctly.

Soc.: Look what follows then. If holiness is a species of justice, then we must, it seems, find out what sort of species of justice holiness is. If you ask me about species – for example, what sort of species even numbers are of number [in general] or which part such numbers 4/8 happen to be [of all numbers], I would say that they are those numbers with not only two unequal parts, but rather with two equal parts. Does it not seem so to you?

Euth.: Yes, to me too.

Soc.: [12e] You too, then, try to teach me in this way what sort of species of justice holiness is, so that we can tell Meletus to stop indicting us for doing wrong and impiety, since I have sufficiently now learned from you which things are pious and holy and which are not.

Euth.: Socrates, it now seems to me that piety and holiness NOTE 9.1 = 12e6 are species of justice, namely [the species] concerned with "taking care" of the gods. The rest of justice is about taking care of humans.

Soc.: Beautiful, Euthyphro. 7/9 Now, to me, you appear to speak beautifully. But there is just one little thing more I am in need of. I do not yet understand what sort of thing you name by this "taking care of". 4/8 You do not mean that the way we take care of other things is the way we take care of the gods. We say umm ... well, for example, we say not everyone knows how to take care of horses but just the horse trainer. Not so?

Euth.: Indeed.

Soc.: And the art of horse training is taking care of horses?

Euth.: Yes.

Soc.: Nor does everyone know how to take care of dogs – but only the dog trainer.

Euth.: So.

Parallel narratives reflect musical structure: In the *Symposium*, the ascent up Diotima's ladder reached the Form of Beauty at the consonant ninth note. Here, at the ninth note, the dialogue's third definition of piety is propounded, now for the first time by Socrates. The definition invokes justice, a cardinal Platonic virtue. Socrates says that holiness is a *morion* of justice and Burnet remarks: "Plato's usual words for 'species' are *meros* and *morion* ... [*eidos* meant] the characteristic 'form' which constitutes the species, and not the species itself regarded as a class or collection of individuals" (1924: 55).

Thus, as in the *Symposium*, the ninth note of the *Euthyphro* is devoted to the most important form of the dialogue: to piety as a species of the form of justice. This climax is more muted than in the *Symposium*, because the *Euthyphro* is shorter, less explicit and more elementary, but correlation with the musical scale is the same in both dialogues.

Socrates confirms that this ninth note was the climax of the dialogue when he later berates Euthyphro: "For just now, when we came to the point, you turned aside!" (*apetrapou*; 14c2).

Alcibiades enters and disrupts the *Symposium* at the same point that the theme of vulgar technical arts enters the *Euthyphro*, that is, after note 9.1. These disharmonious elements are appropriate to transitional notes and lead on to the conflicts in the coming dissonant range.

Note 9.0, consonant (12d3)

At this quite consonant wholenote (a 3:4 ratio), Socrates asserts the strong, Platonistic doctrine that holiness is species of justice. Socrates now harmoniously joins forces with Euthyphro and, in the second person plural, asks "do *we* so assert?" Euthyphro agrees and so also marks this climactic note with a joint and therefore doubly emphatic assertion of higher knowledge.

Note 9.1, consonant (12e6)

Euthyphro marks another note with a definition of holiness. He attempts to clarify which species of justice is involved. The definition above and its refinement here are a quarter-interval apart: narrative structure reflects musical structure.

Soc.: And the art of dog training is taking care NOTE 9.2 = 13b1 of dogs?
Euth.: [13b] Yes.
Soc.: And the art of cow training of cows?
Euth.: Quite so.
Soc.: And holiness and piety are [the art of taking care] of gods, Euthyphro? Is that what you say?
Euth.: I do.
Soc.: Therefore, "taking care of" is in all cases carried out in the same way? Take this, for example. Taking care aims at some good and benefit. Thus you observe that horses 4/5 under the care of a horse trainer are benefited and become better. 4/8 Or don't they seem so to you?
Euth.: They do.
Soc.: And dogs under the care of a dog trainer, and [13c] cows under the care of a cow trainer, and all the others similarly. Or do you think taking care aims at some harm for those under care?
Euth.: My god, not I.
Soc.: So, at some benefit?
Euth.: How not?
Soc.: So, since holiness is a kind of taking care of the gods, it is for the benefit of the gods and making them better? NOTE 9.3 = 13c7 And if you concede this, then after you do something holy, you would have then made (*apergazei*) some one of the gods better?
Euth.: No, by God, I do not!
Soc.: Nor indeed do I, Euthyphro, believe that you meant this. Far from it. But for that sake I was asking you [13d] whatever you could mean by taking care of the gods – since I don't think you meant that.
Euth.: Correct! 4/8 I didn't mean that sort of thing, Socrates.
Soc.: Well. But then which species of taking care of the gods is holiness?
Euth.: Just that, Socrates, of slaves taking care of their masters.

Parallel narratives reflect musical structure: In the *Symposium*, the notes that follow the consonant ninth and lead on to the dissonant tenth notes are transitional, that is, they are harmonious but contain the seeds of the disharmonious passages to come. In particular, Alcibiades, a disruptive force, enters the andron but agrees to preserve the order of the speeches (9.3).

This part of the *Euthyphro* is also transitional. Socrates' questions apparently solicit straightforward agreements from Euthyphro, and Socrates approvingly says in turn that he agrees with him (9.3). This relative harmony between the speakers is appropriate to these relatively consonant notes. However, a new theme is introduced here: various, everyday technical arts such as those of the cow and horse trainers. Diotima's speech particularly contrasted religion and the lower technical arts: "Whosoever has wisdom (*sophos*) in these [spiritual] affairs is a daimonic man; to have it in other matters, as in common arts and crafts, is for the vulgar or mechanical" (203a4–6).

Here, in a discussion of divine knowledge and the gods, these low arts seem jarring and therefore disharmonious.

Note 9.2 (13b1)

A disharmonious discussion of low arts. By assenting, Euthyphro is asserting to an analogy between attending to the gods and attending to dogs. At this note in the *Symposium*, Alcibiades is ridiculing and mocking Socrates; here Socrates may be ridiculing Euthyphro by even suggesting the analogy.

Note 9.3, dissonant (13c7)

The conversation returns to the question of holiness at the note.

Euthyphro here affirms another knowledge claim about holiness: that human attentions do not make the gods better. This passage is neither very consonant nor dissonant: Socrates and Euthyphro agree, but about rejecting a perhaps blasphemous contention.

THE MUSICAL STRUCTURE OF PLATO'S DIALOGUES

Soc.: I understand. It would be, it seems an art of service to the gods.
Euth.: Very much so.
Soc.: Are you able to say then the art that is of service to doctors would be a service aiming to produce *which* effect (*eis tinos ergou apergasian*)? Wouldn't you think health?
NOTE 10.0 = 13e1
Euth.: I would.
Soc.: [13e] What then about the art that which is of service to shipbuilders? Is it an art of service that aims at producing some effect (*eis tinos ergou apergasian*)?
Euth.: Clearly, Socrates, a ship.
Soc.: And the art that serves house-builders would aim at houses?
Euth.: Yes.
Soc.: Tell me then, my good fellow, the art that serves the gods, which effect would it aim to produce (*ergou apergasian*)? It's clear that you know, since you say you, above all others, know best about divine matters (*kallista ge phēs eidenai*) 4/8.
Euth.: And I speak the truth, Socrates.
Soc.: Tell me then, before God, whatever is that splendid effect which the gods produce using us as servants (*ergon ... apergazontai*)?
Euth.: Many, and beautiful ones, Socrates.
Soc.: [14a] And so do generals, my friend. But you could, nevertheless, easily tell me the most important of them: that they produce victory in war. No?
Euth.: How not.
Soc.: NOTE 10.1 = 14a5 And the farmers too, I believe, produce many, beautiful effects. But still, the most important of them is the food that is produced (*apergasias*) SIX-SEVENTHS from the earth.
Euth.: Quite so.
Soc.: What of the many and beautiful effects which the gods produce (*apergazontai*)? What is the most important of this production?
Euth.: But I was saying to you a little earlier, Socrates, that it is a great task (*ergou*) to learn accurately how all that stands. 4/8 [14b] This, however, I say to you simply: that if someone were to know what is pleasing to the gods to say and do – praying and sacrificing – just this is the holy, and such things preserve both individual households and the communities of cities. The opposite of things pleasing to the gods is impiety, which indeed overturns and destroys everything.

Parallel narratives reflect musical structure: The tenth and the eleventh wholenotes are the most dissonant notes in the musical scale. In the *Symposium*, 10.0 and 10.1 are devoted to unflattering comparisons between Socrates and an ugly, piping satyr. Here the comparisons of holiness to low arts continues.

Note 10.0, dissonant (13e1)

The extreme disharmony of Euthyphro's assertion here depends on a Platonic distinction between two kinds of *technai*. Several dialogues separate higher from lower arts: the intellectual or theoretical from the productive or practical.[11] A key difference is that the lower arts, such as house-building, involve manual labour and produce effects or works (*erga*), while the higher arts, such as architecture, produce no separate objects. The *Charmides* compares the virtue *sōphrosunē* to a higher art without *erga* (165d8ff.). If holiness is a species of the virtue of justice, as Socrates defined it at note 9.0, it should have no such *erga*.

Socrates introduces the question of whether Euthyphro thinks holiness is a lower art by using the verb *ap-erga-zesthai*, "to produce an effect", at 9.3. The verb does not appear again for the quarter-interval before this dissonant note, but two of its cognates recur here in the phrase *eis tinos ergou apergasian*. The phrase appears again just after the note and at the next midpoint (cf. also *Euthd.* 291e1, 292a1). This repetition indicates the importance of the issue. By assenting to Socrates' questions, Euthyphro is asserting that sacred relations with the gods are a lower, vulgar art.

At the midpoint, Euthyphro makes particularly pompous assertion: that he is most knowledgeable about the gods.

Note 10.1 and six-sevenths, dissonant (14a5 and a6)

This quarternote nearly coincides with the sixth seventh (which was discussed in the Introduction above). Socrates has asked, sarcastically, about the splendid work, *pankalon ergon,* of the gods (implying they perform a lower, productive art), and now asks about the *ergasia* of farmers (cf. again *Euthd.* 291e8ff.). This note is therefore also marked by the disharmonic association of our relations to the gods with a lower, vulgar art.

Another definition of holiness is asserted midway between the notes.

Soc.: If you wished, Euthyphro, NOTE 10.2 = 14b8 you could have told me the gist of what I was asking much more briefly. [14c] But it's clear you are not eager to teach me. For just now you were nearly upon it and turned away. If you had answered that, I would have already from you have learned about holiness. Now, however, since the asker must follow the one being asked whichever way the one being asked leads, tell me again 4/8 what indeed are the holy and holiness? Do you not say it is some knowledge (*epistēmēn*) of how to sacrifice and pray?
Euth.: I do.
Soc.: And then to sacrifice is to give something to the gods 8/9 and to pray is to ask for something?
Euth.: Very much so, Socrates.
Soc.: [14d] Then, knowledge of asking from and giving to the gods would be, from your statement, holiness.
Euth.: Very pretty, Socrates. You've understood what I was saying.
Soc.: Because I am a devotee (*epimuthētēs*: desirer, lover) NOTE 10.3 = 14d4, my friend, of your wisdom and pay attention to it, so that none of what you say falls to the ground. But tell me what this service is to the gods? You say it is asking from and giving to them?
Euth.: I do.
Soc.: So then would not "asking correctly" be for what we need from them, asking for just these?
Euth.: But what else?
Soc.: [14e] And again, "giving correctly" 4/8 would be of what they happen to need from us, giving these in return to them (*antidōreisthai*). For it would not be technically apt to bear gifts while giving things for which there is no need.
Euth.: You speak the truth, Socrates.

Parallel narratives reflect musical structure: In the *Symposium*, note 10.2 is about Alcibiades' pursuit of Socrates: his repeated invitations, the rejection, the grudging acceptance. It is a disharmonious passage marking a dissonant note. Similarly, here in the *Euthyphro*, Socrates upbraids Euthyphro for not teaching him, that is, for rejecting his request to be taught and disrupting their relationship.

At note 10.3 in the *Symposium*, Alcibiades says Socrates is his only worthy lover (*erastēs*) and begs to be accepted by him. At the same note here, Socrates says he is a "desirer" (*epithumētēs*) of Euthyphro's wisdom, and asks for a student–teacher relationship. Euthyphro's refusal to teach Socrates is like Socrates' refusal to take Alcibiades as a beloved.

Note 10.2, dissonant (14b8)

This dissonant note is marked by the negation of an assertion of higher knowledge. Socrates says Euthyphro has refused to teach him. Socrates' tone is here tense and recriminating. Their relationship is disharmonious.

Socrates here says that Euthyphro has "turned aside" when he was on the point of answering the question about holiness.

Another definition of holiness is asserted midway between the notes (4/8).

Note 10.3, dissonant (14d4)

Euthyphro has just committed to another definition of holiness. Socrates ironically and ambiguously praises his wisdom (*epithumētēs* implies he has not been satisfied), and asks Euthyphro again to try to teach him. This is disharmonious because Socrates is criticizing him for not sharing his supposed wisdom and is trying once again – with some exasperation – to restore their relationship.

Soc.: This art of holiness would then be, Euthyphro, a sort of bartering of the gods and humans with each other.
Euth.: Yes, bartering, if such a name pleases you. NOTE 11.0 = 14e8
Soc.: But nothing is pleasing to me if it does not happen to be true. And tell me, what sort of benefit accrues to the gods from the gifts that they take from us? What they gave us is clear to all. [15a] There is none of our goods that they did not give. But what they take from us, what does it benefit them? Or are we so greedy (*pleonektoumen*) 4/8 in the bartering, that we take all the goods from them and they take none from us?
Euth.: But do you believe, Socrates, that the gods benefit from that which they take from us?
Soc.: But then what could these be, Euthyphro, these gifts of ours to the gods?
Euth.: What do you think, other than the offerings and honours and, as I was just saying, things pleasing to them? NOTE 11.1 = 15b1
Soc.: [15b] Then the holy is pleasing to the gods, Euthyphro, but neither beneficial nor dear to the gods?
Euth.: Oh, I do believe it is more than anything dear to them.
Soc.: Well, here it is again, it seems: the holy is that which is dear to the gods.
Euth.: Most of all.
Soc.: Will you be astonished if, saying that, the statements appear to you not to stay still but walk about, and will you charge me with being the 4/8 Daedalus who makes them walk about, though you yourself are far more technically capable than Daedalus and make then run around in a circle? Or do you not perceive that the statement has gone around us and come again [15c] to the same place? Remember that somewhere before the holy and that which is dear to the gods appeared to us not the same but different from each other. Or don't you remember?
Euth.: I do.

Parallel narratives reflect musical structure: In the *Symposium*, note 11.0 is marked by a very negative and disharmonious passage. Socrates rejects Alcibiades' advances with contempt, causing him to feel anger and *aporia*. The *Euthyphro* also reaches a low point at this note.

In the *Symposium*, Alcibiades receives his fraudulent prize for courage in battle at note 11.1. Here, in the *Euthyphro*, the gods receive honour and gifts from humans, and feel grateful for them, but receive no real benefit (a kind of fraud?).

Note 11.0, dissonant (14e8)

At this very dissonant wholenote, Euthyphro's assertion is again an extreme of disharmony. He here affirms yet another definition of holiness, jarringly comparing holiness to trading or bartering. Money-making, barter and trade are consistently in Plato associated with lower arts and sophistry.[12]

Note 11.1, dissonant (15b1)

Euthyphro asserts that the gods are grateful for holiness and, as Socrates makes clear in an instant, thereby returns to his earlier, already refuted definition.

Soc.: So don't you see (*ennoeis*) NOTE 11.2 = 15c5 that now you say that that which is dear to the gods is holy? Is this anything other than to be "dear to the gods"? Or not?

Euth.: Very much so.

Soc.: Therefore, either our earlier agreement was not right or, if right then, our position now is incorrect.

Euth.: So it seems.

Soc.: From the beginning again, then! We must examine what the holy is, for I will not willingly be frightened off before I learn it. So don't dishonour me! [15d] And in every way 4/8 apply your mind to the utmost and tell me the truth! If any mortal does, you know! And you will not slip free like some Proteus before you tell me. If you did not definitely know what the holy and the unholy are, there is no way you ever would have undertaken to, on behalf of a labourer, charge your father, an elderly man, with murder. NOTE 11.3 = 15d7 The fear of the gods would have kept you from taking the risk of doing something incorrect, and you would have been ashamed before humans. Now I well know (*eu oida*) [15e] that you definitely believe that you know (*hoti saphōs oiei eidenai*) what is holy and what is not. Tell me now, my good man Euthyphro, and do not conceal what you believe!

Parallel narratives reflect musical structure: Both dialogues are negative and disharmonious at 11.2. Alcibiades again compares Socrates to a hubristic satyr and criticizes his speeches. Here, Socrates exposes a fundamental mistake in Euthyphro's views: he has unwittingly returned to an earlier, already refuted view.

At the end of the *Symposium*, Socrates remains awake to continue arguing about tragedy and comedy. Here he says he will not stop pursuing his inquiry.

Note 11.2, dissonant (15c5)

Socrates summarizes Euthyphro's contradictory assertions about holiness, and Euthyphro endorses his summary. This is another example of an elenchus located at a dissonant note.

Note 11.3, dissonant (15d7)

This passage is important for the theory of the marking passages. Socrates makes the connection: charging your father with murder is an assertion of higher knowledge about holiness. Thus the charges are a species of higher assertions. Given that Socrates has now shown Euthyphro's pretensions to know the nature of holiness to be ridiculous, this is a disharmonious passage.

Socrates himself makes a strong assertion here, that he knows that Euthyphro thinks he knows, but this is a characteristically this-worldly assertion.

Euth.: Later, Socrates. Now I'm in a rush – and time's slipping away.

Soc.: What are you doing, my friend? If you go off, you're crushing the great hope 4/8 I had of learning from you about holy and unholy things, and of being rid of Meletus' indictment. [16a] I would have shown him that I'd already become wise about divine matters from Euthyphro and that I would no longer in my ignorance recklessly innovate about such things, and moreover that for the rest of my life I would live better. NOTE 12.0 = 16a4

Parallel narratives reflect musical structure: The conversation breaks up, in both dialogues, at the fourth octad (4/8) before the final note.

Note 12.0, consonant (16a4)

There is a cluster of markers just before the concluding, twelfth wholenote: references to the long-sought definition of holiness, to Meletus' prosecution, and to higher wisdom about the gods.

CHAPTER 7

Extracting doctrine from structure

It is not immediately apparent that new structure leads to new content, that is, that discerning the underlying musical scale of the dialogues will shift ideas about Plato's philosophy. The argument of this chapter is novel and requires some historical context, but has rich dividends.

Aristotle's signature doctrine that "virtue is a mean" has been at the core of the recent revival of virtue ethics. This chapter uses stichometric measurements in a new way to confirm the minority view that Aristotle's doctrine was already present in Plato.

The question below is whether passages ostensibly about one subject may be read as symbols or allusions to something else. This is not a question amenable to logical demonstration. Methodologically, this section employs a mode of interpretation, commonly used in studies of symbolic or allegorical texts, which relies centrally on an argument from coherence: close readings, comparisons and historical context are combined to elucidate the secondary referents of allusive passages. The conclusions reached, however, are strong and the last section below will be devoted to a retrospective analysis of the arguments.

This chapter is part of a larger project that compares passages at the same relative location in different dialogues. A surprising number of themes are shared by these parallel passages (Chs 3, 6).

7.1 Aristotle on virtues and means

One strand of scholarship on Aristotle's doctrine that virtue is a mean interprets it as a borrowing from Plato and ethical discussions in the Academy, implying that Aristotle elaborates a doctrine only alluded to in Plato. Hursthouse, for example, argues that Aristotle "takes over from Plato all the [key] features of the doctrine" (2006: 97). Oates had even earlier argued that Aristotle's doctrine derived especially from the *Philebus*. For him, the Pythagorean metaphysics in the *Philebus* culminates at the end of the dialogue in a defence of the mean, that is, of measure, moderation and symmetry, which has already become an ethical concept:

> [W]ith Plato the mean gives the guiding principle for applying the *peras* to *to apeiron*. Hence Plato sees the mean as symmetry and measure, that which transcends both *to phronein* and *hēdonē* ... in the *Philebus* the mean as an entity or hypostasisation has come to occupy a place beside the good and the beautiful, which are at the apex of the Platonic hierarchy of Ideas.   (Oates 1936: 387–8)[1]

Stichometric measurements will provide new evidence for these contentions, and throw new light on Plato's ethics.

Strikingly, Aristotle himself introduces his doctrine of the mean in the *Nicomachean Ethics* by recalling the Pythagorean metaphysics expounded in the *Philebus*:

> Virtue is a mean (*mesotēs*) since it is able to hit the middle (*mesou*). Vice is many-sided, for, as in the Pythagorean comparison, evil is of the Unlimited and the Good of the Limited ... Thus excess and deficiency are evil and virtue is a mean, ... a ratio (*logō*) defined as a wise man would define it... In terms of being and essence, virtue is a mean; in terms of what is best and good, it is an extreme...   (1106b28–a9)

This definition, and its emphasis on mathematics, wisdom and the sage who attains the mean, will play a role in the following arguments.

The most important mean for Aristotle is that between pleasure and pain. These two basic affects are fundamental to moral choice since they incline the individual to pursue or avoid any particular activity. Thus, the passage above continues: "Concerning pleasure and pain, [for example] ... the mean is *sōphrosunē*, and an excess is licentiousness" (1107b4–7).[2]

As Aristotle summarizes, "moral virtue is about pleasure and pain" (*Eth. Nic.* 1104b8). This is quoted by Theodore Tracy, who reviews why pleasure and pain are "the primary opposites of the moral organism" (1969: 233).

Aristotle clearly thinks of his ethical means in mathematical terms, and uses proportions and geometric lines in expositions of the various virtues.[3] He illustrates this coincidence of mean and extreme, for example, in the long passage about the "great man" who attains to the ethical mean: "The great-souled man is, in terms of his magnitude, an extreme, and in terms of its appropriateness, he is a mean. The small-souled, however, are excessive or deficient" (1123b14–16); "The great-souled man ... is the best. The truly great-souled must be good" (1123b27–9).

Book VI of the *Nicomachean Ethics* is a long defence of the claim that hitting the mean requires *phrōnēsis* and wisdom.[4]

To show that this doctrine is embedded in the musical structure of Plato's dialogues requires an excursion into some recent work on the history of mathematical means.

7.2 Stichometry and the divided line

Greek mathematicians had a rather elaborate typology of various means and proportions. The mean they constructed by the so-called "division into mean and extreme ratio" came at some point to be known as "the golden mean" or "golden section" and was prominent in later Pythagorean and numerological lore. Although Aristotle uses the language of "mean and extreme", and although his doctrine is today sometimes loosely described in terms of a "golden mean", Aristotle never explicitly makes the connection to what in his times would have been a rather obscure mathematical concept. Scholars generally see no connection between Aristotle's doctrine and the mathematicians' golden mean.

Historians of science are, as mentioned in the introduction, accustomed to the idea that studies of primitive pseudo-sciences such as alchemy, astrology and numerology are necessary prolegomena to the study of our modern sciences and mathematics. Plato's dialogues championed reasoned debate, philosophy, mathematics and advanced education, and their achievement is in no way diminished by an admixture of pseudo-science. Writing in the throes of a great mathematical revolution, while advances were being made in his own school, Plato can be excused from too wholeheartedly embracing mathematics. At a time when its applications were being extended far and wide, from music and mechanics to astronomy and architecture, the problem of distinguishing science from pseudo-science in mathematics could remain a problem for later times. Indeed, the problem arises only after the first, historic steps down the path towards science have been taken.

The mathematicians' golden mean occurs in the "pentagram", allegedly an esoteric symbol of the Pythagoreans, constructed by extending the sides of a pentagon to form a five-pointed star (Burkert 1972: 176, 452; Herz-Fischler 1998: ch. III). Euclid's *Elements* contains a number of theorems involving the pentagon and the golden mean and, as discussed in Roger Herz-Fischler's monograph *A Mathematical History of the Golden Number* (1998), these theorems are generally held to have been developed before or during Plato's lifetime.

In his commentary on Euclid's *Elements*, Thomas Heath builds an extensive case for the claim that constructions of the pentagon and the five regular solids among the Pythagoreans before Plato would have led to investigations of the golden mean.[5]

For Heath, this corroborated the assertion in Proclus that Plato himself derived several theorems about the golden mean:

> [T]he problem of the *golden section* ... is no doubt "the section" referred to ... by Proclus ... which says that Eudoxus "greatly added to the number

of the theorems which Plato originated regarding the section." This idea that Plato began the study of the "golden section" as a subject in itself is not in the least inconsistent with [my argument that the problem of finding the golden section] was solved by the Pythagoreans. The very fact that Euclid places it among other propositions which are clearly Pythagorean in origin is significant. (Euclid 1956: vol. 2, 99)[6]

Herz-Fischler's monograph concludes that the key theorems about the golden mean were developed around the time that Plato was writing his dialogues. However, finding little evidence for advanced mathematics in the dialogues, Herz-Fischler supposes they were the work of some other mathematician such as, perhaps, Theaetetus. Whether derived by Plato or one of his contemporaries, there is a historical consensus that the dates make it possible for Plato to have known key theorems about the golden mean.

There is a literature, carefully reviewed by Yuri Balashov and briefly by Herz-Fischler, on the question of whether Plato's divided line, described in the famous passage in the *Republic*, was meant to be divided at the golden mean.[7] Although the golden mean is not explicitly mentioned in the simile nor anywhere else in Plato,[8] these scholars debated whether the passage in the *Republic* is an allusion to a theme that later became prominent. Balashov's review rightly concludes that, although the allusion is possible, such an interpretation is not forced upon us by Plato's text.

Stichometric measurements bring a striking new piece of evidence to this long-standing debate over the divided line. The numerical value of the golden mean is, to three places, 0.618, and thus a unit length divided at the golden mean will be divided at 61.8 per cent.[9] Surprisingly, the *Republic*'s discussion of the divided line lies about 61 or 62 per cent of the way through the text.

The key passage focused on by other scholars, which has the good in some proportion to itself, is at 61.7p (508b13). The calculated location within the text of the golden mean, 61.8p, is nine lines later (508c9). Glaucon there asks for an explanation, and this leads to the long passage about the divided line, which is first mentioned at 62.2p (509d6). By itself, it could be a coincidence that a passage interpreted as an allusion to the golden mean lies near 61.8p, but other dialogues, it will be shown below, also arguably contain allusions to the golden mean near 61.8p.

Euclid's definition of the golden mean is phrased in terms of its technical name: a straight line is said to have been cut in "extreme and mean ratio" (*akron kai meson logon*) when as the whole line is to the greater section, so is the greater to the less (Euclid 1956: bk. II, D. 3). Thus the golden mean is defined by relations between a line and its parts; in various ways they are greater than, less than and equal to each other.

A passage in the *Parmenides* at the location of the golden mean recalls Euclid's language:

- *Parmenides* (61.7–61.8p): The One is equal and greater and less than itself ... And if greater and less and equal, it would be of equal measures and more and less than itself ... and in number less and more (151b5–c7; 61.8p = b7).[10]

The similarity of the content of this passage to Euclid's definition, together with its location, suggests that Plato's dialogues should be surveyed for similar allusions to the golden mean.

7.3 Reading the dialogues in parallel

The following evidence shows that the constellation of themes appearing in Aristotle's discussion of virtue as a mean recur in Plato's dialogues at locations near 61.8p. In particular, Aristotle: (i) makes the mathematical concept of a mean serve as an ethical concept; (ii) says the mean is attained by wisdom; (iii) speaks of great men who succeed in attaining the mean; and (iv) thinks that *sōphrosunē*, for example, is a mean between an excess and deficiency of pleasure.

Given this historical context, it is not surprising that explicit references to "mean" or "middle" or "moderation" occur in several of Plato's dialogues near 61.8p, and connect the term with philosophers or wisdom:

- *Symposium* (61.5–61.8): Diotima explains that neither those already wise, like the gods, nor those entirely ignorant philosophize. Rather, just as Eros is "in the middle", philosophers are "in the middle between both" the wise and ignorant.[11]
- *Philebus* (61.3–61.8p): Socrates asks about pleasures which are great in degree (a continuum). Those with *sōphrosunē* obey the Delphic adage, "nothing in excess" or "everything in moderation". Thus, Socrates says, the greatest pleasures and pains are not virtues.[12]
- *Phaedrus* (61.8–62.1): Socrates remarks at noon that, unlike the Many, they are conversing and not sleeping in "the middle of the day". He proceeds to tell a short myth that has four levels reminiscent of the *Republic*'s divided line.[13]

These three passages repeat "mean" or "moderation" at the location of the golden mean but also suggest that it is peculiarly the philosopher who is associated with these means.

As in Aristotle, the dialogues thus also seem to associate a mean with philosophers who have the virtue of *sōphrosunē* and thus follow some moderate path between the extremes of pleasure and pain. In fact, the theme of pleasure and its moderation consistently recur around 61.8p. The *Cratylus* provides strong evidence because it discusses this theme near 61.8p and nowhere else:

- *Cratylus* (60.8–62.6p): The etymologies of pleasure, pain, desire and *eros*; at 61.8p, the etymology of *euphrosunē*, perhaps "wisdom of the good", but here the good or harmonious movement of the soul with nature.[14]
- *Laws* (61.7–61.8p): The Athenian says that, unlike the Many, those who are pure and chaste win the greatest victory, that is, the victory over pleasure, and live a holy and just life.[15]

- *Timaeus* (60.0–61.6p): The physiological theory of pleasure and pain.[16]

The *Charmides* discusses pleasure in language that recalls the definition of the golden mean:

- *Charmides* (61.8–61.9p): Critias asks if there is a desire, not for any particular pleasure, but for desire itself; this is part of a longer passage about things related to themselves and whether anything could be both "greater and less than itself" (as a line divided at the golden mean).[17]

Some dialogues just place emphatic references to an ideal philosopher near 61.8p:

- *Statesman* (61.7–62.3p): after a long hunt, Socrates first espies the real and kingly statesman (the philosopher) who must be separated from the larger crowd of sophists.[18]
- *Theaetetus* (61.8–62.0): Socrates pauses to express in emphatic terms the reverence and awe he feels for Parmenides, who was both noble and profound (and thus a model philosopher).[19]

Thus the same coherent association in Aristotle between a mathematical mean and, on the other hand, an ethical mean between pleasure and pain attained by wisdom recurs in Plato's dialogues at locations near 61.8p. This makes it more probable that all these passages are allusions to the golden mean like that seen by scholars in the *Republic*'s divided line.

7.4 The logic of the argument and its consequences

Since there is, in some quarters, a facile fascination with the golden mean, it is best to be explicit about the nature of the argument here. It would be simplistic and weak to reason as follows:

1. Some passages in the dialogues allude to the golden mean.
2. Surprisingly, these passages lie close to 61.8p.
3. Therefore, they are in fact allusions to the golden mean.

This argument is wrong-headed in several ways and is not the argument made here. First, it is difficult to prove that a given text in isolation does or does not contain literal evidence for its figurative meanings: allusions are not explicit. Such claims generally must rest on some broader argument from coherence. Thus, it cannot be proved in any rigorous way from these particular texts alone that they are allusions to the golden mean. As Balashov's survey shows, a number of scholars have argued the point back and forth without settling the issue. Second, the measurements of locations in the text have a statistical accuracy only and, by themselves, cannot bear the weight of the extraordinary claim made in step 3.

In short, the arguments for the musical structure of Plato's dialogues do not begin with nor depend on these allusions to the golden mean. They rest, in the first place, on the strong evidence assembled in earlier chapters. On the other hand, the argument about the golden mean does depend on those earlier arguments.

To be explicit, the argument made in this chapter is at once more sophisticated and stronger than the short argument above, but aims only at an incremental addition to what has been established in previous chapters:

1. given that earlier chapters have already established in several ways that the dialogues have a stichometric structure with various musical and mathematical points marked by symbolic passages;
2. given that there is strong contextual evidence that mathematicians within the Academy as well as earlier Pythagoreans knew of and emphasised the importance of the golden mean;
3. given that *other scholars* have argued that the divided line is an allusion to the golden mean;
4. surprisingly, these passages lie close to 61.8p of the way through the text;
5. therefore, this measurement, the strong evidence for stichometric structure, and the strong historical evidence all together make it *more probable* that the other scholars were correct: the divided line is an allusion to the golden mean.

If it is accepted that the dialogues have a stichometric and musical structure with affinities to Pythagoreanism, it is no great step to conclude that they also make allusions to the golden mean, which is involved in geometric constructions attributed to the Pythagoreans.

Observe that this argument relies on the fact that other scholars have interpreted the divided line as an allusion; it does not directly rest on the plausible but debatable claim that the passage is an allusion. Thus it argues from the fact of perceived allusions to an increased probability.

In short, the argument of this chapter aims only at an incremental step. Attempts to evaluate it should begin with the general evidence for stichometric structure presented in earlier chapters.

Only after this argument about the *Republic* is accepted, however, can other dialogues be canvassed for allusions to the golden mean. The argument is conditional: if it is established that one dialogue alludes to the golden mean near 61.8p, then it is possible or probable that other dialogues do so as well. Although it remains a matter of probabilities, the satisfying appearance of other seeming allusions near 61.8p becomes strong confirmatory evidence. It still remains, of course, impossible to establish from the explicit language of the texts alone that they are allusions. However, given that the *Republic* does allude to the golden mean, there is now a substantially heightened probability that these passages in other dialogues are also in fact allusions to the golden mean.

The argument does not aim and cannot go beyond these probabilities: we shall never have literal and explicit evidence that a passage is an allusion. It is nonetheless, given the arguments of previous chapters, improbable both that other experts have argued in print that a passage is an allusion to the golden mean and that the passage merely as a matter of accident lies near the value of the golden mean.

Previous chapters have suggested simple tests for the stichometric structure (measuring the lengths of set speeches, etc.). These passages about the golden mean are not clearly candidates for such tests. The density of Plato's symbolism complicates the issue. It is not the case that means or middles are mentioned only near 61.8p. As Sayre (2006) has noted, "middles" are mentioned near the middle of some dialogues. Moreover, future work will show that there are allusions to other kinds of means in Plato's works.[20]

Once accepted, these arguments have implications for certain areas of historical research. For the history of mathematics, this adds another kind of evidence to the hitherto circumstantial inferences made about knowledge of the golden mean in the Academy. It shows, moreover, that Plato possessed knowledge of the numerical value of the golden mean, since its stichometric location had to be calculated. For the history of philosophy, the ethical passages above confirm the view that central features of Aristotle's doctrine were borrowed from Plato, and connect that doctrine to Pythagoreanism, as Aristotle himself briefly indicated. We learn more about Plato's philosophy by explicating the stichometric structure. In short, structure leads to content.

Moreover, this argument has important ramifications for the textual criticism of Plato's *oeuvre*. Since the value of the golden mean is known precisely, the evidence above provides an important check on the accuracy of the stichometric measurements used here. That is, the discrepancy between the measured location of a passage in the modern text and its location within Plato's autograph (i.e. before any corruptions introduced during its recopying and transmission disturbed the proportions of the original composition) can now be precisely investigated. As the above data show, this discrepancy is generally less than half a per cent. In the *Republic*, the allusion to the golden mean lies at 61.7 per cent of the way through the modern, Oxford text, while in Plato's autograph it lay at 61.8 per cent. In this case, perhaps aided by the fortuitous averaging of the effects due to smaller corruptions that occurs in longer texts (see §2.1), the discrepancy is less than half a per cent.

This means the stichometric structures of the dialogues provide a surprising new technique for evaluating how closely our texts resemble Plato's autographs. Perhaps for the first time, it is possible to reach behind the scribal tradition and gauge the integrity of texts descended from the classical period.

CHAPTER 8
Some implications

The aim of this monograph has been to survey the evidence for the existence of a stichometric, musical structure in the *Symposium* and *Euthyphro*. The following briefly discusses several implications related to the musical structure.

8.1 Summary of the case

The allegorist's dual aims of communication and concealment force interpeters to build strong cases by assembling many reinforcing lines of evidence. A series of salient points are important at the outset of the verification stage, in which the bare existence of the dialogues' musical structure is confirmed:

- the methods employed here are typical of those used by scholars to interpet allegorical texts by authors such as Dante, Spenser and Joyce (§1.8);
- allegory was debated in the circles around Socrates, as is attested by the references in Plato's dialogues and by the Derveni papyrus (Ch. 1).
- symbolism of various kinds and the practice of reserving doctrines were common in antiquity and were especially associated with the early Pythagoreans (Ch. 1);
- the early Academy reported that Plato was a Pythagorean; Sayre, Dillon, Kahn and other scholars argue in different ways that Plato had an innovative Pythagorean philosophy that was not spelled out openly in the dialogues but which can be found there by subtle intepretation (§1.5);
- the theses advanced here are conservative in that they restore the *status quo ante*: Plato was often read as a symbolic writer who reserved his true philosophy through late antiquity and the Renaissance (§1.6);

SOME IMPLICATIONS

- stichometry was routine by the late fifth or early fourth centuries (§2.1);
- simple evidence established a *prima facie* case for line-counting: the climax of Diotima's speech at the top of her ladder is three-quarters of the way through the *Symposium*, the discussion of musical modes and Damon is one-quarter of the way through the *Republic*, and so on (Ch. 2; §3.4);
- objective measurements provided more evidence for line-counting: the lengths of set speeches and the total lengths of the dialogues (Ch. 3);
- the relation of the number twelve to the major musical intervals and the concept of relative consonance were known in the fifth century and by Archytas; Plato's twelve-note scale, quarternotes and relative consonance were discussed by the neo-Pythagoreans (Appendices 1, 2).
- simple, qualitative graphs show that the early speeches in the *Symposium* and the distribution of music-related terminology in the *Republic* are organized around the twelve-note scale (Ch. 2; §3.4);
- test comparisons showed that the consonant eighth and ninth notes are marked with more positive and the dissonant tenth and eleventh notes with more negative concepts in both the *Symposium* and the *Euthyphro* (Ch. 2);
- the guides to strong evidence in Chapters 2 and 6 show that the narrative structures of the dialogues are organized by the twelve-note scale, and that the content of marking passages reflects the relative consonance of the underlying notes;
- parallels between the dialogues show that the same musical scale is used in each, that similar concepts are found at similar relative locations and that the narratives similarly track the consonance of the musical notes (§§3.2–3; Ch. 6);
- the Pseudo-Platonica are a control and show that the methods used here are falsifiable: they can be stringently tested (§3.5).

Chapters 4, 5 and 6 explicated the musical notes in the *Symposium* and the *Euthyphro* in some detail and showed that the musical passages in the twelve-note scale are marked consistently, with species of a single genus of concepts. The appendix on the systematic theory of the marking passages showed that the dialogues explicitly link the various species used to mark the notes.

8.2 Interpreting the dialogues

Although the arguments and ideas in the surface narratives and their dramatic context remain primary, full elucidation of the dialogues will require coupling analysis with the kind of systematic symbolic interpretation practised by Dante and Spenser scholars.

Several long-standing debates over the dialogues are affected by these findings. It has been thought that the *Republic* is a loose composite of tracts written at different times and that, for example, the first book is from Plato's early period. Similarly, the distinct styles of the speeches in the *Phaedrus* and the dialogue's awkward structure have suggested to some that it too may be a composite. Both dialogues, however, are strictly unified by the underlying musical scale and have consistent symbolic schemes. They were written as wholes. If partial drafts were collected from various periods or various sources, they have been assiduously reworked.

The dramatic structure of the dialogues is now also substantially clarified. The literature that charged some dialogues with incoherency, either because they meandered from topic to topic or because the seemed to peter out with no definite conclusions, can now be set aside. Although unconventional, the dialogues have a clear, well-planned structure. They rise to secondary peaks at the third and fourth notes and then climax at the ninth before descending again into disharmony.

New evidence is available to debates over the so-called spurious dialogues, collected in the last volume of the Oxford edition (§3.5). About half of these dialogues do have the same musical structure as the dialogues accepted as genuine. Although this may mean merely that a later imitator had the talent both to discern and reproduce Plato's symbolism, it does raise the likelihood that these dialogues are genuine.

8.3 Problems with anonymity and intentionality

The so-called problem of Platonic anonymity is also transformed. Since Plato never directly speaks in his own voice or endorses the doctrines that appear in the dialogues, inferences about his own philosophical commitments remained more or less conjectural. It is now, however, tempting to interpret the correlation between a dialogue's contents and its musical scale as a running commentary on the surface narrative. Consonant notes are associated with harmonious, positive or more Platonic ideas, which are, in virtue of their location, endorsed or valorized. Conversely, dissonant notes are associated with disharmonious, negative or less Platonic ideas, which are again, in virtue of their location, in some way condemned. In the *Symposium*, for example, this correlation would confirm the view that the second half of Diotima's speech, where the ascent to the Form of Beauty coincides with the consonant ninth note, is the most Platonic passage in the dialogue. In the *Euthyphro*, similarly, Socrates' suggestion at the ninth note that piety is a species of justice would now be taken as the Platonic view. Although this dialogue ends aporetically, the musical symbolism tells us the equation between piety and justice is viewed as favourably as Diotima's ascent. It seems that, for the first time, we can hear Plato's own voice.

This solution to the problem of anonymity, however, generates a new "problem of intentionality". Broadly speaking, should the doctrines inferred from the dialogue's symbolic structures be regarded as Plato's own convictions, as the message he intended to communicate? What were Plato's intentions? Some assert that an author's intentions can never be inferred from a literary text. As a general thesis, this is merely a form of scepticism. The dialogues themselves, however, repeatedly raise and confuse issues surrounding their intentions (even apart from debates over the *Seventh Letter*). In the *Symposium*, for example, the story told in the frame about the origin of the account is deliberately convoluted and problematizes the narrator's reliability and relation to Plato. The explicit aversions to Socratic irony in the dialogues also complicate questions about intentionality. These literary strategies raise the question of whether the musical structures in the dialogues carry authentic doctrine or are merely another layer of puzzles.

This problem of intentionality may be met with two broad responses. Some will be *indifferentists*. They might argue that exposing the symbolic and allegorical layers in the dialogues is equivalent to unearthing new works by Plato, a significant new cache of information about the dialogues and their structure, about Plato's Presocratic inheritance, and about classical philosophy, mathematics, literary theory and music. Its historical significance, these indifferentists may contend, is independent of any connection to Plato's supposed intentions.

On the other hand, *intentionalists* can mount some strong plausibility arguments for taking the symbolically represented doctrines for Plato's own. First, the doctrines cohere with the repeated views of Plato's associates and followers about his beliefs. They definitely asserted that he was a Pythagorean, and the interpretations advanced here may be viewed simply as confirmatory evidence of his contemporaries' claims about his intentions. Second, the doctrines extend and elaborate the hints of Pythagoreanism found in the surface narrative of the dialogues.[1] Those who infer Plato's intentions from those narratives must concede that Pythagoreanism of some sort is a plausible candidate for Plato's philosophy. Third, although reserving doctrines in various ways was common and perhaps even normal among religions, fraternities and guilds at least from the classical period, concealing doctrines as a joke, or a decoy or a philosophical puzzle would be unprecedented in that historical context. As Athenian legal trials show, esoteric knowledge and the preservation of its secrecy could be treated as a grave matter of life or death. Fourth, the scale, the consistency and the coherency of the allegory testifies to its seriousness. It was, with enormous effort and ingenuity, embedded in every work during several decades of literary activity. Fifth, and last, the musical structures are part of a broader symbolic scheme that sheds further light on Plato's philosophy and generally provide more evidence for his Pythagoreanism. Despite these five points, however, legitimate doubt remains about Plato's intentions and both positions have their virtues. This question cannot be settled here.

8.4 Interpreting Plato, Pythagoras and Socrates

A few general conclusions about Plato's philosophy and its relation to Pythagoras and Socrates can, however, be drawn at this point.

The presence of the same musical structure in all the dialogues accepted as genuine suggests that the philosophy expressed there did not, in fundamental ways, develop during Plato's career. Although stylometric data have been interpreted as showing that Plato's dialogues form three groups, early, middle and late, this developmentalism has always had its critics. It is generally not the case that ancient philosophers presented their views as developing over time as, say, modern philosophers or scientists sometimes do. It may seem commonsensical that Plato's philosophy would evolve – he is reputed to have continued writing until his death at eighty-one – but this view has always been open to the charge of anachronism. A few, perhaps unreliable, ancient anecdotes about Plato speak of a single event, some kind of conversion to philosophy or accession to wisdom, and the evidence presented here fits better with this idea (Riginos 1976: 46–7).

It is often thought, in particular, that the theory of Forms is fully developed only in the middle and late dialogues. The musical structures, however, furnish a number of kinds of evidence that the theory of Forms shaped the so-called early dialogues. Most generally, the musical scale itself may be interpreted as a "Form beneath appearances", and seems to show the theory working as a motivation for Plato's literary methods. If, moreover, the marking passages within a dialogue were correctly interpreted as species of a common genus, then they already reveal the core characteristic of a Platonic form, its role as a "one over many". Thus the hints at the ninth note in the *Euthyphro* of the logical terminology associated with the theory of Forms, for one example, should not be seen as fragmentary anticipations of later developments, but as limited glimpses of an already complete theory. Subsequent work will show that such hints are deployed systematically in the so-called early dialogues.

The musical structures seem to conflict with the general views of the Tübinger approach, but to confirm the moderate approach of Sayer, Dillon, Kahn and others (see Ch. 1). Both approaches accept reports of Plato's Pythagorean metaphysics, his so-called "late ontology", and the musical structures make these even more credible. This moderate approach, however, rejects the Tübinger emphasis on some sustained, oral transmission of "unwritten doctrines", and the findings here also tend to undermine that view. First, the Pythagorean doctrines were not "unwritten", but symbolically embedded in the dialogues – as some ancient commentators said. Second, late reports of Plato's Pythagorean doctrines need not now point towards some oral transmission alongside the dialogues. The dialogues themselves could have transmitted these doctrines.

Chapter 1 reviewed the way that Burkert's *Lore and Science in Ancient Pythagoreanism* reshaped the history of Pythagoreanism and its reception. He sceptically assessed the ancient evidence and argued that there was an "expanding tradition" of reports about Pythagoras: more and more seemed to be known as the centuries passed. He concluded that the tradition had been increasingly embellished. Moreover, Burkert rejected the claims of the early Academy that Plato's philosophy had been in some strong way influenced by Pythagoras. Huffman's important volumes on Philolaus and Archytas reinforce and extend this approach to Pythagoreanism.

These views will need to be reconsidered. Although Pythagoras is hardly mentioned in the dialogues, Plato's earlier followers correctly associated him with Pythagoreanism. Moreover, the concealed musical substructure and the use of Pythagorean symbols shows that there was, at least at the time of Plato, a tendency to reserve Pythagorean doctrine, just as was claimed in antiquity. Although many of the later doxographical writings are clearly unreliable, the expanding tradition about Pythagoras may at least in part result from the gradual divulgence of closely held secrets.

Pythagoras has variously been reputed to be the founder of the European tradition in mathematics or a mere legendary miracle worker. The symbolic structures in the dialogues, however, provide a range of early evidence that may reshape this dispute. The structures are, in particular, related to core Pythagorean doctrines such as the "harmony of the spheres", to the theory of relative harmony, and to constructions of the pentagon and regular polyhedra. The general fact that the dialogues have a musico-mathematical substructure seems to conform with the Pythagorean tenet, reported already in Aristotle, that the fabric of reality, beneath appearances, is somehow mathematical. In short, the structures tend to confirm the picture of a tradition with secret doctrines about the musico-mathematical structure of the cosmos.

The musical structures in the dialogues make the historical Socrates even more remote. Debate over the Socratic question, the question of the relation between Plato's portrait and the historical Socrates, has turned in part on whether the so-called early dialogues are closer to Socrates' doctrines and character. If instead of a distinction between early and late, we have only a distinction between elementary and advanced, the simpler "Socratic" dialogues are merely evidence that, as has been suggested, Plato varied the degree to which he revealed the complexities of his philosophy.

The *Apology* has sometimes been thought to be a more or less verbatim, or at least a faithful, account of Socrates' speeches at his trial. It is often supposed to have been written soon after the events, and therefore both to be Plato's first surviving composition and our best evidence for the historical Socrates. The musical symbolism, however, runs through the *Apology* and makes clear that this dialogue is largely a literary creation. The lengths of the speeches, their content and even the brief cross-examination are all correlated with the musical scale. It is not in any simple way evidence for the historical Socrates.

8.5 History of music and mathematics

Plato's use of the mathematically regular scale with quarternotes confirms, for example, Barker's view that such scales were debated at the time of Plato (App. 1). Calculating the locations of the notes within the long texts of the dialogues required translating musical ratios into line counts. This would not be difficult for the enthusiasts who, in the fifth and fourth centuries BCE, were beginning to be called "mathematicians", but for the first time we have evidence of Plato performing elaborate calculations.

The use of the golden mean as a measure of location and as a symbol for virtuous means (Ch. 7) shows a more sophisticated knowledge of mathematics. The golden mean was probably encountered in research on constructing the regular polyhedra called the "Platonic solids". Recognizing its mathematical importance indicated engagement with the more advanced research of the day. This tends to confirm Proclus' assertion that Plato worked on theorems about the "golden section" as well as the widely held view that the related material in Euclid descended from the Academy (Ch. 7). It has been debated whether Plato was merely an armchair philosopher, a mere cheerleader for mathematics (see e.g. Zhmud 1998), or whether he participated in and perhaps directed the Academy's research in mathematics and mathematical astronomy. The musical structures bolster the case for the latter view.

Although Ptolemy's *Harmonics* uses the monochord to demonstrate musical ratios, there is debate about how early this instrument was invented. It is not mentioned explicitly in classical writers, and seemingly only later became important in Pythagorean lore. Nothing detected so far in the musical structures requires the invocation of the monochord. The scales in the dialogues could have been played on a variety of instruments. However, the scale embedded in the dialogues does treat musical pitch as a single, linear continuum (measured by line counts), and is clearly analogous to the monochord. The musical symbolism in the *Republic* seems to allude to a stringed instrument (App. 8), but it may have had more than one string.

More research is needed on ancient theories of relative consonance. Although mentioned in ancient sources, the range of measures employed and the algorithms used to calculate them, their roles in the contending schools of music theory, and their application to quarternotes, for example, is not clear.

It is striking that both Plato and Aristotle assert that the psychological and emotional effects of music depend not just on the particular melody played, but on the scale or key employed.[2] It is likely, therefore, that the twelve-note scale embedded in the dialogues and "sounded" by the relatively harmonious or disharmonious speech at each note was intended to elicit some psychological response. Reading aloud was the norm in antiquity, and the dialogues may, at least in part, have been conceived of as "scores" to be performed by their readers. Aristotle, for example, suggested that music alters souls because the soul itself is or has a harmony.[3] Previous chapters have focused on the literary and symbolic functions of the embedded scales, but the possibility that Plato aimed at some musical effect in his readers will need to be investigated.

8.6 History of literature and literary theory

Platonism inspired much of the European tradition of allegorical literature, and Plato's dialogues can now take their place at its beginning.

I have focused on evidence for Plato's musical symbolism. Apart from the contentions that the musical structure constituted a "Form" beneath the surface narrative and that the various marking passages were species of an overarching genus, a general theorization of the nature of the symbolic scheme has been avoided. Partly, this is because Plato's scheme is *sui generis*, and the close readings of the previous chapters had first to establish its existence. Partly, this is because its relation to later allegorical literature and to the large body of modern literary theory should be considered by experts.

One issue, however, has practical implications. Scholars in translation studies have examined the ways in which allegorical literature has been translated and, in particular, the way that translators unaware of a text's symbolic strategies may render them wholly obscure. A key word, for example, may be repeated throughout a literary work in different contexts and thereby come to be charged with accumulated meaning (e.g. "nothing" in *King Lear*). If a translator fails to notice this and translates the single key word using a range of synonyms in the target language, this kind of symbolism will disappear altogether. These scholars, therefore, have stressed that allegorical texts require special sorts of translation methods. My translations in previous chapters are intended to bring out the symbolism at the locations of the musical notes. Although more recent translations tend to hew more closely to the literal meaning of the dialogues, in general, they still obscure Plato's symbolism and may need revision.

8.7 Ancient book production, papyrology, textual studies

Papyrologists have known for some time that literary scrolls in the classical period could be produced with uniform lines and columns, and that the hexameter line was commonly used as a unit of measure. It is not very surprising that a philosopher with Pythagorean leanings would take advantage of these facts to give his compositions a mathematical organization (as Vitruvius reported; Ch. 2).

As mentioned in Chapter 2, there is some debate about the integrity of Plato's manuscripts. Mapping the musical structure provides a tool for investigating the completeness of each dialogue, but will probably not help with determining whether shorter phrases and sentences are interpolations or whether there are isolated lacunae. The measurements of relative location are accurate only to within a fraction of a per cent. There are some manuscripts, however, that have lost entire columns of the Greek text (see e.g. Brockmann 1992; Böter 1989), which then have to be supplemented from other manuscripts, and the musical structures are fine grained enough to detect or rule out omissions on this scale.

8.8 The forward path

It is difficult to convey the magnitude of the task that lies ahead. This monograph analysed the musical symbolism in two dialogues. A survey confirms that all the genuine dialogues and some of those included among the spuria are structured by the same musical scale. There will be much to be learned by carrying out similar investigations of all the dialogues: first in order to interpret the passages at the musical notes; then to seek broad principles behind their division into species and genera; and finally to determine how these schema shift the philosophical interpretation of each dialogue. These musical patterns involve regular repetitions, and can thus be studied rigorously within each single dialogue. Mastering them will establish a secure foundation for future progress.

Reading the dialogues in parallel and comparing passages at the same relative locations exposes a surprising network of shared symbols, as has been shown already in a preliminary way. Despite the variation of themes, styles and characters, the dialogues often, directly or indirectly, allude to similar concepts in a given "twelfth", as if successive "sections" of the dialogues nod to a regular sequence of topics. These concepts are thus regimented by the musical scale but are not part of the musical symbolism. Earlier chapters may have given the impression that the passages marking the notes were symbols isolated at discrete intervals within the largely non-symbolic surface narrative. The parallel passages show, however, that Plato's symbols are as densely interwoven as Dante's or Joyce's (§2.8). Rigorous study of these will require devising ways of comparing and displaying parallel passages across all the dialogues.

These two projects, mapping the musical structure within each dialogue and building a taxonomy of the parallel passages shared by all the dialogues, will prepare the way for an assessment of the doctrines embedded in the dialogues. The evidence adduced so far, the affinity with the harmony of the spheres and mathematics, is sufficient to certify them as Pythagorean. The doctrines of the early Pythagoreans are, however, known only from fragmentary or from late and often unreliable sources. The symbolic underlevel of Plato's dialogues will now, however, provide a cache of new evidence about doctrines from the fourth-century BCE. Analysing that evidence, placing it within the historical context of Plato's predecessors and followers, and elucidating its relations to the dialogues' musical structure will finally reveal Plato's philosophy.

APPENDIX 1

More musicological background

The most important criticisms of my paper "Plato's Forms, Pythagorean Mathematics, and Stichomtery" (Kennedy 2010) were made by musicologists and led to substantial clarification of the nature of Plato's musical structures. This appendix and the next briefly expand the introductory material in Chapter 2 and examine some issues that will be of interest to experts in Greek music. Appendix 8 examines some evidence in the *Republic* that a monochord inspired Plato's musical scheme.

Novelty

Plato was an innovator. In the *Republic*, he draws an analogy between the "kindred" sciences of astronomy and harmonics that sheds some light on his innovations in music theory (530d6–9). Before Plato, observational astronomy was largely a collection of regularities, which we might call mere surface patterns in the data. In a much-discussed passage in the *Republic*, Socrates criticized this exclusive reliance on the senses and called for a "true astronomy" (c1). This has been interpreted for two reasons as a call to develop deeper geometric models to explain the surface patterns. First, Plato generally emphasized underlying Forms, and, second, astronomical models were in fact developed by Eudoxus, an associate of the Academy. These models were the distant ancestors of Ptolemy's and Copernicus' systems. As Dicks put it:

> [T]here had been accumulating during the sixth and fifth centuries BC a mass of necessarily crude, but nonetheless practically useful, observational material … What was wanted now was for astronomers to … evolve a mathematically based system … this is why [Plato] urged the

> astronomers to concentrate on the mathematical side of their subject and study the real mathematical relations lying behind the visible phenomena. (1970: 107–8)

The *Republic* passes from this call to reform astronomy, from this call to shift from a complicated observational science to one grounded in mathematical regularities, to its discussion of harmonics.

The analogy to music and music theory is clear. Just like astronomy, Greek music had developed an elaborate collection of "regularities", its traditional systems of scales and modes. Just like astronomy these were not systemized or mathematically regular and, crucially, depended on heard consonances, that is, the senses. The mathematically regular scale that structures the dialogues is the counterpart in music of Eudoxus' geometric models in astronomy. Both represent a commitment to simple, mathematical forms that could undergird and systematize the sensory observations.[1]

Directly after the passage on astronomy, the *Republic* criticizes some "Pythagoreans" who investigate music practice. Huffman believes this is aimed at Archytas and shows that Plato was rejecting the music of his day as a foundation for music theory:

> Archytas' close connection to the musical practice of the day confirms and is confirmed by Socrates' famous comment at *Republic* 531c that the Pythagoreans who study music "seek the number in these *heard* concords" and do not ascend to problems ... [Plato is most likely] referring to the Pythagoreans who were his contemporaries and, most notably, Archytas. (2005: 414, emphasis added)

Huffman's interpretation of the "scale" in the *Timaeus* concludes that it is an example of a mathematical, musical construction:

> The sequence [of numbers and ratios in the scale of] the *Timaeus* represents just such a sequence of "concordant" numbers with no references to any audible concords ...
>
> Plato's complaint in the *Republic* is not that the Pythagoreans *started* from the numbers found in heard consonances, but that they did not go on to "ascend to problems" ... Both the astronomy and the harmonics of the *Timaeus* show that Plato himself was perfectly willing to start from motions of heavenly bodies and audible concords, but that he did not focus on the phenomena but rather on the abstract principles that govern them. (1993: 150–51)

Thus it is no objection to say that the mathematically regular scale embedded in Plato's dialogues is not one of the traditional scales or modes of classical Greek music. Innovation is to be expected.

APPENDIX 1: MORE MUSICOLOGICAL BACKGROUND

The importance of twelve

Nonetheless, the genealogy of Plato's twelve-note scale is clear. Unlike the elaborate, traditional scales, the major musical intervals within the scales were grounded in mathematics by the Pythagoreans, and these intervals naturally lead to the use of the number twelve.

As reviewed above, the 6-8-9-12 schema for the major intervals in the octave was well known. It was ascribed to Pythagoras, known to the Pythagorean Philolaus before Plato, embedded in the multi-octave scale discussed in the *Timaeus*, mentioned in the Platonic *Epinomis*, and discussed by Aristotle and Aristoxenus.[2] To exhibit these intervals on an instrument of one or more strings requires dividing the string into twelve equal units. This routine division, which must have been common by Plato's time, naturally suggests the twelve-note "scale" found in the dialogues (see Appendix 2).

The monochord

It was common in later times for music theorists to employ an instrument with a single string, which came to be called a "monochord". There has been a long-standing controversy over when and where the monochord was first developed, since it is not mentioned explicitly by anyone before or during Plato's lifetime but was treated as well known after about 300 BCE.[3] Barker argued (pers. comm.) that the twelve-note scales in Plato's dialogues would naturally emerge from use of the monochord and that they were thus evidence for the use of the monochord in the Academy. David Creese's recent book on the history of the monochord carefully reviews the evidence and tentatively argues for a fourth-century origin (2010: 102).

Scale versus division of the canon

The term "scale" is often taken to denote a musical structure that remains the same from octave to octave. The "scale" in Plato's dialogues is not a scale in this sense. For example, the intervals from note 6 to note 12 and again from note 3 to note 6 are both one octave (i.e. they span a 1:2 ratio). Thus the equal intervals of text between each pair of the major notes from 1 to 12 do not correspond to equal musical intervals in the conventional sense. Plato's twelve-fold musical structure is, in particular, not a single octave with twelve steps (semitones) as in modern equal temperament.

Musicologists prefer to call the "scale" in the dialogues a "division of the canon", where "canon" is the common, ancient term for a monochord. Thus Gaudentius, for example, can say: "if a string has been stretched upon a monochord (*kanonos*) and the monochord is divided into twelve parts, having first struck the whole string, and then the half of it consisting of six parts, the consonance of the whole to the half will be discovered: the octave" (Janus 1962: 341, c. 7, ll 13-17).

Thus the twelve-fold division of the canon was a natural and obvious way to demonstrate the 6-8-9-12 scheme for the major intervals and was explicitly discussed in antiquity. Plato's innovation is to adopt this mathematically regular division as a basis for his allegorical music, but the structure itself was no great innovation.

The preview of the musical symbolism in the *Republic*, as explained in Appendix 8, provides some preliminary evidence that Plato's musical symbolism was inspired by or associated with a monochord.

Here and elsewhere, for brevity, I use "scale" for "division of the canon". Thus I call the musical structure in the dialogues a "scale" even though it does not repeat the same structure in each octave (see below).

Quarternotes and the Harmonikoi

As discussed in Chapter 2, the quarternotes between the twelve major notes were also a much-debated innovation in late-classical musical theory. They are mentioned in the passage about music and astronomy in the *Republic* (*Resp.* 531a4). Aristotle makes the quarternote (*diesis*) the principle of measurement in music (*Metaph.* 1053a12, 1087b33). Aristoxenus said in places that the ear and voice could distinguish no intervals smaller than the smallest *diesis* (*Harm.* 1.14,20), and made it the smallest unit for music: "Let [a tone] be divided in three ways, and the melodious parts of it be the half, the third, and the fourth [*tetarton*, i.e. the quartertone]. Let the intervals less than these all be unmelodic. Let the smallest [the quartertone] be called the 'smallest enharmonic *diesis*'" (*Harm.* I.21,22-8; cf. II.46,1-17).

There is even a precedent for combining these "quarternotes" with a scale constructed by regularly dividing a musical continuum. The passage about harmonic science in the *Republic* is often interpreted as also criticizing a school of musical theorists who are called "harmonists" (*harmonokoi*), and the term "harmonist" is used explicitly in the *Phaedrus* (268d7). Barker gives the best, recent discussion of this school, and here I only summarize a few points relevant as background to Plato's musical scheme.

The harmonists were active by the late fifth century (Barker 2007: 39). They were neither an organized school nor part of a tradition and were not philosophers or mathematicians (*ibid.*: 40, 79). They sought the smallest, audible musical interval but did not regard these intervals as minimal or indivisible (*ibid.*: 34). Most importantly, we are told by several sources, they displayed their musical structures on "diagrams" divided into steps of equal distances, which were sometimes said to be "quartertones": "They may have been no more than a simple line marked off at equal distances representing these successive [quartertones], upon which the notes of a scale were then mapped" (*ibid.*: 42).

These diagrams seem to divide musical intervals into equal subintervals of some kind, and this conflicts with a theorem, ascribed to Archytas, denying the possibility of such divisions. As Barker says, however, Archytas' theorem was in tension with many developments at the time:

> [Archytas' theorem] was held to show, among other things, that it is impossible to divide the span of a [fourth] into equal sub-intervals ... In that case there must be something seriously wrong with the analyses of Aristoxenus, and indeed of the *harmonikoi* too, who talk blithely of quarter-tones, half-tones and the like, and suppose that a tetrachord in enharmonic, for example, contains two intervals of a quarter-tone each and another eight times that size, so that the whole fourth is divisible into ten equal segments.   (*Ibid.*: 304)

The claim here is not that Plato was a harmonist nor that his structure was the same as that used by the harmonists (in part because there is no precise agreement about the nature of the harmonists' diagrams). There are however several analogies:

- The harmonists conceived of the musical continuum as linear or at least could represent it as a line. Plato treated the text of each dialogue as a linear continuum that could be mathematically divided.
- Both the harmonists and Plato inserted quarternotes between the major notes.
- Both the harmonists and Plato considered even smaller divisions (in the *Symposium*, for example, each eighth of each quarter-interval is marked).
- Both the harmonists and Plato treated musical intervals like the octave as if they could be equally subdivided, contrary to musical practice and the theorem ascribed to Archytas.

It will be necessary to re-examine the fragmentary testimonia about the harmonists and to determine their precise relation to Plato's project. The harmonists do show, however, how the musical structure embedded in Plato's dialogues accords well with what is known about the debates over music theory in his day.

Relative consonance

The correlation between the content of Plato's symbolic passages and the relative consonance of the underlying notes is strong evidence for the dialogues' musical structure. The recognition that some notes in a scale are more consonant with a given ground note or tonic is basic to any musical training, both in ancient Greece as well as today. In Greek music, the emphasis on fourths, fifths, tretrachords and so on is just a manifestation of the importance of relative consonance.

There is evidence that the early Pythagoreans investigated relative consonance and constructed algorithms for ranking various pairs of notes as more or less consonant. Huffman (2005: 428ff.) gives an excellent summary of the evidence, and finds, for example, that "The ranking of concords is in fact common in the Pythagorean tradition" (*ibid.*: 432). He concludes that surviving reports of these procedures in Ptolemy and Porphyry go back to Archytas or even to earlier figures in the fifth century.

Several algorithms for calculating relative consonance were known but all agreed on making the octave more consonant than the fifth and the fifth more consonant than the fourth. It is not clear which algorithm Plato used; it is clear which major notes and intervals he ranked as more or less consonant. The algorithm reported by Archytas began by reducing musical ratios to lowest terms: 6:12, for example, became 1:2. Next, the two terms of each ratio were added together and (for some still obscure reason) two was subtracted. The result was a single number for each interval. Lower numbers indicated more consonant intervals. Thus 6:12, 8:12 and 9:12 became 1, 3 and 5, which shows that the octave is more consonant than the fifth and the fifth is more consonant than the fourth. However this procedure may have been derived or justified, it saves the musical phenomena, at least for the major intervals.

Plato was certainly familiar with the major musical intervals and therefore with the concept that notes in a scale will be more or less consonant with a groundnote. Huffman finds some slight evidence that the technical terminology used to describe the mathematical algorithms for calculating relative consonance is echoed in the *Republic* (2005: 437, 442).

Mathematical or acoustic or musical structure

Some have accepted the evidence for the regular structure in Plato's dialogues but question whether it might be a purely mathematical or some merely acoustic structure that falls short of being "musical". There are many reasons, both textual and contextual, for interpreting the dialogue's structure as a musical scale.

Symbolic passages emphatically break the dialogues into twelve major intervals consisting of four subintervals. As above, this structure has clear relations to ancient Greek music theory.

In the *Symposium* the notes were marked with species of "harmony" that, although not exclusively a musical concept, had clear relations to music, which are explicitly mentioned in the dialogue. In the *Euthyphro* too, the notes were marked with concepts related to "harmony".

As shown in an appendix below, the notes in the *Republic* are marked by words associated with music, such as "music", "string", "chord", "orchestra", "mode" and "note", as well as with words associated with mathematics (App. 8).

The correlation between the content of the symbolic passages and the consonance of the notes they mark is, again, strong evidence for the musical nature of the structure.

Finally, the historical context furnishes many reasons for interpreting the structure as a musical scale: the role of music in Pythagoreanism generally and in the *Timaeus*, the harmony of the spheres doctrine (alluded to in the *Republic*'s concluding myth), and so on. There is a clear analogy between an imperceptible musical structure in the cosmos and an allegorical musical structure concealed in a text. The symbols carrying doctrinal content make this connection to Pythagoreanism even more clear.

APPENDIX 2
Neo-Pythagoreans, the twelve-note scale and the monochord

The neo-Pythagoreans reportedly held that there were Pythagorean doctrines concealed in Plato's dialogues (Ch. 1). This section shows that they also encouraged students of Plato to learn about the twelve-note musical scale, quarternotes and the theory of consonance.

Theon's book *On the Mathematics Useful for Reading Plato* has been somewhat neglected by historians of philosophy. It seems to be a general introduction to mathematics, music and astronomy, and does little to connect these to specific passages in Plato's dialogues. Although typical of much Pythagoreanizing Platonism in antiquity, it offers a fascinating and relatively early window on to the resurgence of interest in Plato around the first century, even if Theon often discusses topics that seem to have little relevance to Plato. The following passages show that his music theory is useful for unravelling Plato's allegory.

Theon (fl. 100 CE) was a compiler and included long passages from an earlier lost work by the neo-Pythagorean Thrasyllus (died 36 CE). He is usually identified with the Egyptian Greek who became the court philosopher to the Roman emperor Tiberius and organized Plato's dialogues into the tetrologies still used in some editions today. Tarrant studied Thrasyllus' relation to the developing tradition of Platonism in his *Thrasyllan Platonism* (1993) and his *Plato's First Interpreters* (2000).

Theon's Pythagoreanizing interpretation of Plato is clear in many passages. He thinks of Pythagorean discoveries as essential for reading Plato:

> We will not hesitate, to describe the discoveries made by those before us, as we handed down those transmitted earlier by the Pythagoreans, carrying them as far as the more familiar results – and not claiming to have discovered these ourselves. By transmitting what has been handed down

by those who came before us, we have composed an essential compendium for those intending to understand the works of Plato.
(Theon of Smyrna 1966: 47.10–17)

For example, he stresses the importance of "harmony" and its cosmic dimensions:

> And the Pythagoreans, who Plato follows in many ways, say that music is the combination of opposites, and the unification of pluralities ... Music is not merely an arrangement of rhythms and melodies, but simply a system of the whole. Its *telos* is unification and harmonisation. Indeed, God is the harmoniser of discords, and God's greatest work is using music and medicine to make enemies friends. In music, they say, is the unanimity of things, and moreover the rule of the best over all. And music by nature arises as harmony in the cosmos, good law in the city, and temperance in households. Music is an arrangement and unity of the many.
> (12.10–22)

Although much of Theon's book resembles an elementary textbook, he conceives of his pedagogy as part of an initiation into higher, more mystical studies. These higher levels are not available to all, and in this sense are esoteric:

> And again someone might say that the initiation into philosophy is the handing down of the true mystic rite and of the truly real mysteries. Now initiation has five parts. The preparatory stage is Purification. Participating in the mysteries is not for all who wish to, for there are some whose exclusion is foretold ... (14.18ff.)

A long description of the five stages of the initation follows, and is based on selective use of certain passages in Plato.

The musical sections of Theon's book are concerned with basic theory, but this too is placed in the context of a larger Pythagorean project. For example, as in Plato's symbolism, consonance is a concept that is at once mathematical, musical and philosophical:

> [The Pythagoreans] say some numbers are consonant, and the doctrine (*logos*) concerning consonance is not to be found without arithmetic. Every consonance whatsoever has the greatest strength, for it is the truth in speech (*logoi*), happiness in life, and harmony in nature. And of harmony itself, none will be found in the cosmos without first discovering it among numbers.
>
> But there is also intelligible harmony, and this is more easily understood apart from perception. Now the two sorts of harmony must be discussed: the perceptible harmony in musical instruments and the intelligible harmony among numbers. (46.20–47.8)

Theon uses the monochord to demonstrate his theory of perceptible consonance. He introduces the major musical intervals by comparing the notes sounded by parts of the string to the note sounded by the whole string. This is a straightforward way to proceed and is also the kind of comparison used to establish the relative harmony of the musical notes in Plato's dialogues. For example, Theon says:

> If the single string on this instrument is measured off into four equal parts, the note sounded from the whole string
> - has the ratio of 4:3 with the note sounded from three-quarters [of the string], and the consonance is the fourth,
> - has the double ratio (2:1) with the note from two parts, that is, from half, and the consonance is the octave,
> - has the quadruple ratio (4:1) with the note from one-quarter, and the consonance is the double octave. (57.12–58.5)

Theon discusses at length the question of whether a musical interval can be exactly divided into equal semitones or quartertones. He knows that Archytas' theorem denies this, and also gives a variety of physical reasons that visible intervals of string and audible intervals sung by the voice cannot be exactly divided (70.14ff.). Nonetheless, he concludes in a single line that the interval of the tone can be divided in the intelligible realm of the forms: "But the tone grasped by the intellect (*noēsei lēptos*) can be conceived as divided into two equal parts [i.e. semitones]" (72.19–20). This may in part serve to justify the equal division of the monochord that follows. Although brief, this remark suggests that musical intervals can conceptually or ideally be treated as a series of equal intervals, just as Plato and the harmonists discussed above do (App. 1).

Theon and Thrysullus describe the same twelve-note scale that is embedded in Plato's dialogues in a discussion of notes on the monochord. This scale is not mentioned explicitly anywhere in the surface narratives of Plato's dialogues. It may simply be that the mathematical regularity of this scale made it a convenient means for introducing the major notes and the musical intervals.

Theon relates this division to Pythagorean lore. The numbers one to four as well as the numbers one to ten had some special significance for the Pythagoreans and were called, respectively, the "tetraktys" and the "decad". Theon says his treatment of the twelve-note scale is borrowed from Thrasyllus:

> The division of the monchord (*kanonōs*) is done with the "tetraktys" which is in the decad. The tetraktys is composed of the monad, dyad, triad, and tetrad, that is, 1, 2, 3, and 4. The tetraktys contains the following ratios: 4:3, 3:2, 2:1, 3:1, 4:1 [which are also the most important musical intervals]. Thrasyllus divides the monochord [by moving a "bridge" under the string] as follows:
> - By dividing the length in two at the middle [of the string] he makes

APPENDIX 2: NEO-PYTHAGOREANS, TWELVE-NOTE SCALE, MONOCHORD

the octave, which has a 2:1 ratio [when the whole is compared to the half]. (87.4–10)

Thrasyllus then divides the whole string into thirds and fourths to show that some major notes and intervals can thereby be produced. He then continues with the twelve-fold division:

> The preceding becomes clear if expressed with numbers.[1] If the length of the monochord is twelve, [equal] measures of whatever size, then note 6 will divide the whole string in two and leave 6 divisions on either side. Note 4 will be 4 parts from the beginning. Note 8 will be 4 parts from the end. And 4 divisions will be between these two notes. Note 3 is three lengths from the beginning, and one from note 4. Note 9 is 3 from the end, and one from note 8 [and so on …]. The entire string is Note 12.
> (89.9–24)

Thrasyllus shows that this scale of twelve notes can be used to demonstrate various musical intervals. For example, he says "[The ratio] between the middle note 6 and note 3 is double, which is the octave … [the ratio] between the whole, i.e., note 12, and note 4 is [triple], which is the octave and a fifth … (90.1–12).[2]

In sum, Thrasyllus is doing here what Plato does in the dialogues. Both divide a linear continuum into twelve parts and mark the locations of the more consonant notes. Plato also marks the neutral and dissonant points but this is implicit in Thrasyllus' procedure. The points that remain after singling out the consonant notes are simply the relatively dissonant notes.

There is no hint in these passages that the twelve-note scale is used to structure Plato's dialogues; indeed, much of this music theory is the common property of ancient mathematicians and music theorists. Moreover, interpretation is complicated by the fact that Theon is reporting only parts of Thrasyllus' lost work (Tarrant 2000: esp. 17ff.). Nonetheless, there is a *prima facie* case here that Theon or Thrasyllus recognized the musical allegories in Plato's works:

- the neo-Pythagoreans (correctly) asserted that there were doctrines hidden within Plato's dialogues;
- they (correctly) asserted that these hidden doctrines were Pythagorean;
- they emphasized the importance of musical consonance and quarternotes;
- they emphasized an expansive conception of consonance and harmony, like that used to mark the notes in the *Symposium*;
- they emphasized the importance of the twelve-note, equal division of the canon, although it is not mentioned in Plato; and
- Theon was an esotericist of some kind who emphasized that his book taught only the elementary parts of some higher, mystical lore reserved to a select number.

Less securely, the neo-Pythagoreans may have been early enough to have had access to the dialogues in their classical format, that is, with the regular columns that made detecting the musical structure easier.

Much further research will be required to clarify how strong this case is, and whether or not the neo-Pythagoreans recognized the musical structure of Plato's dialogues. Some conjecture, for example, that the neo-Pythagoreans were merely inspired by Aristotle's views about the relation between Plato and the Pythagoreans in *Metaphysics A*.

APPENDIX 3
Markers between the major notes

For simplicity, most of the discussion above was confined to wholenotes, quarternotes and the sevenths. Much structure remains between these major notes. The following briefly surveys some of the evidence and interprets it; an extended discussion is postponed to subsequent work.

The octaves

Musical notes an octave apart are especially consonant with each other. This interval corresponds to a doubling of a note's pitch or a halving of the instrument's string.

Although there is some uncertainty about calculations of the relative consonance for the early notes in the dialogues, there is some evidence that notes an octave apart are marked in special ways.

On a twelve-note scale, the sixth note is, as mentioned earlier, an octave from the twelfth note (since twelve divided in half is six). In the notation where 1.2 is the quarternote halfway between the first and second wholenotes, successive divisions of twelve by two produce the following series of notes:

12.0, 6.0, 3.0, 1.2, 0.3, 0.1.4, 0.0.6 …

The first three of these notes are very consonant and the more harmonic passages that mark them were discussed above. To facilitate comparisons, the passages marking the other notes in this series in the *Symposium* are briefly described here:

- 1.2: Phaedrus first mentions human love, instead of treating Eros as a god, and first introduces the virtue theme.

- 0.3: Socrates first enters the andron, where the symposium is held, and is asked for his wisdom.
- 0.1.4: Socrates' first appearance in the dialogue, where the narrator begins to recount the story of Agathon's party.
- 0.0.6: The first mention of Aristodemus, said to be Socrates' "lover".

The next note in the series (0.0.3) is briefly marked but not in any emphatic way. The two entrances, at notes 0.3 and 0.1.4 above, especially suggest that these notes play a privileged role within the *Symposium*'s symbolic scheme.

There is also strong evidence that the octaves are especially singled out in the *Euthyphro*, although here it is the legal charges that make their entrances at the octaves and not characters as in the *Symposium*:

- 1.2: Euthyphro first announces that he has charged his father with murder.
- 0.3: Socrates first lists the three, specific charges brought against him by Meletus.
- 0.1.4: Socrates first gives a general description of the charges against him: that he is corrupting the youth.
- 0.0.6: Socrates first mentions the "man" who has charged him, although he is not named until the quarternote a few lines later.

This doubly reinforced evidence for the importance of the octaves shows again that the stichometric structure should be interpreted as a musical scale.

The twelfth wholenote probably has the lowest pitch, which would make the notes in the series of octaves grow progressively higher as they approach the beginning of the dialogue.

Fractions of the whole dialogue

The passages that mark the twelve-note scale and its quarternotes also mark locations that divide the dialogue into some whole number fractions. For example, since the even wholenotes occur at points that divide the dialogue into sixths, marking the twelve wholenotes also automatically marks out the sixths. It is useful to list the fractions that are automatically marked when the twelve-note scale is marked:

1. Whole (12.0)
2. Halves (6.0, 12.0)
3. Thirds (4.0, 8.0, 12.0)
4. Quarters (3.0, 6.0, 9.0, 12.0)
6. Sixths (2.0, 4.0, 6.0, 8.0, 10.0, 12.0)
8. Eighths (1.2, 3.0, 4.2, 6.0, 7.2, 9.0, 10.2, 12.0)

APPENDIX 3: MARKERS BETWEEN THE MAJOR NOTES

The fifths, sevenths, ninths and tenths, however, are not all automatically marked by the wholenotes and quarternotes. Evidence was presented above that the sevenths are marked by symbolic passages in both dialogues. The rest of this appendix collects evidence showing that, in addition, the fifths, ninths and tenths are also marked by symbolic passages that fall between the major notes. Since one-fifth is two-tenths, for example, the markers for the fifths and tenths partially overlap and are treated together.

The ninths

At 177e1, between the major notes, all the symposiasts agree with Socrates that Phaedrus should begin his speech. Such verbal agreements are generally markers for harmony and thus musical notes. The measured location of this passage is 11.1p, that is, it falls at one-ninth of the way through the dialogue. At 22.2p, that is, at two-ninths, the permanent fusion (*suntakeis*) of two lovers is mentioned. Such a combination is usually a strong marker for musical notes. Thus the first two ninths are strongly marked.

The wholenotes and quarternotes in the musical scale are marked with degrees of "harmony", and this was interpreted as a broad category of more or less successful blendings of contraries. The passages at the sevenths were interpreted as instances of temporary mechanical mixture. The evidence collected below shows that the ninths are marked by passages contrasting erotic harmonization with instances of total separation, withdrawal or departure.

- *First ninth, agreement versus mental departure:* All agree (harmony) that Phaedrus should do as Socrates bids: begin leading the symposium by giving an encomium of love.[1] The narrator then says he does not recollect everything Aristodemus said. Later, at 208a4–5, Diotima says that forgetting is an egress or departure of knowledge (177e7, after 1.1).
- *Second ninth, departure versus erotic combination:* The wicked lover departs when the bloom of the body fades; the good lover is abidingly fused (*suntakeis*) with his beloved (183e3, before 2.3, Pausanias).
- *Third ninth, separation versus sexual combination:* The ancient nature of man was threefold: in two kinds of creatures male and female are completely separated, but in the androgynes they are combined (189d5 = note 4.0, Aristophanes).
- *Fourth ninth, departure versus erotic combination:* Eros flees the aged, but is forever together with youth (*aei sunesti*) (195b1, after 5.1, Agathon).
- *Fifth ninth, ugliness spurned versus beauty loved:* The gods make things out of a love of beauty, but ugliness is not loved (201a3, after 6.2, Socrates).[2]
- *Sixth ninth, ugliness spurned versus beauty loved:* Eros spurns and withdraws from the ugly and aims to beget in the beautiful (206e4 = note 8.0, Diotima).

- *Seventh ninth, departure versus acceptance of beautiful Alcibiades:* Coming from the forecourt, Alcibiades stands by the door to the andron uttering his first words: "Will you accept a drunk as a symposiast or should I depart?" (212e1, after 9.1, after Socrates' speech).
- *Eighth ninth, uninitiated versus youths seized by erotic mania:* Alcibiades distinguishes between those whose soul has been seized by an erotic cum philosophical mania (*manias kai baccheias*) and the uninitiated (*bebēlos*) who have never been so seized, and suggests several of the symposiasts had experienced such a mania when young (218b4, before 10.3).
- *Ninth ninth, Socrates' departure with his "lover":* Socrates departs from the symposium, but is followed by his usual companion Aristodemus (223d12 = note 12.0).

The appearance and first words of Alcibiades at the seventh ninth is, given that earlier entrances were specially marked, strong evidence that the ninths too occupy significant locations in the musical scale.

Surviving ancient commentaries on Plato's dialogues often, and seemingly capriciously, interpret isolated passages as if they were symbols for Olympic gods or had some other esoteric content (as will be reviewed in subsequent work). Unlike the repeated patterns studied in this volume, such identifications cannot be rigorously verified and have generally been ignored in modern commentaries. One line of reasoning, however, does suggest the need to re-evaluate these interpretations. It can be only briefly examined here.

Although number symbolism was an important theme in early Pythagoreanism, it is widely agreed that the meanings attributed in extant reports to particular numbers varied significantly and so are unreliable. Burkert's survey of such symbolism, however, does note some persistent associations:

> Certain numbers belong to certain gods; the cult of Apollo and that of Dionysus were dominated by the numbers 7 and 9.   (1972: 474)

> For example, the Carneia [festival of Apollo] lasted 9 days; 9 men gather in each of 9 "sunshades" (tent-like structures ...); Apollo was born on the seventh day of the month, and he is *hebdomagetas* at Aesch. *Sept.* 800... There are 7 bunches of grapes and 7 dolphins on the famous Dionysus cup of Exekias.   (*ibid.*: n.54)

In short, Burkert says that both numbers were associated with both gods. Although the tension between Apollo and Dionysus, respectively the gods of order and disorder, has become a sometimes hackneyed theme of modern criticism, they seem to share seven and nine.

This raises questions about the patterns in the *Symposium*. The first seventh after the beginning of the dialogue is marked by references to Orpheus, who had many mythological associations with Apollo, the god of music. The last ninth before the end of the dialogue is marked by an adjectival form of "Bacchus", an alternate name for Dionysus. This slender evidence for an association between the sevenths and ninths and Apollo and Dionysus can be assessed only by examining other dialogues.

In the *Euthyphro*, the major notes were marked by definite assertions and the sevenths by various failures to assert. The ninths, however, seem to be marked by various states that precede an attempt to make an assertion: ignorance, uncertainty about the future, the need for investigation, and so on. Many of these locations are hypothetical questions or surmises ("If so, what then?") or expressions of ignorance.

- *First ninth, ignorance of the future:* Socrates says that, if his prosecutors are serious it is unclear how his case will turn out – except to soothsayers like Euthyphro (3e3, after 1.1).
- *Second ninth, surmise about the future:* Euthyphro says that, if the prosecutors were to charge him, he would find out their weak spot (5c1, before 2.3).
- *Third ninth, ignorance of the Forms:* Socrates asks Euthyphro to teach him the Form that would enable him to assert what is holy and what not (6e6 = note 4.0).
- *Fourth ninth, ignorance of humans:* Socrates asks if any human, hearing of some injustice, would dispute that a penalty should be paid (8c1, after 5.1).
- *Fifth ninth, need for investigation:* Socrates asks a general methodological question: should assertions be merely accepted because someone asserts them or should they be examined? (9e6, after 6.2).
- *Sixth ninth, words flee before assertion:* Socrates says that, if he had made Euthyphro's assertions, he would be mocked when they – like Daedalus' statues – ran away and did not remain where they were put (11c2 = note 8.0).
- *Seventh ninth, ignorance of meanings:* Socrates asks Euthyphro to "tell me a bit more", saying that he does not yet understand what Euthyphro means by *therapeia* (12e10, after 9.1).
- *Eighth ninth, asking about the gods:* Socrates asks whether Euthyphro defines holiness as a science of giving and asking, of a barter with the gods (14c8, before 10.3).
- *Ninth ninth, no teaching, ignorance of gods:* Socrates bewails that, since Euthyphro will not teach him, he will remain ignorant about divine matters (16a4 = note 12.0).

There is no apparent connection in the Euthyphro between the sevenths and ninths and Apollo and Dionysus.

The fifths and tenths

In the *Symposium*, the fifths are marked by species of harmony and *krasis*. In music theory, two notes whose pitches were in a 1:5 ratio do have a degree of consonance.[3]

- First fifth, Athenian laws a *krasis* or median: Pederasty is encouraged or discouraged by foreign cities, but Athenian laws do both in a way that is "difficult to understand" (182d5, before 2.2, Pausanias).
- Second fifth, fusion of two lovers into one: Hephaestus' offer to fuse two, true lovers is repeated (192e8, after 4.3, Aristophanes).[4]
- Third fifth, poverty has sex with resource, conception of *eros*: Penia waylays Poros in the garden at the gods' party (203b7, before 7.1, Diotima).
- Fourth fifth, Socrates conquers all, crowned by Alcibiades: Alcibiades says that, although Agathon's writing has recently won a prize, Socrates' speech wins for all time. He then retrieves some ribbons from Agathon's head and crowns Socrates. Speech and speeches have often figured as sites for harmonization. The dominance of one ingredient over another in mixtures and blends is an extreme form of harmonization, a "conquering" (213e3, after 9.2, Alcibiades' banter).[5]

It is difficult to interpret the more concisely marked fifths in the *Euthyphro*. The first two involve assertions about divine knowledge, which suggests that here too the fifths are consonant and so are marked in ways similar to the major notes. The next two, however, although part of discussions about holiness and the gods, are difficult to pick out from the surrounding argumentation. They are not emphatically marked.

- First fifth, divine knowledge: Socrates has long thought it worth much to know about the gods (5a6, before 2.2).
- Second fifth, Euthyphro asserts divine knowledge: According to Euthyphro's argument, the gods dispute about justice and morals (7e1, after 4.3).
- Third fifth, love and action, passion: Socrates asks, "Is not that which is loved in some state either of becoming or suffering?" He applies this to piety, "being loved by all the gods", in a few lines (10c7, before 7.1).
- Fourth fifth, attendance aims at good: *Therapeia* aims at the good, even when attending to horses (13b9, after 9.2).

It is similarly difficult to interpret the tenths in both dialogues, which seem marked in a tenuous way. Part of the problem is that they overlap with the fifths and with the sixth wholenote (5/10 is 6/12). Thus only four candidate passages in each dialogue remain to form the basis for an interpretation. It may be that the tenths, however, which are only faintly consonant with the twelfth, are only faintly marked or not at all. In the *Symposium*, the fifths were marked harmoniously, the sevenths by mixtures, and the ninths by separations. This suggests decreasing degrees of harmonization.

APPENDIX 4

The central notes

The sixth and therefore central wholenotes in the *Symposium* and the *Euthyphro* are marked in various ways, as shown above, but also share a novel, more subtle kind of symbolism. Its importance is twofold. First, the sixth wholenote is the most consonant in the twelve-note scale, and this symbolism serves to reinforce its emphatic marking. Second, the location of this structure corroborates the measured locations of the exact centre, and even helps identify the central sentence in each of the dialogues.

The following arguments are sequestered in an appendix because confirming them would require surveying more than the two dialogues discussed here. The musical patterns reviewed in earlier chapters could be rigorously established because they consisted of musical symbols regularly repeated throughout entire dialogues. The interpretations of single phrases sketched here are offered as suggestive hypotheses for future investigations.

These structures are not, strictly speaking, part of the musical structure of the dialogues. However, Huffman has perceptively argued (pers. comm.) that the sixth and central notes should be more emphatically marked than the annotations in previous chapters suggest. There is, in fact, a great deal of subtle symbolism packed into these central passages. I conjecture that Plato's resort to more subtle symbolism at the centres of the dialogues, which are perhaps easy to locate in an approximate way, was another strategy aimed at avoiding any over-obvious evidence for his stichometric structures. Forms should lie beneath appearances.

Scholars of classical literature are familiar with so-called "ring structures" (see e.g. Louden 1999). In English, a speech might be opened by saying "Topics A, B and C will be discussed", and then closed with "So, as promised, topics A, B and C were discussed". In both cases, the topics are given in the same order. In classical Greek and elsewhere, the convention in a wide variety of contexts was to reverse the second list, as if mentally retracing the journey: "So, as promised, topics C, B and A were discussed". Concepts or episodes in such a circular order – A, B, C, C, B, A – form a ring structure.

The evidence below suggests that Plato places a "loose ring structure" around the centres of the *Symposium* and *Euthyphro*.[1] The elements are not repeated in the same words but are paraphrased, and the order of the second list is very loose, almost a jumble.

It is better to begin with the *Euthyphro* because the passage at the centre is shorter and more obviously peculiar, although the evidence will seem rather tenuous until a similar pattern is seen in the *Symposium*.

At the centre of the *Euthyphro*, without much provocation, Socrates abruptly interrupts his long interrogation to summarize the legal and ethical issues. The key, repeated concepts are marked below with capital letters. The translation has been again, sometimes awkwardly, modified to bring out the similarities between phrases marked by the same letters. Individual underlined words indicate repeated concepts, and the long underlined phrase marks the central sentence of the dialogue. The point of the following is that a number of concepts are repeated before and after the note at 6.0:

Soc.: [9a] Come now, my dear Euthyphro, teach (A: TEACH) me too so that I may become wiser. (B: WISDOM) What proof (C: CLEAR SIGN) is there for you that all the gods 4/8 believe (D: ALL GODS THINK) your neighbour died unjustly (E: UNJUSTLY), who killed a man (F: MURDERER) while he was labouring, was bound by the master of the deceased, and died on account of the bindings (just before the man who bound (G: BOUND, 3 REPETITIONS) him could ask the priests what should be done about him), and indeed, that on behalf of such a one it is correct for a son to charge and prosecute a father CENTRE, TWO ASSERTERS OF DIVINE KNOWLEDGE NOTE 6.0 for murder (F: MURDERER). Come, [9b] try to show me clearly (C: CLEAR SIGN) what about this indicates, more than anything, that all the gods believe (D: ALL GODS THINK) that this action is correct. And if you show this properly, I will never cease to sing the praises of your wisdom (B: WISDOM).

Euth.: But that's probably no small task, Socrates; since I could show you that quite clearly (C: CLEAR SIGN).

Soc.: I understand; 4/8 I seem to you to be a slow learner (A: TEACH) or slower than the judges: since you will show (G: SHOW, 3 REPETITIONS) them clearly it is an unjustice (E: UNJUSTLY), and that the gods all (D: ALL GODS THINK) hate such things.

In this passage, words for death or murder occur some five times before the note but not afterwards.[2]

A similar and similarly loose pattern can be seen at the centre of the *Symposium*. Using the same conventions as above, the central passage is:

Once Agathon had spoken (A: END OF SPEECH), Aristodemus said, all of those present applauded noisily (B: STRONG APPROVAL OF SPEECH) 7/8, as the youth had spoken so suitably both for himself and for the god.

Then Socrates said, with a glance toward Eryximachus, "So do I seem to you," he said, "son of Acumenus, to have feared back then a fear not to be feared, (C: FEAR, 3 REPETITIONS) or rather was I not speaking prophetically (D: SOCRATES IS PROPHET) just now when I said that Agathon would speak marvellously (E: AGATHON SPEAKS WELL) and I would find myself at a loss (F: SOCRATES' APORIA)?"

CENTRE: ERYXIMACHUS ASSERTS DIVINE KNOWLEDGE
SOCRATES IS PROPHET, SO HARMONISES WITH DIVINE
THE GOODMAN SPEAKS GOOD; AGREE/DISAGREE

"The other [point]," NOTE 6.0 replied Eryximachus, [198b] "that he would speak well (*Agathon eu erei*), you seem to me to have spoken prophetically (D: SOCRATES IS PROPHET); but as to your being at a loss (F: SOCRATES' APORIA), I do not think so." "And how, you fortunate man," said Socrates, "should I or anyone else whosoever not be at a loss (F: SOCRATES' APORIA), when about to speak after the delivery of such a beautiful and variegated speech? (E: AGATHON SPEAKS WELL) Now, some of its other bits 1/8 were not uniformly marvellous, but who would not be amazed hearing the beauty of the words and phrases (B: STRONG APPROVAL OF SPEECH) at the end? (A: END OF SPEECH) Since I was considering that I would not be able to speak [198c] as beautifully (BEAUTY, 3 REPETITIONS), not even close to it, I was on the verge of running away (C: FEAR) ..."

Once again, the paragraph after the centre shares many of the concepts with the preceding paragraph.[3]

In sum, the only claim made here is that in both dialogues, the paragraphs before and after the central note share many of the same concepts, although the order of the latter is, very roughly, reversed. In this sense, a loose ring structure surrounds and serves to mark the centre of the musical scale.

APPENDIX 5

Systematic theory of the marking passages

This appendix aims to give a specific and rigorous answer to the question of which terms and concepts count as markers of the *Symposium*'s musical notes. It collects, repeats and systematizes earlier annotations. This material is central to the second stage of interpretation, in which all the musical symbols are explicated, but not for verifying the existence of the musical scale.

Analysing Plato's symbolic scheme is difficult. Its methods and aims are novel. Its interpretation depends on familiarity with the theory of Forms, Pythagorean music theory and mathematics. It was designed to be subtle, and its obscurity has been compounded by differences in language, culture and conceptual schemes.

This appendix systematically surveys the various symbols used in the *Symposium*. It collects them into a number of categories and shows that each category is a species of harmonization. Even with the accompanying annotations, the glosses inserted into the left-hand text of the dialogue in Chapters 2 and 3 may have appeared arbitrary. The following is a systematic argument, explaining and justifying the interpretation of each passage.

The symbolic scheme of the dialogues is *sui generis*. This appendix introduces the methodology used to gloss particular notes by tracing the successive stages of their interpretation.

Deciphering the symbolic scheme of a single dialogue begins with a survey of the locations corresponding to the small whole number ratios favoured by the Pythagoreans, that is, of the passages at three-quarters, two-thirds, one-half, one-third and one-quarter of the way through the entire dialogue. In the *Symposium*, these passages describe kinds of combination or unities: the unity of a form and its participants, copulation, androgynes and so on.

A careful survey of the entire dialogue will show that various sorts of combination are lodged at the twelfths and the quarter-intervals between them. This pattern corresponds to a known Greek musical scale and, together with Eryximachus' theory of music and harmony, leads to an interpretation of the passages as species of harmonization.

Two sorts of problems arise at this point. There seem to be both too many and too few passages describing harmonies. First, a scattering of passages between the major notes and thus outside the musical pattern seem to be instances of harmony. Further study reveals that these surplus harmonies lie at mathematically significant points, at one-seventh, two-fifths, and so on, and can be interpreted as secondary, relatively consonant points within the musical scale. In the second place, however, a minority of the passages at the twelfths or quarternotes do not seem to fit into the larger pattern: they do not seem to be species of harmony.

The method for resolving these apparent defects in the general musical pattern is best illustrated with a concrete example. The very first note in the dialogue (0.0) and some of the subsequent octads are marked with the concept "reciting or practising speeches". This is not obviously a species of harmony, and its tenuous connection to that genus probably deliberately marks the note in a subtle way. This passage is an apparent counter-example to the general rule that the major notes are marked with species of harmony.

As discussed above (§2.8), however, Diotima later resolves this puzzle when she says that our memories of individual pieces of knowledge can be refreshed by repeatedly practising them, perhaps in the same way that a piece of music is practised over and over again:

> [W]ith regard to our knowledge, some persists and some perishes in us ... What we call "practising" (*meletan*; e.g. practising speeches) implies that our knowledge is departing; since forgetfulness is an egress of knowledge, while practising substitutes a young one in place of that which departs, and so saves our knowledge enough to make it seem the same. Every mortal thing is saved in this way; not by keeping it exactly the same forever, like the divine, but by replacing what goes off or is antiquated with something young, which is like the same. Through this device, Socrates, a mortal thing participates of immortality ...
> (207e5–b3)

Diotima's word for "practising" (*meletan*) is a cognate of the word used for practising speeches at note 0.0 (*ouk ameletētos*). She is here saying that "practising or reciting speeches" is to our knowledge as sexual reproduction is to our bodies. The similarity lies in that both are ways for mortals to participate in or share in immortality: either by replacing our memories with new ones or by replacing ourselves with our offspring. Now "participation", the "fitting together" in the *krasis* of mortal and immortal or in the relation of a particular with an eternal Form, is an important species of harmony and marks several major notes (see below). Diotima therefore explicitly makes reciting speeches into a species of harmonization. Note 0.0 is not, therefore, a counter-example to the general pattern of marking the wholenotes with species of harmony.

This method for resolving the puzzle has several general implications. Interpreting isolated symbols may depend on conceptual *connections* made elsewhere in the dialogue. Thus, for another example, when Diotima says that "beauty is a harmony with the divine", passages about beauty elsewhere in the dialogue become exemplars of a species of harmonization.

These connections may be interpreted as clues. Plato has deliberately obscured the regular pattern of notes by marking them with a wide range of *prima facie* unrelated species. On the other hand, when their connections are not straightforward, he supplies just the clues needed to understand how the passages fall under a common genus. In the *Euthyphro*, when Socrates emphasizes that the legal charges depend on an implicit assertion of higher knowledge about the good or the gods, this is a clue. All reiterations of the charges in the dialogue therefore count as members of a species that marks the notes. In short, a patient and careful reader who exploits all the clues will be able to perceive the regularity of the embedded pattern, that is, the Form.

During the past generation of Plato scholarship, progress was often made by analysing the dramatic context of the arguments in the dialogues. The musical scales, however, stretch through the whole of each dialogue and therefore through the different speeches made by the dialogue's various characters. In the case of these clues, context is not essential. A connection made at one point in the dialogue may be important for interpreting symbols throughout a dialogue.

The following surveys the species of harmonization and lists, for each of them, which concepts and which notes it embraces. The general glosses explain the range of passages, and foreground particularly clear or paradigmatic instances of each species.

Each marking passage contains a blend or mixture of elements, each of which is more or less harmonious, and so there is generally more than one category of concepts at each note.

I. Musical harmony

The Greek word *harmonia* has, as mentioned, a broad range of reference and includes many kinds of "fitting together". Its special musical sense, the blending of different musical pitches, is not one of the chief concepts used to mark notes in the *Symposium*. In contrast, in the *Republic*, references to ordinary, vocal and instrumental music play an important role in its symbolic scheme.

Explicit reference to musical harmony is made at 3.2, a very consonant quarter-note between two of the most consonant wholenotes. This passage is also important because it establishes connections between music and *eros*. Eryximachus says there that music implants *eros* and *homonoia*, and is knowledge of erotics. In short, musical harmony is effected by erotic harmony; it is a sort of friendship between contrary pitches. Agathon reinforces this connection at note 5.3, when he says that Eros is skilful at composing music. This dialogue, therefore, does not take musical harmony as a paradigm of harmony, but rather sees it as another kind of erotic harmonization.

References to vocal and instrumental music recur at notes 10.0 and 10.1 in Alcibiades' speech, but there mark the notes negatively. The music of Marsyas, an ugly satyr, and piping were viewed negatively in some quarters (see the annotations to 10.0).

Alcibiades does say that the prose of Socrates' speeches is a kind of music made without musical instruments. Since speeches and the broad range of things described by *logos* and its cognates (arguments, agreements, etc.) are sites of harmonization in the *Symposium*, this makes explicit the idea that *logos* may be a kind of music. That is, something like the musical harmonization of opposing ideas may occur in a speech, and this is in fact the structure of many marking passages. *Clear instance*: Note 3.2 shows that the species of musical harmony can mark a consonant note. In short:

- musical harmony is a species of harmony, and may mark notes (e.g. 3.2);
- musical harmonization is effected by erotic harmonization (3.2);
- ordinary music, especially piping, may mark disharmony (10.0, 10.1);
- prose speech and other instances of *logos* may be harmonized (10.0).

II. Harmonization as "fitting together" into one

The clearest general kind of marking passage describes the combination of two opposites or two parts into one whole. The following surveys a number of species.

Unification and unity: two becoming one
The explicit use of "unity" or of "two becoming one" marks the locations of a number of musical notes.

Clear instances: Hephaestus makes an offer to the two lovers at note 4.3: "being two you will become one". This is summarized some eight OCT lines later: "from two, one will emerge" (192e8–9). It is unusual to have such a strong marker lodged so far from a major note. In fact, this later summary falls at two-fifths (= the end of line 192e8), and marks this consonant point in the dialogue. Thus this marker appears twice in order to mark two nearby notes, 4.3 and 2/5.

- Socrates and Aristodemus will be "two together" (0.2).
- Eros is a Uniter, attempting to make "one from two" (4.2).
- Hephaestus will weld two lovers into one (4.3, 2/5).
- Unity of form of beauty (9.0).

Physical combination

Several notes describe processes or results of physical combination.

Clear instance: Notes in Aristophanes' speech are marked by bodily combination. His androgynes are a physical combination, or primitive unity, of two genders.

- Aristophanes' androgynes combine genders (4.0, 4.2).
- Apollo's healing of severed creatures (4.2).
- Hephaestus will weld two lovers into one (4.3).
- Agathon says Eros makes a home in soft souls, a disharmonic *krasis* (5.2).

Combining opposites

Some notes seem to emphasize the harmonization – the combination or agreement – of diametrically opposite pairs of qualities. *Clear instance:* Socrates argues a single writer can combine abilities to compose comedy and tragedy (two opposed genres).

- Agreement of wise and unwise in frame's notes (0.0, 0.1, 0.2, 0.3).
- Freely choosing slavery for virtue (2.3).
- Aristophanes' androgynes combine genders (4.0, 4.2).
- *Krasis* of pleasure and pain (10.1).
- Socrates is compelling agreement about combining comedy and tragedy (before 12.0).

Diatribein or social mixing

Tribein, as mentioned in the annotations to octad 0.0.4, may mean "rubbing", "kneading" or "grinding", and thus *diatribein* may be "rubbing away", "spending time" or even "mixing socially" (LSJ). At note 11.3 in the *Phaedo*, cognates of *tribein* also occur twice, and the second is a kind of mixing (117a6–7). This suggests the verb and its cognates may be a symbol for mixing or harmonization. Although speculative, it is easy to see why this word might function as a Pythagorean symbol. It seems cognate to the Greek word for "three", a number important in Pythagorean numerology. Moreover, Socrates and some of his followers were known for wearing a well-worn or rustic, toga-like garment called a *tribōn* (LSJ; Socrates' *tribōn* is mentioned at *Symp.* 219b6).

Clear instances: This verb is used twice in the closing line of the *Symposium* and twice in the opening line of the *Euthyphro*.

- Spending time with Socrates (0.0.4).
- Eryximachus suggests spending time with speeches (1.1).
- *Diatribein* is repeated twice at the note (12.0).
- Note 0.0 of the *Euthryphro* also uses *diatribein* twice.
- Note 11.3 of the *Phaedo* also uses *diatribein* twice.

III. Homologia or verbal agreement

The characters in the *Symposium* often agree with each other at the locations of the musical notes. These agreements are symbols for yet another kind of harmonization: a fitting together of the words or sentiments of the characters. Eryximachus connects verbal agreement to musical harmonization when he says that musical harmony is a type of "agreement" (*homologia*; 187a8–b7).

Sometimes, however, agreement with a verbal request or invitation is not expressed verbally. For example, when Agathon asks Socrates to sit with him, Socrates simply walks over and sits (0.3).

An agreement may thus express or represent an "agreement of minds" between the dialogue's characters, and it may be either the verbal or mental agreement that marks the note. As mentioned above, Eryximachus also says that music implants *homonoia* (3.1), and this connects the agreement or similarity of minds to musical harmonization.

Several varieties of agreements may be distinguished.

Agreement with invitations or requests or orders
- The narrator is asked to halt and halts (0.0).
- The narrator agrees to recite the speeches (0.1).
- Aristodemus agrees to go to Agathon's party (0.2).
- Socrates agrees to sit with Agathon (0.3).
- Eryximachus says he will obey Aristophanes (5.0).
- Phaedrus agrees to allow Socrates to ask questions of Agathon (6.1).
- Disharmony: Socrates is grudgingly persuaded to accept Alcibiades' invitation (10.2).

Agreement with assertions or opinions
- Phaedrus agrees with Eryximachus to moderate the drinking (1.0).
- Socrates says all will agree to make speeches (1.1).
- Eryximachus says he agrees with Pausanias about Eros (3.2).
- Loud approval at the end of Agathon's speech (6.0).
- Eryximachus agrees that Socrates is a prophet (6.0).
- Agreement and negative agreement that gods are happy and beautiful (7.0).
- Socrates and Diotima agree about love being begetting in beauty (8.0).
- Approving applause at the end of Socrates' speech (9.1).
- Socrates is compelling agreement about combining comedy and tragedy (before 12.0).

Agreements to maintain the order of speeches
- All agree to drink moderately, and so preserve order (1.0).
- All agree to give speeches from left to right (1.1).
- Eryximachus and Aristophanes agree to swap turns at the midpoint between 3.0 and 3.1 (to avoid interrupting the speeches).

- Agathon agrees to stop talking with Socrates and give his speech (5.1).
- Socrates is urged to speak and agrees (6.1).
- Alcibiades agrees with Eryximachus to speak in an orderly, "just" way from left to right (9.3).
- Disharmony: Agathon says he will move closer to Socrates, disrupting or restoring the arrangement of speakers; jokes about maintaining the order (11.3).
- Disharmony: Socrates disagrees with the suggested change of seating order because it will alter the speaking order (11.3).
- Disharmony: Order breaks up at midpoint (11.3.4).
- Socrates, Aristophanes, Agathon preserve the left to right order of speaking (before 12.0).

Disharmony: elenchus, disagreement, criticism

Although all the major notes are marked by kinds of harmony, this may be more or less successful, that is, more or less harmonious. When agreement is partial or – as in an elenchus – when it is agreed that the interlocutor has disagreed with his own earlier statements, then the passage is a symbol for relative disharmony. Extreme disharmony may be marked by disagreements: criticism, ridicule, and so on.

- Agathon criticizes the previous speakers (5.0).
- Eryximachus partially disagrees with Socrates (6.0).
- Socrates' elenchus of Agathon (6.3).
- Diotima's elenchus of young Socrates: Eros not a god (7.0).
- Diotima's elenchus of Aristophanes' definition of love as a pursuit of the whole (7.3).
- Alcibiades knowingly breaks agreements with Socrates, runs away (10.1).
- Alcibiades criticizes Socrates' speeches: ridiculous and common (11.2).
- Jocular disagreements about seating and speaking order (11.3).

IV. Erotic harmony: love, friendship and sex

Eros can combine or mediate between opposites. Eryximachus once again makes this explicit: a doctor produces love, which makes extreme elements friends and lovers (3.1). Not every reference, therefore, to the god Eros or to love marks a note in the *Symposium*. Only Eros or love when it functions as some sort of harmonization serves as a symbol.

Sex is, inevitably, a kind of erotic "fitting together" (e.g. at 3.0 and 8.0), but *eros* can also lead to emotional and mental harmonization and these relationships also mark notes (e.g. at 9.2).

An important marker in this dialogue is *eros* as a path to virtue. This may not, at first, appear to be a kind of harmonization, but is so for two reasons. First,

APPENDIX 5: SYSTEMATIC THEORY OF THE MARKING PASSAGES

as argued in Chapter 7, virtue is a mean, and a mean is a middle ground where opposites meet and are blended and harmonized. Thus, when Eros propels lovers toward virtues, he is teaching them to balance and moderate the vicious extremes. Second, such a virtue is also conceived of as participation in goodness, and participation in forms is another kind of harmonization (see below).

Eros as bond, unification, partnership

Eros is sometimes declared the agent of harmonization, as a "uniter" or "partner". Sometimes, however, we see erotic bonds in action, as when Socrates declares his long-standing love for Alcibiades (9.2).

- Each Eros is a partner (*sunergon*) of each Aphrodite (2.0).
- Eros is a Uniter, attempting to make one from two (4.2).
- Agathon says Eros makes a home in soft souls, a disharmonic *krasis* (5.2).
- Eros is best partner (*sunergon*; 9.1).
- Alcibiades and Socrates bicker, declare love (9.2).
- Alcibiades asks Socrates to be his erotic partner (*sullēptora*; 10.3).
- Socrates will not forsake Alcibiades in battle, saves his life (11.1).
- Socrates and Aristodemus, his lover or friend, leave the symposium (12.0, cf. 0.0.6).

Eros as a path to the virtuous mean, to beauty

The virtues and beauty are also discussed below.

- A man in love avoids shameful acts (1.2).
- Alcestis avoids shame because of love (1.3).
- Achilles is courageous because of love (1.3).
- Pausanias says heavenly love makes us zealous for virtue (3.0).
- Eryximachus says it is good to gratify the good (3.1, 3.2, 3.3).
- Eryximachus says the doctor produces love, which reconciles extreme elements (3.1).
- Eryximachus says Eros produces the virtues on earth and in heaven, and produces happiness (3.3).
- Disharmony: Eros not beautiful (6.3).
- Diotima says men love only the good (7.3).
- Right method of pederasty leads to the form of beauty (9.0).
- Disharmony: Alcibiades' offer to trade sex for moral edification (10.3).

Sex

- Eryximachus says it is good to gratify the good (3.1, 3.2, 3.3).
- Women-courters, adulterers and so on (4.2).
- Agathon says Eros is a skilful "poet", creator of life (5.3).
- Eros is the child of Resource and Poverty, combines properties of both (7.1).
- Love is not of beauty, but of begetting in beauty (8.0).

- Reproduction is something immortal in mortals (8.0).
- Practising speeches is like reproduction, replaces old with new (8.1).

Erotic disharmony, lovers' quarrels

As before, a harmonization may be less successful and then serves as a marker for disharmony.

- Disharmony: Socrates twice rejects Alcibiades' advances (10.2).
- Disharmony: a youth pursues an older lover (10.2).
- Disharmony: Alcibiades offers to trade sex for moral edification (10.3).
- Disharmony: Alcibiades' advances are rejected again (11.0).
- Jealous squabbling between Socrates, Agathon, Alcibiades (11.3).

Other relationships

The relationship between teacher and student in Plato generally may have an erotic component. In this dialogue, references to teaching relationships recur at musical notes, and are another kind of erotic relationship.

- Aristophanes says he will teach "human nature" to avoid impiety to Eros (4.0).
- Agathon says Eros is the teacher of all crafts (5.3).
- Marsyas is the teacher of Olympus the flute player (10.0).

V. Beauty, the virtues, and means

The *Symposium* culminates at note 9.0 in Diotima's description of the transcendent Form of Beauty. She told us at the previous wholenote, however, that beauty is a "harmony" with the divine (8.0). Thus invocations of beauty are a species of harmony and will mark musical notes.

As mentioned above, virtues as means are also a kind of harmonization. The passages at the notes repeatedly connect virtue to beauty. Socrates suggests that good things are beautiful (6.3). Pausanias thinks, as a sophist might, that performing an action beautifully makes it virtuous (2.0). In short, the virtues may be understood as species of harmonization either because they are means and kinds of participation in goodness or because they are kinds of beauty, a harmony with the divine.

Beauty

- Pausanias says that aiming at virtue makes action beautiful (3.0).
- Disharmony: Pausanias says beautiful actions are virtuous (2.0).
- Good things are beautiful (6.3).
- Eros is bent on beauty (7.1).

APPENDIX 5: SYSTEMATIC THEORY OF THE MARKING PASSAGES

- Theory: Beauty is harmony with divine (8.0).
- Love is not of beauty, but of begetting in beauty (8.0).
- Participation of one form of beauty in many bodies (8.3).
- Single Form of Beauty, all beautiful things participate in it (9.0).
- Disharmony: Socrates is like an ugly satyr (10.0, 11.2).

Virtues

- Theory: many notes are marked with the idea that harmonies of various kinds will restore virtue.
- Theory: to have virtues is to have a divine soul (after 8.2).
- Theory: Pausanias says that aiming at virtue makes action beautiful (3.0).
- Theory: Pausanias says Eros makes us zealous for virtue (3.0).
- Diotima says those pregnant in soul conceive virtues, these are inventors, poets and so on; to have virtues in the soul is divine (8.2).
- *Phronēsis* is the greatest part of virtue; justice, temperance (8.2).
- Alcibiades says Socrates is wise and steadfast (11.0).
- Disharmony: Alcibiades' fraudulent prize for courage (11.1).
- Alcibiades gives Socrates justice, tells of his courage in saving Alcibiades' life (11.1).
- Shame avoided, virtue restored by harmonies:
  - Shame of Eros' neglect remedied by agreement to praise (1.1).
  - A man in love avoids shameful acts (1.2).
  - Alcestis avoids shame because of love (1.3).
  - Achilles is courageous because of love (1.3).
  - Weak: Pausanias says virtue depends on beautiful action (2.0).
  - Weak: Pausanias says shame is avoided by *kosmiōs* action (2.1).
  - Weak: Pausanias says virtue comes from custom (2.2).
  - Freely choosing slavery (*krasis*) and exchanging sex for virtue (2.3).
  - Eryximachus says it is good to gratify the good (3.1, 3.2, 3.3).
  - Eryximachus says Eros produces the virtues on earth and in heaven, and produces happiness (3.3).
  - Aristophanes says his teaching relationship will avoid shameful neglect of Eros (4.0).
  - Aristophanes has Zeus sever and Apollo "fit together" the creatures to avoid impiety (4.1).
  - Diotima says men love only the good (7.3).
- Truth
  - The *Symposium* does not explain the *Sophist*'s theory that assertions are made true by a harmonization of predicate and subject, as reviewed in Chapter 6.
  - Socrates wants to speak only the truth (6.1).
  - Socrates says truth cannot be contradicted (6.3).
- Disharmony: vice as lack of harmony.
  - Orpheus is weak and soft without *eros* (1.3).

- Disharmony: ethical relativism.
  - Pausanias says virtue depends on beautiful, correct action (2.0).
- Means: philosophers and Eros are "intermediates" (near 204b1).
  - Eryximachus recommends moderate drinking (1.0).
  - Philosophers and Eros as means (Phi: before 7.2).

VI. Participation in Forms

The most consonant note (9.0) is marked by a vision of the transcendent form of beauty and the participation in it of beautiful things.

- *Participation* of one Form of Beauty in many bodies (8.3).
- *Shared forms* are brothers (8.3).
- *Negative description* of Form of Beauty (9.0).
- *Single Form of Beauty*, in which all beautiful things participate (9.0).
- *Reciting speeches*, participates in immortality.
  - Practising is *krasis* with immortal (after 8.1).
  - Giving speeches is a kind of *diatribein* (1.1).
  - Request to recite speeches (0.0).
  - The narrator recites philosophical speeches (0.1).
  - Socrates should recite a defence speech (0.2).

VII. Arts of harmony

A major theme of the dialogue is that certain arts aim at producing harmonizations.

Erotics
- Eryximachus says erotics harmonizes opposites and creates rhythm and harmony (3.2).
- Eryximachus says medicine is the erotics of evacuation, repletion (3.1).
- Eryximachus says the doctor produces love, which reconciles extreme elements (3.1).
- Prophecy, an art, oversees the communion of gods and men, supervises the health of loves, and is a craft of friendship and erotics (3.3).
- Eryximachus says Agathon and Socrates are experts in erotics (5.0).
- Agathon says Eros is the teacher of all crafts, and so taught Apollo (archery, medicine, divination), Muses (music), Hephaestus (metalwork), Athena (weaving) and Zeus ("pilotage of gods and men") (after 5.3).
- Those pregnant in soul with virtues are craftsmen, inventors, poets (8.2)
- Initiation into erotics begins at 8.3, following steps of ladder at octads (8.3)

- Right method of pederasty leads to form of beauty (9.0)
- Socrates honours erotics and *eros* (9.1)

Music
- Eryximachus says music implants *eros* and *homonoia*, and is knowledge of erotics (3.2).
- Agathon says Eros is skilful in all composing related to music (5.3).

Medicine
- Eryximachus says medicine gratifies the good and not the bad (3.1).
- Eryximachus says medicine is erotics of evacuation, repletion (3.1).
- Eryximachus says the doctor produces love, which reconciles extreme elements (3.1).
- Apollo heals the severed creatures (4.1).

Prophecy
- Prophecy, an art, oversees the communion of gods and men, supervises the health of loves, is a craftsman of friendship and love, which knows human erotics (3.3).
- Eryximachus agrees that Socrates is a prophet (6.0).
- Diotima is a prophet.

VIII. Disharmony

It is useful to collect the various ways that disharmony may be represented.

Killing, battle, war
- Orpheus dies at the hands of women (1.3).
- Hephaestus fused lovers together after death in Hades (4.3).
- Socrates is compared to Marsyas, who was horribly killed (10.0).
- Alcibiades compares his advances to a battle charge (10.2).
- Alcibiades compares his advances to battle (11.0).
- Socrates saves Alcibiades in battle (11.1).

Aporia or mixed positive and negative emotions
- The lovers' *aporia* at Hephaestus' offer (4.3).
- *Aporia* versus pleasure (5.0).
- Socrates' fear and *aporia* after Agathon's speech (6.0).
- Love is acquisitive, *aporia* (7.2).
- *Krasis* of pleasure and pain (10.1).
- Alcibiades' anger and *aporia* (11.0).

Hubris

- Alcibiades complains of Socrates' hubris (11.0, 11.2).
- Socrates thinks he is superior (11.3).

Negative terms

- Agathon's cluster of negative words (5.3).
- Eros' negative qualities at note (7.1).
- Negative description of form of beauty is positive (as in "negative theology", here the negations indicate a supreme goodness beyond the capacity of our language; 9.0).

Miscellaneous

- Pausanias' relativism (2.0).
- Pausanias' dualism between two loves (2.0).
- Adultery and scandal from lack of customary action (2.1).
- Scandalous behaviour by lovers (2.2).
- Exchanging sex for money, patronage (2.3).
- Aristophanes asks not to be mocked (5.0).
- Agathon's cluster of rhetorical effects (5.1).
- Agathon's cluster of words for softness (5.2).
- Agathon says Eros makes a home in soft souls, a disharmonic *krasis* (5.2).
- Socrates threatens to disrupt speaking order (6.1).
- Socrates does not want to be mocked (6.1).
- Eros is not a god (7.0).
- Amputating limbs (7.3).
- Humans, even our knowledge, are always perishing; we are never the same (8.1).
- Lover's quarrel: Alcibiades bickering with Socrates (9.2).
- Alcibiades' fraudulent prize for courage (11.1).

APPENDIX 6

Structure in Agathon and Socrates' speeches

It was mentioned in Chapter 5 that the speeches of Agathon and Socrates have a parallel structure:

- *Cross-examination* (of Agathon: 194c7ff.; of the younger Socrates, 201 e6 ff.).
- *Introduction* and Previewed Structure (Ag.: 194e4–195a5; Soc.: 201d8ff.; cf. 199c3ff.).
- *Part 1: Nature and origins of Eros*
- (A) *Nature* (Ag.: 195a5ff.; Soc.: 202d8ff.).
  Transition (Ag.: 196b4–5; Soc.: 204c8–d2).
- (B) *Goodness* (esp. the four cardinal virtues; Ag.: 196b6ff.; Soc.: 204d4ff.).
  Transition (Ag.: 197c1–4; Soc.: 206b1ff.).
- *Part 2: Works of Eros* (peroration and vision; Ag.: 197c3ff.; Soc.: 206b7ff.).

At 207a5–c7, Socrates or Diotima shifts from the use of *eros* to its cause. Since Socrates says his speech will have two major parts, this transition probably marks a subsection of the second part. At 197c3, Agathon introduces the second part of his speech by saying Eros is also a "cause". So, in both speeches, to explain how something causes is a way of describing its *erga*, its works or functionings.

Although Alcibiades has not heard the earlier speeches, it may be that his speech shares the same structure as the two preceding speeches by Agathon and Socrates, at least in some rough and confused way. Alcibiades proceeds from Socrates' nature (comparison to a satyr, etc.), to his virtues (resistance to Alcibiades' charms, temperance, etc.), and then to his works (the battles scenes and feats of endurance). But the parts of Alcibiades' speech are not clearly marked, and this remains uncertain.

APPENDIX 7
Euripides and line-counting

Modern scholars have found some evidence that Euripides counted the lines of his characters' speeches and integrated these into a larger framework within each play. Euripides scholars might want to reconsider this evidence in the light of Plato's musical schemes.

Euripides' dramas have often been criticized for lacking the perfection of form associated with Sophocles and Aeschylus, and have thus had a rather variable reputation in modern times (Michelini 1987). Csapo (2004), for example, makes Euripides a champion of the New Music, which deliberately rejected the austere order and elite values of his predecessors. There is, however, a contrasting but compatible view that Euripides coupled the apparent disorder of his plays to an underlying order. The view that he was simply a sloppy or second-rate craftsmen was challenged in the 1950s by Walther Ludwig. As Anne Norris Micheleni's review of modern criticism of Euripides says, he:

> demonstrated in precise detail the deeply ingrained tendency in Euripides toward an orderly and formal style, with discrete elements of the work clearly distinguished and the underlying logical architecture – whether of grammar, motivation, or plot – in plain view. Ludwig demonstrates the importance of self-consciousness to such a style ...   (1987: 32)

Ludwig assembled evidence for three underappreciated aspects of Euripidean drama: its clarity, integrity, and arithmetical planning. Opposing those from Aristotle to Schlegel who condemned his compositions, Ludwig's analysis of the plays found evidence for a clear design:

> Instead of a lack of diligence in the construction of his plays, a consummate art of dramatic form will become visible, a form which Euripides

APPENDIX 7: EURIPIDES AND LINE-COUNTING

created with conscious effort according to a stylistic ideal peculiar to himself ... the speech of Euripides' *Electra*, [for example,] seems rather like a geometrically-planned French garden ... (Ludwig 1954: 6)

But each part of the play ... receives its form (*Gesetz*) from the whole of the play and always remains a member of an integrated totality. The clear relations between the individual sections order these parts into the tectonics of a transparent system. (*Ibid.*: 8–9)

Ludwig traces this *Ökonomie des Ganzen* (*ibid.*: 12, etc.) in several of Euripides' plays. He examines the lengths of various scenes and speeches for regular and parallel patterns. The messenger's speech beginning at line 774 in the *Electra*, for example, is found to consist of three distinct parts, the first of which is exactly half as long as the remainder (*ibid.*: 16). The chance that this might be an accident is reduced by comparing this pattern to a messenger's speech beginning at line 1122 in the *Ion*, which has a similar distribution of lines. Ludwig also argues that the two scenes share a parallel structure (*ibid.*: 18–19). The combination of the internal coherence of the patterns with their repetition in a range of works (*ibid.*: 13, 21, 25, 28, 55–6, 58, 60–61, etc.) leads Ludwig to conclude that the scenes have a strictly parallel architecture: "Such an *Arithmetic der Komposition* represents the final development of a stylistic ideal aimed at clarity ... the relations in the matter of the play are reflected in an abstract, formal scheme and, through this reflection, achieve a perfect clarity (*Eindeutigkeit*)" (*ibid.*: 9).

Ludwig may be criticized on several fronts. He is little concerned with the historical context of Euripides' work, nor, as Micheleni (1987) says, with any motivation beyond an abstract aesthetics of form. Moreover, he tends to assume that his analyses of the structure in various parts of the plays show that the whole too is structured, but he does not exhibit this overall structure.

Ludwig's conclusions were carried further, perhaps too far, by Werner Biehl, the editor of the Teubner editions of Euripides' *Ion*, *Trojan Women*, *Orestes* and *Cyclops* as well as author of several volumes of textual criticism and commentary. Through several decades, his editions of the plays argued, like Ludwig, that they had a precise mathematical structure (*Planungsökonomie*). He also, however, spelled out the overall structure of the plays. His evidence was summarized in his 1997 volume *Textkritik und Formanalyse zur euripideischen Hekabe*. It is impossible to do justice to Biehl's dense and learned analyses without expounding the plays, and a short discussion must suffice here before turning to criticism of his methods and conclusions.

Euripides' plays have various natural divisions, for example, where one actor stops and another begins or where the chorus interrupts the action. While establishing the text of the plays, Biehl found that several of these natural divisions contained the same number of lines. This led to an elaborate investigation and to the strong claim that the plays' architecture had been precisely planned. Both the divisions between the actors as well as various events within the longer speeches were allotted places according to a mathematical scheme that encompassed the entire play. These schemes are laid out in large diagrams in Biehl's monograph. They lead to conclusions such as:

> These results may already provide sufficient indications that, both in the conception of the total work and within the units of verse, a planned numerical regularity (*Gesetzmäßigkeit*) must be taken into account ... one will finally be able to see a confirmation that a completely conscious and thorough, integrated plan ... was intended by Euripides ...
> (1997: 205)

> Obviously, Euripides already had a finished and integrated plan before his eyes when conceiving the text, just as he had, down to the details, thoughts about the content and concrete images for the form of the dramatic action. (*Ibid.*: 270)

Biehl argued that knowledge of these structures affected the interpretation of the action of the play, signalling correspondences between events and demarcating phases in the development of a character (*ibid.*: 208). He denied that these mathematical structures would have been perceptible to the audience in the theatre but thought they would have opened up new dimensions of interpretation to the "reader of the text" (*ibid.*: 240).

Although some scholars have tentatively endorsed Biehl's claims,[1] no consensus has formed and it is best to remain cautious. Two criticisms can be directed against his work. First, as with Ludwig's work, Biehl does not sufficiently motivate the architecture he finds in the plays. Although he does connect it to the unfolding action, the mathematical organization remains for his Euripides an end in itself with little historical context. Second, Biehl claims an extraordinary and not entirely plausible level of precision. Although an expert in textual criticism, these claims must raise suspicions given the state of the manuscript tradition. In the wake of the work of Ludwig and Biehl, it is probably best to adopt a moderate position of the kind we find in Lloyd (1992). He acknowledges that Euripides' speeches have lengths that suggest some sort of counting or planning, and briefly suggests that over-precise claims should be avoided.

APPENDIX 8
Data from the *Republic*

This appendix introduces and contextualizes a sample of the evidence used to produce the diagrams of the *Republic*'s musical structure in Chapter 2, and has the limited aim of establishing the plausibility of the methods employed there.

The terms related to music, mathematics, and measurement used to mark the musical notes in the *Republic* fall into the following categories:

(a) Instrument: *kataskeuē*, etc.
(b) String: *chordē*
(c) Tension: cognates of *teinō*, etc.
(d) Expert musician or craftworker: the player, plucker, measurer.
(e) Measurement: *metrein* and cognates.
(f) Division or sectioning of the string: *temnein* and a wide variety of cognates.
(g) Ratio or concord of the lengths or notes: *logos, sumphonos*, etc.
(h) Plucking the String: *apopsallō*, etc.
(i) Vibration or dissonance.
(j) Operation or functioning: *ergon, dunamis*, etc.
(k) Hearing and listening: *akouō* etc.
(l) Music, note, harmony: a wide variety of specialist terms.

This may seem to be an arbitrary collection of terms. It may not at once be clear, for example, why words for division or cutting were interpreted as musical terms. These and arguably similar terms, however, are used in the discussion of the monochord in Ptolemy's *Harmonics*, as the following passages show.

Ptolemy's monochord consisted of a string stretched over a frame with movable bridges:

> [T]he string stretched over (*diateinomenē chordē*) what is called the *kanōn* will show us the ratios (*logous*) of the concords more accurately and readily ... [the string's] limits (*peratōn*) are appropriately placed so that the limits of the plucked sections between them, into which the whole length is divided (*horizetai*), have suitable and clearly perceptible points of origin.   (Ptol. *Harm.* bk I, ch. 8; Ptolemy 1930: 17, ll20ff.)[1]

Although sometimes used as a synonym for "monochord", *kanōn* strictly denoted the ruler used to measure the string:

> Let us think of a *kanōn* on a straight line (*eutheian*)... and, at its limits, bridges that are in all respects equal and similar ... To the string we shall now fit a measuring-rod *(kanōnion)* and use it to divide up the length ... so that we may make comparative measurements (*parametrēseis*) more readily.   (Ptol. *Harm.* bk I, ch. 8; Ptolemy 1930: 18, ll9ff.)[2]

The familiar Pythagorean idea that consonances and harmonies between musical notes correspond to ratios between string lengths can now be demonstrated. For example, the note sounded when the whole string is plucked can be compared to the note produced by three-quarters of the string:

> When ... the measuring-rod has been divided in the ratios of the concords ... by shifting the bridge to each point of division (*tmēma*) we shall find that the differences (*diaphoras*) of the appropriate notes agree most accurately with the hearing. For if [one] distance (*diastaseōs*) is constructed of four parts of which [another] is three, the notes corresponding to them will make the concord of a fourth.
>   (Ptol. *Harm.* bk I, ch. 8; Ptolemy 1930: 18, ll15ff.)[3]

Thus Ptolemy's description of the monochord uses many of the kinds of terms that appear at the locations of musical notes in the *Republic*, and shows that the above list is coherent.

The calculated location of note 1.0 in the *Republic* is 348e7. The marking passage for this note stretches from 348a to 353a and includes terms such as:

(a) Instrument: lyre (349e11).[4]
(b) String: musical string (*chordōn*; 349e12), vine-branch (353a1).
(c) Tension: stretching against (*antikatateinantes*; 348a7), overreach in stretching and loosening musical strings (349e11–12), overreaching (349b8ff., many times).
(d) Musician cognates: (349e1ff., seven times).
(e) Measurement: count up and measure: *arithmein, metrein* (348a9, b1).
(f) Division, sectioning, cognates of *temnō*: cut-off (*apotemnontas*; 348d7), cutting a section of the vine (*apotemois*; 353a1), three knives (353a1ff.)

APPENDIX 8: DATA FROM THE *REPUBLIC*

(g) Ratio, concord, harmony: *logos* (348a6), tuning or harmonizing the lyre (*harmottomenos*; 349e10).

(h) Vibration or dissonance, alternation between contraries, stasis: dissension/discord/hate/fighting versus agreement and love (*stasis*, etc. versus *phila*, etc.; 351d2ff.), inner opposition and self-hatred in the city and individual (351e10ff.).

(i) Operation or functioning: *dynamis* (351e8), *ergazesthai* (352a7), *ergon* (352e1, 3a7, 1b)

(j) Music: musician or cognates (349e1ff., seven times), harmonizing the lyre (*harmottomenos*; 349e10).

The calculated location of note 3.0 in the *Republic* is 399b1. The marking passage for this note stretches from 397a to 403c and includes terms such as:

(a) Instrument: "trumpets and flutes and shepherd's pipes and the sounds of all instruments" (397a6ff.), triangles, harps, flutes and instruments with many strings or many harmonies are banished, only the lyre, the cither and shepherd's pipes, the instruments of Apollo retained (399c10ff.).

(b) String: "many-stringed" instruments (399d4ff.), etc.

(c) Tension: looseness (*chalarai*; 398e10).

(d) Expert musician or craftworker: musician (398e1, 402b9, 402d8).

(e) Measurement and size: three, four, foot (unit of measurement; verse in metre is measured language) (400a5ff.), big versus small (402a9ff.).

(f) Division, sectioning, cognates of *temnō*: *skutotomon* (397e5ff., three times).

(g) Ratio, concord, harmony: harmony and rhythm (397b6ff., 398d2ff., 399a5ff., 399e8ff., 401d6ff., 404d12–e1), *logos* (398b7, 403c5).

(h) Vibration or dissonance, alternation between contraries, stasis: musical modes for war and peace (399a3ff.), violent versus voluntary (399c2), *kakos* versus *kalos* and so on (401b1–d2), manic *eros* versus *eros* for beauty and cosmos (403a5ff.).

(i) Operation or functioning: *ergon* (400a4, 401a3, c6).

(j) Music: various sounds (397a4, etc.), songs and tunes (398c1–2), the musical expert Damon (400b1ff.), musical modes (398e1ff.), musical education (401d4ff.).

Although the issue will need to be investigated further, the clusters of terms used to mark the notes in the *Republic* therefore seem to form a complex symbolic representation of playing a stringed instrument like the monochord. Recall that the *Republic* speaks of banning many-stringed instruments at 399c7.

APPENDIX 9
OCT line numbers for the musical notes

As discussed in Chapter 7, the measured locations of the musical notes on the *Symposium*'s musical scale are surprisingly accurate, despite the changes the text may have undergone during its transmission. The Stephanus pages have significantly variable lengths but, in the *Symposium* and not generally in other dialogues, the interval between quarternotes is coincidentally about one Stephanus page.

This accident does, however, make it clear that the Stephanus numbers prevented rather then helped the detection of the musical structure of the dialogues. Here, the distance between quarternotes in the range from 0.1 to 1.2 is very nearly one Stephanus page (see below). Suppose a reader had noticed the repeated pattern of motions and agreements in the frame, and began examining other passages at similar intervals, using the Stephanus page numbers as a measure (and so looking for symbols around c3–8 on succeeding pages). Already by notes 2.0 and 2.1, the error between the actual location of the notes and the location found using the Stephanus numbers would be about half a page. Using the Stephanus page numbers as a measure would thus obliterate any trace of symbols repeated at equal intervals.

As mentioned above, files containing the Greek texts of some of Plato's dialogues (with all the significant points marked) are available online.

Wholenotes and quarternotes in *Symposium*:

Note 0: 172a1	1q: 173c3	2q: 174c8	3q: 175c7
Note 1: 176c7	1q: 177c8	2q: 178d5	3q: 179d8
Note 2: 180e5	1q: 182a4	2q: 183a8	3q: 184b3
Note 3: 185b6	1q: 186c1	2q: 187c8	3q: 188d1
Note 4: 189d5	1q: 190d6	2q: 191d7	3q: 192d8
Note 5: 193d7	1q: 194e4	2q: 195e7	3q: 197a2
Note 6: 198a8	1q: 199b4	2q: 200c1	3q: 201c5
Note 7: 202c7	1q: 203d1	2q: 204d5	3q: 205d10

APPENDIX 9: OCT LINE NUMBERS FOR THE MUSICAL NOTES

Note 8:   206e4   1q: 208a1   2q: 209a6   3q: 210b1
Note 9:   211b4   1q: 212c2   2q: 213c3,   3q: 214c1
Note 10: 215c2   1q: 216c6   2q: 217c8   3q: 218d2
Note 11: 219d6   1q: 220d6   2q: 221d8   3q: 222e7
Note 12: 223d12

Wholenotes and quarternotes in *Euthyphro*:

Note 0:   2a1   1q: 2b11   2q: 2d2   3q: 3b2
Note 1:   3c6   1q: 3d9   2q: 4a9   3q: 4c2
Note 2:   4d4   1q: 4e7   2q: 5b2   3q: 5c5
Note 3:   5d9   1q: 6a3   2q: 6b7   3q: 6d1
Note 4:   6e5   1q: 7a10   2q: 7c4   3q: 7d7
Note 5:   8a4   1q: 8b8   2q: 8d1   3q: 8e6
Note 6:   9b1   1q: 9c3   2q: 9d6   3q: 10a3
Note 7:   10b7   1q: 10c13   2q: 10e7   3q: 11a8
Note 8:   11c3   1q: 11d6   2q: 12a4   3q: 12b9
Note 9:   12d3   1q: 12e6   2q: 13b1   3q: 13c7
Note 10: 13e1   1q: 14a5   2q: 14b8   3q: 14d4
Note 11: 14e8   1q: 15b1   2q: 15c5   3q: 15d7
Note 12: 16a4

Fifths in *Symposium*:

One: 182d5   Two: 192e8   Three: 203b7   Four: 213e3

Fifths in *Euthyphro*:

One: 5a6   Two: 7e1   Three: 10c7   Four: 13b9

Sevenths in *Symposium*:

One: 179d2   Two: 187b4   Three: 194c1   Four: 201e6
Five: 209c1   Six: 216d4

Sevenths in *Euthyphro*:

One: 4b10   Two: 6b2   Three: 8b2   Four: 10a9
Five: 12a7   Six: 14a6

Ninths in *Symposium*:

One: 177e7   Two: 183e3   Three: 189d5   Four: 195b1
Five: 201a3   Six: 206e4   Seven: 212e1   Eight: 218b4

Ninths in *Euthyphro*:

One: 3e3   Two: 5c1   Three: 6e6   Four: 8c1
Five: 9e6   Six: 11c2   Seven: 12e10   Eight: 14c8

Notes

1. The nature and history of philosophical allegory

1. The recent interest in ancient allegory is treated in books by Lamberton (1986), Ford (2002), Boys-Stones (2003), Sedley (2003) and Struck (2004). There is some older work that attempted to resist the tendency in histories of literature to underplay ancient allegory, including Buffière (1956), Pepin (1958), Detienne (1962) and Coulter (1976).
2. See Plut. *De aud. po.* 19e–f; Lamberton (1986: esp. 20, 48); Ford (2002); Struck (2004: esp. ch. 1).
3. See Rankin (1986) for a discussion of Antisthenes, his Homeric criticism and allegory that was written before the impact of the Dervini papyrus was felt.
4. Ford (2002: 258, 201 n.51, 224 n.47); cf. Pl. *Symp.* 209c7–d4 on Homer and Hesiod.
5. The authenticity of this dialogue is discussed in §3.5.
6. Succeeding chapters and an appendix will discuss the significance of the passages at the centres of the dialogues. The first line in this quotation is the calculated centre of the *Cratylus*.
7. Stroumsa provides a helpful perspective on the religious resonances of the new philosophies of nature: "The peculiarity of Greek esotericism lies in the fact that revelation [of the kind found in Christianity] was unknown in the Greek religious world; in such a context what is kept hidden is the *arcana naturae*, not the *arcana dei*" (2005: 2).
8. For Speusippus, see Tarán (1981); for Xenocrates, DL (I.4, para. 13); for Heraclides, Gottschalk (1980); for Aristotle, Ross's editions of his fragments (Aristotle 1952, 1955). For Pythagoreanism in the Academy generally, see below.
9. Burkert (1972: 1–14) summarizes earlier work on Pythagoreanism and Kahn (2001) provides a recent assessment. C. J. de Vogel (1966: ch. 8) usefully compares doctrines ascribed to Plato and Pythagoras.
10. Thesleff (1961) surveys, and Thesleff (1965) collects, the Hellenistic literature on Pythagoras.
11. See Aristotle's fragments (Aristotelis 1955) and Arist. *Metaph.* A, M, N.
12. "Plato himself hardly ever speaks of the Pythagoreans by name, which is a curious fact on any theory" (Field 1930: 178).
13. Reviewed in Krämer (1990) and Findlay (1974), which both include collections of relevant passages in Plato and of the later reports about the unwritten doctrines.

14. Dillon accepts the view of Proclus (*In Ti.* I.76, 1–2) that Crantor, who died about 290 BCE, "perhaps makes his most distinctive contribution to the history of Platonism, the idea of a commentary" (Dillon 2003: 218).
15. Xenocrates allegorizes the Olympic gods, Hades is air, etc.; see Dillon (2003).
16. See Burkert (1972), Dillon (2003), among others.
17. Plotinus, *Enn.* IV.2.2, VI.8.22, VI.8.19, III.4.5, III.7.13. See also Charrue (1978).
18. For Proclus, see *In R.*, 73.13–28, 74.22, 79.4, 83.15.
19. There is an older but vigorous and valuable retelling of this movement in Farrar (1961).
20. Another useful recent study that traces the history and epistemology of esotericism in Jewish thought is Halbertal (2007).
21. For similar passages, see Stroumsa (2005: 4).
22. Fowler is primarily concerned to apply the same techniques to allegories in the *Fairie Queen*, but provides an array of evidence and arguments responding to Hieatt's critics.
23. Two volumes by S. K. Heninger are of special note. In *Touches of Sweet Harmony* (1974) he surveyed Renaissance Pythagoreanism and its impact on the arts of the day; in *Sidney and Spenser* (1989) he gave a close reading of the Pythagorean structures of a range of poems.
24. See the articles "number symbolism, modern studies in", "number symbolism, tradition of" and "pun", among others.

2. Introducing the dialogues' musical structure

1. Files containing the Greek texts of some of Plato's dialogues (with all the significant points marked) are available online.
2. Pl. *Leg.* 958e9–59a1 is discussed at Ohly (1928: 93).
3. Sometimes later manuscripts contain "false" line counts; apparently, the numbers were simply copied from earlier texts with different line lengths. According to Edward Maunde Thompson, "in the Codex Urbinas of Isocrates, and in the Clarke Plato of AD 888, at Oxford, indications of partial stichometry have been traced" (1912: 67–71). See also August Pauly (1929: vol. IIIA.2, 2487–9).
4. For pictures and an introduction for non-specialists, see, for example, Thompson (1912). Some believe that classical literary scrolls were manufactured in expensive, standardized lengths, and that authors would thus have had an incentive to plan their compositions so that they would fit into a standard scroll and not waste large blank spaces. William Johnson (2004) finds no evidence for such standardization in the later papyri from Oxyrhyinchus. The columns and lines in classical literary papyri were typically fairly uniform (see the illustration, *ibid.*: x; also Birt 1882) and this would have made it easier for authors (and their readers) to maintain accurate counts. Birt went so far as to conclude that this was the norm: "That no classical writer could compose a work without disposing or planning it" (dass kein classischer Schriftsteller zu componieren vermocht hat ohne zu disponieren) (1882: 342).
5. Callimachus' catalogue, compiled about a century after Plato's death, recorded the stichometric totals for each of the scrolls in the library of Alexandria (Ohly 1928; Blum 1991: 157–8). Francesca Schironi (2005) argues that a critical edition of Plato was made at Alexandria. See also Blum (1991: 201).
6. Some set speeches in Euripides' plays have similar lengths and he has been suspected of counting the number of lines even in these larger textual units. See Appendix 7.
7. As mentioned above, the paragraphs a–e, for example, are also of variable length and are occasionally omitted altogether. In the *Republic* and the *Laws* there are gaps in the Stephanus page numbers between books.
8. One argument is that the symbols at the locations of the early notes are appropriate to their

locations (see below). Thus Plato had already fixed the length of the entire dialogue at the time the passages at the early notes were composed.

9. For general histories of ancient Greek music, see Barker (1984), West (1992).
10. Theon of Smyrna (1966: 47.18–49.5) = Tarrant (1993: T13); Theon of Smyrna (1966: 85.8–93.11) = Tarrant (1993: T14a).
11. The Greek word *harmonia* originally applied to a wide range of things "fit together". Its special musical sense slowly became more pronounced during and after the fifth century BCE (Barker 1982: vol 1, xxff.).
12. The whole sentence is "Some say the soul is a harmony, for a harmony is a *krasis* and synthesis of opposites" (Arist. *De an.* 407b30–32).
13. See, for example, R. B. Rutherford (1995) on "separatists" versus "unitarians", Jonathan Lear (1992), A. H. Lesser (2003) and A. Krohn (1876) on the *Republic*.
14. The distinction between a harmony, *krasis* or synthesis of ingredients, on the one hand, and a mixture, on the other, is common but the Greek terms used to describe these kinds varied, as Aristotle's shifting usage shows. In *De Anima*, for example, he uses "synthesis" and "mixture" loosely, and sometimes slides from one to the other (e.g. 408a13–18). In *De Generatione et Corruptione*, in contrast, he uses "mixture" to mean "a thorough blend", and "synthesis" to mean a mere co-location of ingredients (327a30ff., e.g. 328a8–9). For Aristotle's loose terminology, see Joachim's edition of *Gen. corr.* (Aristotle 1926: 175ff., 185) and Polansky (2007: 105ff.). Here, "synthesis" is always a synonym for "harmony", and "mixture" implies combination without such blending.
15. For a general discussion, see West (1992).
16. For the traditional seven-string lyre, see the Homeric Hymn to Hermes, ll. 20–67, the Aristotelian *Problemata*, 19.32, and Horace's Ode 3.11. For the association of the seven-string lyre with Orpheus, see e.g. Nichomachus of Gerasa's *Harmonics* in Janus (1962: 266, ll. 1ff.). Barker says "we know from vase-paintings and allusions in poetry that there were only seven [strings] on the traditional tortoiseshell lyre" (2007: 276).
17. The ratio between a note at one-seventh and the twelfth note is just 1:7, and this is not a small whole-number ratio (nor is seven in the Pythagorean tetraktys). The seven-seventh is the same as the twelfth note on the musical scale, and would therefore be in harmony or "unison" with it. Thus, only the first to sixth sevenths are marked by mixture.
18. "There is no doubt that by kithara they meant a box lyre, as used by citharodes" (West 1992: 51).
19. See, among others, Thompson (1912). There may also have been no indications of change in speaker.
20. Short blocks of text easily counted by hand were duplicated many times and combined; the computer correctly counted the total. The texts of some dialogues were also separated into several parts to check that the computer's counts of the parts exactly added to its counts for the whole (linearity preserves ratios).
21. They excluded the large number of "invisible characters" in the Unicode files from the counts by examining each character's hexadecimal representation.
22. The question is reviewed in Böter (1989). Brockmann (1992: 5–16) and Irigoin (1997) contain historical surveys of modern textual criticism of Plato's dialogues. S. R. Slings's work on the text of the *Republic* is collected in Slings (2005). The older edition of the *Republic* by Adam (1902) contains a convenient overview of the categories and locations of its textual problems (see Index III under "Manuscripts", Adam 1902).
23. In this volume, I show only that Plato was counting some unit of text. I will give the evidence that he was counting syllables and hexameter lines in a future work.
24. The number of letters per standard line is discussed by Birt (1882), Graux (1878) and Ohly (1928). Birt concluded: "This standard line (Normalzeile) of circa 35 letters therefore ... dominated book production unchanged through at least five hundred years from Dionysius' copy

NOTES

of Thucydides until the time of Justinian" (1882: 202). Schanz examined the ninth-century Clarke codex of Plato's dialogues at Oxford and argued that the partial stichometric notations in its margins descended from earlier copies. His analysis found that scribes had employed average line lengths of 35.56 letters in the *Cratylus* and 34.32 letters in the *Symposium*.

It was sometimes common, especially in and after the Hellenistic period, for the actual lines employed in papyri to have lengths different from the thirty-five-letter line that served as a conventional unit of measurement, as Birt (1882: 210ff.) and Blum (1991) discuss.

25. Aristotle discusses the theory of inductive arguments in many places, including *An. post.* I.1, 71a5ff.; *Rh.* I.2, 1357b25ff.
26. Such a density of symbolism comports with the common view that Plato is a teleologist. Although the conversations in the dialogues can seem meandering, for many or most passages it is possible to specify a reason why they lie where they do.

3. Independent lines of evidence

1. Socrates' shorter first speech is 99.9 per cent of one-third of the second speech. Socrates' second speech (243e9–257b6) has 21,508 characters, and one-third of this is 7,169 characters. The first speech has 7,163 characters (237a7–241d1). The speeches contain prologues, interludes and quotations. If the prologue of the first speech (237a7–b1) is not counted, then the first speech has 6,743 characters, which is close to one-twelfth of the dialogue (6,744). Lysias' speech early in the *Phaedrus* is criticized for its lack of organization; its length is 5,750 characters, which is not close to one-twelfth of the entire dialogue.
2. Ten-twelfths of the total dialogue in *Menexenus* is 20,610 letters, and the speech is 20,601 letters, or 99.95 per cent of ten-twelfths. The speech lasts from 236d4 to 249c8.
3. These speeches will be annotated in following chapters. For convenience, their OCT line numbers are summarized here. Pausanias' speech begins at 180c4, shortly before the two-twelfths point at 180e5, and ends at 185c3, three OCT lines after the three-twelfths point at 185b7. Eryximachus' speech (with the exchanges about hiccups) begins at 185c5, shortly after three-twelfths, and ends with some repartee with Aristophanes at 189c1, shortly before the four-twelfths point at 189d6. It is not possible to say exactly where this speech ends. Aristophanes' speech begins at 189c2, shortly before the four-twelfths point, and ends at 193e2, three OCT lines after the five-twelfths point at 189d7. Socrates begins responding to Agathon at 198a4, four lines before the central six-twelfths point at 198a8. After some banter, Socrates agrees to give a proper speech at 199b2–7 which is at the six-twelfths and a quarternote point (199b4). After quizzing Agathon and reporting his conversation with Diotima, Socrates stops at 212c3, which is one OCT line after the nine-twelfths and a quarternote point (212c2). The *Symposium* contains 83,481 characters and Socrates' speech 20,809 characters. Alcibiades agrees to give a speech at 214c6, shortly after the nine-twelfths and three quarternotes point (214c1) and stops at 222b7, shortly before the eleven-twelfths and three quarternotes point at 222e7.
4. See note 3.
5. The conclusion of Agathon's speech is at 197e8; the centre of the dialogue is four OCT lines later at the six-twelfths point, 198a4. There is complicated symbolism at the centre of the dialogue, as discussed in later chapters.
6. The three-twelfths point of the *Phaedo* is at 72c8; the conclusion of the cyclic generation arguments is at 72c5–e2, that is, at the three-twelfths point. The *Phaedo*'s argument for immortality from recollection begins at 72e3, immediately after the three-twelfths point, and concludes at 77c6–d5, that is, at the four-twelfths point (77c8).
7. In the *Euthyphro*, the first definition of holiness is at 5d8–e2, that is, at the three-twelfths

point (d9). The second definition of holiness is at 6e10–7a1; the four-twelfths point is at the word "paradigm" at e4–5.
8. In the *Apology*, the investigation begins at 21b8–9, that is, at the two-twelfths point, which is at the word *sophos* in line b9. Socrates concludes his discussion of his investigations at 23c1 and turns to his own teachings at the next line (*pros de toitois ...*); the four-twelfths point is at this line, 23c2.
9. Measurements of the total lengths of dialogues are less accurate than measurements of relative locations, as discussed in Chapter 2.
10. Pl. *Resp.*: calculations place the centre of the dialogue at 472b8 = 50.0p, which is the passage about the ideal just man; Zeus at 472e8; philosopher-kings at 473c11 = 50.5p; "*hegemon*" at 474c1–3.
11. Pl. *Phdr.*: the calculated centre is within the passage 252e1–3b2, at the phrase "[humans] participate in god" (253a4–5).
12. Pl. *Symp.*: Zeus at 197b3; "hegemon" at 197e2–3, cf. d3; "spectacle" at 197d5–6; prophet at 198a4–a10. The centre of the *Symposium* is in this passage at a8.
13. Pl. *Cra.*: centre at 412e3; the passage 411d4–413d2 considers the listed terms. *Nous* is *autokratôr* at 413c5–7.
14. Pl. *Apol.*: wiser at 29b4; injustice at b6; philosophy at c8; the god at d3–4; the centre at c4.
15. Pl. *Euthd.*: philosophy at 288d6ff.; knowledge at d8ff.; immortality at 289b1; the centre at 289b2.
16. Pl. *Euthphr.*: justice at 8e7; wiser at 9a2; what the gods believe at 9a8–b1; and praising wisdom at 9b3; the centre at 9a8.
17. Pl. *Grg.*: wisdom at 487c5 and e4; justice at 488b2–6; 50.0p is between these passages at 488a7, where Socrates behaves like a philosopher.
18. Pl. *Ti.*: 56c3–7; centre at 56e3.
19. Many examples could be given, including: Sayre's cutting in half at the halfway point of the *Statesman* (284e2 = 6/12 exactly), "try to cut this into three" at the two-thirds point of the *Philebus* (48d4 = 8/12 exactly), three kinds at the one-third point of the *Symposium* (189d7, 4/12 = d5).
20. Pl. *Ap.*: 10/12 = 38a1, 11/12 = 40a5.
21. Pl. *Phd.*: 10/12 = 108b2, 11/12 = 113c1; wicked souls in Hades at 108a7ff.; earth a hollow 109a9ff.; underworld 111c5ff.; Tartarus at 113b4 etc.; River Styx at 113c1–2.
22. Pl. *Phdr.*: 10/12 = 270d7, 11/12 = 275a7; blind rhetoric at 270e2; persuasive rhetoric 271c10ff.; no truth 272d2ff.; writing 274c5ff.
23. Pl. *Resp.*: 10/12 = 573e4; 11/12 = 599c7; tyrant 566a10ff.; poets 595a1ff. This range does include the three proofs that the just life is the best or happiest (580b1ff.), which are evaluated by judges as in a theatrical contest.
24. Pl. *Symp.*: 10/12 = 215c1, 11/12 = 219d5; Alcibiades begins at 215a4; Satyr simile at 215b4ff.; seduction 217a2ff.; rejection 219c6ff.
25. Pl. *Ti.*: 10/12 = 80d7; 11/12 = 86d3; old age and death, 81c6ff.; diseases of body, 81e6–86b1, and of soul, 81e6ff.
26. Pl. *Ap.*: 8/12 = 33d3; 9/12 = 35d3; theism at d5ff.
27. Pl. *Phd.*: 8/12 = 97e4; 9/12 = 103a6; the theory of Forms exposited from 100b1; the proof of immortality finishes between the nine- and ten-twelfths points at 106e5ff.
28. Pl. *Phdr.*: 8/12 = 261c6; 9/12 = 266b1; the four aspects of dialectics are at 262b5–9, 263b6ff., 264b2ff. and 265d3ff.
29. Pl. *Resp.*: 8/12 = 524d3; 9/12 = 549e6; ascension at 521d; study of One at 525a1; sciences from 526c7; dialectics from 532d7; nuptial number from 546b4; transformation begins at 547c5, where the discussion of timocracy also begins; timocracy as a mixture at 548c3–5 and 550b5; timocracy concludes at 550c1.

30. Pl. *Symp.*: 8/12 = 206d8, 9/12 = 211b2; contact with Beauty at 206d2ff.; form of the One at 211b1.
31. Pl. *Ti.*: 8/12 = 68e2; 9/12 = 74e5; demiurge at 68e1ff., divination at 71d5ff., body constructed at 74d6ff.
32. Note 2.0 = 373d9, note 3.0 = 399b1. The lines were "smoothed" by the software.
33. The slight notches visible on the flanks of the peak at note 3.0 mark the locations of the quarternotes.
34. There is perhaps a theoretical possibility that very long lists (on the order of the length of the text itself) or very short lists of *hapax legomena* might be constructed in ways that led to some pattern.
35. There are older surveys of the pseudo-Platonica in Schaarschmidt (1866) and Heidel (1976). For recent debates, see Döring *et al.* (2005).
36. See Plato (1999) on the *Cleitophon* and Denyer (2001) on the *First Alcibiades*. There is a stronger inclination to doubt the authenticity of the *Epinomis*. Leonardo Tarán (1975) thought that neither ancient testimony nor the style of the *Epinomis* proved it inauthentic, but argued that doctrinal differences between it and the canonical dialogues suggested its spuriousness. A. E. Taylor (1960: 14ff., 497ff.) and others have defended its authenticity.

4. An emphatic pattern in the *Symposium*'s frame

1. For the *Symposium*, I have followed the Greek of Burnet's OCT edition or of Dover's edition in the Cambridge Greek and Latin Series (1980). I am much indebted to the linear commentaries of Dover (1980), Bury (1932) and Rowe (1998). For the *Euthyphro*, I have followed the newer OCT edition of Duke *et al.* (1995) and Burnet's commentary (1924). All errors that remain are my own. With polysemous terms such as *kalos* and *logos*, it was not possible to be consistent.
2. "Tē dē tēs kinēseōs taksei rhuthmos onoma eiē tē de autēs phōnēs ... harmonia ...".
3. "*Sophia*" does occur between 0.0 and 0.1. There is complicated, dense symbolism in this first quarter-interval. In general, arguments about symbols at the locations of notes do not imply that similar symbols do not occur between notes (see §2.8).
4. The first two notes involve requests to recite the speeches given at Agathon's party, and it was, no doubt, the erotic subject matter of the speeches that contributed to their memorization and the requests. At the first quarternote, Apollodorus' delight in philosophy or perhaps the *phila* involved in philosophical pursuits leads to the agreements.

    In the third passage, both the suggestion that Aristodemus attend Agathon's party and his willingness to go without an invitation attest to the friendship between Aristodemus and Socrates. We have already been told explicitly that Aristodemus was some kind of lover of Socrates (*erastēs*; 173b3). Thus the agreement is at least in part produced by their friendship or "*eros*" for each other. In the fourth passage, Agathon invites Socrates to share his couch. This initiates the flirtation between them and, in the context of classical Greek symposia, may have had erotic or seductive overtones. Socrates complies, and in the course of the dialogue will make his reciprocal interest in Agathon clear. Arguably, in all three passages, the agreement is produced by *eros*, just as Eryximachus' theory holds.
5. Although the evidence is too extensive to collect here, Plato elsewhere uses words with the syllable *mel*, such as *ameletētos*, to refer to music, perhaps because of its connection to "melody" (*melos*).
6. There is also an allusion to Homer, but material in the commentaries will not be repeated.
7. Following Dover (1980: 83–4).
8. This quarternote is harmonically significant and may therefore be an appropriate place both

for Socrates' entrance and for his first exchange with Agathon. As mentioned in the comments on note 0.2, this passage is four "octaves" from the twelfth note. Thus Socrates enters the dialogue at the "fifth octave", and enters the andron at this "fourth octave" (see Appendix 3).
9. Normally we would translate the two negatives in a positive way, but they are preserved here since Plato will use clusters of negatives as part of his symbolism (cf. note 5.3).
10. For Archytas, see, for example, Huffman (2005: esp. 19, 73–4, 235ff., 332ff.). For later evidence see Iambl. *VP* 31.
11. Forms of the words "pleasure" and "pain" appear (*aêdês*, 176c8; *chalepon*, d1).
12. In the *Phaedo*, note 0.1 has the "*krasis*" between pleasure and pain (59a6–7). Note 0.2 has pleasure and pain "joined" together but does not repeat the word "*krasis*" (60b3–c1).
13. Preserving the cluster of negatives.

5. Making the *Symposium*'s musical structure explicit

1. Thus Eros as human love enters three "octaves" from the twelfth note (twelve halved three times is one-and-a-half). Socrates entered the dialogue at five octaves and entered the andron at four octaves from the twelfth note. This passage, however, seems to be dominated by negative concepts such as shame. This may be because this region in the musical scale is not very consonant.
2. It is likely that this note would have been considered dissonant, since note 1.3 (= 1.75/12) corresponds to an irreducible ratio of 7/48.
3. I take no position here in the debate over whether Plato's image of the sophists is just or accurate.
4. The distinction here between harmonization and unity may lie in this. Harmonization involves, as Aristotle has it (see Ch. 2), a mutual homogenization of properties; unification produces a single substance.
5. There is an undeveloped hint of a less sophistic, more Platonic doctrine here. Although custom is apparently the foundation of virtue, "good men" follow custom voluntarily.
6. Omitting *philosophias* at 183a1.
7. 183b2, reading *autou*.
8. Pausanias has mentioned philosophy before, but only in passing: "philosophy and gymnastics" (182c1).
9. The lover as erotic guide is at 2.3.4 and the gratification theme is at 3.0 (and at earlier notes).
10. This substantive has a wide range of meanings. It is literally "a common thing", but may here be "partnership" or "association" (LSJ). In Aristophanes' speech, the androgynes are a "combined" or *koinos* sex (189e1, 3, …), so that the adjective there implies a kind of "harmonization" or unity. At the beginning of this marking passage, another art of the heavens, astronomy, is mentioned, and is also made a science of erotic relations (6/8).
11. Eryximachus does not articulate any real theory of harmony or its various species, and is therefore portrayed as an erudite, but not clear, thinker. He does not, for example, explain how harmony can be agreement without difference (cf. Aristotle's theory in *De Generatione et Corruptione*, discussed in Ch. 2).
12. The phrase "*krasis* and harmony" is thus a hendiadys, naming one thing through two words.
13. This is approximate because there is no sharp cut-off between the speeches and the banter. It may be that the friendly interchange between Eryximachus and Aristophanes, and its blurred boundaries, are a way of "harmonizing" or "fitting together" the two speeches, which would be appropriate to this consonant range.
14. If justice is a form of harmony, as in the *Republic* (e.g. 443d6ff., 433b3ff.), then a justified cut made by the god of justice may, paradoxically, create a kind of harmony.
15. The structure of the three remaining speeches and their interrelations are complicated, and a

full discussion would distract from the central goal here: to exposit direct and clear evidence for the musical scale.
16. Effeminate: lines 30ff., 95ff., 134ff., 185ff., 218ff.; promiscuous: 35; cross-dressing: 135ff., 160ff., 250ff.; passive: 35ff., 155ff.; soft or tender: 185–92.
17. Aristophanes' play leaves no doubt that Agathon is being denigrated as a passive: 200ff. (cf. Henderson 1991: 209ff.), esp. paras 460 and 462). See also Dover (1989).
18. Reading *aganos* at 197d5.
19. Some would say that the twelfth note itself is more consonant, but this is a matter of terminology. When the twelfth note is played with itself, there is strictly no "con-sonance", but only "unison".
20. These notes have a 2:3 and a 3:4 ratio with the twelfth note.
21. See Appendix 6 for references.
22. It will be argued in Chapter 6 that in the *Euthyphro* predication is a kind of harmonization. Socrates' discussion here of "possessing properties" may refer to that species of harmony, but it would be the only clear instance in this dialogue.
23. Other forms of the Greek word Diotima uses for "hush" mean a "religious or holy silence". Socrates uses the word at 214d5. The Pythagoreans were known for prizing religious silence (see e.g. Burkert 1972: 179).
24. See e.g. *Alc.* I, 106e6–7.

6. Parallel structure in the *Euthyphro*

1. As discussed briefly in the next section, a disjunction is just one kind of assertion or proposition in modern logic, but is not always so in ancient logic, where a disjunction may instead just be a failure to assert something definite.
2. The sixth seventh is a puzzle. It nearly coincides with note 10.1. This does not appear to assert a disjunction or difference, but simply that a farmer grows food from the earth ("Many and fair, too, are the works of the farmer ... but his chief work is the production of [6/7] food from the earth?"). In the *Symposium*, the sixth seventh is marked by a passage that compares Socrates to a satyr: ugly and ignorant on the outside, but good when opened. Perhaps, in the *Euthyphro*, producing "fair" food from dirt makes a similar contrast.
3. The debate about whether Aristotle is discussing "words or things" can be set aside here.
4. The *Euthyphro* marks some of the dissonant sevenths with disjunctive assertions. Ordinarily, in modern logic, the disjunction "p or not-p" is a single proposition and is always true. In Aristotle, as the much-contested discussion of the sea battle (*Int.* IX) shows, this proposition may not always be true. Thus a disjunction may not be an assertion involving synthesis, and would therefore be appropriate to mark the lack of synthesis at a dissonant musical note. But it is not necessary here to enter into the theory of complex propositions.
5. This section collects and repeats some of the later commentary.
6. The name "Apollodorus" means, etymologically, "gift of Apollo" (cf. 172a6).
7. Although their brevity makes them difficult to confirm, there may be etymological puns at work here. The *Cratylus* associated Euthyphro with etymology (396d5).
8. Another word with the stem -*mel*- is repeated twice.
9. The note falls at the phrase *all' homose ienai*, whose symbolic or etymological sense, if any, is uncertain.
10. Fear and pleasure, that is, the basic forces of aversion and attraction, straddled note 1.0 in the *Symposium*. Here, a quarter-interval later, the same forces straddle this note.
11. For some examples, see Pl. *Plt.* 258d4ff., *Grg.* 449d8ff. and *Phlb.* 55d1ff. For an overview see Dodds (1959: 196ff.) and Roochnik (1998).
12. Cf. *Soph.* 223c6ff. with *emporikē* at 223d11, etc.; *Euthd.* 288e2ff. Recall also the swipe at the

7. Extracting doctrine from structure

1. The key passages in the *Philebus* are 64d9ff. and 66a6ff.
2. Aristotle refers to the *Philebus* at 1172b29ff.
3. Examples of his mathematical imagery include 1106a27ff. on "continuous and divisible" and means as "middles" versus "mean terms" in proportions, 1131a4ff. on justice and proportions between parts of a line, and so on.
4. Aristotle conceives of the philosopher as virtuous, and therefore happy in human terms, but also as enjoying the higher happiness of intellectual contemplation. Happiness is "activity according to virtue", and wisdom is the most pleasurable of activities agreeing with virtue (*Eth. Nic.* 1177a13, 24). The philosopher and contemplation are treated at 1177a25ff. and 1178a4ff.
5. In Greek mathematics, the terms "mean" and "extreme" each play two roles. First, a mean may be the middle or something near the middle of a line or some other geometric object; an extreme is some kind of boundary or end. Thus a mean point in a line may also be an extreme of the two flanking segments. Second, however, in proportions, if a is to b as b is to c then b is a "mean" term and both a and c are "extreme" terms.
6. See Burkert (1972: 452 n.26) and Herz-Fischler (1998: 90–95).
7. As reviewed by Balashov (1994) and Herz-Fischler (1998: 84–5), Brumbaugh, Gibson, Des Jardins, and Dreher hold that the *Republic* does allude to the golden mean; Cherniss opposes; Balashov holds that it is possible but unproven.
8. Burkert (1972: 453 n.28) sees tenuous evidence in a vague passage in the Platonic *Hippias Major*, but see Herz-Fischler (1998: 85).
9. Notation and terminology vary slightly. Sometimes the golden mean is said to be the reciprocal of 0.618, that is, 1.618. Which number is dubbed the golden mean is arbitrary. The value of the golden mean is found by solving a quadratic equation. If $1:x :: x:(1-x)$ then $x^2 + x - 1 = 0$; the positive root of that equation is $(\sqrt{5} - 1)/2$.
10. The discussion of great and small lasts from 149d8 to 151e2. Perhaps this whole passage alludes to the golden mean.
11. *Symp.*: Eros is *en mesō* at 203e5 = 61.0p, but philosophers and Eros are *hoi metaksu* at 204b1 and b5; 61.8p = 204b6.
12. *Phlb.*: 61.8p at 45e7; *mēden agan* at 45e1. The Delphic Oracle was a temple to Apollo, a deity important to the Pythagoreans.
13. *Phdr.*: *mesēmbria* at 259a2, a6 and d8; 61.8p = 258e7. The four levels are: the sun and gods above; the singing cicadas overhead who are messengers to the gods; conversing philosophers; and the slumbering Many below with their inert *dianoia*.
14. *Cra.*: 419b5–420b5; 61.8p = 419d7.
15. *Leg.*: victory at 840c5, holy and just at d8; 61.8p = 840d8.
16. *Ti.*: 64c7–65b3; 61.8p = 65b7.
17. *Chrm.*: 167e1(= 61.8p)–e2; greater and smaller at 168b10–c2, 64.0–64.4p.
18. *Plt.*: 61.8p at 291b2; separating the two groups at c5–6.
19. *Tht.*: 183e3(= 61.8)–184a1.
20. It will be argued, for example, that passages at $1 - 0.618$ are also marked with references to the golden mean. In geometric constructions of the Platonic solids, lines were marked at both 0.618 and $1 - 0.618$.

8. Some implications

1. For example, the *Timaeus*, the *Philebus* and the closing myth of the *Republic*.
2. See e.g. *Resp.* 398e2ff. and Arist. *Pol.* (VIII, 5–7). By "scale or key" is meant the "mode".
3. Arist. *Pol.* (VIII, 5.4–10, esp. 5.10). Cf. the *Phaedo*'s doctrine of the soul.

Appendix 1: More musicological background

1. Barker (2007: 294ff.) discusses the relation of Archytas and Aristoxenus to the musical practice of their times.
2. See Creese (2010: 93ff.). For Pythagoras and Philolaus, see Huffman (1993: 54, 167ff.); Pl. *Ti.* 34b10ff.; *Epin.* 991a6–b4; Arist. *Metaph.* 1093a28–b5. Gibson (2005: 684 n.16) concludes that this last passage shows that Aristotle knew the 6-8-9-12 schema.
3. See Burkert (1972: 375 n.22), Barker (1982), West (1992) and Barker (2007) for earlier, contrary views and a brief survey of the debate.

Appendix 2: Neo-Pythagoreans, the twelve-note scale and the monochord

1. In the following, I use numbers to name each note instead of the Greek names used by Thrasyllus. His terminology is, from the "beginning" to the "end" of his string: note 3 = *hyperupatē*, note 4 = *hypatē mesē*, note 6 = *mesē*, note 8 = *nētē diezeugmenē*, note 9 = *hyperbolaia*, note 12 = *proslambamenos*.
2. Interestingly, in this paragraph some intervals are counted down from the twelfth note and some short lengths of string are compared to each other rather than always to the whole string.

Appendix 3: Markers between the major notes

1. The word for begin, *katarchō*, may have religious overtones: to begin a sacrifice, and so on (LSJ).
2. Socrates refers back to 197b4, where Agathon said the gods make things by approaching Eros. At that point, Agathon refers back to the beginning of his own speech, which is at 4/9.
3. These "fifths" should not be confused with the musical interval a "fifth", which corresponds to a 3:2 ratio.
4. Hephaestus offers to fuse the lovers at note 4.3, and is there quoted by Aristophanes as if in direct discourse. The offer is repeated about eight lines later by Aristophanes speaking in his own voice. The marker for 2/5 falls at the phrase "from two, one emerges", and explains why this strong reference to harmonization occurs after and close to the quarternote.
5. See e.g. Arist. *Gen. corr.* 328a23ff.

Appendix 4: The central notes

1. There are affinities between these ring structures and role of the centre in Pythagorean cosmology, but this appendix concentrates on the textual evidence alone.
2. The phrase at the centre of the *Euthyphro*, "ought to prosecute for and charge with", is teasingly peculiar. Since they were written by the author of the *Cratylus*, it may not be inappropriate to examine their etymologies. The translation's "ought to" is *orthōs*, which means "correct", from its root meaning of "upright". Socrates then uses, perhaps for emphasis, two nearly

synonymous words for "prosecute", *epeksienai* and *episkēptō* (*hendiadys*) at the calculated centre of the dialogue. The roots of the first word mean "to go out upon", and so "pursue" or "prosecute". The second word is uncommon and is used only here in this dialogue (see *Thesaurus Lingua Graecae*, www.tl.uci.edu). Its root means "lean on" or "fall down" (a king leans on a staff called a "sceptre"), and its legal meaning is "lay a strict charge upon" or perhaps "come down hard on". The two parts of the phrase at the centre of the dialogue thus have almost opposite etymologies, one indicating "out and up" and the other "falling down". If we take *orthōs* in its sometime literal sense as "upright", the phrase might be rendered "to go out and upright and down".

The word for "binding" is repeated three times before the centre; the word for "show" is repeated three times after the centre. The directions up and down were important in Pythagorean cosmology. Does the symbolism suggest, as in the *Timeaus* and elsewhere, some sort of creation or emanation at the centre: constriction, unfolding and then appearances? Does the ring structure symbolize some concentric flow from a central creation? These questions cannot be rigorously answered on the slim evidence presented here.

3. The etymology of a phrase at the centre of the *Symposium* is also intriguing. The dialogue contains a series of unrecognized puns on Agathon's name, whose root meaning is *agathos* or "good", a key term in Platonism. A part of the central phrase runs "Agathon speaks good" (*Agathōn eu erei*; 198a9). Speaking, speeches and saying have been treated as sites of harmonization (e.g. *homologia*) at some of this dialogue's musical notes, which indicates that Agathon's "speaking" may have a deeper metaphysical meaning here too (cf. the role of *logos* in Stoicism, Neoplatonism, etc.). Construing the phrase in a metaphysical sense, it may be suggestively rendered "the Good speaks the good" or even "good flows from the Good".

Cognates of "fear" are repeated in the sophistic jingle before the centre. Fear in Plato and Aristotle is an aversive emotion or force. After the centre, forms of "beautiful" are repeated three times, and the beautiful in this dialogue is something desired or pursued. Is this also some symbolism for emanation: repulsion, flowing out of good, dispersal of beauty?

Appendix 7: Euripides and line-counting

1. Huys (2000) wrote in a brief review in *Les Etudes Classiques*: "[Biehl's book on the Hecuba analyses the] 'quantitative form,' that is, the numerical architecture according to which Biehl says Euripides consciously structured not only the lyrical parts but also the trimeter scenes. For instance, within the agon scenes, the number of lines spoken by Polymestor (ll. 1132–82) equals those in Hecuba's discourse (ll. 1187–237). By applying more complex schemes, Biehl successfully reveals arithmetic structures where they are less manifest and shows the relations that these structures have with the dramatic meaning envisaged by the poet ... even if this study does not convince the sceptics on many points of detail, it remains a testament to the impressive erudition and extraordinary prudence of a great philologist."

Appendix 8: Data from the *Republic*

1. Also Barker (1984: 291).
2. Also Barker (1984: 292).
3. *Ibid.*
4. Here, line numbers refer to Slings's newer edition of the *Republic* (2003).

Bibliography

Adam, J. 1902. *The Republic of Plato*. Cambridge. Cambridge University Press.
Alline, H. 1915. *Histoire du Texte de Platon*. Paris: Librairie Ancienne Honore Champion.
Alpers-Goelz, R. 1976. *Der Begriff SKOPOS in der Stoa und seine Vorgeschichte*. Hildesheim: Georg Olms.
Annas, J. 1981. *An Introduction to Plato's Republic*. Oxford: Clarendon Press.
Aristophanes 2004. *Thesmophoriazusae*. Oxford: Oxford University Press.
Aristotelis 1955. *Fragmenta Selecta*. Oxford: Clarendon Press.
Aristotle 1926. *On Coming-to-be and Passing-away*. Oxford: Clarendon Press.
Aristotle 1952. *Select Fragments*, W. D. Ross (ed.). Oxford: Clarendon Press.
Aristotle 1982. *De Generatione et Corruptione*. Oxford: Clarendon Press.
Aristoxenus 1974. *Aristoxenou harmonika stoicheia*. Hildesheim: Georg Olms.
Balashov, Y. 1994. "Should Plato's Line be Divided in the Mean and Extreme Ratio?" *Ancient Philosophy* 14: 283–95.
Barker, A. 1982. "Aristedes Quintilianus and Constructions in Early Music Theory". *Classical Quarterly* 32(1): 184–97.
Barker, A. 1984. *Greek Musical Writings*. Cambridge: Cambridge University Press.
Barker, A. 2001. *Scientific Method in Ptolemy's Harmonics*. Cambridge: Cambridge University Press.
Barker, A. 2007. *The Science of Harmonics in Ancient Greece*. Cambridge: Cambridge University Press.
Barnes, J. 1993. *The Presocratic Philosophers*. London: Routledge.
Bergsten, G. 1969. *Thomas Mann's "Doctor Faustus": The Sources and Structure of the Novel*. Chicago, IL: University of Chicago Press.
Berti, E. 1966. "Contributo allo studio dei manoscritti platonici del Critone". *Studi Classici et Orientali* 15: 210–20.
Betegh, G. 2004. *The Derveni Papyrus: Cosmology, Theology and Interpretation*. Cambridge: Cambridge University Press.
Biehl, W. 1997. *Textkritik und Formanalyse zur euripideischen Hekabe: Ein Beitrag zum Verständnis der Komposition*. Heidelberg: Universitätsverlag C. Winter.
Birt, T. 1882. *Das Antike Buchwesen*. Berlin: Verlag von Wilhelm Hertz.
Blum, R. 1991. *Kallimachos: The Alexandrian Library and the Origins of Bibilography*. Madison, WI: University of Wisconsin Press.

Bodéüs, R. 2000. *Aristotle and the Theology of the Living Immortals*. Albany, NY: SUNY Press.
Böter, G. 1989. *The Textual Tradition of Plato's Republic*. Leiden: Brill.
Boys-Stones, G. R. (ed.) 2003. *Metaphor, Allegory, and the Classical Tradition: Ancient Thought and Modern Revisions*. Oxford: Oxford University Press.
Brandwood, L. 1992. "Stylometry and Chronology". In *The Cambridge Companion to Plato*, R. Kraut (ed.), 90–120. Cambridge: Cambridge University Press.
Brisson, L. 2004. *How Philosophers Saved Myths*. Chicago, IL: University of Chicago Press.
Broadie, S. 2003. "Aristotelian Piety". *Phronesis* 48(1): 54–70.
Brockmann, C. 1992. *Die handschriftliche Überlieferung von Platons Symposion*. Wiesbaden: Ludwig Reichert Verlag.
Buffière, F. 1956. *Les mythes d'Homère et la pensée grecque*. Paris: Les Belles Lettres.
Burkert, W. 1972. *Lore and Science in Ancient Pythagoreanism*. Cambridge, MA: Harvard University Press.
Burkert, W. 1987. *Ancient Mystery Cults*. Cambridge, MA: Harvard University Press.
Burnet, J. 1924. *Plato's Euthyphro, Apology of Socrates, and Crito*. Oxford: Oxford University Press.
Burnet, J. 1977. *Plato's Phaedo*. Oxford: Clarendon Press.
Burnyeat, M. F. 2007. "The Truth about Pythagoras". *London Review of Books* 29(4): 3–6.
Bury, R. G. 1932. *The Symposium of Plato*. Cambridge: Heffer.
Bury, R. G. 1897. *Plato's Phaedo*. Cambridge: Cambridge University Press.
Charrue, J. M. 1978. *Plotin, Lecteur de Platon*. Paris: Belles lettres.
Cole, T. 1991. *The Origins of Rhetoric in Ancient Greece*. Baltimore, MD: Johns Hopkins University Press.
Coulter, J. A. 1976. *The Literary Microcosm: Theories of Interpretation of the Later Neoplatonists*. Leiden: Brill.
Creese, D. 2010. *The Monochord in Ancient Greek Harmonic Science*. Cambridge: Cambridge University Press.
Csapo, E. 2004. "The Politics of the New Music". In *Music and the Muses: The Culture of "Mousike" in the Classical Athenian City*, P. Murray & P. J. Wilson (eds), 207–48. Oxford: Oxford University Press.
Denyer, N. 2001. *Alcibiades*. Cambridge: Cambridge University Press.
Detienne, M. 1962. *Homère, Hésiode et Pythagore: poésie et philosophie dans le pythagorisme ancien*. Bruxelles-Berchem: Latomus.
Dicks, D. R. 1970. *Early Greek Astronomy to Aristotle*. Ithaca, NY: Cornell University Press.
Diels, H. & W. Schubart 1905. *Anonymer Kommentar zu Platons Theaetet*. Berlin: Weidmannische Buchhandlung.
Diels, H. & W. Kranz 1959. *Die Fragmente der Vorsokratiker*. Berlin: Weidmannsche Verlagsbuchhandlung.
Dillon, J. M. 1977. *Middle Platonists*. London: Duckworth.
Dillon, J. M. 2003. *The Heirs of Plato: A Study of the Old Academy (347–274 BC)*. Oxford: Clarendon Press.
Dodds, E. R. 1928. "The Parmenides of Plato and the Origin of the Neoplatonic 'One'". *Classical Quarterly* 22: 129–42.
Dodds, E. R. 1959. *Plato: Gorgias*. Oxford: Clarendon Press.
Döring, K., M. Erler & S. Schorn 2005. *Pseudoplatonica*. Stuttgart: Franz Steiner.
Dörrie, H. 1976. *Von Platon zum Platonismus*. Opladen: Westdeutscher.
Dover, K. J. 1989. *Greek Homosexuality*. Cambridge, MA: Harvard University Press.
Dover, K. 1980. *Plato: Symposium*. Cambridge: Cambridge University Press.
Duke, E. A. et al. (ed.) *Platonis: Opera*. Oxford: Clarendon Press.
Euclid 1956. *The Elements*, T. Heath (ed.). New York: Dover.
Eudoxos 1966. *Die Fragmente des Eudoxos von Knidos*, F. Lasserre (ed.). Berlin: De Gruyter.

Farrar, F. W. 1961. *History of Interpretation*, Bampton Lectures 1885. Ann Arbor, MI: Cushing-Malloy.
Field, G. C. 1930. *Plato and His Contemporaries*. London: Methuen.
Findlay, J. N. 1974. *Plato: The Written and Unwritten Doctrines*. London: Routledge & Kegan Paul.
Ford, A. L. 2002. *The Origins of Criticism: Literary Culture and Poetic Theory in Classical Greece*. Princeton, NJ: Princeton University Press.
Fowler, A. 1964. *Spenser and the Numbers of Time*. London: Routledge & Kegan Paul.
Gibson, S. 2005. *Aristoxenus of Tarentum and the Birth of Musicology*. London: Routledge.
Gottschalk, H. B. 1980. *Heraclides of Pontus*. Oxford: Clarendon Press.
Gouk, P. 1999. *Music, Science and Natural Magic in Seventeenth-Century England*. New Haven, CT: Yale University Press.
Graux, C. 1878. "Nouvelles recherches sur la stichometrie". *Revue de philologie, de litterature et d'histoire anciennes* 2(2): 97–143.
Halbertal, M. 2007. *Concealment and Revelation: Esotericism in Jewish Thought and its Philosophical Implications*. Princeton, NJ: Princeton University Press.
Halliwell, S. 1998. *Aristotle's Poetics*. London: Duckworth.
Hamilton, A. C. 1991. *The Spenser Encyclopaedia*. London: Routledge.
Hankinson, R. J. 1994. *The Sceptics*. London: Routledge.
Harris, J. R. 1893. *Stichometry*. London: C. J. Clay.
Heath, M. 1989. *Unity in Greek Poetics*. Oxford: Clarendon Press.
Heath, T. 1981. *A History of Greek Mathematics*. New York: Dover.
Heidel, W. A. 1976. "Pseudo-Platonica". In *Plato's Euthyphro*, G. Vlastos (ed.), 1–78. New York: Arno Press.
Henderson, J. 1991. *The Maculate Muse: Obscene Language in Attic Comedy*, 2nd edn. New York: Oxford University Press.
Heninger, S. K. 1974. *Touches of Sweet Harmony: Pythagorean Cosmology and Renaissance Poetics*. San Marino: Huntington Library.
Heninger, S. K. 1989. *Sidney and Spenser: The Poet as Maker*. University Park, PA: Pennsylvania State University Press.
Herz-Fischler, R. 1998. *A Mathematical History of the Golden Number*. New York: Dover.
Hieatt, A. K. 1960. *Short Time's Endless Monument: the Symbolism of the Numbers in Edmund Spenser's "Epithalamion"*. Oxford: Oxford University Press.
Hoefmans, M. 1994. "Myth into Reality: The Metamorphosis Of Daedalus and Icarus". *L'Antiquite Classique* 63: 137–60.
Hösle, V. 2008. "Did the Greeks Deliberately Use the Golden Ratio in an Artwork? A Hermeneutical Reflection". *La Parola del Passato* 362: 415–26.
Huffman, C. A. 1993. *Philolaus of Croton: Pythagorean and Presocratic*. Cambridge: Cambridge University Press.
Huffman, C. A. 1999. "The Pythagorean Tradition". In *The Cambridge Companion to Early Greek Philosophy*, A. A. Long (ed.), 66–87. Cambridge: Cambridge University Press.
Huffman, C. A. 2005. *Archytas of Tarentum: Pythagorean, Philosopher and Mathematician*. Cambridge: Cambridge University Press.
Hursthouse, R. 2006. "The Central Doctrine of the Mean". In *The Blackwell Guide to Aristotle's Nicomachean Ethics*, R. Kraut (ed.), 96–115. Oxford: Blackwell.
Huys, M. 2000. Review of Werner Biehl, *Textkritik und Formanalys zur euripideischen Hekabe: Ein Beitrag zum Verständnis der Composition*. *Les Études Classiques* 68: 97–8.
Irigoin, J. 1997. *Tradition et Critique des Textes Grecs*. Paris: Les Belles Lettres.
Janko, R. 2001. "The Derveni Papyrus: A New Translation". *Classical Philology* 96(1): 1–32.
Janko, R. 2009. "Socrates the Freethinker". In *A Companion to Socrates*, S. Ahbel-Rappe & R. Kamtekar (eds), 48–62. Chichester: Wiley-Blackwell.

Janus, C. 1962. *Musici scriptores graeci: Aristoteles, Euclides, Nicomachus, Bacchius, Gaudentius, Alypius et melodiarum veterum quidquid exstat*. Hildesheim: Georg Olms.
Johnson, W. A. 2004. *Bookrolls and Scribes in Oxyrhynchus*. Toronto: University of Toronto Press.
Kahn, C. H. 1996. *Plato and the Socratic Dialogue: The Philosophical Use of a Literary Form*. Cambridge: Cambridge University Press.
Kahn, C. H. 2001. *Pythagoras and the Pythagoreans: A Brief History*. Indianapolis, IN: Hackett.
Kamtekar, R. 2004. "What's the Good of Agreeing? Homonoia in Platonic Politics". *Oxford Studies in Ancient Philosophy* **26**: 131–70.
Kennedy, J. B. 2010. "Plato's Forms, Pythagorean Mathematics, and Stichometry". *Apeiron* **43**(1): 1–32.
Kingsley, P. 1995. *Ancient Philosophy, Mystery, Magic*. Oxford: Clarendon Press.
Krämer, H. J. 1990. *Plato and the Foundations of Metaphysics*. Albany, NY: SUNY Press.
Kraut, R. (ed.) 1992. *The Cambridge Companion to Plato*. Cambridge: Cambridge University Press.
Kraut, R. 2006. *The Blackwell Guide to Aristotle's Nichomachean Ethics*. Oxford: Blackwell.
Krohn, A. 1876. *Der Platonishe Staat*. Halle: R. Mühlmann.
Laks, A. & G. W. Most (eds) 1997. *Studies on the Derveni Papyrus*. Oxford: Clarendon Press.
Lamberton, R. 1986. *Homer the Theologian: Neoplatonist Allegorical Reading and the Growth of the Epic Tradition*. Berkeley, CA: University of California Press.
Landels, J. G. 1999. *Music in Ancient Greece and Rome*. London: Routledge.
Lang, F. G. 1999. "Schreiben nach Mass. Zur Stichometrie in der antiken Literatur". *Novum Testamentum* **41**(1): 40–57.
Lasserre, F. 1954. *Plutarque: De La Musique*. Olten: Urs Graf-Verlag.
Lear, J. 1992. "Inside and Outside the Republic". *Phronesis* **37**(2): 184–215.
Ledger, G. R. 1989. *Re-counting Plato: A Computer Analysis of Plato's Style*. Oxford: Clarendon Press.
Lesser, A. H. 2003. "The Unity of Plato's Phaedo". *Philosophical Inquiry* **25**(3/4): 73–85.
Liddell, H. G., R. Scott, H. S. Jones & R. McKenzie 1996. *A Greek–English Lexicon*, 9th edn. Oxford: Oxford University Press.
Lloyd, M. 1992. *The Agon in Euripides*. Oxford: Clarendon Press.
Long, A. A. (ed.) 1999. *Cambridge Companion to Early Greek Philosophy*. Cambridge: Cambridge University Press.
Louden, B. 1999. *The Odyssey: Structure, Narration, and Meaning*. Baltimore, MD: Johns Hopkins University Press.
Ludwig, W. 1954. *Sapheneia: ein Beitrag zur Formkunst im Spätwerk des Euripides*. Stuttgart: Universität zu Tübingen.
Maclean, H. & A. L. Prescott 1992. *Edmund Spenser's Poetry*. New York: Norton.
Merlan, P. 1968. *From Platonism to Neoplatonism*. The Hague: Martinus Nijhoff.
Michelini, N. N. 1987. *Euripides and the Tragic Tradition*. Madison, WI: University of Wisconsin Press.
Minar, E. L. 1942. *Early Pythagorean Politics in Practice and Theory*. Baltimore, MD: Waverly Press.
Moutsopoulos, E. 1959. *La Musique dans l'oeuvre de Platon*. Paris: Presses Universitaires de France.
Murray, P. & P. J. Wilson (eds) 2004. *Music and the Muses: The Culture of "Mousike" in the Classical Athenian City*. Oxford: Oxford University Press.
Munxelhaus, B. 1976. *Pythagoras musicus: zur Rezeption der pythagoreischen Musiktheorie als quadrivialer Wissenschaft im lateinischen Mittelalter*. Bonn-Bad Godesberg: Verlag fur Systematische Musikwissenschaft.

Nails, D. 2002. *The People of Plato: A Prosopography of Plato and other Socratics*. Indianapolis, IN: Hackett.
Neuse, R. 1966. "The Triumph over Hasty Accidents: A Note on the Symbolic Mode of the Epithalamion". *Modern Language Review* **61**(2): 163–74.
Numenius of Apamea 1973. *Fragments*, E. Des Places (ed.). Paris: Societé d'Edition "Les Belles Lettres".
Oates, W. J. 1936. "The Doctrine of the Mean". *Philosophical Review* **45**(4): 382–98.
Ohly, K. 1928. *Stichometrische Untersuchungen*. Leipzig: Harrassowitz.
Oram, W., E. Bjorvand & R. Bond (eds) 1989. *The Yale Edition of the Shorter Poems of Edmund Spenser*. New Haven, CT: Yale University Press.
Pauly, A. 1929. *Pauly's Reale-Encyclopaedie der Classischen Altertumswissenschaft*. Stuttgart: Metzlersche.
Pepin, J. 1958. *Mythe et Allegorie: Les origines grecques et les contestations judeo-chretiennes*. Paris: Aubier.
Pfeiffer, R. 1968. *History of Classical Scholarship: From the Beginnings to the End of the Hellenistic Age*. Oxford: Clarendon Press.
Plato 1578. *Opera quae extant*, H. Stephanus (ed.).
Plato 1924. *Plato's Euthyphro, Crito, and Apology of Socrates*, J. Burnett (ed.). Oxford: Clarendon Press.
Plato 1959. *Gorgias*, E. R. Dodds (ed.). Oxford: Clarendon Press.
Plato 1999. *Cleitophon*, S. R. Slings (ed.). Cambridge: Cambridge University Press.
Plato 2003. *Platonis Rempublicam*, S. R. Slings (ed.). Oxford: Clarendon Press.
Polansky, R. M. 2007. *Aristotle's De Anima*. Cambridge: Cambridge University Press.
Praechter, K. 1973. "Richtungen und Schulen im Neuplatonismus". In *Praechter: Kleine Shriften*, H. Dörrie (ed.), 165–221. Hildesheim: Olms.
Proclus 1970. *A Commentary on the First Book of Euclid's Elements*, G. Morrow (trans.). Princeton, NJ: Princeton University Press.
Pruche, B. (ed.) 1968. *Basile de Césarée: Sur le Saint-Esprit*. Sources Chrétienne 17. Paris: Cerf.
Ptolemy 1930. *Die Harmonielehre des Klaudios Ptolemaios*, I. Düring (ed.). Gothenburg: Elanders boktr. aktiebolag.
Rankin, H. D. 1986. *Anthisthenes Sokratikos*. Amsterdam: Adolf M. Hakkert.
Richter, L. 1961. *Zur Wissenschaftslehre von der Musik bei Platon und Aristoteles*. Berlin: Akademie-Verlag.
Riginos, A. S. 1976. *Platonica: The Anecdotes Concerning the Life and Writings of Plato*. Leiden: Brill.
Roochnik, D. 1998. *Of Art and Wisdom: Plato's Understanding of Techne*. University Park, PA: Penn State University Press.
Ross, W. D. 1951. *Plato's Theory of Ideas*. Oxford: Clarendon Press.
Rowe, C. J. 1998. *Plato: Symposium*. Warminster: Aris & Phillips.
Runia, D. T. 1986. *Philo of Alexandria and the Timaeus of Plato*. Leiden: Brill.
Rutherford, R. B. 1995. *The Art of Plato: Ten Essays in Platonic Interpretation*. London: Duckworth.
Sayre, K. M. 2006. *Metaphysics and Method in Plato's Statesman*. Cambridge: Cambridge University Press.
Sayre, K. M. 1983. *Plato's Late Ontology: A Riddle Resolved*. Princeton, NJ: Princeton University Press.
Schaarschmidt, C. 1866. *Die Sammlung der platonischen Schriften zur Scheidung der Echten von den Unechten*. Bonn: A. Marcus.
Schanz, M. 1881. "Zur Stichometrie". *Hermes* **16**(2): 309–15.
Sedley, D. 2003. *Plato's Cratylus*. Cambridge: Cambridge University Press.
Sedley, D. & G. Bastianini 1995. *Corpus dei Papiri Filosofici Greci e Latini*. Florence: Olschki.

Schironi, F. 2005. "Plato at Alexandria: Aristophanes, Aristarchus, and the 'Philological Tradition' of a Philosopher". *Classical Quarterly* **55**(2): 423–34.
Slings, S. R. 2005. *Critical Notes on Plato's Politeia*, G. Boter & J. van Ophuijsen (eds). Leiden: Brill.
Spenser, E. 1977. *The Faerie Queene*. Harlow: Longman.
Stroumsa, G. G. 2005. *Hidden Wisdom: Esoteric Traditions and the Roots of Christian Mysticism*. Leiden: Brill.
Struck, P. 2004. *Birth of the Symbol: Ancient Readers at the Limits of their Texts*. Princeton, NJ: Princeton University Press.
Tarán, L. 1975. *Academica: Plato, Phililp of Opus, and the Pseudo-Platonic Epinomis*. Philadelphia, PA: American Philosophical Society.
Tarán, L. 1981. *Speusippus of Athens*. Leiden: Brill.
Tarrant, H. 1993. *Thrasyllan Platonism*. Ithaca, NY: Cornell University Press.
Tarrant, H. 2000. *Plato's First Interpreters*. London: Duckworth.
Tarrant, H. & D. Baltzly (eds) 2006. *Reading Plato in Antiquity*. London: Duckworth.
Taylor, A. E. 1960. *Plato: The Man and his Work*. London: Methuen.
Theon of Smyrna 1966. *Expositio Rerum Mathematicarum ad Legendum Platonem Utilium*, E. Hiller (ed.). Stuttgart: Teubner.
Thesleff, H. 1961. *An Introduction to the Pythagorean Writings of the Hellenistic Period*. Abo: Abo Akademi.
Thesleff, H. 1965. *The Pythagorean Texts of the Hellenistic Period*. Abo: Abo Akademi.
Thesleff, H. 2009. *Platonic Patterns*. Las Vegas, NV: Parmenides Publishing.
Thompson, E. M. 1912. *An Introduction to Greek and Latin Palaeography*. Oxford: Clarendon Press.
Tigerstedt, E. N. 1974. *The Decline and Fall of the Neoplatonic Interpretation of Plato: An Outline and Some Observations*. Helsinki: Societas Scientariarum Fennica.
Tigerstedt, E. N. 1977. *Interpreting Plato*. Stockholm: Almqvist & Wiksell.
Tracy, T. J. 1969. *Physiological Theory and the Doctrine of the Mean in Plato and Aristotle*. The Hague: Mouton.
Vlastos, G. 1991. *Socrates: Ironist and Moral Philosopher*. Ithaca, NY: Cornell University Press.
Vogel, C. J. de 1966. *Pythagoras and Early Pythagoreanism: An Interpretation of Neglected Evidence on the Philosopher Pythagoras*. Assen: Van Gorcum.
Vogel, M. 1963. *Die Enharmonik der Griechen*. Düsseldorf: Verlag der Gesellschaft zur Forderung der Systematischen Musikwissenschaft.
Wachsmuth, C. & O. Hense (eds) 1884–1912. *Ioannis Stobaei Anthologium*, vols I–V. Berlin: Weidmann.
Wallis, R. T. 1972. *Neoplatonism*. London: Duckworth.
West, M. L. 1992. *Ancient Greek Music*. Oxford: Clarendon Press.
Winnington-Ingram, R. P. 1932. "Aristoxenus and the Intervals of Greek Music". *Classical Quarterly* **26**(3/4): 195–208.
Wood, A. S. 1969. *Captive to the Word: Martin Luther, Doctor of Sacred Scripture*. Exeter: Paternoster.
Zhumd, L. 1997. *Wissenschaft, Philosophie und Religion im fruhen Pythagoreismus*. Berlin: Akademie Verlag.
Zhumd, L. 1998. "Plato as Architect of Science". *Phronesis* **43**(3): 210–44.
Zuckert, C. H. 2009. *Plato's Philosophers: The Coherence of the Dialogues*. Chicago, IL: University of Chicago Press.

Index

Academy (Plato's) 15, 19, 250
allegory
  anti-allegorical turn 22–3
  defined 3
  enigma 7
  etymological 3
  hyponoia 7, 21
  and literalism 22
  and Luther 22
  philosophical tradition 3
  and Platonism 251
  rhetorical tradition 2, 12
  and Socrates 5ff.
  and Spenser 26ff.
  symbol 8ff., 47–8
  turn towards in Platonism 20ff.
anonymity (Platonic) 246ff.
Antisthenes 6
Archytas 254, 257
Aristotle 5, 14, 15, 31, 34, 37, 50, 250, 255
  logic and music 181
  and mixture 38
  relation to Plato 48
  virtues and means 236ff.
Aristophanes 13
Aristoxenus 34
astronomy (Plato's criticism of) 253–4
"at a note" vs. "near a note" 41

Balashov, Y. 239
Barker, A. 255ff.
Basil the Great 24

bias, confirmation 50
Biehl, W. 289–90
Burkert, W. 9, 11, 14ff., 49, 248–9
Burnyeat, M. 14

canon, division of *see* scale
central notes in dialogues 271ff.
Christianity
  esotericism in 23ff.
  Protestantism 22, 24
  Reformation 22–3
  Roman Catholicism 22
Clement of Alexandria 24
Cole, T. 10
consonance
  algorithms for measuring 35, 250, 258
  correlation with narrative 38
  correlation with positive concepts 56, 180
  harmony, distinguished from 38
  and quarternotes 35
  relative 35, 257ff., 292
  and Theon of Smyrna 261ff.
counter-examples 47, 275
Creese, D. 255

Daedalus 219
Dante 23, 25
decad 262
definitions of opposites 203
Derveni papyrus 2, 3, 4, 6, 13
developmentalism in Plato 248
Diagoras 13–14

INDEX

dialogues, Plato's
  central notes 271ff.
  corruptions in 45
  density of symbolism in 47
  interpretation in antiquity 18ff.
  musical nature of structure 1, 29ff., 258–9
  narrative *see* narrative structure
  spurious 36, 60, 246
  textual criticism of 45, 251ff.
  total lines in 45
  twelve-note scale used in 33
  unity of 246, 251
diesis see quarternote
Dillon, J. 17–18, 248
disharmony *see* harmony
dissonance *see* consonance
divided line (*Resp.*) 238ff.
Dörrie, H. 18ff.

erotics 62
esoteric doctrines 16, 23ff.
Eudoxus 253
Euripides 288ff.
explication vs. verification 29, 46
elenchus 37, 44, 47
enigma *see* allegory
etymology *see* allegory
Euclid 238–9, 250
explication vs. verification 29

falsifiability 50, 60
Ficino, M. 22
fifths (one-fifth of entire dialogue) 40, 269–70
Ford, A. 4, 7
Forms (Plato's) 1, 36, 46
  in early dialogues 248
Fowler, A. 26–7

golden mean *see* Pythagoreanism

harmonikoi 256ff.
harmony and *harmonia*
  and climaxes of Diotima's speech 43
  consonance, distinguished from 38
  definition 36, 276
  disharmony marks dissonant notes 44
  and duality 84
  Eryximachus' theory of 36, 43
  and *krasis* 36, 75, 103
  and motion 61, 177
  and ratios 32–3, 40, 292

  and rhythm 62
  tribein as a symbol for 69, 77, 177, 187
  symbols marking notes 36, 51
  and synthesis 36
  and unity 84
Heath, T. 238–9
Herz-Fischler, R. 239
hexameter *see* stichometry
Hieatt, A. K. 25ff.
Huffman, C. 9, 15–17, 249, 254, 257
Hursthouse, R. 236–7
hyponoia see allegory

Iamblichus 21–2
inductive arguments 46, 49–50
intentionality 246ff.
intervals and harmony 33

Janko, R. 12–14

Kahn, C. 16–18, 248
Kingsley, P. 7
krasis (linguistic) 45
krasis (musical) *see* harmony

Lamberton, R. 6
letter-counting *see* stichometry
line-counting *see* stichometry
literalism 22
logic (relation to music) 181ff.
Ludwig, W. 288ff.
Luther, M. 22
lyre 292
  seven strings 39

Macrobius 21
Metrodorus 6
mixture
  Eryxhimachus' theory 39
  Greek theory of 38
  relation to logical assertion 181ff.
monochord 58, 250, 255–6, 260ff., 291ff.
mystery religions 9, 24, 261

narrative structure
  clarified 1, 246
  correlation with consonance of notes 38
  disjointed in dialogues 1, 37
  not disturbed by symbols 51
  dramatic climaxes at notes 41
  and musical structure 4
  organized by twelve-note scale 1, 33ff.

negation and dissonance 117, 123
neo-Platonism vs. Platonism 21–3, 24
neo-Pythagoreanism 14, 20–21, 27, 51
   on consonance 261ff.
   twelve-note scale and monochord 260ff.
ninths (one-ninth of entire dialogue) 267–9
notation for wholenotes, quarternotes and octads 40
Numenius 14, 20

objections and responses 48ff.
octad (one-eighth of quarter-interval) 83, 111
   Agathon's virtues and 43
   defined 35, 40
   Diotima's ladder and 42, 149
   notation 40
octave
   6-8-9-12 schema 33, 255–6
   from middle to end of dialogue 33
   symbolic passages at 71, 265
Orpheus 39–40, 83, 119
   seven-stringed lyre 39–40

parallel passages 54, 183ff., 240–41
Philolaus 15
Plotinus 21–2
Porphyry 21–2
Proclus 21–2
prose
   a kind of music 63, 161, 277
   and stichometry see stichometry
Protestantism see Christianity
Ptolemy 250, 291
pun 87, 107, 109
punctuation (in Plato's autographs) 44–5
Pythagoras 10, 27
   Plato and 15ff., 248–9
Pythagoreanism
   6-8-9-12 octave schema 255
   aesthetics 28, 30
   and Aristotle 15, 49
   ethics 75
   golden mean or phi 139, 238–43, 250
   harmony of the spheres 1, 29
   musical theories criticized 254
   and Orpheus 39
   pentagram and pentagon 238
   and Plato 14ff., 248–9
   ratios and harmonies 40
   and relative consonance 257ff. , 292
   and reserve 8ff.

revival 28
self-control in 75
and silence 177
Timaeus not Pythagorean 15
and unwritten doctrines 16, 49
and virtue as a mean 237

quarternotes (notes at quarter intervals) 34, 250
   diesis 256
   and equal division of interval 256–7, 262
   and *harmonikoi* 256
   notation for 40
   and uncertainty about consonance 145

references, backward 69, 96, 99
reformation see Christianity
reserve
   and *argumentum ex silentio* 50–51
   doctrine of 8ff.
rhetoric 12
rhythm 62
ring structures 271ff.
Roman Catholicism see Christianity

Sayre, K. 16, 18, 248
scale
   and division of the canon 32, 255–6
   genus, overarching 36
   outline for speeches 42
   same in all genuine dialogues 33
   symbols not precisely correlated with 48
   equal division of scale 33, 256–7, 260ff.
   twelve-note scale in Plato 32
   twelve-note scale in neo-Pythagoreans 260ff.
Sedley, D. 3
seventh notes
   and lyre 39
   marked by mixtures in *Symp.* 38ff., 43
   marked by failed assertions in *Euthphr.* 180ff.
Socrates and allegory 5ff., 14
softness 117, 121
sophists 84, 119
speeches, set
   lengths and locations 41, 52–3
   structured by speeches 42
Spenser 23, 25ff.
spurious dialogues see dialogues
Stephanus pages 31–2
   irregularities in 294

INDEX

stichometry
  algorithm for line-counting 45
  common in classical period 31
  and divided line 238ff.
  error analysis and averaging 45
  and Euripides 288ff.
  hexameter lines 31, 45
  letter-counting vs. line-counting 45
  partial vs. total 31
  prose 31, 45
  relative measurements 45
  thirty-five letters per line 45, 53
  total length of dialogues 53–4
  uniform lines and columns 31–2, 64
  verifying measurements 243
Stroumsa, G. 23ff.
Struck, P. 4–5, 8
structure of Plato's dialogues *see* dialogues
symbol 8
  density in dialogues 47
  correlation with scale 48
symbols marking musical notes
  species of a single genus 36

typology 274ff.
synthesis *see* harmony

Tarrant, H. 20–21, 260ff.
technē 96, 99
  low arts with *erga* 225, 227
tenths (one-tenth of entire dialogue) 269–70
tetraktys 262
textual criticism *see* dialogues, Plato's
Theon of Smyrna 33–4, 260ff.
Thrasyllus 33, 260ff.
translations, need for new 251
tribein *see* harmony
Tübingen school 16–17, 49, 248
typology of symbols 274ff.

unwritten doctrines and Plato 16, 49

verification *see* explication
Vitruvius 27

wholenote (at each twelfth) 33, 35
  notation for 40